Praise for
The History of the Death Penalty in Colorado

"Written by one of the most distinguished death penalty scholars in the world today, *The History of the Death Penalty in Colorado* is a comprehensive and engaging resource for students, attorneys, legislators, and anyone considering the pros and cons of the death penalty, both in Colorado and on a national scale. The book will be of interest to readers far beyond Colorado's borders for many years to come."

—ELIZABETH A. ZITRIN JD, PRESIDENT, WORLD COALITION AGAINST THE DEATH PENALTY

"*The History of the Death Penalty in Colorado* provides a model of what is needed in every state to preserve the historical record of our fights over executions. It's my personal hope that Colorado will soon end the death penalty, thus making the story of its ultimate abolition the only supplement this book ever needs."

—MIKE FARRELL, HUMAN RIGHTS ACTIVIST AND ACTOR (*M*A*S*H*)

"Michael Radelet's meticulous research and insight are critical to our understanding of capital punishment. No scholar has done a better job of exploring and navigating the pitfalls of the death penalty at the state, national, and international level."

—DOUGLAS K. WILSON, COLORADO PUBLIC DEFENDER

"A compelling account of a key issue in Colorado history and an important service to the state of Colorado."

—SCOTT PHILLIPS, UNIVERSITY OF DENVER

TIMBERLINE BOOKS

Stephen J. Leonard and Thomas J. Noel, editors

The Beast
BENJAMIN BARR LINDSEY WITH HARVEY J. O'HIGGINS

Colorado's Japanese Americans
BILL HOSOKAWA

Colorado Women: A History
GAIL M. BEATON

Denver: An Archaeological History
SARAH M. NELSON, K. LYNN BERRY, RICHARD F. CARRILLO, BONNIE L. CLARK, LORI E. RHODES, AND DEAN SAITTA

Denver's Lakeside Amusement Park: From the White City Beautiful to a Century of Fun
DAVID FORSYTH

Denver Landmarks and Historic Districts: Second Edition
THOMAS J. NOEL AND NICHOLAS J. WHARTON

Dr. Charles David Spivak: A Jewish Immigrant and the American Tuberculosis Movement
JEANNE E. ABRAMS

Enduring Legacies: Ethnic Histories and Cultures of Colorado
EDITED BY ARTURO J. ALDAMA, ELISA FACIO, DARYL MAEDA, AND REILAND RABAKA

Frank Mechau: Artist of Colorado, Second Edition
CILE M. BACH

The Gospel of Progressivism: Moral Reform and Labor War in Colorado, 1900–1930
R. TODD LAUGEN

Helen Ring Robinson: Colorado Senator and Suffragist
PAT PASCOE

The History of the Death Penalty in Colorado
MICHAEL L. RADELET

Ores to Metals: The Rocky Mountain Smelting Industry
JAMES E. FELL, JR.

Season of Terror: The Espinosas in Central Colorado, March–October 1863
CHARLES F. PRICE

A Tenderfoot in Colorado
R. B. TOWNSHEND

The Trail of Gold and Silver: Mining in Colorado, 1859–2009
DUANE A. SMITH

The History of the **Death Penalty** in Colorado

MICHAEL L. RADELET

To Claire –
With admiration for all
your hard work doing mitigation!
Michael L Radelet
March 2017

UNIVERSITY PRESS OF COLORADO
Boulder

Published by University Press of Colorado
5589 Arapahoe Avenue, Suite 206C
Boulder, Colorado 80303

Printed in the United States of America

The University Press of Colorado is a proud member of the Association of American University Presses.

The University Press of Colorado is a cooperative publishing enterprise supported, in part, by Adams State University, Colorado State University, Fort Lewis College, Metropolitan State University of Denver, Regis University, University of Colorado, University of Northern Colorado, Utah State University, and Western State Colorado University.

∞ This paper meets the requirements of the ANSI/NISO Z39.48-1992 (Permanence of Paper).

ISBN: 978-1-60732-511-6 (cloth)
ISBN: 978-1-60732-512-3 (ebook)

Library of Congress Cataloging-in-Publication Data
Names: Radelet, Michael L., author.
Title: The history of the death penalty in Colorado / Michael L. Radelet.
Description: Boulder: University Press of Colorado, 2016. | Includes bibliographical references.
Identifiers: LCCN 2016032566 | ISBN 9781607325116 (cloth) | ISBN 9781607325123 (ebook)
Subjects: LCSH: Capital punishment—Colorado—History. | Criminal justice, Administration of—Colorado—History. | Executions and executioners—Colorado.
Classification: LCC HV8699.U6 R66 2016 | DDC 364.6609788—dc23
LC record available at https://lccn.loc.gov/2016032566

Cover photograph by the author

In memory of
Ann Radelet Schneidewind
1948–2012

Teach me to feel another's woe
To hide the fault I see
And mercy to others show
That mercy shown to me.
—Alexander Pope

CONTENTS

FOREWORD

Sister Helen Prejean, C.S.J.

I have known Prof. Michael Radelet for over thirty years, and I know him well. Over those years we have shared many laughs and tears and innumerable moments of exhaustion, exasperation, and elation. He was among those who helped me, tirelessly, with the scores of footnotes that are found in my two books, *Dead Man Walking* (1994) and *Death of Innocents* (2006). He is known around the world as an impeccable academic with a firm handle on facts and figures relating to the death penalty in the United States and around the globe. But perhaps more importantly, he is the only academic I know who has walked the walk, working directly with scores of death row inmates, their families, and friends and family members of homicide victims. He can write the academic papers but is never far from the lived experiences of the real people whose life stories are behind the numbers.

In the pages that follow, Professor Radelet has performed an invaluable service by giving us a comprehensive (and downright interesting) history of the death penalty in Colorado, where he has lived since 2001. He begins with the forty-year history of public executions in the state and outlines the history of resistance and dissent, both private (such as when numerous wardens refused to participate in hangings) and public (such as when legislators—from both sides of the aisle—conducted sporadic campaigns to increase or decrease the death penalty's use). He ends with a series of complex questions that Colorado citizens and legislators will need to face in determining the future of the state's execution chamber.

Colorado's experience with executions, from its beginning up to the present, is riddled with inconsistencies and contradictions. On one hand, Colorado is one of the few death penalty states in the United States with a history of abolition (1897–1903), an experiment that ended only when legislators saw a need to placate lynch mobs and eliminate the bad press that the state was getting because of lynching activity. The state's attempts to prevent botched executions—a concern that today is delaying executions from California to Florida—dates back over 125 years, when the state first started to tinker with the gallows, going so far as to employ an "upright jerker" that launched inmates skyward rather than dropping them through a trap door. And in 2009 the legislature came within one vote of abolishing the death penalty and using the monies saved to fund continued investigations of unsolved homicides. On the other hand, efforts to maintain and expand the death penalty have also prevailed at times, such as in 1995, when the legislature attempted to increase the number of death sentences by removing juries from making the life-and-death decisions, only to see the Supreme Court reject this idea in 2002. In 2013 a decision made by current governor John Hickenlooper made it likely that no executions will be held until after he leaves office in January 2019. It remains to be seen, though, whether and when the death penalty in Colorado will be tabled on a permanent basis.

Of course, many of the incidental details surrounding the death penalty in Colorado are today lost to history. Our ancestors did not have mitigation specialists or people who could construct detailed life histories that might provide clues as to why the offender did what he did. Private thoughts by governors or prosecutors or judges or prison workers were rarely recorded. We have few ideas about how the execution was received by family members of the victims or the family members of the inmates, although these effects must have lasted, at least in some cases, for multiple generations in both families.

Arguably the top pro–death penalty argument today is a justification based on retribution, or simply summarized as "he deserves it." Execution, we are told, is "just desserts." This whole justification overlooks the truth that many of those whom we send to death row and execute today, just like the victims who did not deserve their horrible deaths, did not "deserve" being born with fetal alcohol syndrome, abusive parents, a childhood of poverty, or the horrible and unforeseen consequences of mental illness or alcohol and drug addiction. No one, it seems, was asking what these future offenders "deserved" while they were being raised with so many strikes against them. Too few of us cared.

As I see it, human beings do not have the wisdom or skills to determine what other people "deserve" with the accuracy necessary to separate who shall live and who shall die. There are too many unknowns and unknowables. In fact, determining whatever the offenders might hypothetically "deserve" is woefully inexact. But whatever the offenders may or may not "deserve," we have more than enough data today to conclude that we do not "deserve" to kill. With the death penalty today infected by racial bias, arbitrariness, erroneous convictions, lousy legal representation, and a host of other faults, the claim that the death penalty is "reserved for the worst of the worst" is patently untrue. The record of the death penalty in the United States and Colorado is a record of errors. Beyond any doubt, we are making these godlike decisions without godlike skills.

"What's past is prologue," wrote Shakespeare in act 2, scene 1 of *The Tempest*, a phrase now carved on the exterior of the National Archives in Washington, DC. Indeed, history is not determinative, but it certainly does set the context for the present. Today, the future of the death penalty in the United States is far from certain, but histories like the one portrayed in this book—the history of a move toward the death penalty's disuse and abandonment—can tell us a great deal about where the death penalty is headed. While the final chapter of capital punishment in Colorado is yet to be written, one can only hope that the list of those executed in Colorado will not include any new additions in the years to come.

HELEN PREJEAN, C.S.J.
New Orleans
May 2016

FOREWORD

Stephen J. Leonard

Christ and Hammurabi did not see eye to eye. More than seventeen centuries before Christ, Hammurabi, king of Babylon, promulgated a code of justice, which, although favoring the rich and well born, marked an advance in civilization. By balancing the crime and the punishment—"an eye for an eye and a tooth for a tooth"—Hammurabi offered a way to curb unlimited retribution and vendettas among members of the upper crust. Matthew, in his gospel 5:38, reports Christ's far more merciful view: "You have learned how it was said: 'Eye for eye and tooth for tooth.' But I say this to you: offer the wicked man no resistance." And a few sentences later, Matthew quotes Christ: "Love your enemies."

Today, much of Hammurabi's Code is defunct and forgotten, but notions of a life for a life and even more Draconian punishments from ancient times still shape the jurisprudence of some countries such as Iran, Saudi Arabia, and Pakistan, which together executed more than 1,400 people in 2015. China, North Korea, and several other countries do not even reveal their numbers. Among the disciples of Hammurabi, the United States, where fewer than 30 people were executed in 2015, ranks low. Capital punishment has clearly become "unusual punishment" in the United States and most other advanced countries. After two thousand years, Christ and others of like mind are scoring victories in some places, but the debate continues.

In this book, Michael Radelet, a sociology professor at the University of Colorado Boulder, covers more than 150 years of Colorado's history showing how citizens have employed legal capital punishment as a response to serious crime. He also touches on, but does not detail, Coloradans' once considerable addiction to lynching (illegal use of capital punishment), a topic I covered in *Lynching in Colorado, 1859–1919* (Boulder: University Press of Colorado, 2002). Instead, Radelet focuses on more than 100 instances in which accused miscreants were executed after receiving legal or at least open and ostensibly fair trials. He tells of attempts to abolish the death penalty, of tortuous hangings, and of changing fashions in execution—hanging including hanging with the heart cut out (to make sure the departed was truly, really dead), gas, and lethal injection.

Radelet reports public executions such as that in 1886 of an African American—Andrew Green—in Denver, where an estimated 15,000 people watched Green slowly strangle. That circus-like spectacle led to the abolition of public executions in Colorado. He recalls the agony of Eddie Ives, a man so light that it was difficult to kill him by hanging. Flummoxed prison officials hanged him twice and perhaps a third time before he died. That botched execution brought a reform of sorts—the use of gas instead of hanging as a means of execution. Radelet also recounts the 1939 fate of accused murderer Joe Arridy, a man with the mental capacity of a young child who was gassed after a flawed trial.

Much of this is largely forgotten, although Andrew Green has been remembered thanks to William M. King's book *Going to Meet a Man: Denver's Last Legal Public Execution, 27 July 1886* (Boulder: University Press of Colorado, 1990) and Joe Arridy was belatedly pardoned in 2011 by Colorado governor Bill Ritter. Colorado history is sugared with stories of triumph and romance, of the picturesque and the pleasant. Remembering choking people to death and recalling how men (no woman has been legally executed in Colorado) gasped and struggled to break their restraints as they were forced to breathe cyanide gas does not appeal to most sane people. Executions make ephemeral front-page stories and then are quickly shelved in a usually locked closet of the mind wherein also lurks the Marquis de Sade.

Unappealing history, however, is sometimes necessary. For letting us know about a chapter of our past that remains open in our present, Michael Radelet is to be thanked. He has not written a polemic, although polemicists may use it. Rather, it is a book of inconvenient truths—hot coals that will make readers think. Meticulously researched and concisely written, it is a welcome addition to the University Press of Colorado's Timberline Series, which for more than a decade has showcased scholarly works on Colorado.

STEPHEN J. LEONARD
Coeditor with Thomas J. Noel
of the Timberline Series

ACKNOWLEDGMENTS

There is a long list of people who deserve thanks for their magnificent help in producing this manuscript. First and foremost is Hugo Adam Bedau (1926–2012), who taught me how to think and write about the death penalty. M. Watt Espy (1933–2009), a self-employed and autodidactic death penalty expert from Headland, Alabama, unselfishly shared his research with me and taught me to teach by using the power of stories that are impossible to make up. Hopefully the family and friends of these scholars will see their work live on in the following pages.

Since moving to Colorado in 2001 I have had the privilege of working with many inspirational colleagues in the Institute of Behavioral Sciences at the University of Colorado, under the spectacular leadership of Richard Jessor, Jane Menken, and Myron Gutmann. They have created an environment where a person's IQ goes up twenty points just by entering the building.

I was privileged to begin to work on Colorado death penalty cases back in the late 1980s, when Colorado public defenders David Wymore and the late Terri Brake showed me how special their office was. Doug Wilson, who became head of the Colorado Public Defender's Office in 2006, continued that instruction, both through cases we worked on together and in informal discussions over many glasses of good Colorado beer. Colorado defense attorneys Phil Cherner, Craig Truman, and my former student Effie Seibold (née Hindson) also taught (and continue to teach) me what was going on, as do state attorneys Stan Garnett in Boulder and Bob Grant in Adams County. One of these days I hope to write something on the death penalty that will turn Bob into an abolitionist.

A host of academics—beginning with Werner Einstadter, when I completed my MA at Eastern Michigan University, and Bob Perrucci, who directed my PhD studies at Purdue—have had lifelong impacts on the way I do my work. More recently, I have greatly benefited from conversations about the death penalty with Profs. Jim Acker (University at Albany–SUNY), Roger Hood (University of Oxford), Stephen Leonard (Metropolitan State University of Denver), Bill Schabas (Middlesex University London), and San Francisco–based attorney Elizabeth Zitrin, president of the World Coalition Against the Death Penalty. Ditto for Robert Perske and the folks at The ARC chapter in Colorado Springs, who took the little-known case of Joe Arridy, executed in Colorado in 1939 despite severe developmental disabilities, and won a full posthumous pardon for him in 2011.

I am indebted for the opportunity to work with scores of individuals who lost a loved one to murder in Colorado and where the murder has never been solved. The Reichert family in Greeley (Don, Jerri, and Mark) has taught me much over the years, as has Howard Morton, now executive director emeritus of Families of Homicide Victims and Missing Persons.

Jane Thompson, associate director of faculty services and research at the William A. Wise Law Library at the University of Colorado Boulder, has been a wonderful friend for many years, frequently showing me bags and bags of new tricks that she and her computers can do when researching some piece of death penalty trivia. Martha Quillen at the Salida Regional Library and John Major and Lynne Garell at the Bud Werner Memorial Library in Steamboat Springs are among the dozens of librarians throughout the state who also seemingly dropped everything to help me track down information. This book would not have been possible without the assistance of researchers at the Colorado State Archives and especially at the Stephen H. Hart Library and Research Center at History Colorado (formerly the Colorado Historical Society) in Denver. I also thank Stacey Cline, Director of the Museum of Colorado

Prisons in Cañon City and Laurie Kilpatrick, Public Information Officer of the Colorado Department of Corrections, for their help.

Pat Furman, Ann Roan, Hollis Whitson, and Mary Claire Mulligan—four exceptionally dedicated and talented Colorado death penalty attorneys—read drafts of this book and made oodles of helpful suggestions. I would like to say that any legal errors in the book are theirs and theirs alone, but that would not be right (or accurate). Their comments have been tremendously helpful.

I completed this book while on sabbatical leave from the University of Colorado during the 2014–2015 academic year, and I will always be grateful to CU for giving me the opportunities to do this sort of work. CU even threw in free use of the university's flat in London for a month. Out-of-pocket expenses were covered by a grant from Proteus Action League, Amherst, Massachusetts. I thank Prof. Lis Semel at the University of California, Berkeley School of Law (Boalt Hall) for providing office space for me in October 2014; my coauthor and friend Glenn Pierce at Northeastern for putting up with my frequent visits to Boston (and Alan Agresti and Jacki Levine for giving me a key to their flat in Brookline); and Saul Lehrfreund and Parvais Jabbar for hosting me at London's Death Penalty Project in January and February 2015.

Portions of this book first appeared in two articles in the *University of Colorado Law Review*: Michael L. Radelet, *Capital Punishment in Colorado, 1859–1972*, 74 U. COLO. LAW REV. 885 (2003), and Stephanie Hindson, Hillary Potter, & Michael L. Radelet, *Race, Gender, Region and Death Sentencing in Colorado, 1980–1999*, 77 U. COLO. LAW REV. 549 (2006). These excerpts (edited and updated) are reprinted with permission of the *University of Colorado Law Review*.

The folks at the University Press of Colorado, especially Acquisitions Editor Jessica d'Arbonne and Diane Bush, have been wonderful to work with. As soon as I met Jessica in 2014 I knew that I had found the right publisher. I never even thought about a Plan B.

Finally, for all her tolerance, support, and wisdom, I thank my wife, Lisa, the love of my life, whom I met in the 1980s while she was working with death row inmates in Texas and I was doing the same in Florida. It made for some mighty romantic courting. As our many friends know, since then she has prevented me from making well over 9,000 errors (one for each day of our marriage) and still counting.

The History of the **Death Penalty** in Colorado

CHAPTER 1

INTRODUCTION

As this book goes to press in 2016, democratic governments throughout the world are commemorating the 800th anniversary of the signing of the Magna Carta, which Lord Alfred Denning, the most respected British judge of the twentieth century, described in 1965 as "the greatest constitutional document of all times—the foundation of the freedom of the individual against the arbitrary authority of the despot."[1] Yet, one type of punishment that is increasingly criticized for its imposition based on "the arbitrary authority of the despot" is the death penalty. While the death penalty today has little in common with the death penalty as it was practiced when the Magna Carta was signed, or even when its 750th or 700th anniversaries were celebrated fifty and one hundred years ago, questions about its use and value seem to be escalating, in Colorado and throughout the world, at exponential rates.

At the time of this writing, at the end of 2015, Colorado's death penalty had become such a trivial component of the state's criminal justice system that it is now quite possible that we will never see another execution in

1. *See, e.g.*, ANTHONY ARLIDGE & IGOR JUDGE, MAGNA CARTA UNCOVERED (2014); Magna Carta Trust, *Magna Carta Today: Why Celebrate 800 Years*, accessed July 15, 2016, http://magnacarta800th.com/magna-carta-today/objectives-of-the-magna-carta-800th-committee/.

DOI: 10.5876/9781607325123.c001

the state. After all, by 2016 there were only three inmates on death row in Cañon City, and the only one who is anywhere close to being put to death is Nathan Dunlap, convicted of killing four people in an Aurora restaurant in 1993.[2] In 2013 Colorado governor John Hickenlooper indefinitely halted his execution, a move that effectively imposed a moratorium on all executions in the state.[3] For murders committed between January 1, 2000 and December 31, 2015, prosecutors sought the death penalty against eighteen men and one woman (plus against one of those men a second time). In 2009 and again in 2013, the Colorado General Assembly came close to passing abolition bills. Its members may do so again in the near future, a current or future governor could commute all the death sentences to prison terms with a stroke of the pen, or the courts could easily tinker with these sentences, rendering Colorado's executioner permanently unemployed. This book will cover the history of Colorado's struggles with the death penalty, but with the death penalty still legally permissible, the final chapter of this history has not yet been written.

DEFINING AND COUNTING LEGAL EXECUTIONS

To assemble a complete list of Colorado executions, decisions have to be made on how to accurately distinguish a legal execution (performed after a trial under statutory authority) from a lynching (in which a mob or group performs an execution without recognized legal authority). In a seminal book closely related to the death penalty, distinguished Colorado historian Stephen J. Leonard, from Metropolitan State University of Denver, documented some 175 lynchings in Colorado between 1859 and 1919, including two in which the victims were burned to death and one in which a woman was lynched.[4] Sometimes a perfunctory trial before a vigilante court preceded the lynching, but that extralegal trial should not cause today's historians to classify the hanging as a legal execution.

---

2. *See* appendix 2, case no. 17.

3. Karen Augé & Lynn Bartels, *Nathan Dunlap Granted Temporary Reprieve by Colorado Gov. Hickenlooper*, DENVER POST, May 23, 2013, at 1.

4. *See* Stephen J. Leonard, *Avenging Mary Rose: The Lynchings of Margaret and Michael Cuddigan in Ouray, Colorado, 1864*, COLO. HERITAGE 37 (Summer 1999): 34–47; STEPHEN J. LEONARD, LYNCHING IN COLORADO, 1859–1919 (2002), at 3 (hereinafter LEONARD).

On the other hand, five cases from 1859 to 1860 that are treated as legal executions in this book arguably could be classified as lynchings,[5] and Leonard does so; but they are included in the inventory of legal executions in this book because they were, in a real sense, at least quasi-legal. Strictly speaking, these five executions occurred without statutory authority. In each, however, the prisoner received a semi-formal trial; lay citizen volunteers acted as judge, defense attorney, prosecutor, and jurors; and there were attempts by those in charge to provide the prisoner with minimal due process protections, such as the opportunity to cross-examine witnesses. The five defendants in these questionable cases were tried, convicted, and condemned to death in forums known as People's Courts and will be discussed in the next chapter.

There is no question about the legality of the proceedings that caused ninety-eight other Coloradans to be hanged, gassed, or (in one case) injected with lethal chemicals. Only two of these executions occurred in the past fifty years. The last was that of Gary Lee Davis, who was put to death on the gurney in the Colorado State Penitentiary in Cañon City in 1997.[6] His immediate predecessor to be executed, Luis José Monge, fired his attorneys, forfeited his appeals, and in 1967 became the last prisoner to be asphyxiated in Cañon City's gas chamber.[7] While no one knew it at the time, Monge's execution marked the end of an era in death penalty history for both Colorado and the United States, and there were no more executions anywhere in the fifty states for nearly a decade. Five years after Monge's death, the US Supreme Court handed down its decision in *Furman v. Georgia*,[8] which, in effect, invalidated all but a few death penalty statutes nationwide.[9] Thereafter, most states resisted making the ban permanent and enacted new death penalty statutes—some of which withstood constitutional scrutiny[10]—and in 1977 Gary Gilmore in

5. *See* appendix 1 (case nos. 1–5). Indeed, these five cases are included on Leonard's list of Colorado lynchings, so there is some overlap in our work. LEONARD, at 3.

6. *See* appendix 1, case no. 103.

7. *See* appendix 1, case no. 102.

8. 408 U.S. 238 (1972).

9. After *Furman* was handed down, there were still some questions about some narrowly defined and/or mandatory capital statutes. MICHAEL MELTSNER, CRUEL AND UNUSUAL: THE SUPREME COURT AND CAPITAL PUNISHMENT 299–302 (1973).

10. Gregg v. Georgia, 428 U.S. 153 (1976).

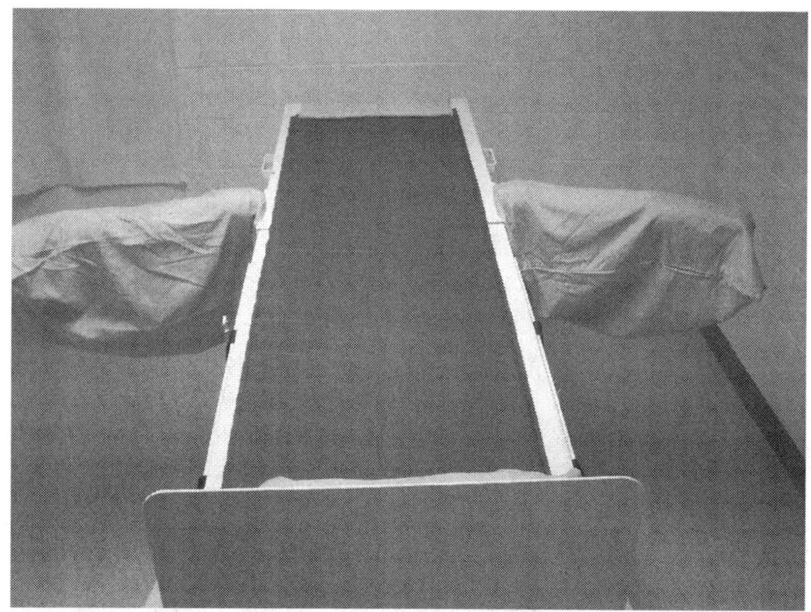

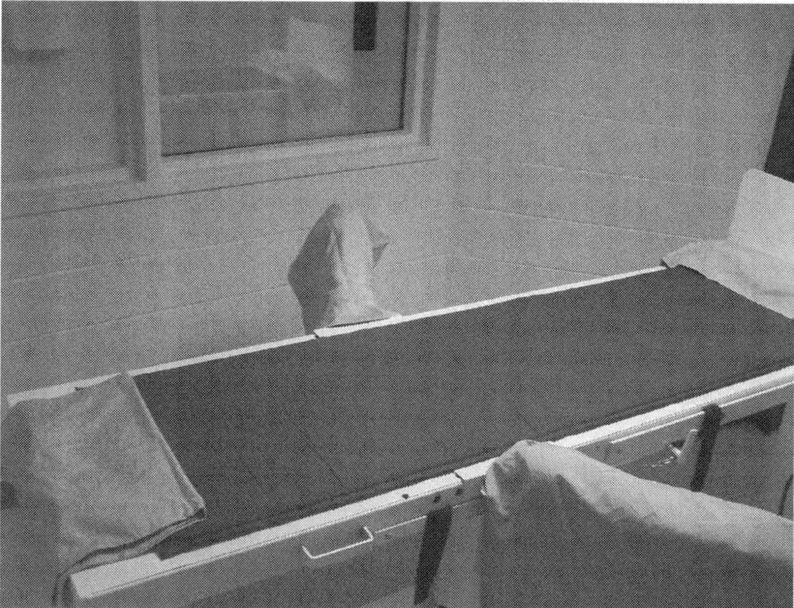

FIGURE 1.1. *Colorado's modern execution gurney at the Colorado State Penitentiary, used for the execution of Gary Lee Davis in 1997. The security devices on the gurney have been covered so that locking mechanisms are not revealed. Photo courtesy of the Colorado Department of Corrections (Adrienne Jacobson, Public Information Officer).*

Utah became the first "post-*Furman*" and "post-Monge" prisoner to be executed in the United States.[11]

Between January 1, 1977 and the end of 2015, there were 1,422 executions in the United States. Only one of these executed inmates—Gary Lee Davis—went to his death in Colorado, although that low "success" rate has not stopped a considerable number of politicians and prosecutors from trying their best and spending millions of dollars to increase the number.[12]

Assembling a comprehensive list of those executed in Colorado's history is neither a simple nor a straightforward task, but this job has now been completed. Appendix 1, at the end of this book, gives a chronological list of all those who were executed in Colorado and a short description of each case.[13] Before November 1890, Colorado executions occurred in counties, and before 2003 there was never a statewide "master list" that could give students of the death penalty the names, dates, and places where executions were carried out under county authority.[14] The best single source for execution data, both in Colorado and in other states, comes from the scholarship of the late M. Watt Espy, an Alabama researcher whose work in documenting executions is regarded by most scholars as incomplete yet definitive.[15] As a starting point, Espy supplied his data for this project, which included the names and dates

---

11. Like Monge, Gilmore dropped his appeals and asked to be executed.

12. For a complete and up-to-date list of all those executed in the United States since 1976, see http://www.deathpenaltyinfo.org/views-executions, accessed July 15, 2016.

13. For longer descriptions of each Colorado execution, *see* R. MICHAEL WILSON, LEGAL EXECUTIONS IN THE WESTERN TERRITORIES, 1847–1911: ARIZONA, COLORADO, IDAHO, KANSAS, MONTANA, NEBRASKA, NEVADA, NEW MEXICO, NORTH DAKOTA, OKLAHOMA, OREGON, SOUTH DAKOTA, UTAH, WASHINGTON AND WYOMING 56–66, 205–6 (2010); R. MICHAEL WILSON, LEGAL EXECUTIONS AFTER STATEHOOD IN ARIZONA, COLORADO, NEVADA, NEW MEXICO, AND UTAH: A COMPREHENSIVE REGISTRY 96–195 (2012).

14. This list was first made available in Michael L. Radelet, *Capital Punishment in Colorado, 1859–1972*, U. COLO. L. REV. 74 (2003): 885–1010.

15. *See, e.g.*, Francis X. Clines, *A Dismayed Historian of the Gallows*, N.Y. TIMES, Nov. 18, 1992, at A16. Espy passed away in 2009. His papers are now permanently housed in the M. E. Grenander Department of Special Collections and Archives at the University at Albany, SUNY. *See* http://library.albany.edu/speccoll/findaids/eresources/findingaids/apap301.xml, accessed July 15, 2016.

of approximately 90 percent of the executions included in appendix 1. Extensive searches in the Colorado State Archives, Stephen H. Hart Library and Research Center at the Colorado Historical Society (now called History Colorado), the Denver Public Library, and Norlin Library at the University of Colorado Boulder, as well as in several smaller libraries throughout the state, were conducted to supplement the Espy data and to collect information on each execution. In several cases in which the race of the executed prisoner's murder victim was unknown, information was obtained from death certificates from the Health Statistics Section, Colorado Department of Public Health and Environment.

GENERAL PATTERNS IN COLORADO EXECUTIONS

Using this methodology, and including the five executions that resulted from decisions made by People's Courts, a total of 103 legal executions between the beginning of 1859 and the end of 2015 were identified. Only men were executed,[16] all of whom were convicted of murder.[17] Table 1.1

---

16. Although Colorado has never executed a woman (and this research project has not identified any woman sentenced to death in Colorado's history), there was at least one lynching that claimed the life of a woman. On January 19, 1884, Michael and Margaret Cuddigan were lynched in Ouray after being arrested (on skimpy evidence) of killing a ten-year-old foster child who was in their care. Margaret was twenty-one at the time of her death and was seven months pregnant. *See* Stephen J. Leonard, *Avenging Mary Rose*, 37; LEONARD, at 73–86. There is also a possibility that a Hispanic woman was lynched in Trinidad in 1873. LEONARD, at 74.

17. Although every person legally executed in Colorado since 1859 was convicted of murder, there were other crimes that at one time or another also carried the death penalty. A mandatory conviction of first-degree murder and a discretionary death penalty was legislated for those convicted of causing a death by anarchy. *See* COLO. REV. STAT. § 40-23-14 (1963). The 1861 Session Laws mandated that those performing abortions in which the woman died also faced a mandatory conviction for murder and a discretionary death penalty. *See id.*, § 40-2-23. The 1861 session laws made the death penalty mandatory for those convicted of perjury that resulted in the conviction and execution of an innocent person. Act of Nov. 5, 1861, § 80, 1861 Colo. Terr. Sess. Laws 290, 306. *See also* COLO. REV. STAT. § 35-1717 (1908). In 1939, in the wake of the 1932 New Jersey kidnapping of the son of aviator Charles Lindbergh, the General Assembly made kidnapping in which the victim suffers bodily harm a capital offense. *See* Act of Apr. 3, 1939, § 1(a), 1939 Colo. Sess. Laws 319. Finally, prisoners serving a life sentence faced a death sentence for assault while attempting to escape. "Every person undergoing a life sentence in the state penitentiary who, while escaping or attempting to escape, commits an assault with intent

summarizes these executions, breaking them into five categories: (1) county authority, pre-statehood (ten cases), (2) county authority after statehood (fifteen cases), (3) hangings under state authority (forty-five cases), (4) asphyxiations under state authority in the gas chamber (thirty-two cases), and (5) the only execution since 1967, Colorado's sole lethal injection.[18] Table 1.1 also lists the date of the offense, date of execution, the day of the week on which the execution occurred, and the number of months between the crime and the execution.

As shown in Table 1.1, on eight occasions, two men were executed on the same day[19] and twice the state executed three people on a single day.[20] One of the double executions claimed the lives of Louis and John Pacheco, who are the only brothers to be executed in the state.[21] Table 1.2 categorizes some of the data from Table 1.1 so that various trends by decade can be examined. During the 1930s—the busiest decade for Colorado's executioners—twenty-five executions took place, seven in 1930 alone. Colorado's execution total was also in double figures in the 1880s (thirteen), the 1890s (twelve), and the 1940s (thirteen). There were, however, only ten executions in the last half of the twentieth century and only ten executions from 1950 through 2015. In contrast, in the past twenty years (1996–2015), Texas, with 427 executions, has averaged twice that number *per year*. As Bob Grant, one of Colorado's top death penalty prosecutors over the past three decades, has regularly pointed out, debating the death penalty in Colorado is a lot different than debating it in Texas.

Table 1.2 also collapses data from Table 1.1 to calculate the average time between the crime and the execution. Prior to 1869, when there were few places to confine prisoners, executions typically occurred within two months of the crime. During the next ninety years, prisoners' executions generally occurred within one or two years of the capital offense. By the 1960s, however, the average prisoner in Colorado waited

---

to commit bodily injury upon the person of another with a deadly weapon or instrument, or by any means of force likely to produce great bodily injury, shall be guilty of a felony, and upon conviction thereof, be punishable by death." COLO. REV. STAT. § 40-7-49 (repealed).

18. In 1988 Colorado changed its method of execution from the gas chamber to lethal injection. *See* Act of May 29, 1988, § 1, 1988 Colo. Sess. Laws 671.

19. *See* appendix 1, case nos. 7, 8, 15, 16, 31, 32, 39, 40, 54, 55, 59, 60, 72, 73, 78, and 79.

20. *See* appendix 1, case nos. 35–37 and 63–65.

21. *See* appendix 1, case nos. 72 and 73.

TABLE 1.1. Chronology of Colorado executions—1859–2015 (ordered by date of execution)

Case	Name	Date of crime	Date of execution	Day of execution	Months between crime and execution
County authority—Pre-statehood—Hanging (N = 10)					
1	Stoefel	04-07-1859	04-09-1859	Saturday	0
2	Young	03-12-1860	03-15-1860	Thursday	0
3	Gredler	06-12-1860	06-15-1860	Friday	0
4	Gordon	07-20-1860	10-06-1860	Saturday	3
5	Waters	11-30-1860	12-21-1860	Friday	1
6	Van Horn	Oct. 1863	12-18-1863	Friday	2
7	Foster	01-05-1866	05-24-1866	Thursday	5
8	Stone	01-05-1866	05-24-1866	Thursday	5
9	Smith	02-16-1868	02-18-1870	Friday	24
10	Myers	08-10-1871	01-24-1873	Friday	17
Executions in counties—State law—Hanging (N = 15)					
11	Miller	08-26-1876	02-02-1877	Friday	6
12	Nunez	10-04-1877	03-14-1879	Friday	17
13	Simms	01-25-1880	07-23-1880	Friday	6
14	Salisbury	04-29-1880	06-17-1881	Friday	14
15	Rosengrants	06-18-1880	07-29-1881	Friday	13
16	Gilbert	10-02-1880	07-29-1881	Friday	10
17	Coleman	07-05-1881	12-16-1881	Friday	5
18	Woods	05-25-1882	06-23-1882	Friday	1
19	Garcia	04-15-1883	12-20-1884	Saturday	20
20	Hibbard	Nov. 1883	04-24-1885	Friday	17
21	Clements	08-17-1885	12-03-1885	Thursday	4
22	Minich	10-13-1884	02-05-1886	Friday	16
23	Green	05-19-1886	07-27-1886	Tuesday	2
24	Femenella	03-11-1888	08-23-1888	Thursday	5
25	Ortiz	03-30-1889	07-16-1889	Tuesday	4
State authority—Cañon City—Hanging (N = 45)					
26	Griego	06-03-1890	11-08-1890	Saturday	5
27	Joyce	07-04-1890	01-17-1891	Saturday	6

continued on next page

TABLE 1.1.—*continued*

Case	Name	Date of crime	Date of execution	Day of execution	Months between crime and execution
28	Davis	01-07-1891	09-22-1891	Saturday	8
29	Smith	June 1891	12-14-1891	Monday	6
30	Lawton	08-17-1891	05-06-1892	Friday	9
31	Jordan	01-23-1893	05-11-1895	Saturday	28
32	Augusta	07-19-1892	05-11-1895	Saturday	34
33	Taylor	01-19-1895	12-13-1895	Friday	11
34	Ratcliff	05-06-1895	02-07-1896	Friday	9
35	Holt	11-20-1895	06-26-1896	Friday	7
36	Noble	11-20-1895	06-26-1896	Friday	7
37	Romero	11-20-1895	06-26-1896	Friday	7
38	Galbraith	03-09-1904	03-06-1905	Monday	12
39	Andrews	12-31-1903	06-16-1905	Friday	18
40	Arnold	12-31-1903	06-16-1905	Friday	18
41	Johnson	04-08-1905	09-13-1905	Wednesday	5
42	McGarvey	09-24-1906	01-12-1907	Saturday	4
43	Alia	02-23-1908	07-15-1908	Wednesday	5
44	Lynn	05-14-1908	10-08-1908	Thursday	5
45	Wechter	02-11-1911	08-31-1912	Saturday	19
46	Hillen	10-24-1913	06-24-1915	Thursday	20
47	Quinn	10-24-1914	01-28-1916	Friday	15
48	Cook	03-09-1912	02-26-1916	Saturday	48
49	Bosko	04-11-1919	12-10-1920	Friday	20
50	Borich	03-31-1922	08-18-1922	Friday	5
51	McGonigal	06-01-1922	04-26-1924	Saturday	23
52	Shank	09-16-1925	09-18-1926	Saturday	12
53	Casias	06-19-1926	11-12-1926	Friday	5
54	Noakes	07-21-1926	03-30-1928	Friday	20
55	Osborn	07-21-1926	03-30-1928	Friday	20
56	Ives	11-22-1928	01-10-1930	Friday	14
57	Weiss	02-14-1929	05-28-1930	Wednesday	15
58	Fleagle	05-23-1928	07-10-1930	Thursday	26
59	Royston	05-23-1928	07-18-1930	Friday	26

continued on next page

TABLE 1.1.—*continued*

Case	Name	Date of crime	Date of execution	Day of execution	Months between crime and execution
60	Abshier	05-23-1928	07-18-1930	Friday	26
61	Herrera	06-29-1929	08-20-1930	Wednesday	14
62	Moya	01-27-1930	12-12-1930	Friday	11
63	Ray	03-14-1930	01-30-1931	Friday	11
64	Walker	03-14-1930	01-30-1931	Friday	11
65	Halliday	03-14-1930	01-30-1931	Friday	11
66	Foster	July 1931	12-11-1931	Friday	5
67	Farmer	01-06-1931	03-18-1932	Friday	14
68	Maestas	09-09-1931	05-27-1932	Friday	9
69	Moss	03-10-1932	03-10-1933	Friday	12
70	Jones	Oct. 1932	12-01-1933	Friday	14
STATE AUTHORITY—CAÑON CITY—ASPHYXIATION (N = 32)					
71	Kelley	10-17-1933	06-22-1934	Friday	8
72	L. Pacheco	02-27-1934	05-31-1935	Friday	15
73	J. Pacheco	02-27-1934	05-31-1935	Friday	15
74	Belongia	12-16-1934	06-21-1935	Friday	6
75	McDaniels	07-15-1935	02-14-1936	Friday	7
76	Aguilar	08-15-1936	08-13-1937	Friday	12
77	Arridy	08-15-1936	01-06-1939	Friday	29
78	Catalina	03-15-1938	09-29-1939	Friday	18
79	Agnes	11-20-1937	09-29-1939	Friday	22
80	Leopold	12-04-1938	12-08-1939	Friday	12
81	Coates	10-13-1938	01-10-1941	Friday	27
82	Stephens	10-09-1939	06-20-1941	Friday	20
83	Sukle	09-30-1939	05-22-1942	Friday	32
84	Fearn	04-22-1942	10-23-1942	Friday	6
85	Sullivan	01-09-1942	09-20-1943	Monday	20
86	Honda	05-03-1942	10-08-1943	Friday	17
87	Potts	04-03-1943	06-22-1945	Friday	27
88	Silliman	01-22-1944	11-09-1945	Friday	22
89	Martz	12-06-1943	11-23-1945	Friday	24

continued on next page

TABLE 1.1.—*continued*

Case	Name	Date of crime	Date of execution	Day of execution	Months between crime and execution
90	Brown	05-12-1945	05-23-1947	Friday	24
91	Gillette	12-26-1946	06-20-1947	Friday	6
92	Battalino	07-07-1947	01-07-1949	Friday	18
93	Schneider	09-20-1947	12-16-1949	Friday	27
94	Berger	01-26-1948	10-26-1951	Friday	45
95	Martinez	11-28-1954	09-07-1956	Friday	21
96	Graham	11-01-1955	01-11-1957	Friday	14
97	Leick	12-01-1953	01-22-1960	Friday	74
98	Early	04-25-1958	08-11-1961	Friday	40
99	Wooley	06-16-1959	03-09-1962	Friday	33
100	Hammil	08-27-1958	05-25-1962	Friday	45
101	Bizup	03-25-1960	08-14-1964	Friday	53
102	Monge	06-29-1963	06-02-1967	Friday	47
State authority—Cañon City—Lethal injection (N = 1)					
103	Davis	07-21-1986	10-13-1997	Monday	135

four years after the crime before his execution. Before the 1970s, the longest time between the commission of the crime and execution came in the case of Leroy Adolph Leick, executed in January 1960 after a six-year battle fought mainly over his mental competence for execution.[22] Gary Lee Davis, the only person in Colorado executed after 1967, lived for just over eleven years after his crimes, ten of them on death row. In sharp contrast to the time on death row served by those executed prior to 1972, the average time between sentencing and execution for the 1,320 inmates executed in the United States from 1977 to 2012 was eleven years, four months; for the 43 inmates executed in 2012, fifteen years, ten months; and for the 39 inmates sent to their deaths in 2013, fifteen-and-a-half years.[23]

22. *See* appendix 1, case no. 97.

23. Tracy L. Snell, *Capital Punishment, 2013—Statistical Tables*, table 10, Bureau of Justice Statistics, Dec. 19, 2014 (NCJ 245789). This time span would be even longer if those who gave up their appeals and asked to be executed were removed from the analysis. Of the 1,422 people executed in the United States between 1977

TABLE 1.2. Colorado executions by decade, 1859–2015 (N = 103)

	Number of executions	*Average number of months between crime and execution*
1859	1	0.0
1860–69	7	2.3
1870–79	4	12.8
1880–89	13	9.0
1890–99	12	11.4
1900–09	7	9.6
1910–19	4	25.5
1920–29	7	15.0
1930–39	25	14.5
1940–49	13	20.8
1950–59	3	26.7
1960–69	6	48.7
1970–79	0	—
1980–89	0	—
1990–99	1	135
2000–09	0	—
2010–15	0	—

TABLE 1.3. Day of the week of executions (N = 103)

	1859–1889	*1890–2015*
Sunday	0	0
Monday	0	4
Tuesday	2	0
Wednesday	0	4
Thursday	5	3
Friday	15	57
Saturday	3	10
Total	25	78

Table 1.3, also collapsing case-by-case data from Table 1.1, shows that about 70 percent of Colorado executions (N = 72) occurred on Fridays. This finding holds for both executions under county authority (1889 and earlier) and those conducted in and after 1890 under state authority. This occurred because Colorado statutes required that the trial judge, or the state Supreme Court if the case was appealed, designate a week during which the execution should be conducted. The sheriff or warden, however, had discretion to determine the exact day and hour. The Colorado Supreme Court defined that "week" as beginning at midnight Saturday and ending at midnight the following Saturday.[24] Friday executions allowed the prisoner to live most of the

and December 31, 2015, 143 (10.1 percent) gave up their appeals and asked to be put to death. http://www.deathpenaltyinfo.org/views-executions, accessed July 15, 2016.

24. *In re* Tyson, 22 P. 810, 812 (Colo. 1889); Mora v. People, 35 P. 179, 182 (Colo. 1893).

week and eliminated the need for those employees involved in the execution to work on weekends.[25]

Table 1.4 shows that three-quarters of those executed in Colorado—79 out of 103—were sentenced to death for killing one victim. Five were convicted of killing four people, including three codefendants who killed four people during a bank robbery in Lamar in 1928.[26] In 1957 the state executed John Gilbert Graham, the only person put to death for killing more than four people, after his conviction for blowing up an airliner in 1955.[27]

TABLE 1.4. Number of homicide victims for each executed inmate*

Number of victims	*Number of cases (N = 103)*	*Case numbers*
1	79	—
2	15	7–8, 21, 28, 38, 48, 49, 50, 51, 52, 67, 72–73, 83, 88
3	3	34, 93, 98
4	5	58–60, 66, 102
44	1	96

* These numbers reflect only the number killed in the time immediately surrounding the capital homicide. The defendant might not have been convicted of, or sentenced to death for, each of the murders. Nor do these tallies reflect prior homicides.

Before being moved to Cañon City, hangings were popular social events. Table 1.5 displays the estimated attendance at executions conducted in public and open to all interested citizens. The accuracy of these estimates is debatable, but there is no doubt that hangings were popular social events, often attracting several thousand spectators—some of the biggest crowds ever assembled at the time—from the local community and distant towns and cities.[28] As discussed below, by the 1880s, the popularity of executions and their festive atmosphere prompted politicians to turn them into private events. The largest crowd to witness an

25. Another explanation with religious origins was brought to my attention by Prof. John Bessler: "There is no recorded explanation of why executions in the United States took place only on Fridays. Historians believed that after Christ's crucifixion occurred on that day, ecclesiastical courts began fixing Friday for legal executions. The custom continued in England and was brought to the United States." April Moore, Folsom's 93: The Lives and Crimes of Folsom Prison's Executed Men 205 (2013).

26. *See* appendix 1, case nos. 58–60.

27. *See* appendix 1, case no. 96.

28. One cannot help but wonder how crowds of this size managed before the invention of porta-potties.

TABLE 1.5. Attendance at selected public hangings

Date	*Defendant*	*Location*	*Spectators (est.)*
04-09-1859	Stoefel	Denver	1,000
06-15-1860	Gredler	Denver	3,000–4,000
10-06-1860	Gordon	Denver	Several thousand
12-18-1863	Van Horn	Central City	Thousands
05-24-1866	Foster & Stone	Denver	"Not less than 3,000"
02-18-1870	Smith	Central City	2,000
01-24-1873	Myers	Denver	3,000
03-14-1879	Nunez	Pueblo	1,200–1,500
07-23-1880	Simms	Fairplay	800
06-17-1881	Salisbury*	Colo. Springs	Over 1,000
07-29-1881	Rosengrants & Gilbert	Leadville	5,000
12-20-1884	Garcia	Pueblo	4,000
12-03-1885	Clements	Saguache	5,000
02-05-1886	Minich	Leadville	7,000
07-27-1886	Green	Denver	15,000–20,000
08-23-1888	Fermenella*	Buena Vista	1,500
UNKNOWN NUMBER OF WITNESSES			
03-15-1860	Young	Denver	
12-21-1860	Waters	Denver	
02-02-1877	Miller	W. Las Animas	
12-06-1881	Coleman*	Gunnison	
06-23-1882	Woods	Durango	
04-24-1885	Hibbard	Trinidad	
07-16-1889	Ortiz	Antonito	

* Three executions were held within the fences of local jails and hence were only "semi-public."

execution assembled in Denver in 1886 and watched as Andrew Green slowly strangled to death.

Finally, Table 1.6 shows the race of the defendant and the victim in Colorado death penalty cases. Ten of those executed were African American, and fifteen others were members of other racial or ethnic minorities (Hispanic, Asian, or "other"). In other words, nearly a quarter of those put to death in Colorado (25/103) were members of racial or ethnic minority groups. No white person has ever been put to death in

TABLE 1.6. Defendant-victim racial/ethnic combinations*

Race of defendant and victim	*Number*
W-W	76
H-W	7
B-W	6
W-B&W	1
Other-W	2
B-B	4
H-H	5
W-H	1
A-A	1
TOTAL	103

W = white; B = black; H = Hispanic; A = Asian

Colorado for a crime that victimized an African American.

SENTENCED TO DEATH BUT NOT EXECUTED

In the course of this research, approximately one hundred cases were found in which men in Colorado were sentenced to death but never executed. There is no evidence that any woman has ever been sentenced to death in the state. These cases, ordered by the year in which the death sentence was imposed, are listed in appendix 2. However, this list is no doubt incomplete.[29] Some inmates who were sentenced to death may have had their sentences commuted even before reaching the prison, others may have died of natural causes soon after the death sentence was imposed, some of these cases were not appealed or even reported in newspapers that are accessible today, or for other miscellaneous reasons they have disappeared into history. Interestingly, while cases that resulted in an execution are relatively easy to identify, those where a death sentence was imposed but not carried out are not found in any central source,

29. Research of this sort has been made possible only in the past few years, as newspapers have become increasingly digitized and searches are becoming easier. As more and more digitized newspapers become available, this list will no doubt be expanded. Currently, by far the best place to access newspapers (digitalized or on microfilm) is at the Stephen H. Hart Library in Denver.

I found one case where it was reported that the defendant was sentenced to death, when in fact he was not, showing that one cannot always believe everything that is printed in the newspaper. In September 1878, the *Rocky Mountain News* reported that Wright Dunham was found guilty of murder and would therefore be sentenced to death. *Dunham to Die: Found Guilty of Murder in the First Degree*, ROCKY MTN. NEWS, Sept. 27, 1878, at 4. *See also Murder at Deer Trail*, PUEBLO WEEKLY CHIEFTAIN, May 2, 1878, at 1. However, at sentencing in October 1878, Dunham was sentenced to life. *Dunham Sentenced for Life*, ROCKY MTN. NEWS, Oct. 22, 1878, at 4. Apparently, the earlier coverage of the case was just an ambiguous prediction or an assumption that he would be sentenced to death.

and those who committed the murders—perhaps as it should be—have been forgotten. Executing an inmate guarantees that he or she will be remembered forever.

To identify these cases, I searched in Westlaw, Lexis, and the Colorado Historic Newspapers Collection[30] for terms such as "sentenced to death" or "sentenced to be hanged." This strategy is admittedly hit-and-miss. Once a lead was uncovered, it was not uncommon for the relevant names to be misspelled or information about the case (e.g., date of offense, date of death sentence) to be too cryptic to use. Also useful were the Colorado State Penitentiary Records housed at the State Archives in Denver.[31] These records are microfilmed copies of handwritten entries for each prisoner ever housed in the Colorado State Penitentiary, which opened in Cañon City in 1871. However, going through the microfilmed copies of these records is extremely time-consuming, the handwriting is often impossible to read, and the quality of the copies is often poor. Nonetheless, this source did contain information on perhaps a dozen cases.

For the Denver cases, the indexes to the *Denver Post* and the *Rocky Mountain News* proved to be indispensable.[32] These indexes are digitized copies of typed 3 × 5 cards compiled by scores of researchers and volunteers over the years, originally filed in the Western History Collection of the Denver Public Library. Although these indexes are incomplete and have virtually no information on cases outside the Denver metropolitan area, they are invaluable.

OUTLINE OF THE FOLLOWING CHAPTERS

The book is organized in roughly chronological order, with exceptions here and there for discussions of events or cases that took several years to unfold. Chapter 2 begins when the city of Denver was founded and Euro-Americans first started to settle in the area. Very soon after the city was formed the hangings began, and five cases in which men were exe-

---

30. *See* Colorado Historic Newspapers, http://www.coloradohistoricnewspapers.org/, accessed July 15, 2016,.

31. *Corrections Records*, COLORADO STATE ARCHIVES, accessed July 15, 2016, https://www.colorado.gov/pacific/archives/corrections-records.

32. *See* University of Colorado Boulder Libraries, accessed July 15, 2016, http://ucblibraries.colorado.edu/how/newspapers.htm.

cuted after being sentenced to death by People's Courts are recounted. Colorado was recognized as an official territory of the United States in 1861, and the next section looks at the ten cases that ended in hangings prior to statehood in 1876. Counties continued to hang people for thirteen years thereafter, with some of the hangings becoming rambunctious public spectacles, which partially fueled abolitionist sentiments in the late 1880s. Meanwhile, the General Assembly continued to tinker with Colorado's death penalty statute and moved executions to a central location in Cañon City, where they are still held today. Prison officials also invented a hanging machine, where the inmate was launched upwards rather than made to fall through a trap door, as well as a rather complex hydraulic apparatus that allowed the prisoner to stand on a platform, where his weight would trigger a device that effected his hanging without any involvement by an executioner or other prison personnel. The chapter ends when the death penalty ended: the 1897 formal abolition of the death penalty in Colorado.

The twentieth century did not begin happily for death penalty opponents, as several lynchings persuaded the General Assembly to bring back the death penalty in 1901. Chapter 3 begins with this reenactment of capital punishment, which clearly was done in an effort to reduce the number of lynchings, not to reduce homicide rates or render help to the families of the victims. This chapter takes us through the debates over the death penalty regularly held in the State Capitol building in the twentieth century, although the primary change made by the General Assembly was to scrap the hanging machine and install a gas chamber in 1933. After Colorado executed Luis José Monge in 1967, executions both in Colorado and throughout the United States stopped, and it seemed for a time like the ban would be permanent.

Chapter 4 describes the efforts made in Colorado after 1967 to ensure that its death penalty would not go away. The state enacted a revised death penalty statute in 1974, and the national moratorium on executions ended in 1977. Twenty years later, Gary Lee Davis was executed via lethal injection in Cañon City. As of the end of 2015, he and Monge remain the only two people executed in Colorado in the last fifty years.

Plenty of politicians, prosecutors, and citizens are unhappy with the fact that Colorado's execution gurney is collecting dust, although as described in chapter 5, public and political support for the death penalty has been quite volatile. This chapter brings us into the twenty-first century and that century's first major death penalty event. In 2002 the US Supreme Court threw out Colorado's use of three-judge panels, which had been introduced in 1995, largely because legislators thought that juries were too hesitant to impose death sentences. With falling homicide rates, increasing public ambivalence about capital punishment, and the exponential rise in the cost of death penalty prosecutions, only three inmates were added to Colorado's death row in the first fifteen years of the new century (one of whom has since been resentenced to life).

Most significantly, in 2013 Gov. John Hickenlooper announced, in effect, that no one would be executed as long as he was in office, and chapter 6 takes us into the Hickenlooper era. In 2014 he not only announced that he had become a firm opponent of the death penalty, but he was also reelected to another four-year term. Supporters of the death penalty tried to make his anti–death penalty stand an issue in the election, but their antagonism had little or no effect. On the other hand, two of the three inmates on Colorado's death row were put there as a result of their roles in the murder of the son of a current state legislator, Rhonda Fields, and her son's fiancée. In 2010 Fields was elected to the Colorado House of Representatives. She has vowed to keep fighting until those two murderers are executed and is running for a seat in the Colorado Senate in 2016.

The final chapter, an epilogue, does not report the end of the death penalty story in Colorado, although numerous signs indicate that it might very well go away in our lifetimes. A case that might have major effects on future debates is that of James Holmes, convicted of killing a dozen people in an Aurora movie theater in 2012. At trial in the summer of 2015, almost everyone agreed that Holmes was severely mentally ill, but he failed in his bid to be found not guilty by reason of insanity. Nonetheless, three jurors were sufficiently concerned about the severity of his mental illness that the jury failed to reach a unanimous sentencing decision, so Holmes was spared a trip to death row. A generation ago many claimed we needed the death penalty to deter criminal homicides, but no one has ever seen capital punishment as a deterrent to schizophrenia.

And so there are many unanswered questions about the future of the death penalty in Colorado. Perhaps the best way to make predictions is to look where we have been.

CHAPTER 2

HANGINGS IN THE NINETEENTH CENTURY

HANGINGS IN PRE-TERRITORIAL DAYS, 1859–1860

The history of capital punishment in the place that we now call Colorado is as old as the history of European settlement in the area. Its roots began in 1859, when the first murder ever recorded in the new settlement of Denver was avenged by the hanging of the confessed perpetrator, John Stoefel. At the time, Denver, having existed for only six months, comprised part of Arapahoe County, Kansas Territory. Despite a low population, some one thousand spectators reportedly attended the execution. Stoefel was driven in a two-horse wagon to a cottonwood tree near Cherry Creek, a rope was put around his neck, and he dropped to his death when the wagon was driven out from underneath him.[1] A fortnight later, the inaugural issue of the first Denver newspaper, the *Rocky Mountain News*, published news about the crime and execution.[2]

Colorado did not become an official legal entity until February 1861, when Congress passed a bill creating the Territory of Colorado. Thus, reasonable people may disagree about whether Stoefel in 1859 and

---

1. Olga Curtis, *Denver's First Murderer*, DENVER POST (Empire Magazine), May 7, 1978, at 66.

2. *Murder and Execution*, ROCKY MTN. NEWS, Apr. 23, 1859, at 3. At its beginning, the newspaper was published as a weekly.

DOI: 10.5876/9781607325123.c002

four others (Moses Young, Marcus Gredler, James Gordon, and Patrick Waters) who were hanged in Denver in 1860 should be counted among the tally of legal executions in what would later become the state. The legal proceedings that determined the guilt and sentence for the five men were, at best, only quasi-legal. At the time, the nearest operative court system was in Leavenworth, Kansas. Given the distance and the absence of railroad transportation, Colorado simply lacked an effective, legally sanctioned criminal justice system. Hence, ad hoc People's Courts developed and were used in Denver in the pre-territorial days between 1859 and 1861.[3] These tribunals varied slightly in structure from case to case, but they usually had one man serving as a judge and twelve others as jurors.[4] In at least one of these cases, the court summoned twenty-four prospective jurors and permitted the prosecutor and defense to each strike six.[5] Given these efforts to ensure some measure of due process, and the implausibility or impracticality of any alternative, the five men executed in pre-territorial days under the authority of these People's Courts are included in the tally of legal executions in this book, although they could just as easily be considered extrajudicial lynchings. The line between legal and extrajudicial executions can sometimes be a bit fuzzy.

These same criteria led to the exclusion of other defendants whose hangings followed perfunctory trials in jurisdictions in which, and at times when, legitimate legal remedies within a formal criminal justice system existed. Take, for example, the hanging of Joseph (Jack) Carr on November 6, 1869, in Evans, Weld County. After a quarrel, he shot the owner of a local hotel, who was a former member of the Territorial Legislature. When apprehended shortly after the murder, Carr was

---

3. Francis S. Williams, *Trials and Judgments of the People's Courts of Denver*, COLO. MAG. 27 (1950): 294; STEPHEN J. LEONARD, LYNCHING IN COLORADO, 1859–1919, at 15–29 (2002) (hereinafter LEONARD).

4. B. Richard Burg, *Administration of Justice in the Denver People's Courts*, JOUR. OF THE WEST 7 (1968): 510–21. In addition to the five defendants who were hanged under the jurisdiction of People's Courts, Burg also describes the case of William F. Hadley, who was sentenced to death by a People's Court on June 25, 1860. However, on the eve of his execution, Hadley bribed a guard, escaped, and was never heard from again. *Id.* at 515. *See* appendix 2, case no. 1.

5. *See* appendix 1, case no. 5.

> taken back, a people's court was organized, with Capt. R. Sopris as judge, a jury empaneled, and after a trial lasting half an hour, the jury returned a verdict of murder in the first degree, and the judge sentenced him to be hung to [*sic*] the nearest tree, which was done.[6]

To today's eye, this proceeding is merely a vigilante court with perfunctory hearings followed by lynch-mob justice. Furthermore, unlike in earlier years, the Territory of Colorado had an active death penalty statute after November 1861.[7] Thus, it is not included in the catalog of legal executions presented in this book.

The five death sentences handed down by the People's Courts were carried out quickly and in public. The first three executions occurred two or three days after the crimes were committed, but the fourth, that of James Gordon, took seventy-eight days. This was because Gordon temporarily escaped. Once caught and brought back to Denver, he was tried the next day in front of one thousand spectators, promptly convicted, and sentenced to death. Four days later he was dead. The fifth, Patrick Waters, went to his death twenty-one days after the murder but only two days after his trial. There were reportedly one thousand witnesses to Stoefel's execution, three thousand or four thousand who saw Gredler hang, and "several thousand" who watched as Gordon's life was ended. Meanwhile, the 1860 population of Denver, where all these hangings took place, was only 2,603.[8] Those early hangings were major social events, roughly akin to what might occur if the Denver Broncos today played in the Super Bowl . . . and played it in front of 6 million spectators. Even without cell phones or the Internet, news traveled fast.

HANGINGS IN COLORADO TERRITORY, 1863–1876

An 1866 newspaper description of the first Denver execution under territorial law noted that "[p]revious to this the exigencies of the times

---

6. *Murder of Daniel Steele at Evans*, ROCKY MTN. NEWS, Nov. 8, 1869, at 4. *See also* CAROL REIN SHWAYDER, 1 WELD COUNTY—OLD & NEW A32 (1983); LEONARD, at 64–65.

7. Act of Nov. 5, 1861, § 80, 1861 Colo. Terr. Sess. Laws 290, 306.

8. Denver Parks Collections, Denver Parks Timeline, pageformer.com/pageformer/dpl/parks/resc.html.

threw the administration of justice for capital offenses into the hands of the people and People's Courts, which, on account of the absence of places wherein to confine notorious criminals, were obliged to dispense justice in a very summary manner."[9] In other words, the primary justification for Colorado executions in the 1860s was that Colorado settlers at the time lacked not only a functioning criminal justice system but also jails or prisons (other than distant federal prisons) that could house those convicted of the most serious crimes for long periods of time.[10] That justification disappeared with the opening of a territorial prison in Cañon City in 1871.[11] Supporters of the death penalty then shifted their justifications to the punishment's purported deterrent effects, while voices in opposition focused on religious principles and the immorality of revenge. A debate in the *Rocky Mountain News* in 1867 provides examples of the arguments from both sides. A lengthy letter to the editor complained that the death penalty was "clearly opposed to the divine precepts of Jesus . . . [and] at variation with every principle of justice."[12] The author denounced the death penalty as pure retaliation and revenge and pointed to several European countries to show that the use of the death penalty was in decline. Adding a point still heard in death penalty debates today, the author argued that imprisonment for life "is a more horrible thing to contemplate, in many instances, than

---

9. *Justice Appeased*, ROCKY MTN. NEWS, May 30, 1866, at 1.

10. Denver did not have a jail until 1861, three years after the city was founded. LEONARD, at 106.

11. Cañon City is located in south central Colorado, approximately one hundred miles southwest of Denver and forty miles west of Pueblo. Thomas Macon, a member of the Territorial Legislature from Cañon City, was instrumental in the decision to locate the prison at Cañon City. At the time, both Denver and Golden were fighting over which city would be named the capital of the new state. Representative Macon supported Denver over Golden, and this support won him enough votes from legislators in northern Colorado to have the prison located in Cañon City. The prison was originally opened as a federal penitentiary but was deeded to the state in 1876, when Colorado attained statehood. ROSEMAE WELLS CAMPBELL, FROM TRAPPERS TO TOURISTS; FREMONT COUNTY, COLORADO, 1830–1950 (1972), at 46. For a brief history, *see* Gerald E. Sherard, *A Short History of the Colorado State Penitentiary*, accessed July 15, 2016, https://www.colorado.gov/pacific/sites/default/files/A%20Short%20History%20of%20the%20Colorado%20State%20Penitentiary.pdf.

12. Laura de Forch Gordon, *Capital Punishment*, ROCKY MTN. NEWS, Apr. 22, 1867, at 2.

death."[13] In response, the editors of the *Rocky Mountain News* focused primarily on the death penalty as a means of deterring future murderers from criminal violence, explaining,

> It is a fact well known to all our pioneer settlers, that were it not for the visitation of the death penalty upon notorious offenders, our city would at one period have been so completely sunken in the wicked depravity of crime, as to have made it utterly impossible for a quiet, peaceable man, much less a God-fearing, law abiding one, to reside in it.[14]

Notably, this debate lacks any discussion of two leading modern justifications for the death penalty: retribution and the need to execute killers to help ease the grief of the families of the murder victim. Instead, these nineteenth-century justifications for the death penalty focused on religious principles (religious arguments were heard on both sides of the issue), deterrence, and the need to execute killers because a shortage of prison cells meant they could not be kept in prison for long periods of time.

Gov. William Gilpin signed into law the first legislation authorizing the death penalty in the Territory of Colorado on November 5, 1861,[15]

---

13. *Id.*

14. *Id.* The editorial board of the *Rocky Mountain News* retained their support for the death penalty until February 12, 2007. *A Mythical Penalty: Abolition of Death Sentence Would Only Recognize Reality*, ROCKY MTN. NEWS, Feb. 12, 2007, at 34. Two years later, the newspaper ceased publication.

15. *See* Roxane J. Perruso, *And Then There Were Three: Colorado's New Death Penalty Sentencing Statute*, U. COLO. L. REV. 68 (1997): 194 (hereinafter Perruso); Act of Nov. 5, 1861, div. IV, § 20, 1861 Colo. Terr. Sess. Laws 290, 293. For two years prior to that bill, provisional laws also punished murder with a mandatory death sentence. *See* Provisional Laws and Joint Resolutions Passed at the First and Called Sessions of the General Assembly of Jefferson Territory, part 1, § 2 (1860).

There are two unpublished papers in the Stephen H. Hart Library in Denver that give valuable background information on the death penalty in Colorado. *See* John O. Sindall, *Capital Punishment in Colorado* (1973), and Robert W. Gordon, *A Legislative History of Capital Punishment for the Territory and State of Colorado, 1861 to 1965* (1965).

The fact that the outstanding papers of Sindall and Gordon found their way into the Hart Library is amazing. In 2015 the "Gordon" who authored the above paper could not be located, although he is not the same as the well-known historian by the same name, now a professor of law at Stanford University. Sindall, on the other hand, lives today in Concord, Massachusetts. His seminal paper on the death pen-

which was codified in 1868.[16] The first legal execution under territorial authority took the life of William S. Van Horn, who was hanged before a crowd of "thousands" in Central City on December 18, 1863. Van Horn had to be transported to Denver before his trial to avoid being lynched. Nearly two-and-a-half years passed until the next two men were hanged, Franklin Foster and Henry Stone. On May 24, 1866, after listening to the hymn "Rock of Ages," the men were dropped simultaneously from the scaffold in front of some three thousand witnesses.

Only two other men were sent to the scaffold under territorial law: George Smith in 1870 and Theodore Myers in 1873. Like Van Horn, Smith was hanged in Central City, thirty-five miles west of Denver, a town that had been originally settled by gold miners. Central City, with a population of roughly 10,000, was well known for some pugnacious citizens: the county museum reports, "In 1861 alone Central City recorded 217 fist fights, 97 revolver fights, 11 Bowie knife fights and one dog fight. Amazingly, no one was killed."[17] Smith was executed only after a bitter legal fight that included an unsuccessful appeal to the Colorado Supreme Court[18] and failed clemency petitions to both the governor and, while the governor was traveling out of state, the acting governor. His execution occurred a full two years after the murder—the longest time prior to execution that any condemned prisoner lived until 1895.

HANGINGS IN COUNTIES AFTER STATEHOOD, 1877–1889

When Colorado became a state in 1876, its death penalty statute was a mess. The 1868 capital statute was amended in a bill signed by Gov. Edward M. McCook on February 11, 1870.[19] However, the 1870 statute contained a loophole that allowed those accused of murder, if they played their cards right, to avoid ever meeting the executioner. This was

---

alty in Colorado was the first paper he ever wrote as a freshman at Metropolitan State University of Denver. He completed his PhD in philosophy at the University of Sydney, Australia, and spent his career as an administrator at Harvard University.

16. COLO. TERR. REV. STAT. ch. XXII, § 20 (1868).

17. Gilpin County Museum, *Central City, Colorado—A Brief History*, accessed July 15, 2016, http://www.centralcitycolorado.com/history.php.

18. Smith v. People, 1 Colo. 121 (1869).

19. *See* Act of Feb. 11, 1870, 1870 Colo. Terr. Sess. Laws 70.

because the 1870 legislation permitted defendants to avoid the death penalty by pleading guilty and avoiding a jury trial. As Roxane J. Perruso explains,

> The legislation . . . limited the availability of the death penalty to cases *in which the jury* found not only that the defendant was guilty of murder, but also that the killing was deliberate, premeditated, or committed during the perpetration (or attempted perpetration) of a felony.[20]

The 1876 Denver trial of Filomeno Gallotti and two of his associates ("the Italian Murderers") for a quadruple murder exposed this problem. The murders were especially atrocious, and the defendants escaped several lynching attempts before their trial. Future Colorado governor and US senator Charles S. Thomas served as Gallotti's defense attorney.[21] Thomas successfully argued that no jury could be impaneled following a defendant's guilty plea, which negated the possibility of a death sentence. Consequently, the three defendants were promptly sentenced to life imprisonment.[22]

Before this issue was resolved, Colorado achieved statehood and in 1877, the state's first legislature adopted both the 1868 death penalty statute and the 1870 provision amending it.[23] On February 2, 1877, an African American named James Miller, after being harassed at a dance hall by a white patron, killed another white man who was also at the dance hall. He eventually became the first prisoner legally executed in

---

20. Perruso, at 194 (emphasis added). *See also* Hill v. The People, 1 Colo. 436 (1872).

21. Paul H. Gantt, The Case of Alfred [*sic*] Packer, the Man Eater 146 n.213 (1952) (hereinafter Gantt). Thomas served as governor between 1899 and 1901 and as a senator between 1913 and 1921. *Id.*

22. *Id.* at 81. A similar issue recently led a New York court to invalidate a portion of the then-current New York death penalty law. The statute allowed for the imposition of a death sentence only by a jury. Defendants pleading guilty to capital murder (which is allowed only on the consent of the prosecutor and the permission of the judge) cannot be sentenced to death. The New York Court of Appeals has ruled that this provision coerces guilty pleas and punishes the right to trial by jury—at least in cases where the prosecutor has filed a notice of intent to seek a capital sentence. It invalidated one death sentence imposed under the statute on this ground. *See* People v. Harris, 779 N.E.2d 705 (N.Y. 2002).

23. Perruso, at 195 (citing Colo. Gen. Laws ch. XXIV, div. IV, § 615 (1877); Colo. Gen. Laws ch. XXIV, div. XV, §§ 868, 869 (1877).

the state of Colorado.[24] The execution was held in West Las Animas.[25] Because Miller pled not guilty, he was unable to win the type of relief won by the Italian Murderers. As we see throughout the history of Colorado's death penalty, and indeed up until the present, Lady Luck plays a major role in determining who is and who is not a recipient of the executioner's services.

The murder for which Miller was convicted occurred on August 26, 1876—just twenty-five days after Colorado became a state.[26] However, the first murder in the new state that resulted in a death sentence occurred just a few days earlier, although the defendant was never hanged because of what many modern observers would no doubt call the luckiest "legal technicality" in the state's death penalty history. Here, Malachi Moneyhan—his surname is spelled at least six different ways in newspapers, prison records, the records of the Colorado Supreme Court, and the cemetery in which he was laid to rest—was sentenced to death for killing Patrick Fitzpatrick.[27] But luckily for Malachi—his first name is spelled consistently—the indictment in his case inconsistently spelled the victim's name as "Fitzpatrick" or "Fitz Patrick." That incongruity was enough for the Colorado Supreme Court to toss out the conviction.

In 1881 the legislature attempted to close the avenue through which the Italian Murderers escaped the gallows by repealing the provisions of the 1870 statute. In its place it adopted

> a new statute with essentially the same provisions but adding a proviso that in case a defendant pleaded guilty of murder, a jury should pass on the question whether the murder was deliberate and premeditated or not. Thus in the case of a positive finding, the death penalty could be imposed.[28]

This corrective action, however, was itself flawed, because by repealing the 1870 statute, the convictions of all those sentenced under its authority could not be sustained.[29] The Colorado Supreme Court revealed a

---

24. *See* appendix 1, case no. 11.
25. In 1886 "West" was removed and the town was renamed Las Animas.
26. *See* chapter 1, table 1.1.
27. *See* appendix 2, case no. 5.
28. GANTT, at 81 (citing Colo. Laws 1881, at 70).
29. *Id.* at 82.

similar flaw in an 1882 decision. The Colorado legislature had repealed a larceny statute in 1881 without a "savings clause" to maintain the applicability of the statute to all crimes committed prior to its repeal.[30] In an 1883 case titled *Garvey v. People*, the Colorado Supreme Court held that any murder conviction under the 1870 statute could not be sustained because the amended statute did not contain a savings clause, thus prohibiting the retroactive application of the new 1881 statute.[31] The new statute could not apply to Albert Garvey, so he was set free.[32]

The 1883 *Garvey* decision also effectively spared the life of one of Colorado's most notorious felons, alleged cannibal Alferd Packer. On April 13, 1883, one month prior to the *Garvey* decision, Packer was sentenced to death after being convicted for the murders of five companions. In 1885 the Colorado Supreme Court invalidated Packer's death sentence under *Garvey* but allowed the state to try him under Colorado's manslaughter statute, which had not been altered by the legislature.[33] In 1886 Packer was convicted on five counts of manslaughter and sentenced to eight years on each count, for a total of forty years. He served fifteen years before being paroled in 1901.[34]

After *Garvey*, the legislature finally corrected the statute in 1883 to allow capital punishment of defendants who pled guilty.[35] For the first time, this statute established degrees of murder, setting a penalty of ten years to life for those found guilty of second-degree murder.[36] As summarized by the Colorado Supreme Court,

> The statute defining the crime of murder and providing for its punishment was last amended by the legislature of 1883. As amended the stat-

---

30. *See id.* at 82; Hirschburg v. People, 6 Colo. 145 (1882).

31. 6 Colo. 559 (1883).

32. GANTT, at 82.

33. Packer v. The People, 8 P. 564 (Oct. 1885); GANTT, at 82. *See also* Alfred Packer, COLO. STATE ARCHIVES, accessed July 15, 2016, https://www.colorado.gov/pacific/archives/alfred-packer.

34. *See* https://www.colorado.gov/pacific/archives/alfred-packer, accessed July 15, 2016. Packer died in 1907. *Id.* In 1968 students at the University of Colorado Boulder voted to name the cafeteria in the University Memorial Center (Student Union Building) the Alferd G. Packer Memorial Grill, with the motto "Have a friend for lunch."

35. WILLIAM M. KING, GOING TO MEET A MAN 13–14 (1990) (hereinafter KING).

36. Perruso, at 195 (citing Colo. Gen. Stat. ch. XXV, div. IV, § 709 (1883)).

> ute divides the crime of murder into two degrees, and requires the jury trying any person indicted for said crime, if they find him guilty thereof, "to designate by their verdict whether it be murder of the first or second degree." The amended statute further provides that "every person convicted of murder of the first degree shall suffer death, and every person convicted of murder of the second degree shall suffer imprisonment in the penitentiary for a term not less than ten years. Laws 1883, p. 150.[37]

Meanwhile, public executions—whether by lynching or after being authorized in a legal trial—were becoming more controversial. To be sure, they were important social events in the community that served an entertainment function. Legal executions regularly attracted audiences of between one thousand and five thousand spectators.[38] By far, the largest number of witnesses to an execution gathered in Denver on July 27, 1886, when thousands watched as Andrew Green died for the murder of a streetcar driver.[39]

Debate in Denver over whether hangings should be public accelerated in the month before Green's execution. By that time, several eastern cities—including Boston, New York, and Philadelphia—had abolished public hangings, and some Colorado civic leaders feared that the spectacle of a public hanging would tarnish the image of the progressive, cosmopolitan city that Denver hoped to cultivate.[40] England abolished public hangings in the 1860s:

> The exclusion of the crowd from the execution scene on the one hand appeased [the] squeamishness' that was part of the developing Victorian middle-class culture of sensibility, and on the other meant that hanging could be carried out as a more orderly, bureaucratic affair, over which the state had firmer control.[41]

A year before Green was put to death, state representative Lafe Pence of Ouray had tried to abolish public hangings following the lynching of

---

37. Kearney v. People, 11 Colo. 258, 258; (1888).

38. *See* table 1.5.

39. *See* appendix 1, case no. 23.

40. KING, at 91.

41. LIZZIE SEAL, CAPITAL PUNISHMENT IN TWENTIETH-CENTURY BRITAIN: AUDIENCE, JUSTICE, MEMORY (2014), at 13 (hereinafter SEAL) (author's citations omitted).

a woman in his city.[42] Editorials in the *Denver Tribune-Republican* urged the sheriff to conduct the hanging in private, but other editorials in the *Rocky Mountain News* urged the sheriff to open the event to the public.[43] As a compromise, the sheriff allowed the public to witness Green's execution but did not announce its site beforehand. Instead, the site became known only on the day of Green's death (near Cherry Creek, between the Broadway and Colfax bridges), when carpenters arrived to construct the gallows. By the time they finished the job—still several hours before the hanging—some three thousand spectators had assembled, with several thousand soon to join them.[44]

Green was hanged with a "twitch-up" gallows. This method of execution was thought to inflict less suffering on the prisoner and run a lower chance of blunder than the more traditional "long-drop" gallows. With a long-drop hanging, the prisoner drops with a rope around his neck, and his weight causes death through strangulation or, if the drop comes to an abrupt stop, a broken neck.[45] With the twitch-up method, a weight greater than that of the condemned man's body causes the death.[46] In Green's case, the executioner attached a 310-pound weight to the rope, which was strung through a series of pulleys on a horizontal beam. After Green and the choir sang "Why Not Tonight," followed by a ten-minute farewell speech and a closing song by Green and the choir, "Nearer My God to Thee,"[47] the weight fell, taking with it the slack in the rope around

---

42. *Id.* at 92–93; Leonard, *Avenging Mary Rose: The Lynchings of Margaret and Michael Cuddigan in Ouray, Colorado, 1864*, COLORADO HERITAGE 37: 34–47 (1999).

43. SEAL, at 92–98.

44. *Id.* at 119.

45. Hangings cause relatively instantaneous death if the victim's spinal cord is severed. However, this happens in only a minority of hangings. More often, the rope cuts off blood supply to the brain, thereby taking several minutes before death comes, or the prisoner is asphyxiated, causing him to gasp for breath for several moments while he slowly suffocates. If the drop is too long, the prisoner is decapitated. Consequently, hanging as a method of execution was always controversial. STUART BANNER, THE DEATH PENALTY: AN AMERICAN HISTORY 44–48 (2002) (hereinafter BANNER). It was hoped that the twitch-up method of hanging would increase the proportion of executed prisoners who succumbed to a broken neck. *Id.*

46. *Id.* at 92.

47. *Denver Disgraced: The Scenes at the Hanging of Andy Green Disgraceful in the Extreme*, LEADVILLE HERALD DEMO., July 28, 1886, at 1.

his neck, and Green shot up into the air.[48] The launch, however, failed to break Green's neck, so the crowd of fifteen to twenty thousand[49] watched for some twenty-three minutes as Green slowly strangled to death.[50] In the aftermath, as William M. King notes, "the abolition of public hangings in Colorado, because of the Denver experience with Andrew Green, was an idea whose time had surely come."[51]

Overall, in the three decades prior to 1890, the death penalty invoked heated public debates in Colorado. Although some western lore and many television Westerns often depict a citizenry that welcomed frequent executions, in fact, less than one execution per year occurred in the territory and state, and they were always controversial. Eventually, increasing opposition to the festive atmosphere surrounding public executions led to their demise.

THE MOVE TO CENTRALIZE EXECUTIONS IN CAÑON CITY

The botched execution of Andrew Green and the number of spectators who witnessed and later argued about it, not to mention the pageantry surrounding it, added enormous fuel to the movement to abolish public hangings in Colorado. The outrage sparked by the circus and party atmosphere did not alone lead to the uproar by opponents of public executions. Rather, the perception of an "image problem"—a belief that public hangings were bad for Colorado's national image—similarly drove the growing opposition to public executions. As King observes,

> Hanging people in the public square had no place in a modern society that emphasized order and control; it effected an unsavory image, was bad for long-term growth and development, and should therefore be opposed by progressive-minded people.[52]

48. The rope used to hang Green was manufactured by a St. Louis company that specialized in making rope for this purpose. One hundred feet of the rope was ordered for Green's hanging, leaving enough left over to be used for the hanging of Nicolai Femenella (*see* appendix 1, case no. 24), two years after Green's death. KING, at 117.

49. KING, at 119, 131.

50. *Id.* at 150.

51. *Id.* at 142.

52. *Id.*

Or, as Stuart Banner puts it,

> Public executions would be widely criticized in the nineteenth century, and much of the criticism would be directed at the crowd, who would be accused of drunkenness, irreverence, rowdiness, and similar sins. Respectable Americans of the nineteenth century would come to feel embarrassment at the idea of attending an execution, and a superiority to the sort of person who would attend.[53]

And so it was clear that the days of public executions were numbered.

To make executions less visible to the public, critics of public hangings urged legislators to "centralize" hangings by moving them all to one location and conducting them under the authority of the state rather than the counties. A growing desire to search for ways to apply the death penalty more humanely and with limited involvement of prison personnel accompanied this increasing cultural opposition to public executions. Six months after Green's death, Gov. Benjamin H. Eaton called for legislation outlawing public executions. However, it took two more years for the legislature to act. On April 19, 1889, Gov. Job A. Cooper signed a bill moving all executions to within the walls of the state penitentiary in Cañon City.[54] Those who most strenuously objected to the new law included Colorado State Penitentiary warden J. A. Lamping, who saw executions as incompatible with the rehabilitative goals of the prison.[55] The last public hanging in Colorado took the life of Jose Abram Ortiz[56]

---

53. BANNER, at 37.

54. *Id.* at 151; Act of Apr. 19, 1889, § 1, 1889 Colo. Sess. Laws 118. The law repealed all previous death penalty statutes and took effect ninety days after the governor signed it: July 19, 1889. However, the repeal took effect immediately on the date the governor signed the law in April. There was no savings clause. Consequently, two defendants sentenced to death for murders committed in May and June 1889 later had their convictions and sentences vacated by the US Supreme Court. *See In re* Medley, 134 U.S. 160 (1890); *In re* Savage, 134 U.S. 176 (1890).

55. William Hazlett, *Capital Punishment Has Bloody History*, ROCKY MTN. NEWS, Dec. 19, 1960, at 24. At least one later warden agreed. Harry C. Tinsley, who supervised seven executions, 1955–1964, told the *Rocky Mountain News* that he thought "[a]n execution serves to upset the order and dignity of a prison." William Hazlett, *Hand of Every Person Guides Executioner*, ROCKY MTN. NEWS, Dec. 20, 1960, at 6.

56. *See* appendix 1, case no. 25.

in Conejos on July 16, 1889, three months after Governor Cooper signed the new legislation, but three days before the ban took effect.[57]

Because of the fierce opposition to public executions, the 1889 legislation not only prevented the public from attending executions but also from learning any details about them. Thereafter, the warden in charge of the execution no longer announced the day and time of the execution in advance. The legislation mandated that state officials keep all details about the execution secret,[58] although some officials violated the rule at irregular intervals. Furthermore, the 1889 legislation permitted only a small group of spectators to witness each execution and prohibited the spectators, like the prison workers, from divulging any details.[59] The legislation mandated that immediately after the execution, "a *post mortem* examination of the body of the convict shall be made by the attending physician and surgeon."[60] Several other states passed similar secrecy laws at roughly the same time, but occasionally these laws were flouted and prison officials and others in attendance leaked details about a given execution, such as information about the inmate's demeanor in his last moments.[61]

The new laws particularly aimed to restrict access to executions by women and children. Before 1890 children frequently attended public executions in Colorado; parents and other adults who believed the

---

57. *Judicially Hanged: Ortiz, the Mexican Murderer, Suffers the Penalty of Law for His Crime*, ROCKY MTN. NEWS, July 17, 1889, at 1. The last public execution in the United States took place before a crowd of ten thousand to twenty thousand spectators in Owensboro, Kentucky, in 1936. BANNER, at 156.

58. This provision was repealed on March 29, 1897, by the same bill that abolished the death penalty.

59. The number of spectators at executions varied considerably, although exact numbers are not available. For example, thirty people witnessed the hanging of E. J. Farmer in 1932. *See* appendix 1, case no. 67. The next year, sixty legislators and state employees watched as Nelivelt Moss was hanged. *See* appendix 1, case no. 69. In 1933 fifteen physicians were permitted to witness the execution of William Kelley, who was the first person to die in Colorado's gas chamber. *See* appendix 1, case no. 71. There were fifty spectators present when Paul J. Schneider was executed in 1949. *See* appendix 1, case no. 93. Before Pete Catalina was put to death in 1939, Warden Roy Best invited twenty inmates to watch as the gas chamber was tested by killing a pig. *See* appendix 1, case no. 78. It was thought that watching the pig gasp for its final breaths would deter the prisoners from future criminality.

60. Act of Apr. 19, 1889, § 5, 1889 Colo. Sess. Laws 120.

61. BANNER, at 163.

death penalty had a deterrent effect considered the experience uniquely instructive. The elimination of public executions effectively ended this opportunity. Banner attributes the masculinization of executions partly to positions of power, with men more likely than women to have the jobs and connections necessary to secure invitations to hangings.[62] In addition, changing social mores led to the perception of attending executions as an unfeminine activity.

HANGINGS IN CAÑON CITY IN THE 1890S

The transition of executions from counties to the state penitentiary was not a smooth one. When the legislature charged the state prison, against Warden Lamping's wishes, with the responsibility of conducting executions after 1890, no one coveted the duty of serving as the hangman. Consequently, an attempt was made to build a hanging machine that would not require a prison worker or volunteer citizen to spring open a trap door on the gallows and otherwise supervise the execution. At the same time, authorities wanted a hanging machine that accomplished its mission quickly and did not cause prolonged suffering for the inmate.

On November 8, 1890, Noverto Griego, convicted of killing a merchant in Trinidad, became the first of forty-five prisoners to be hanged in Cañon City.[63] In supervising the execution, Warden Lamping followed the law by not disclosing in advance the time of the hanging and keeping secret all of the details of the hanging after it occurred. The warden could invite only six people—all men—to attend each execution, none of whom represented the press and all of whom were sworn to secrecy.[64] "Newspaper men of every description were positively forbidden admittance, and the utmost secrecy was observed until after the execution,

---

62. *Id.* at 159.

63. *See* appendix 1, case no. 26.

64. *The Crime Expiated: Noverto Griego Probably Pays the Penalty of His Awful Deed Today*, TRINIDAD DAILY NEWS, Nov. 7, 1890, at 4. "The law requires that only the penitentiary Warden, the prison physician and one assistant, one friend of the condemned man whom he may name, the Sheriff of the county in which the murder took place, and a jury of six men to be selected by the Warden shall witness the execution." *Graves to Hang Himself*, N.Y. TIMES, Jan. 24, 1892, at 16.

when it was readily ascertained who the witnesses were and that everything had worked well."[65]

As seen in Table 1.2, during the 1890s, eleven more hangings occurred in the prison at Cañon City after Griego's death. The next hanging, in January 1891, took the life of James Joyce.[66] According to the *Rocky Mountain News*, the "surgeons" declared that the execution was "the most successful and painless execution that has ever been performed in America."[67] They credited Lamping for this achievement and particularly applauded a hydraulic process that was used in the hanging. In effect, this invention, "which is intended to do away with the repugnant duties of the executioner,"[68] required the prisoner to hang himself. The *Rocky Mountain News* described the machine with these words:

> The criminal . . . stepped upon a small carpeted platform, two feet by three feet . . . and the plug was drawn out of the can in the adjacent room, and as the water, weighing some forty pounds, trickled away it lessened the weight on the end of an iron rod until that dropped off, and Joyce's soul took its flight into eternity.[69]

The "Do-It-Yourself-Hanging-Machine," described by one author as a "Rube Goldberg-like contraption,"[70] was next used eight months later on William H. Davis,[71] who had been convicted of killing his foster mother and her paramour.[72] A few months after Davis's death, the *New York*

---

65. *Hung for Murder: The Brute Who Slugged Poor Underwood Stretches Hemp*, PUEBLO CHIEFTAIN, Nov. 9, 1890, at 1.

66. *See* appendix 1, case no. 27.

67. *Without a Tremor*, ROCKY MTN. NEWS, Jan. 18, 1891, at 1.

68. *Graves to Hang Himself*.

69. *Without a Tremor*.

70. ANDREW J. FIELD, MAINLINER DENVER: THE BOMBING OF FLIGHT 629 215 (2005) (hereinafter FIELD).

71. *See* appendix 1, case no. 28.

72. This time newspapers credited Deputy Warden George E. Dudley for the invention of the new machine. *Hanged in Prison*, ROCKY MTN. NEWS, Sept. 23, 1891, at 1. "This death machine is the only one of its kind on record. It is the invention of a tender-hearted Deputy Warden who had been assigned to cut the rope at a previous execution, but who, rather than perform that duty, set his wits at work to invent a contrivance which would do the undesirable work for him. This he did. His conscience is now serene." *Graves to Hang Himself*.

Times printed a more detailed description of Colorado's unique hydraulic "upright jerker":

> In the centre of the death chamber is a platform about four feet square, raised, perhaps, five inches above the level of the stone floor. Over this platform dangles the noose. The hangman's rope runs over a pulley wheel at the ceiling and disappears through a small aperture into the adjoining room. To the end of the rope, in this second room, is attached an iron weight of 370 pounds. This weight is supported, six feet from the floor, by a cross beam which may be likened to the beam of a large pair of balancing scales. On its end opposite the weight is suspended a small wooden cask containing about two gallons of water. This water cask may be moved from right to left and an exact balance thereby given to the cask and the iron weight. In the bottom of the cask is a wooden plug and connected with it is a small, strong cord leading from the plug to the platform in the death chamber.
>
> When . . . [the condemned inmate] steps on the platform . . . [h]is weight on the platform removes the plug from the cask, the water rushes from it until the cask is sufficiently lightened, and then the heavy weight on the opposite end of the beam drops on a thick mattress on the floor.[73]

When the weight dropped, the prisoner, attached by his neck to the other end of it, abruptly flew skyward. This twitch-up method of hanging led to the expression that the inmate was "jerked to Jesus."[74]

The deputy warden did not receive lasting credit for his invention. By 1971, the *Denver Post* reported that the machine was "[c]reated by a convict, whose name has now been forgotten." Cary Stiff, *The Do-It-Yourself Hanging Machine*, DENVER POST (Empire Magazine), June 13, 1971, at 45.

The inmate discussed in the above *New York Times* article was Dr. T. Thatcher Graves, who was then on death row for the murder of Mrs. Josephine A. Barnaby. Graves subsequently won a new trial from the Colorado Supreme Court. Graves v. People, 18 Colo. 170; 32 P. 63 (1893). However, in 1893 he took his own life while awaiting that trial. *Dr. Graves Death: End of the Barnaby Murder Defendant*, ROCKY MTN. NEWS, Sept. 4, 1893, at 1 and appendix 2, case no. 19.

73. *Graves to Hang Himself*.

74. *See, e.g.*, appendix 1, case nos. 17 and 42. In the former case, reference to being "jerked to Jesus" can be found in DUANE A. SMITH, ROCKY MOUNTAIN BOOM TOWN, A HISTORY OF DURANGO 51 (1980). This means that the twitch-up method of hanging in Colorado predated the 1890 centralization of execution hangings in

The upright jerker was used in several other states as early as the 1830s. New York, New Jersey, Illinois, South Carolina, and Pennsylvania used various forms of the contraption, in modified forms, although without the hydraulic component.[75] In Connecticut, 50 pounds of "shot" were put in a cylinder, and when it poured out, it triggered a lever that held a weight of 312 pounds. When that weight fell, the inmate soared to his death.[76]

After Davis's execution in September 1891, the state hanged nine other men from the gallows in Cañon City before the end of the nineteenth century. No executions occurred between May 1892 and May 1895 because Gov. Davis Waite opposed the death penalty,[77] but seven took place during 1895 and 1896. These included two men hanged on May 11, 1895, for separate crimes: Thomas Jordan, who shot a coworker,[78] and Peter Augusta, who killed a man in a lover's triangle.[79] The attending physician described the executions as "the most skillful that had been made in his seventeen years' experience as prison surgeon," even though Jordan's neck did not break and he dangled from the gallows for eleven minutes before death was pronounced.[80]

A reporter who witnessed the executions for the *Denver Post* would no doubt disagree with the assertion that the hangings were "skillful." Readers were told that the person to be hanged was ushered until he was standing on "the fatal trap." Then, this is what happened to Jordan:

Cañon City; the latter case, involving the last man to be legally hanged in Colorado (1933), indicates that the twitch-up gallows was used throughout the entire history of hangings in Cañon City.

75. BANNER, at 171.

76. *Forced to Execute Himself. The South Windsor Murderer Pays the Extreme Penalty. First Trial of the New Automatic Gallows in the Connecticut State Prison Successful*, N.Y. TIMES, Dec. 18, 1894, at 3.

77. In discussing the execution of Thomas Jordan, who was put to death soon after Governor Waite left office, the *Rocky Mountain News* reported, "Governor Waite's position upon capital punishment was well known. He was opposed to it, and during his administration it was practically admitted that Jordan would be safe from the noose of the hangman." *The Condemned*, ROCKY MTN. NEWS, May 12, 1895, at 1.

78. *See* appendix 1, case no. 31.

79. *See* appendix 1, case no. 32.

80. *Two Men Executed*, TRINIDAD DAILY NEWS, May 14, 1895, at 1.

> One minute, two minutes, three minutes, four minutes, it seemed almost an eternity. Suddenly there was a noise and the body shot into the air with tremendous force. Almost to the ceiling it went and then it fell back again until the slack of the rope tightened and the neck was given an awful wrench. But Thomas Jordan was not dead. Three times his body convulsed and his legs were drawn up. Two doctors held his wrist and it was seven minutes after he shot into the air before the heart ceased to beat and the limbs grew still and cold. The corpse swung a few minutes more; then it was carried from the room.[81]

One wonders how many readers of the *Post* that evening lost their appetites for dinner.

Jordan's attorneys vigorously contested his execution; he was the first prisoner hanged at Cañon City to appeal his conviction to the Colorado Supreme Court.[82] Concerns about his sanity were so paramount that Gov. Albert W. McIntire visited Jordan on death row so he could ascertain first-hand whether clemency was in order.[83]

Meanwhile, Colorado's death row received the most socially prominent citizen in its history, although this inmate was never executed. Dr. Thomas Thatcher Graves, a lawyer who had graduated first in his class from Harvard Medical School, was sent to a death cell in Cañon City in 1892 after being found guilty in what was then the longest murder trial in the history of the United States. Graves was convicted of killing a former patient, friend, and wealthy widow, Josephine Barnaby, whose estate he controlled and managed and whose will promised him a substantial financial benefit. In 1893 Graves won a new trial, but he committed suicide soon thereafter and the new trial was never held.[84]

Another unusual case from this era sent a Ute Indian, "Pablo the Ute," to death row for killing a woman named Eweep, another Indian. On appeal, Pablo argued that he should not have been tried in state court since both he and the victim were Indians, even though the murder was not committed within the boundaries of the Indian reservation. This

---

81. *Swung into Eternity*, DENVER POST, May 13, 1895, at 8.
82. Jordan v. People, 19 Colo. 417; 36 P. 218 (Colo. 1894).
83. *The Condemned*.
84. *See* appendix 2, case no. 19.

argument was unsuccessful.[85] Three weeks after losing the decision, still on death row, Pablo died from tuberculosis.

Four men were executed in 1896; the latter three were codefendants who were all executed on the same day. But the first execution of the year, on February 7, involved Benjamin Ratcliff. A single parent, he had been involved for several years in disputes with the school board in a rural area near Fairplay. When one school board member circulated a false rumor that Ratcliff was involved in an incestuous relationship with his daughter, Ratcliff appeared at a school board meeting and shot and killed all of its members.[86]

After Ratcliff was hanged, there was just one more execution day in Cañon City in the 1800s. But on that day—June 26, 1896—three men died. It was one of only two times in Colorado history that three people were hanged on the same day, and arguably, the ripple effect from a triple execution added to abolitionist sentiment.[87] The hangings took the lives of William Holt, Albert Noble, and Deonicio Romero, ex-cons convicted of killing police officer John Solomon during a robbery in Trinidad. When the three died, a total of thirty-seven men had been executed (including those condemned to death by the People's Courts) in Colorado. This represents 36 percent of those put to death in Colorado through 2014.

---

85. See appendix 2, case no. 26.

86. While the public's attention is often and rightfully directed toward the families of homicide victims, we have little information about what the families of current and former death row inmates experience. In the case of the Ratcliff family, Benjamin's crime and execution was a guarded family secret until the 1970s, when one of his granddaughters became curious after stumbling on a list of people executed in Colorado. As a result, in 2010 one of Ratcliff's great-grandsons, Chris Andrew, published a book titled *The Legend of Benjamin Ratcliff: From Family Tragedy to a Legacy of Resilience*. It is a magnificent piece of work, detailing the family's history and the secret that Ratcliff's grandchildren did not discover for eighty years, and it gives readers insights into the execution's aftermath. The book ends in 2010, when a large group of Ratcliff's descendants assembled at what once was the Ratcliff homestead, not far from the murders, for the first Ratcliff family reunion.

87. *See* appendix 1, case nos. 35–37. The second execution of three men on one day occurred on March 14, 1930, when three bank robbers—Claude Ray, John Walker, and Andrew Halliday—were hanged in Cañon City for murdering a sheriff in Eads, approximately 110 miles east of Pueblo.

THE ABOLITION OF THE DEATH PENALTY IN 1897

While no one knew it at the time, the triple execution of Holt, Noble, and Romero in 1896 proved to be the end of an era in Colorado. Not only were they the last to be executed in Colorado in the nineteenth century, they were the last before the state abolished the death penalty.

Nationally, in 1846 Michigan became the first state in the United States, and indeed the first English-speaking jurisdiction in the world, to abolish the death penalty. Rhode Island and Wisconsin soon followed in 1852 and 1853, respectively. Iowa temporarily abolished the death penalty in 1872 but restored it in 1878. Maine abolished the death penalty in 1876, resurrected it in 1883, and abolished it for good in 1887. Colorado followed as the next state to experiment with abolition.[88]

Efforts to abolish the death penalty in Colorado, led mainly by religious leaders, greatly accelerated in the mid-1890s. On March 15, 1893, by a 19–13 vote, the state Senate passed a bill abolishing the death penalty,[89] but the State House of Representatives defeated the measure two weeks later, 30–19.[90] On February 28, 1895, a bill abolishing the death penalty passed without debate in the Senate.[91] The *Denver Post* applauded the move, although the editors added that the bill would strengthen the anti–death penalty position if it also removed any hope of a pardon for the prisoner.[92] Ultimately, the bill died in the House of Representatives,[93] but it successfully resurfaced two years later. This time it passed in both legislative chambers.

The debate resurfaced in the legislative session of 1897 when Rep. Eugene Engley introduced H.B. 74, which proposed to abolish the death penalty and substitute for it a punishment of life imprisonment. Representative Engley argued that rich men were never hanged, and that in the recent case of Dr. Graves,[94] something like 1,100 of the 1,200

---

88. Iowa, Maine, and Wisconsin totally abolished the death penalty; Michigan retained it for treason until 1963; and Rhode Island retained it for murder of a guard by a lifetime prisoner. HUGO ADAM BEDAU, THE DEATH PENALTY IN AMERICA, CURRENT CONTROVERSIES 9 (1997).

89. S.J. Res. 962–63, 9th Leg. (Colo. 1893).

90. *The Capital Punishment Bill*, ROCKY MTN. NEWS, Apr. 1, 1893, at 8.

91. *No Work for Hangman*, ROCKY MTN. NEWS, Mar. 1, 1895, at 8.

92. *Capital Punishment*, DENVER POST, Mar. 1, 1895, at 4.

93. H.R.J. Res. 853, 10th Leg. (Colo. 1895).

94. *See* appendix 2, case no. 19.

potential jurors had to be dismissed because of their strong feelings against the death penalty. He told his colleagues, "Judicial murder is as wicked as any murder, and should be made as punishable as if committed without judicial sanction."[95] On the other hand, Rep. Andrew Park from Pueblo opposed the bill, pointing out that the average time served for those sentenced to life in prison was only nine years and predicting that abolition would increase both the number of capital crimes and the number of lynchings.[96] On February 17, the abolition bill—along with a measure to ban the wearing of top hats in movie theaters—passed in the House on a 43–15 vote.[97]

A month later, the Senate took up the bill but without much discussion. Notably, John Cleghorn, warden of the state penitentiary in Cañon City, traveled to Denver to speak against the bill, warning that if the death penalty were abolished there would be no way to prevent further murders by the forty prisoners then at Cañon City serving life sentences.[98] However, the Senate ultimately voted 21–11 in favor of the bill.[99]

On March 29, 1897, Gov. Alva Adams signed H.B. 74, which abolished the death penalty for all crimes and substituted life imprisonment with hard labor (but parole eligibility) for those convicted of first-degree murder.[100] The law took effect ninety days after the governor signed it.[101] However, "Any murder which shall have been committed before this Act takes effect shall be inquired of, prosecuted and punished in accordance with the law in force at the time such murder was committed."[102] Therefore, three men were sentenced to death later in 1897 for murders that predated June 29, 1897—after the death penalty abolition bill was signed but before it took effect. Two of these were men who killed two

95. *Capital Punishment*, DENVER POST, Feb. 5, 1897, at 2.

96. *Id. See also The House*, ROCKY MTN. NEWS, Feb. 6, 1897, at 8.

97. This did not apply to murders committed prior to the passage of the bill. *In the Legislature*, ASPEN DAILY TIMES, Feb. 18, 1897, at 1.

98. *Wants Capital Punishment*, DENVER POST, Mar. 25, 1897, at 1.

99. *No More Hangings*, DENVER POST, Mar. 26, 1897, at 6.

100. Act of Mar. 29, 1897, § 1, 1897 Colo. Sess. Laws ch. 35; *Hanging Is Abolished*, DENVER POST, Mar. 29, 1897, at 1; *No More Hanging by Law*, ROCKY MTN. NEWS, Mar. 30, 1897, at 10. The act also abolished the secrecy requirements surrounding executions imposed by the 1889 legislation.

101. *Hanging Is Abolished*.

102. 1897 Colo. Sess. Laws ch. 35.

deputy sheriffs in 1896[103] and the third was a man who committed a murder in April 1897.[104] Governor Adams subsequently commuted all three death sentences.

For three years following abolition, no strong efforts were made to restore the death penalty. In early 1899, Boulder's *Daily Camera* editorialized, "There is no call for a revival of that relic of barbarism, capital punishment. Colorado, in the vanguard of progress, must take no step backward."[105] Two years after signing the abolition legislation, Governor Adams applauded the repeal in his annual message to the legislature, calling it "the most forward step in criminal legislation that has yet been taken in Colorado."[106] However, by 1901, more and more leaders were calling for the death penalty to be reinstated. For example, at one debate in Denver in early 1901, Rev. G. B. Vosburgh, the pastor of the First Baptist Church, claimed that the number of murders in Arapahoe County had risen significantly since the death penalty was abolished. He added some pertinent phrases from the Old Testament, such as "Whoso sheddeth man's blood by man also shall his blood be shed."[107]

THE AFTERMATH: SOME WELL-PUBLICIZED LYNCHINGS

Unfortunately for death penalty opponents, angry mobs viewed the abolition of the death penalty as a justification to return to lynching. Despite the optimism of death penalty foes when the death penalty was scrapped, three lynchings early in the new century rekindled efforts to bring the executioner back. The first occurred in Cañon City in January 1900, after four prisoners escaped from the state penitentiary, murdering a guard in the process.[108] All four men were soon recaptured. When

---

103. *See* appendix 2, case nos. 29 and 30.

104. *See* appendix 2, case no. 31.

105. Editorial, BOULDER DAILY CAMERA, Jan. 31, 1899, at 2.

106. Message of Gov. Alva Adams, S.J. Res. 39, 41, 12th Leg. (Colo. 1899). Adams also noted that of the twenty-five inmates condemned to death since executions were moved to the state penitentiary, thirteen were reprieved by the courts or the governor. *Id.* at 40.

107. *Minister Wants Death Penalty*, ROCKY MTN. NEWS, Jan. 18, 1901 at 6.

108. One of the escaped convicts was Anton Woode, who was convicted of murder on April 8, 1893 and sentenced to twenty-five years in prison. The murder was committed when Woode was eleven years of age. The complete story of this case is

Thomas Reynolds, the one who had actually killed the guard, returned to Cañon City, an angry mob of five hundred citizens seized him, put a rope around his neck, and strung him from the nearest telegraph pole.[109] When Gov. Charles S. Thomas and Secretary of State Charles Stonaker heard the news, Stonaker recognized at once that the lynching would fuel renewed debate over the death penalty:

> Lynching is a horrible thing . . . but this affair has been horrible from the start. If lynching was ever justifiable, it was in this case, but I cannot put myself in the position of indorsing [*sic*] it . . . Capital punishment will never be restored. The people have outgrown it. It was useless. It was not a deterrent of crime. It is merely an end of the criminal.[110]

Nonetheless, within a few days, the *Denver Times* renewed its call for restoration of the death penalty:

> The Cañon City citizens who took the law into their own hands felt that there has been too much leniency shown criminals in this state, where sentimentality has overbalanced common sense. Prisoners at the penitentiary are accorded too many privileges, and escape, legal or otherwise, has been made too easy. The people of Cañon City believed that in self-protection, an object lesson should be given these prisoners . . . The lynchers also had in mind a hint to the legislature that if the law does not provide adequate punishment for criminals the people will.[111]

---

found in DICK KRECK, ANTON WOODE: THE BOY MURDERER (2006). When he arrived at the prison, he was the youngest inmate in the United States. For more details, including a picture of the young boy, *see* Diana Anderson, *Anton Woode*, accessible in the research files at the Ryoal Gorge Regional Museum and History Center, Cañon City.

109. *Reynolds Lynched at Cañon City*, ROCKY MTN. NEWS, Jan. 27, 1900, at 1; *A Rope Awaits Wagoner: Convict Reynolds Lynched Last Night*, DENVER POST, Jan. 27, 1900, at 1; *No Inquest over Reynolds' Remains*, DENVER TIMES, Jan. 27, 1900, at 1.

110. *What the Governor Thought of Lynching*, ROCKY MTN. NEWS, Jan. 27, 1900, at 8.

111. *Restore Capital Punishment*, DENVER TIMES, Jan. 28, 1900, at 12. Several other newspapers from throughout the state echoed the call for reinstatement. *Restore Capital Punishment*, DENVER TIMES, Jan. 29, 1900, at 4 (quoting excerpts from editorials from ten other Colorado newspapers).

How the newspaper knew what the lynchers had in mind was not revealed, but, no doubt, they had a pretty good finger on the pulse of a sizeable chunk of the community.

Four months later, a mob of roughly six thousand citizens of Pueblo lynched Calvin Kimblern, an African American suspected of killing two young girls. No investigation was ever undertaken to identify the lynchers; the coroner refused to investigate the death because, he said, Kimblern was not a human being. Governor Thomas justified the lynching as "a natural outburst of indignation of the people of Pueblo."[112] He pointed out that because no death penalty existed, Kimblern would have received a prison sentence for the crimes, and people seeking a commutation of Kimblern's sentence would then harass a future governor. Thus, he reasoned, the absence of the death penalty, not toxic racism, was the cause for the lynching.[113]

Newspapers around the state echoed this theme. On the day after Kimblern's lynching, the *Denver Post* quoted editorials in the *Denver Republican*, the *Colorado Springs Gazette*, and the *Pueblo Chieftain* calling for restoration of the death penalty: "The horror of the lynching at Pueblo has shocked the public, but it is the legitimate outcome of the abolishment of capital punishment. No punishment short of death would have fitted Kimblern's atrocious crime . . . Repealing the law providing for the death penalty was at least a piece of silly sentimental folly."[114] Added the *Rocky Mountain News*,

> To prevent the recurrence of such horrors the death penalty should be restored . . . In the case of such crimes as those committed by Kimblern a jury may be relied upon to fix the penalty at death, and the certainty that it will do so will stop the blackening of Colorado's fair name with lynchings.[115]

The final straw came six months later. On November 8, 1900, a white girl named Louise Frost, described in various reports as between eleven and thirteen years old, was sexually assaulted and murdered in Limon,

---

112. LEONARD, at 146.
113. *Id.* at 143, 146–47.
114. *Capital Punishment Must Be Restored*, DENVER POST, May 4, 1900, at 4.
115. *Restore Capital Punishment*, ROCKY MTN. NEWS, May 24, 1900, at 4.

allegedly by a sixteen-year-old black youth named John Preston Porter, Jr. After Porter's apprehension in Denver, local newspapers quickly announced that his guilt was unquestionable,[116] and a mass meeting of citizens from the Limon area "decided that the negro shall be hanged, but that no torture shall be permitted."[117] Calls for the return of capital punishment quickly resurfaced. Wrote the *Denver Post*,

> [T]he laws of Colorado, since the repeal of the law legalizing hanging, provide no adequate punishment for such inhuman brutes as those who commit outrageous crimes like that at Limon. Indeed, with capital punishment abolished there is in such cases a direct invitation to the outraged people to take the law into their own hands and visit upon the head of the brutal murderer such condign punishment as cannot fail to shock the whole community . . . A few more object lessons will doubtless convince the people of the state that capital punishment should be restored to the statute books. While it may be true that ordinary life or long term imprisonment may be a fit punishment for the crime committed, there are times when nothing short of the death penalty will satisfy the demands of justice.[118]

Back in Limon, mobs began to search all trains coming from Denver to see if Porter was being brought back to the city for trial.[119] On November 15, the *Rocky Mountain News* announced that Porter had confessed, with the headline "Porter Condemned to Death by His Own Confession."[120] The next day, the newspaper wrote, "In addition to deciding that the execution would be a hanging the men of Lincoln county voted to notify all negroes of bad character to leave the county. Notices will be posted. If they do not go they will be quietly escorted across the border."[121] That afternoon, a crowd of three hundred met the train carrying Porter as it arrived in Limon, brought him to the site of the murder, and tied him

116. *Guilt Points Its Finger at Porter*, ROCKY MTN. NEWS, Nov. 13, 1900, at 1.

117. *Sheriff Fears a Lynching: John Porter, the Murderer of a Little Girl, to be Kept at Denver*, N.Y. TIMES, Nov. 16, 1900, at 5.

118. *Punishment for the Limon Ravisher*, DENVER POST, Nov. 13, 1900, at 4.

119. *Determined Men Search the Trains for Porter*, ROCKY MTN. NEWS, Nov. 13, 1900, at 2.

120. *Porter Condemned to Death by His Own Confession*, ROCKY MTN. NEWS, Nov. 15, 1900, at 1.

121. *Mob Much Disappointed*, ROCKY MTN. NEWS, Nov. 16, 1900, at 2.

with chains to a piece of railroad iron that had been stuck in the ground. By then, the crowd had swelled to approximately seven hundred spectators, all male.[122] Two hours after his arrival in Limon, the father of the victim took a torch, lit the fire, and Porter was burned at the stake.[123]

As described on the front page of the *New York Times*:

> For an instant the body stood erect, the arms were raised in supplication while burning pieces of clothing dropped from them. The body then fell away from the fire, the head lower than the feet still fastened to the rail.
>
> This was not expected, and for a few minutes those stolid men were disconcerted; they feared that the only remaining chain would give way. If this had occurred the partly burned human being would have dashed among them in his blazing garments. And not many would have cared to capture him again. But the chain held fast.
>
> The body was then in such a position that only the legs were in the fire. The cries of the wretch were redoubled, and he again begged to be shot. Some wanted to throw him over into the fire, others tried to dash oil upon him. Boards were carried, and a large pile made over the prostrate body. They soon were ignited, and the terrible heat and lack of air quickly rendered the victim unconscious, bringing death a few moments later.[124]

For twenty minutes, Porter slowly burned to death, screeching and begging to be shot. When he finally died, the men in the crowd bid each other good night and went home without lingering to discuss what they had just done.

As historian Stephen Leonard characterized the horror, "In less than half a century the 1859 People's Court had devolved into a mob shaking with pure enjoyment as they roasted a human being."[125] The following Sunday, ministers throughout Denver condemned the mob action, but

---

122. *The Colorado Lynching: District Attorney Says Public Opinion Will Not Permit Punishment of the Mob*, N.Y. TIMES, Nov. 18, 1900 at 4.

123. *Fearful Revenge for Murder of Louise Frost*, ROCKY MTN. NEWS, Nov. 17, 1900, at 1; JOHN H. MONNETT & MICHAEL MCCARTHY, COLORADO PROFILES: MEN AND WOMEN WHO SHAPED THE CENTENNIAL STATE 205–14 (1996). When asked to comment on the lynching, Gov. Charles S. Thomas (1899–1901) stated, "My opinion is that there is one less negro [*sic*] in the world." *Thomas is Waggish*, BOULDER DAILY CAMERA, Nov. 17, 1900, at 2 (quoted in LEONARD, at 149).

124. *Boy Burned at the Stake in Colorado*, N.Y. TIMES, Nov. 17, 1900, at 1.

125. LEONARD, at 124.

several also called for the reintroduction of capital punishment as a method to deter future lynchers.[126] Again, some newspapers called for a repeal of the law that had abolished capital punishment.[127] As the spotlight shifted to the debate of capital punishment, the pressure to condemn the lynchers—especially for killing a black person—lessened.

So ended the history of the death penalty in Colorado in the nineteenth century. To be sure, death penalty foes had a victory, but the supporters of executions vowed to do their best to ensure that the victory was short-lived.

126. *Colorado Lynching*; *Oppose Mob Rule*, DENVER TIMES, Nov. 19, 1900, at 16.

127. *See, e.g.*, *Once More, the Death Penalty*, DENVER TIMES, Nov. 17, 1900, at 4; *The Porter Burning*, DENVER TIMES, Nov. 19, 1900, at 7 (presenting excerpts from editorials from several newspapers from throughout the state); *Whether to Restore the Death Penalty*, DENVER TIMES, Jan. 28, 1901, at 6.

CHAPTER 3

TWENTIETH-CENTURY EXECUTIONS AND DEBATES

THE REINSTATEMENT OF THE DEATH PENALTY IN 1901

At first, it appeared that Colorado's abolition of the death penalty would be long lasting. In 1899 Governor Adams stated, "I think that a candid investigation will convince even the man who has been most in favor of a gallows as a permanent state institution that, for the purpose of punishing murder and executing the laws, the repeal of the death penalty was the most forward step in criminal legislation that has yet been taken in Colorado."[1] However, he was wrong. Just four years after Colorado's death penalty was scrapped, the issue came back for legislative debate. Leading newspapers, fearing that the lynch mobs might fuel a national perception that Colorado was uncivilized or barbaric, attempted to frame the problem of mob violence as the absence of capital punishment rather than the barbarism of the populace. The sponsor of the legislation to bring back the death penalty "referred feelingly to the parents of Louise Frost," while a death penalty opponent accused those who supported the bill of "cold and deliberate murder."[2]

---

1. Cary Stiff, *Lynching Spurred End to Capital Punishment Repeal*, DENVER POST, Nov. 1, 1966, at 52.

2. *Calls Them Murderers*, DENVER POST, Feb. 9, 1901, at 10.

DOI: 10.5876/9781607325123.c003

Fortunately, an eight-page pamphlet outlining the pros and cons of the 1901 debate survives.[3] Written by the Rev. Victor E. Southworth from the Church of Humanity in Denver and published by the Colorado Anti-Capital Punishment Society, it begins by listing the six main arguments voiced by those who advocated for the return of hanging: (1) precedent, (2) incapacitation and the certainty that executed offenders would not offend again, (3) the financial savings if the state does not have to pay for long imprisonment of the offender, (4) retribution and "eye for an eye," (5) the inability to rehabilitate those convicted of the worst murders, and (6) deterrence. Southworth's pamphlet addresses each of these arguments and points to, among other things, the inability of avoiding erroneous executions. He concludes by posing some important and well-worded questions that could easily be repeated, word-for-word, by contemporary death penalty abolitionists:

> In order to prevent murder must we dip our pen in human blood to write the law? In order to inspire the public with respect for human life must we refuse to show mercy ourselves? Must we kill a few men officially in order to frighten ourselves and our neighbors into peaceable and kindly conduct towards one another? Must we manifest hatred to encourage love and have an exhibition of brutality to teach kindness?[4]

But in the end, Reverend Southworth's arguments did not prevail. On February 8, 1901, the state House of Representatives voted 41–24 to reinstate capital punishment. The bill passed the state Senate on March 29.[5] Gov. James B. Orman would neither sign the reinstatement bill nor veto it, and so, on July 31, 1901, it became effective without his signature.[6] Colorado's executioner was back in business.

---

3. Victor E. Southworth, *A Protest against the Death Penalty*, pamphlet, 1901, Stephen H. Hart Library and Research Center, Denver, CO.

4. *Id.* at 8.

5. *Passed the Senate*, DENVER POST, Mar. 29, 1901, at 2.

6. Act of May 2, 1901, ch. 64, sec. 2, § 1176, 1901 Colo. Sess. Laws 153–54. In declining to veto the bill, Governor Orman said he believed it would be repealed by the next legislature and that he had doubts about the constitutionality of the bill's provisions. *Kills Two Bills: Capital Punishment Becomes a Law Through Lapse of Time*, ROCKY MTN. NEWS, May 1, 1901, at 12.

As before, the new law permitted few witnesses to attend the executions[7] and dictated that virtually all aspects of the hangings remain secret.[8] The mandatory death penalty was abandoned; juries were now asked to decide whether to sentence those convicted of first-degree murder to death or imprisonment for life at hard labor. The new law rendered defendants under the age of eighteen at the time of conviction ineligible for the death penalty[9] as well as those convicted solely on circumstantial evidence. To the regret of today's students of the death penalty, the law also specified that "[n]o account of the details of any such execution, beyond the statement of the fact that such convict was on the day in question duly executed according to law at the state penitentiary, shall in any manner be published in this state."[10] We therefore have only inconsistent and often sketchy accounts of what an inmate's last hours were like.

After the new capital punishment statute was enacted, only five more lynchings occurred within Colorado's borders.[11] This decline in lynchings was a national phenomenon, but to supporters of the death penalty in Colorado, the decline was a direct consequence of the return of the state-employed hangman.[12] Whether the death penalty deterred homicide remained (at the time) an open question, but the pro–death penalty newspapers and legislators were, no doubt, pleased at the death penalty's resurrection and its apparent effect as a deterrent to would-be lynch mobs.

---

7. The statute specified that the warden "shall invite to be present thereat the sheriff of the county wherein the conviction was had, the chaplain and physician of the penitentiary, two practicing surgeons, residents of the state, the spiritual adviser [*sic*] of the convict, if any, and six reputable citizens of the state, of full age." Act of May 2, 1901, § 6, 1901 Colo. Sess. Laws 155–56.

8. Those who violated the secrecy provision were subject to a fine of between $50 and $500 or by one to six months in jail. *Id.* § 9, at 157.

9. *Id.* sec. 2, § 1176, at 154. In 2005 the US Supreme Court held that the death penalty was unconstitutional for those who had not reached their eighteenth birthday at the time of the crime (age at the time of conviction was not relevant). Roper v. Simmons, 543 U.S. 551 (2005).

10. *Id.* § 6, at 156.

11. Stephen J. Leonard, Lynching in Colorado, 1859–1919, 174 (2002).

12. The flawed logic is sometimes summed up in the Latin phrase *post hoc, ergo propter hoc*, or "after this, therefore because of this."

HANGINGS (AND BOTCHED HANGINGS) IN CAÑON CITY, 1905–1932

Sixty-five people were put to death in Colorado between 1905 and 1967, with just over half (thirty-three) sent to the hereafter with a noose. Growing concerns about botched hangings, which most often occurred when the inmate slowly strangled rather than dying from a broken neck, prompted the state to execute prisoners after 1933 (N = 32) by asphyxiation in the gas chamber. This section will review the hangings and the reasons behind Colorado's change in its method of execution.

In the first thirty-three years of the twentieth century, Colorado executed an average of one man per year with its twitch-up hanging machinery in Cañon City. In February 1905, in *Andrews v. People*, a unanimous Colorado Supreme Court held that the new death penalty statute was constitutional.[13] J. Newton Andrews, however, was not the first to be hanged pursuant to its provisions. That distinction belongs to Azel Galbraith,[14] whose execution was delayed pending the outcome of the *Andrews* case. Galbraith, convicted of killing his wife and their eight-year-old son, was jerked to his death on March 6, 1905.

The state next hanged Andrews and his codefendant, Fred Arnold.[15] They were convicted of entering a Denver home in a robbery attempt, murdering a sixty-three-year-old resident, and wounding her son. At age nineteen, Arnold remains the only teenager and the youngest person ever executed in the state. Before 1972, Colorado never specified a minimum age at the time of the commission of the crime for a person to be eligible for execution. Instead, the minimum age—eighteen—was when the person became eligible to be sentenced to death. Hence, in 1933 Walter Reppin was sentenced to death for the murder of a gas station attendant that occurred when he was only seventeen. However, by the time he pleaded guilty and stood for sentencing, he had passed his eighteenth birthday, making him eligible for a death sentence. He was sent to death row, although he was ultimately resentenced to life.[16]

---

13. Andrews v. People, 33 Colo. 193; 79 P. 1031 (Colo. 1905).
14. *See* appendix 1, case no. 38.
15. *See* appendix 1, case nos. 39 and 40.
16. *See* appendix 2, case no. 60.

The state also executed a fourth man in 1905: a former deputy sheriff named Joseph Johnson, who was hanged for the murder of a prominent Democratic politician in Trinidad.[17] We can assume that as a deputy sheriff, Johnson was almost certainly knowledgeable about the state's new death penalty law, but its message of deterrence did not sink in.

At least one case from the early 1900s took the life of a man who, at least in today's eyes, was undoubtedly afflicted with severe mental problems. In 1908 Giuseppe Alia entered St. Elizabeth's Catholic Church in Denver and shot and killed the officiant, Fr. Leo Heinrichs. Alia was a native of Italy who did not speak English, with few (if any) friends in Denver. The Italian government and the Catholic Church strongly opposed his execution. Nonetheless, "four expert brain specialists [said] Alia was perfectly sane,"[18] and at trial, only the Italian counsel, Dr. Baron Tosti, expressed a belief that Alia was insane, basing his opinion on the belief that the murder was committed without apparent motive.[19] The insanity defense failed. Alia was hanged with little fanfare only five months after the murder.[20] Today a plaque in the church commemorates Father Leo's death.

After Alia, six more men were hanged before 1920. In 1915 the state sent Harry Hillen to his death for the senseless murder of a real estate agent during a robbery in Denver.[21] Hillen confessed to the murder, explaining that it was triggered "because he [the victim] snarled at me. I can't stand snarls."[22] In 1916 Oscar Cook was executed nearly four years after he murdered a saloonkeeper and a Denver police officer. The four years that passed before he stood on the twitch-up gallows was, at the time, a longevity record for Colorado's executed inmates. In large part, the delay in his execution was attributable to a decision by the Colorado Supreme Court granting him a new trial in 1914. Until the moment of his death, Cook continued to steadfastly insist that he was not the gunman.

---

17. *See* appendix 1, case no. 41.

18. *Trial of Priest's Slayer*, N.Y. TIMES, Mar. 9, 1908.

19. *Father Leo's Slayer Guilty*, N.Y. TIMES, Mar. 13, 1908.

20. *See* appendix 1, case no. 43; *Fr. Leo Heinrichs, Priest of the Eucharist*, CATHOLIC TRADITION, accessed July 15, 2016, http://catholictradition.org/Priests/fr-heinrichs.htm.

21. *See* appendix 1, case no. 46.

22. *Shot Chase Dead When He Snarled, Bandit Confesses*, ROCKY MTN. NEWS, Oct. 28, 1913, at 1.

The state executed seven inmates in the 1920s, the first four of whom were convicted of double murders.[23] Four of the seven received their sentences for domestic murders, which resulted from jealousy or lovers' quarrels.[24]

Two cousins, Raymond Noakes and Arthur Osborn, were the last two hanged in the 1920s.[25] The two men killed a neighbor, Fred N. Selak, after an argument over access to a road on Selak's property. In newspaper and other accounts, Selak was referred to as a "hermit," a "wealthy recluse," and "a yodeler extraordinary."[26] He was hanged in the woods near his Grand Lake home, and Noakes and Osborn returned to his cabin after the murder and stole some vintage coins. They were arrested when they tried to spend the money, which was immediately recognized for its uniqueness. Selak's body was found nearly a month after the murder—still hanging from the tree—after Noakes and Osborn were arrested, confessed, and told the authorities where to find the body.

Prison warden F. E. Crawford and Chap. J. Willis Hamblin made two trips from Cañon City to Denver to plead with Gov. William Adams to spare the cousins' lives.[27] Like his brother, former Colorado governor Alva Adams, William was a staunch foe of the death penalty. Nonetheless, he denied the requests for commutations. After the executions, the boys' aunt predicted that the hangings would abolish the death penalty in Colorado.[28] Indeed, on the same day as they were executed, the *Rocky Mountain News* reported that a branch of "the National Society for the Abolition of Capital Punishment" would soon open in Colorado.[29]

In October 1929, the country's worst prison riot to date occurred in Cañon City, taking the lives of eight guards and five convicts. One of those murdered was Colorado's executioner, John J. ("Jack") Eeles, seventy-seven, a veteran guard who was widely disliked by prisoners, primarily for his well-known role in serving as the state's executioner

---

23. *See* appendix 1, case nos. 49–52.

24. *See* appendix 1, case nos. 50–53.

25. *See* appendix 1, case nos. 54 and 55.

26. ROBERT C. BLACK III, ISLAND IN THE ROCKIES: THE HISTORY OF GRAND COUNTY, COLORADO, TO 1930 368 (1969).

27. *Noakes, Osborn Hanged*, ROCKY MTN. NEWS, Mar. 30, 1928, at 1.

28. *Fight on Death Penalty Looms*, DENVER POST, Mar. 30, 1928, at 3.

29. *Death Penalty Foes Convene*, ROCKY MTN. NEWS, Mar. 30, 1928, at 2.

for the prior three decades.[30] None of those involved in the riot was sentenced to death. Over seventy years would pass until the next correctional officer in Colorado, Eric Autobee, was murdered while on duty. He was killed at Limon Correctional Facility in 2002.[31]

Colorado executed seven people in the single year of 1930, the same number of people who had been executed during all of the 1920s. Eddie Ives was the first person put to death by the hangman selected to replace Eeles.[32] It did not go well. By then, the weight that jerked the prisoner into the air had increased to 600 pounds;[33] a later source claimed that it was increased to 1,000 pounds.[34] When the state hanged Ives, who weighed only eighty pounds, the hanging rope came off the pulley and Ives "flew up to the ceiling, then dropped back to the floor."[35] This mishap required a second attempt to hang Ives, which resulted in his slow strangulation.[36]

---

30. WAYNE K. PATTERSON & BETTY L. ALT, SLAUGHTER IN CELL HOUSE 3: THE ANATOMY OF A RIOT, 78 (1997). Since the state's hanging machine did not require an executioner, it is likely that Eeles's role was to organize the hangings and prevent any kinks. Furthermore, the fact that it was well known that Eeles was involved in the hangings showed that the secrecy supposedly surrounding hangings was far from leakproof.

31. Kieran Nicholson, *Inmate Kills Corrections Worker, State Says Officer Is 1st Killed by Prisoner Since '29*, DENVER POST, Oct. 20, 2002, at B1. This case, in which Edward Montour was initially sentenced to death, will be discussed further in chapter 5.

32. *See* appendix 1, case no. 56.

33. *Lethal Gas Chamber Soon Will Be Built at State Pen*, ROCKY MTN. NEWS, May 21, 1933, at 3.

34. A 1,000-pound weight was (reportedly) used to hang Claude Ray, John Walker, and Andrew Halliday in 1931. Charles T. O'Brien, *Three Manter Bandits Hanged; Noose Fails to Break Necks and Slayers Strangle to Death*, DENVER POST, Jan. 31, 1931, at 1.

35. Frances Melrose, *Little Eddie Ives Played Big Role in Changing Execution*, ROCKY MTN. NEWS, Jan. 17, 1977, at 8. *See also* Alice Spencer Cook, *The Man Was Hanged Twice*, DENVER POST (Empire Magazine), Apr. 6, 1958, at 6.

36. Botched hangings were not unheard of in Colorado's past. When James Miller was hanged in 1877, the entire trap door on the scaffold fell beneath him, and Miller's feet came to rest on it when he dropped. The trap door had to be removed so he could dangle freely. *See* appendix 1, case no. 11. In 1881 the rope broke as W. H. Salisbury was being hanged, forcing the executioners to hang him a second time. *See* appendix 1, case no. 14. Later that year, the trap door failed to open during the hanging of Thomas Coleman; he had to be removed from the gallows while repairs (which later proved successful) were made. *See* appendix 1, case no. 17. The secrecy provisions surrounding Colorado executions makes it impossible to determine how many executions conducted at Cañon City were "botched." We do know, however,

FIGURE 3.1. *Eddie Ives, executed January 10, 1930. He was hanged a second time after a botched first attempt. Photo courtesy of the Colorado State Archives.*

Ives had been convicted of killing Denver police officer Harry Ohle and slightly wounding a second officer, Robert Evans. The men were shot as they searched for illegal liquor at a Denver speakeasy. Also killed that night was Louvenia Reese, the African American wife of the speakeasy's proprietor. She had no prior connection with Ives and was killed by a stray bullet as Ives started shooting. Apparently, because the authorities needed only one murder conviction to win a death sentence against Ives, no charges were filed against him for Reese's murder.

In a bizarre twist, a nurse named Farice King was among those who cared for Officer Evans at Denver General Hospital. On the day that Evans was scheduled for release, King entered his room with a gun and mortally wounded him before badly wounding herself. As it turned out, about a dozen years before Ohle's murder, Evans and King had been romantically involved. But much to the agony of King, Evans had ended

---

that during one asphyxiation, the spectators had to scatter when the gas chamber leaked. *Death Chamber at Pen Tested*, ROCKY MTN. NEWS, Dec. 5, 1939, at 1. *See* appendix 1, case no. 78.

the relationship a year before the shooting. Eventually, it was revealed that Evans was actually named "John Bobzine," who fifteen years earlier had walked out on a wife and family in Iowa before changing his name and moving to Denver. At trial, King was sentenced to life imprisonment, but the sentence was commuted and she was freed in 1934.[37]

In addition to Ives, six other men were hanged in 1930. Harold Weiss and Emelio Herrera faced the executioner for killing their wives in domestic arguments[38] and William Moya was convicted of killing his landlord during a robbery.[39] The other three were codefendants—one was hanged on July 8 and the other two were hanged eight days later.[40] They were members of a four-person gang of robbers led by brothers Ralph Emerson Fleagle (named after the famous writer and poet) and William Harrison Fleagle (a.k.a. "Jake," named after the former president). Working from a base in western Kansas, the brothers and their accomplices (who usually joined them for only one or two crimes) staged a series of stick-ups of various targets (e.g., banks, trains, and gambling establishments) in several states, ranging from the Midwest to California. With eyes focused on the First National Bank in Lamar, Colorado, they recruited a Californian named Harold Royston and a former bootlegger named George Abshier to help with the job. During the robbery, in May 1928, the bank president shot and wounded Royston, and both the bank president and his son were murdered in the return fire. The robbers grabbed $220,000 and two hostages and fled.

Safely back at their hideout in western Kansas, the Fleagle brothers drove to a nearby town and pleaded with a local physician, W. W. Wineinger, to treat the wounded Royston. They drove to their hideout in Wineinger's car. Then, after the doctor treated Royston's wounds, the bandits shot and killed him. The body of one of the hostages (the other had been released uninjured) was found shortly thereafter.

The authorities soon arrested four other men, and eyewitnesses confirmed that they had the right culprits. They almost certainly would have been hanged had it not been for pure luck. About a year after the mur-

37. Alan Prendergast, *Love Crazy*, WESTWORD (Denver), Oct. 9, 2003, at 29.

38. *See* appendix 1, case nos. 57 and 61.

39. *See* appendix 1, case no. 62.

40. *See* appendix 1, case nos. 58–60.

ders, the Federal Bureau of Investigation matched a fingerprint found on Wineinger's car with one in their files for Jake Fleagle. Agents then determined that both brothers had been making some huge bank deposits. The Fleagle family told the police that Ralph was living in Illinois, and the authorities quickly located and arrested him. For several weeks he would not talk, but he agreed that he would name his accomplices if the prosecutor agreed not to seek death in his case. With that agreement, he fingered Howard Royston as an accomplice, and Royston was arrested and offered a full confession that led to the arrest of Abshier.

The four innocent men who likely would have been sentenced to death were cleared and released. In separate trials, each defendant was convicted and sentenced to death (true to his word, the prosecutor did not seek death for Ralph Fleagle, but the jury sentenced him to hang nonetheless). The Colorado Supreme Court scheduled him as the first to hang. After he was dead, "The body was cut down and taken to the prison hospital, where the heart was removed by a surgeon to comply with a state law."[41]

Royston and Abshier were hanged eight days later, although the 600-pound weight on the rope failed to break their necks.[42] In October, the police tracked Jake to Branson, Missouri, where he was shot dead while being taken into custody.[43]

Four more executions followed in 1931, including one of only two triple executions in Colorado's history, which, like the case of the Lamar bandits,[44] resulted from a botched bank robbery. Claude Ray, John Walker, and Andrew Halliday robbed a bank in Manter, Kansas, and shot and killed a sheriff in Eads, Colorado, just west of the border between the states, as they attempted their escape.[45] Roy Best, the acting director of the Colorado State Police and future warden at Cañon City, was one

41. Charles T. O'Brien, *Ralph Fleagle Dies on Gallows*, DENVER POST, July 11, 1930, at 1, 4. I have not found any other evidence to suggest that inmates' hearts were removed after an execution.

42. Fred S. Warren, *Lamar Bandits Are Avenged! Bandits Strangle to Death as Rope Fails to Break Their Necks*, DENVER POST, July 19, 1930, at 1.

43. For general information on the case, *see* COURTNEY RYLEY COOPER, TEN THOUSAND ENEMIES 112–25 (1935); Kathleen Van Buskirk, *Outlaw for My Neighbor: The Jake Fleagle Story*, WHITE RIVER VALLEY HIST. QUARTERLY 7 (Fall 1979), accessed July 15, 2016, http://thelibrary.org/lochist/periodicals/wrv/V7/N1/F79e.htm.

44. *See* appendix 1, case nos. 58–60.

45. *See* appendix 1, case nos. 63–65.

of the officers who worked on the case. In the last execution of 1931, the state hanged quadruple murderer James Foster, convicted of pouring gasoline on his wife and three children and lighting them afire.[46]

THE ADOPTION OF THE GAS CHAMBER IN 1933

The early 1900s were not bereft of efforts to abolish the death penalty. For example, in 1916 the State Federation of Women's Clubs proposed an abolition bill. A heated argument broke out at the meeting of the Denver Ministerial Alliance when members were asked to support the bill. In the debate, the Rev. John H. Houghton, rector of St. Mark's Episcopal Church, left no doubt about where he stood on the measure: "Look at this disgraceful Bulger [an accused murderer][47]—I would hang him tomorrow. A man not worth one-ninety-thousandth [*sic*] part of a cent to the community. He should be hanged like a dog."[48] Similar debates raged in other states. Kansas abolished the death penalty in 1907, Minnesota in 1911, Washington in 1913, Oregon in 1914, North Dakota in 1915 (except for murder committed by a prisoner already serving a life sentence), South Dakota in 1915, Tennessee in 1915 (except for rape), and Missouri in 1917.[49] In Colorado, however, efforts to reform the death penalty in the years surrounding World War I failed.

Reform efforts in Colorado accelerated again during the Depression in the 1930s and focused on improving the techniques of executions or abolishing the practice altogether. Colorado's twitch-up execution apparatus never worked with the perfection hoped for by its inventors.

---

46. *See* appendix 1, case no. 66.

47. *See* appendix 2, case no. 48.

48. *Hang Bulger Like Dog, Cries Church Rector*, ROCKY MTN. NEWS, Jan. 4, 1916, at 12. James C. Bulger was a "soldier of fortune" who participated in several wars in the early twentieth century and in 1902 was an organizer of the first regiment of Theodore Roosevelt's Rough Riders. On May 6, 1914, he shot and killed the part owner of the Savoy Hotel in Denver, for which he was sentenced to death. On April 3, 1916, the Colorado Supreme Court affirmed the conviction and on November 13, 1916, Gov. George Carlson commuted his death sentence to a term of 131 years. He was finally paroled on December 1, 1960, after forty-five years behind bars. *Canon City Convict, 80, Wins Freedom*, ROCKY MTN. NEWS, Nov. 6, 1961, at 25.

49. HUGO ADAM BEDAU, THE DEATH PENALTY IN AMERICA, CURRENT CONTROVERSIES 9 (1997).

Although it is difficult to say with certainty, William King reports that "in forty of the forty-four instances where this method was employed in Colorado between 1890 and 1933 . . . death by strangulation was the result; in only four instances did the neck of the felon actually break."[50]

The botched execution of Eddie Ives fueled cries for a more dependable, if not more humane, execution method. Former warden Thomas Tynan (who served from 1909 to 1927) reportedly told one newspaper, "Colorado has one of the most ghastly hanging machines possible. More than half the men executed at Cañon City have not been hanged at all. They have strangled."[51] Supporters of changing the method of execution also included Tynan's cousin, Warden F. E. Crawford, "a kindly and considerate man who abhorred executions and who regarded hanging as a form of punishment out of the Middle Ages."[52] During his tenure, from 1927 to 1931, Crawford was in charge during the 1929 prison riot (when he was injured by some ricocheting buckshot)[53] and also supervised a dozen hangings, including that of Ives. In fact, before the hanging, he had personally traveled to Denver to plea with Gov. William Adams to spare Ives's life.

More Colorado legislators became dissatisfied with the state's death penalty, and efforts to completely outlaw capital punishment resurfaced. In 1933 President Franklin D. Roosevelt joined those calling for the abolition.[54] In March 1933, by a 20–12 vote, the Colorado Senate passed a

---

50. WILLIAM M. KING, GOING TO MEET A MAN 92. Actually, forty-five men were hanged in Cañon City between 1890 and 1933 (see table 1.1). Unfortunately, King does not provide the source for these tallies. Andrew Field states "only two of the forty-five men put to death in the device died as intended." ANDREW FIELD, Mainliner Denver 215 (2005). Again, no source for these tallies is provided. Another report states, "Only two of the last fifteen hanged on the queer gallows have received broken necks." *Killer Strangles in Fourteen Minutes on Colorado Gallows*, DENVER POST, Dec. 2, 1933, at 1. Data presented in appendix 1, taken from newspaper accounts—which may or may not be accurate—indicate whether or not the inmate's neck was broken in thirty-two of the forty-five hangings. Of the thirty-two, it was reported that the neck was broken in twenty-two cases. Of the last ten hangings where the type of death was reported, only two men had their necks broken.

51. *Id.* at 38.

52. W. T. Little, *What about Executions before 1890?* ROCKY MTN. NEWS, July 6, 1965, at 76.

53. PATTERSON & ALT, at 50.

54. STUART BANNER, THE DEATH PENALTY: AN AMERICAN HISTORY 224 (2002) (hereinafter BANNER, THE DEATH PENALTY).

bill abolishing the death penalty.[55] This bill, amidst two hundred others that dealt with a broad range of non–death penalty issues, ultimately died without action in the state House of Representatives on May 8, when they voted to adjourn.[56] But earlier that year, both the Senate[57] and the House of Representatives passed legislation formally switching the state's method of execution from hanging to asphyxiation. Arguably, this reform defused opposition to the death penalty by furthering the belief that executions could be made more "humane," thereby challenging abolitionists' claims that executions were inherently cruel. On March 31, 1933, Gov. Edwin C. Johnson signed the bill, changing the method of execution for all capital offenses committed after that date.[58] Suddenly, Colorado was in the market for a gas chamber.

Nevada adopted the gas chamber in 1921 and first used it in 1924. Hence, when Colorado began its search for a new method of execution, lethal gas, as the most modern method available, was seen as the most technically advanced and civilized. In 1933 Colorado became the second state to adopt asphyxiation in the gas chamber as its official means of execution.[59]

In May 1933, Warden Roy Best visited Carson City, Nevada, to inspect that state's execution apparatus. Once he knew what he wanted—a huge three-seat model—he secured the approval of Governor Johnson and turned to the Denver firm of Eaton Metal Products, paying them $2,500 to handle the construction.[60] Eaton usually built boilers and petroleum tanks, but soon they found themselves with a side business

55. *Measure to Abolish Death Penalty is Passed by State Senate and Sent to House*, ROCKY MTN. NEWS, Mar. 18, 1933, at 5; *Death Penalty Bill May Save Doomed Men*, DENVER POST, Mar. 29, 1933, at 2.

56. S. 86, 1933 Leg., Evening Sess. (Colo. May 8, 1933); *Vote for Adjournment Kills Scores of Bills in General Assembly*, DENVER POST, May 9, 1933, at 4.

57. *Colorado Senate Approves Lethal Gas for Executions*, DENVER POST, Feb. 2, 1933, at 4.

58. Act of Mar. 31, 1933, ch. 61, 1933 Colo. Sess. Laws, 420–22; *Governor Signs Lethal Gas Bill*, ROCKY MTN. NEWS, Apr. 1, 1933, at 1.

59. By 1955, a total of eleven states had turned to lethal gas as the execution method. BANNER, at 199.

60. *$2,500 For Death House*, ROCKY MTN. NEWS, June 15, 1933, at 14; Maurice Leckenby, *State Pen Death Chamber Nearing Completion Here*, ROCKY MTN. NEWS, Sept. 24, 1933, at 6. A later report stated that the chamber cost $9,500. Fred Baker, *New Gas Chamber Takes First Life in Test Run—A Pig*, ROCKY MTN. NEWS, Apr. 5, 1955, at 44.

FIGURE 3.2. *Colorado's second gas chamber, in which eight prisoners died between 1956 and 1967. Photo by author.*

of constructing gas chambers. Eventually, they built gas chambers for all but one of the eleven states that adopted that method of execution.[61] Colorado used its three-seat gas chamber—nicknamed "Roy's

61. Cary Stiff, *The Death House by the Side of the Road*, DENVER POST, May 16, 1971, at 18. Eaton built all the gas chambers used in the United States except the one used

Penthouse" in honor of Warden Best[62]—for twenty-two years.[63] To the extent that concerns over painful and lingering deaths caused by bungled hangings threatened the future of Colorado's death penalty, the introduction of the gas chamber probably helped preserve the legality of the death penalty in the state.[64]

ASPHYXIATIONS, 1934–1967

On June 22, 1934, William Cody Kelley became the first prisoner to be asphyxiated by cyanide gas in Colorado's gas chamber.[65] Kelley and an accomplice were convicted and sentenced to death for the beating death of a rancher. But the accomplice's death sentence was commuted, and he spent fifteen years in prison running a business and building a savings account before being released.[66] Apparently, the preparations by prison authorities for the new execution method led to success. Echoing a theme that newspapers claimed in several other cases,

---

in North Carolina. *Id. See also*, *Execution Chamber Styles*, ROCKY MTN. NEWS, Feb. 27, 1938, at 6 (includes picture of Denver workman putting the final touches on the gas chamber that would soon be installed in San Quentin, California); Cary Stiff, *Denverite "Refined" Death*, DENVER POST, Sept. 15, 1966, at 88; Bill Pardue, *Denver Firm Receives Inquiries On Gas Chambers*, ROCKY MTN. NEWS, Dec. 6, 1976, at 43; THOMAS J. NOEL & KEVEN E. RUCKER, EATON METAL PRODUCTS: THE FIRST 80 YEARS 26–32 (1998) (erroneously reports that John Gilbert Graham was the first person to be executed in the state's second gas chamber).

62. Stiff, *Denverite "Refined" Death*.

63. In 1955 the state constructed a new location at the prison for executions, and the builders deemed the original gas chamber too big and bulky for the new building. A lean, trim one-seat model, also built by Eaton Metal Products, replaced the old three-seater. Stiff, *Death House*; *State's New Gas Chamber to Claim 1st Victim Friday*, ROCKY MTN. NEWS, Sept. 2, 1956, at 5. The new gas chamber cost $9,000. Baker, *New Gas Chamber*. This new gas chamber, in which eight prisoners eventually died, now sits outside the prison museum in Cañon City, available for tourists to visit and inspect. By the time the new chamber was constructed, Colorado's original gas chamber had been moved to a children's playground in a park in Cañon City and eventually was turned into a grain storage building. It has since been discarded.

64. Colorado had two double executions in its gas chamber (1934 and 1939), but no triple executions with the gas chamber. The two triple executions in the state's history (1896 and 1931) were by hanging. There were also six double hangings (1866, 1881, 1895, 1905, 1928, and 1930).

65. *See* appendix 1, case no. 71.

66. *Id. See also*, appendix 2, case no. 61.

the *Rocky Mountain News* described the execution as "far quicker and much more humane than any of the hangings which have preceded it."[67] Warden Best, pleased with the machine he helped design, pronounced the execution "the most successful and painless one ever conducted at the penitentiary."[68] Still, the proclaimed success did not entirely eliminate problems. In 1939 prison officials described the double execution of Pete Catalina[69] and Angelo Agnes[70] as "the quickest and most humane execution we ever had."[71] Ironically, the public later learned that the gas chamber leaked during the execution, forcing spectators to flee the room.[72] Two years later, the *Denver Post* claimed that the execution of Joe Coates[73] was "the easiest and quickest death of any of the fourteen men" who died in Colorado's gas chamber.[74] Clearly, the prison officials and the newspapers wanted to assure the public that prisoners were being executed with as little pain as possible.

The next two men to die in the gas chamber were sentenced to death for killing a rancher and his son and wounding the rancher's wife in a robbery near Greeley. The killers, Louis and John Pacheco, died sitting in two of the three chairs in Roy's Penthouse. The two, Mexican Americans born in Colorado,[75] remain the only brothers executed in the state.[76]

By any measure, the most controversial execution in the history of the state also took place in the 1930s, when the state executed a developmentally disabled inmate named Joe Arridy (pronounced Ah-REE-day) for the rape and murder of a young Pueblo girl.[77] Arridy's conviction rested solely on the basis of his purported confession. In addition

---

67. Wallis M. Reef, *Kelley Meets Swift Death by Lethal Gas*, ROCKY MTN. NEWS, June 23, 1934, at 1.

68. Charles T. O'Brien, *Kelley Executed in New Gas Cell*, DENVER POST, June 23, 1934, at 1.

69. *See* appendix 1, case no. 78.

70. *See* appendix 1, case no. 79.

71. *Agnes and Catalina Executed Together in Lethal Chamber*, DENVER POST, Sept. 30, 1939, at 1.

72. *Death Chamber at Pen Tested*, ROCKY MTN. NEWS, Dec. 5, 1939, at 1.

73. *See* appendix 1, case no. 81.

74. *Coates Begs for Prayer in Death Chair*, DENVER POST, Jan. 11, 1941, at 1.

75. *See* appendix 1, case nos. 72 and 73.

76. In 1928 cousins Raymond Noakes and Arthur Osborn, who had been raised like brothers, were hanged. *See* appendix 1, case nos. 54 and 55.

77. *See* appendix 1, case no. 77.

to Arridy, the state also executed Frank Aguilar, who possessed the murder weapon and whose guilt was never in doubt, for the crime.[78] Notably, during Aguilar's execution, one of the witnesses, Adlai S. ("Ad") Hamilton, a Pueblo resident and conductor for the Missouri Pacific Railroad, suffered a heart attack and died.[79] Although Aguilar's execution was otherwise routine, Arridy's stay on death row significantly differed from the experiences of other condemned inmates. While on death row he became close friends with Warden Best, who ultimately spoke out against his execution and purchased toys and picture books to help Arridy pass the time.[80] History later showed that the execution was a horrible mistake. As will be discussed further in chapter 5, in January 2011, Arridy was granted a posthumous pardon by Colorado governor Bill Ritter after his innocence was determined.

Colorado executed thirteen individuals during the 1940s. At least one of those executions took the life of yet another inmate who had a profound intellectual disability, John Sullivan.[81] Even the sheriff who investigated the crime concluded that Sullivan was a "decidedly subnormal person."[82] The Colorado Supreme Court wrote, "The experts were . . . practically unanimous in saying that [the] defendant's intellect was below 'the average normal level;' that he was 'of inferior intelligence' and 'mentally' below eighteen years of age."[83] Sullivan's attorneys had challenged the execution by arguing that Colorado banned the death penalty for those under age eighteen. The court reasoned that "[t]his has nothing to do with 'age' as used in the statute . . . Had the legislature intended 'mental age' it would have used no such equivocal language."[84]

At mid-century, Colorado began to see a discernable downturn in the number of executions, and that trend continues to this day. Indeed, in the past sixty-five years (through 2015), there have been only ten executions in the state, and only two in the past fifty years.

---

78. *See* appendix 1, case no. 76.

79. "Last night's attack was apparently caused by the excitement of the execution." *Puebloan Witness, Dies at Execution*, PUEBLO CHIEFTAIN, Aug. 11, 1937, at 1.

80. *See* ROBERT PERSKE, DEADLY INNOCENCE? 125 (1995).

81. *See* appendix 1, case no. 85.

82. *Handyman Is Held in Slaying of Woman at Manitou Springs*, DENVER POST, Jan. 12, 1942, at 5.

83. Sullivan v. People, 111 Colo. 205; 139 P.2d 876, 877 (Colo. 1943).

84. *Id.*

The last execution in the 1950s involved perhaps the most notorious killer in the history of the state, John Gilbert Graham.[85] On November 1, 1955, Graham planted twenty-five sticks of dynamite in his mother's suitcase as she departed on a United Airlines flight from Denver to Portland, Oregon. Eighteen minutes after the plane departed from Stapleton International Airport, the suitcase exploded, killing his mother—Daisie E. King—and forty-three others on the plane. It was the first case of sabotage involving a commercial airplane in the United States. At the time, there was no federal law that made blowing up an airplane illegal, so the case was tried under state jurisdiction in a Denver courtroom.[86] Despite the magnitude of the crime, the motive was simple: Graham's troubled relationship with his mother. This was insufficient to convince any psychiatrists who saw Graham during a thirty-day pretrial stay at the Colorado Psychopathic Hospital[87] that his initial insanity plea had any merit.

The April 1955 trial became famous for its innovative use of cameras. It was filmed and recorded from a special booth in the courtroom that hid the equipment and camera operators from view. Denver news shows regularly broadcast prerecorded excerpts from the ongoing trial, which the jurors were forbidden to see.[88] According to the *Denver Post*, "When the trial was over, the judge, the jury foreman, and prosecution and defense attorneys said that to their knowledge the broadcast did not distract anyone and did not interfere with the fairness of the trial."[89] Graham was tried only for the murder of his mother.[90]

The final jury was composed of seven men and five women. Women did not have a right to sit on juries in Colorado until 1944, although some occasionally did before then at the discretion of the trial judge.

---

85. *See* appendix 1, case no. 96.

86. FIELD, at 29, 67.

87. FIELD, at 111–12; James A.V. Gavin & John M. McDonald, *Psychiatric Study of a Mass Murderer*, AMERICAN JOUR. OF PSYCH. 115 (1959): 1057.

88. Howard Pankratz, *Colo. A Leader in Courtroom Cameras*, DENVER POST, Dec. 12, 2002, at 7A.

89. *Id.*

90. "In 1956, Colorado law required that jurors in capital cases be sequestered 'during all recesses from the time the jury is selected until discharged by the trial court.' In 1984, this requirement was eliminated and Colorado judges were given the discretion to decide when to sequester a jury. In 1998, the rule was amended a second time to limit sequestration to 'extraordinary cases.'" FIELD, at 145.

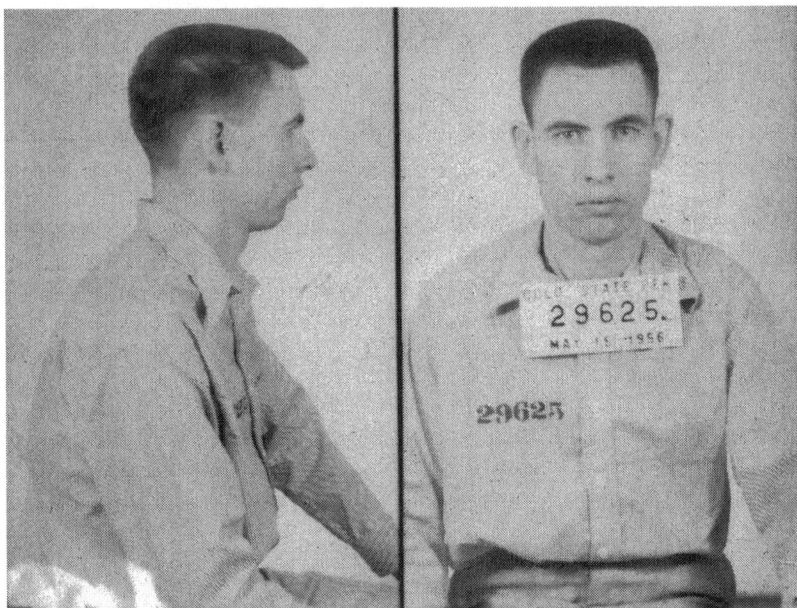

FIGURE 3.3. *John Gilbert Graham, executed January 11, 1957. His forty-four victims make him the worst mass-murderer in Colorado's history. Photo courtesy of the Colorado State Archives.*

On November 3, 1914, Colorado voters were asked in a ballot initiative to allow a three-fourths jury verdict in civil cases and permit women to serve on juries. The voters said no.[91] But in 1944, with 60 percent in favor, Colorado voters amended the state constitution to permit women to serve as jurors.[92]

Graham's full confession was introduced at trial, assuring a guilty verdict and a death sentence. After the trial was finished, he attempted to stop all the appeals of his conviction and sentence so that he could quickly go to the gas chamber. He was executed on January 11, 1957.[93] In

91. See *Colorado Three-Fourths Jury Verdict and Women Jurors, Measure 3 (1914)*, BALLOTPEDIA, accessed July 15, 2016, http://ballotpedia.org/Colorado_Three-Fourths_Jury_Verdict_and_Women_Jurors,_Measure_3_%281914%29.

92. HOLLY J. MCCAMMON, THE U.S. WOMEN'S JURY MOVEMENTS AND STRATEGIC ADAPTATION: A MORE JUST VERDICT 149–55 (2012).

93. Margaret Vandiver has described the execution of another man named John Graham, whose experience, although different from that of any person in Colorado, is well worth remembering. Graham, who was African American, was convicted of

2005, fifty years after the murders, the case was the subject of a book by Denver attorney Andrew J. Field.[94]

After Graham's execution in 1957, Colorado's gas chamber was not used again for the next three years. In the interim, the biggest crime news in the state was a botched kidnapping that became a non–death penalty case. On February 9, 1960, one of the state's most prominent citizens, forty-four-year-old Adolph ("Ad") Coors, was kidnapped and murdered while driving to work at the Coors Brewery in Golden. Coors was the grandson of the founder of Coors, and in 1960 was one of four in the family who controlled and ran the brewery. His abandoned car was found a short distance from his home in Jefferson County. A ransom note was delivered to his wife, Mary, demanding $500,000; but while Mary was prepared to pay the money, she never again heard from the kidnapper. Within a few days, the kidnapper was identified as Joseph Corbett, Jr., a man with a reported IQ of 148 who had recently escaped from a California prison while serving a sentence for manslaughter. Coors's body was not found until September 11, and on October 29, Corbett was arrested in Vancouver, British Columbia.

With no eyewitnesses nor a confession, the state decided not to seek the death penalty, but at trial in Golden in March 1961, Corbett was convicted of first-degree murder and sent off to Cañon City.[95] He was released in 1980, after serving nineteen years, but he returned to prison for another seventeen months for a parole violation. He lived in Denver until August 2009, when he took his own life.[96]

Six men were put to death in Cañon City in the 1960s, all of whom were convicted of especially aggravated murders. The first individual

---

the rape of a fourteen-year-old white girl that occurred near Ocala, Florida, in 1931. Graham first met his lawyers at the beginning of the hour-long trial. The jury deliberated three minutes before returning a death sentence. Eight days later, Graham was executed in the state's electric chair in Raiford. Margaret Vandiver, *The Quality of Mercy: Race and Clemency in Florida Death Penalty Cases, 1924–1966*, UNIV. OF RICHMOND L. REV. 27 (1993): 315–43, at 336–37.

94. FIELD, at 145.

95. Jerry Grunska, *The Kidnap-Murder of Adolph Coors III*, HISTORICALLY JEFFCO 17 (2004): 2–8; DAN BAUM, CITIZEN COORS: A GRAND FAMILY SAGA OF BUSINESS, POLITICS, AND BEER 57–63 (2000).

96. Kevin Vaughan, *Adolph Coors Murder: Notorious Killer's Quiet End*, DENVER POST, Aug. 30, 2009, at A19.

executed during this decade was Leroy Leick, who killed his wife after an unsuccessful two-year attempt to hire someone to do the job for him.[97] In 1961 David Early was executed for the murder of a Denver attorney and the attorney's wife and child.[98] The murders occurred only four days after Early's release from a federal penitentiary. Harold Wooley was executed for the murder of an affluent Denver man[99] and Walter Hammil was convicted of the sexual assault and murder of an eleven-year-old Denver boy.[100] John Bizup, who spent eighteen of his life of thirty years in and out of reform schools and jails, was executed in 1964 for the murder of a Pueblo cab driver.[101]

For the three years following Bizup's execution in 1964, Colorado did not host any executions, and nationally there were only seven in 1965, one in 1966, and one in the first five months of 1967. Then, in June 1967, Luis José Monge[102] became the sixth (and last) person to be executed in Colorado in the 1960s. Monge gave up his appeals and asked to be executed following a conviction for killing his wife, Dolores, who was pregnant with their eleventh child. He also killed three of their ten children but was not tried for those crimes.

Monge's was a curious case, and we are fortunate that journalist Stephen H. Gettinger has given us a lengthy account to help understand it.[103] Monge was born in Puerto Rico but moved to Brooklyn at age eleven, after his parents died, and lived with a series of relatives. After military service, he was employed as a driver-salesman for a Denver furniture company. While outwardly a devoted husband and father, he began sexually abusing his daughter Janet, who told Dolores and Anna, the oldest sibling. Monge promised to stop, and apparently tried very hard to do so, but in June 1963, Anna confronted him as he molested Janet as she slept. Monge feared public discovery and lost all self-control.

---

97. *See* appendix 1, case no. 97.

98. *See* appendix 1, case no. 98.

99. *See* appendix 1, case no. 99.

100. *See* appendix 1, case no. 100.

101. *See* appendix 1, case no. 101.

102. *See* appendix 1, case no. 102.

103. STEPHEN H. GETTINGER, SENTENCED TO DIE: THE PEOPLE, THE CRIMES, AND THE CONTROVERSY 1–20 (1979).

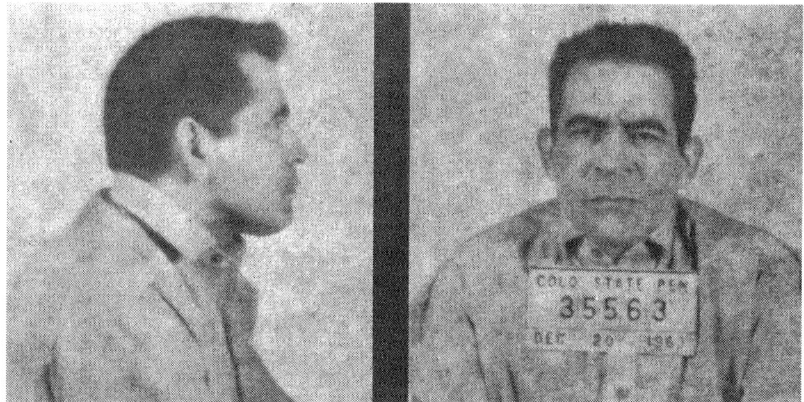

FIGURE 3.4. *Luis José Monge, executed June 2, 1967. The last person executed in Colorado—and the United States—before the US Supreme Court invalidated all death penalty statutes in 1972. Photo courtesy of the Colorado State Archives.*

In an ill-advised attempt to cover up his sex crimes, Monge repeatedly struck Dolores with a fire poker, killing her; stabbed a daughter; choked a son; and killed another son with the fire poker. He then called police and admitted what he had done.

Ten days later, Monge attempted to plead guilty, but his attorneys convinced him to enter an insanity plea. That plea eventually failed—no doubt partly because Monge, filled with remorse, continuously insisted that he was sane and ready to accept his punishment. He admitted his guilt, waiving the guilt phase of his trial, and a jury was seated to determine the penalty. Meanwhile, the trial judge arranged a surprise meeting between Monge and his seven surviving children. All was forgiven. He was still their father, and they still loved him dearly. Nonetheless, during the penalty phase, Monge directed his attorneys not to rebut any of the prosecution's arguments, and he was quickly sentenced to death.

Once on death row, the surviving children regularly made the 120-mile trip to Cañon City to visit their father. Monge lost an initial appeal in the Colorado Supreme Court, and then dismissed his attorneys and made it clear that he did not want any further appeals to be filed. Nonetheless, early in 1967, another attorney filed an appeal in the case. But when this appeal attracted wide newspaper coverage—the attorney claimed that Monge wanted to be executed at high noon in front of the Denver City Hall—Monge and his family ordered the attorney to cease work on the case. Given the national litigation over the death penalty, it was almost certain that Gov. John Love would have granted a temporary reprieve had Monge requested it. But Monge, not wanting to put his family through any further pain, was ready to die.

After sharing a final meal with his surviving children, Monge went to the gas chamber on June 2, 1967. He was the second of only two inmates in the United States to be executed that year. On the eve of the execution, seventy protestors denounced the death penalty in a rally at the state capitol. As he was being led into the gas chamber, Monge handed Warden Wayne Patterson a picture of Christ and asked that the warden present it to his (Patterson's) mother. As it turns out, Patterson's mother, a steadfast death penalty opponent, had been corresponding with Monge and the other condemned inmates, lending them whatever support she could while they were under her son's command.[104]

Unbeknownst to Coloradoans at the time, Monge would be the last person ever asphyxiated in Colorado, the last person executed in the state for thirty years, and the last person to be executed in the United States for the next ten years.

THE SUCCESSFUL EFFORT TO (AGAIN) END THE DEATH PENALTY

During the 1950s and 1960s, Colorado's death penalty faced both political and legal challenges. Colorado legislators attempted to abolish the death penalty on several occasions. In addition to legislators, many prominent figures supported these efforts, including prison wardens, district attorneys, governors, and leaders in the religious community. This movement ultimately failed, however, largely because of several heinous murders in Colorado and elsewhere in the United States in the mid-1960s that

---

104. WAYNE K. PATTERSON & BETTY L. ALT, KEEPER OF THE KEYS: A WARDEN'S NOTEBOOK 139–145 (2003). Journalist Cary Stiff, who had done extensive reporting on the death penalty for the *Denver Post*, decided that after witnessing Monge's execution, he would never witness another. "When the time came, [Monge] marched into the gas chamber and sat down without protest. So that was unsettling a little bit. I knew what was going to happen. There were no cries, no screams, no throwing up. It was very mechanical. I found that even more obscene." Quoted in Sarah K. Duran, *Witnesses Prepared for Execution*, BOULDER DAILY CAMERA, Oct. 12, 1997, at 1.

FIGURE 3.5. *Grave marker for Luis José Monge, Woodpecker Hill, Greenwood Cemetery, Cañon City. This is the only grave marker on Woodpecker Hill with bullet holes in it. Monge was the last person executed in Colorado—and the United States—before the US Supreme Court invalidated all death penalty statutes in 1972. Photo by author.*

shifted sentiment toward death penalty support. On the other hand, efforts throughout the country to urge the US Supreme Court to review the constitutionality of the death penalty had more success.

There were several attempts in the Colorado legislature to abolish the death penalty in the 1950s and 1960s. For example, in February 1955, Castle Rock Republican Ed G. Seidensticker and Arapahoe County Democrat Byron Johnson introduced abolitionist legislation in the state House of Representatives.[105] A month later, the House came "within a whisker" of passing the ban,[106] first approving the abolition bill, but

---

105. *House Measure Bans Death Penalty in State*, Rocky Mtn. News, Feb. 24, 1955, at 16.

106. *Bill to End Capital Punishment Returned to House Committee*, Rocky Mtn. News, Mar. 29, 1955, at 44. The 1955 abolition bill failed by only one vote. Field, at 148.

soon thereafter returning it to a dead-end committee for further study.[107] Similarly, in 1957 a bill championed by the Women's International League for Peace and Freedom and sponsored by Republican Rena Mary Taylor of Palisade passed a House committee on a 6–5 vote,[108] but the bill failed by a substantial margin in the full House.[109]

Yet, the issue stubbornly persisted. In many ways, the death penalty comprised part of a wide array of civil rights and human rights issues that Americans were reexamining at the time—a reexamination that included debates about the rights of racial and ethnic minorities and the role of women. In 1959 the Senate overwhelmingly defeated an abolitionist measure introduced by Everett Cook (D-Cañon City). Senator Cook estimated that the abolition of the death penalty would save taxpayers more than $750,000.[110] Two years later, an abolitionist bill, as well as a bill establishing a statewide referendum on the issue, failed in the Senate Judiciary Committee.[111] In 1964 the Senate rejected a referendum that imposed a five-year moratorium on the death penalty after heated debate over biblical directives on capital punishment.[112] Ultimately, a resolution calling for a referendum on a constitutional amendment to abolish the death penalty passed the Senate in 1964, but it failed to muster enough votes to pass through a House committee.[113]

This bill appeared again in the 1965 legislative session, this time introduced by Republican Reps. John Mackle of Longmont and Ruth Clark of Fort Collins. On its initial reading, it passed the House by an "overwhelm-

---

107. The vote to bury the bill was 34–29. *House Move Kills Death Penalty Ban*, DENVER POST, Mar. 29, 1955, at 3.

108. *Bill Voiding Death Penalty Squeaks by House Group*, ROCKY MTN. NEWS, Feb. 27, 1957, at 41; *House Will Debate Capital Punishment*, ROCKY MTN. NEWS, Mar. 2, 1957, at 34; *House Kills Bill Banning Death Penalty in Colorado*, ROCKY MTN. NEWS, Mar. 5, 1957, at 5.

109. The vote was 36–23. *Bill to Ban Death Penalty Turned Down by House*, DENVER POST, Mar. 5, 1957, at 14.

110. Tom Gavin, *Senate Dumps Death Penalty Measure Again*, ROCKY MTN. NEWS, Mar. 5, 1959, at 5.

111. The measures failed by identical 5–2 votes. *Anti-Death Penalty Bill Dies*, ROCKY MTN. NEWS, Mar. 2, 1961, at 24.

112. This bill was defeated on a 23–9 vote. Dan Thomasson, *Senate Defeats Moratorium on Death Penalty*, ROCKY MTN. NEWS, Feb. 18, 1964, at 5.

113. *Plan to Bar Death Penalty Is Introduced*, ROCKY MTN. NEWS, Jan. 22, 1965, at 44.

ing" margin.[114] Ten days later, the Senate also gave its approval. Another Republican—Sen. Donald E. Kelley of Denver—provided leadership on the issue.[115] The resolution provided that all offenses committed after January 1, 1967, would carry a maximum sentence of life imprisonment. However, it was contingent upon voter approval. Citizens would vote as part of the 1966 general election, eighteen months after the legislature's action. When Governor Love signed the legislation on May 6, 1965, he set the stage for a spirited debate on the issue throughout the state.[116]

By then, the death penalty was authorized for five crimes, although no one (at least insofar as this author has been able to determine) except those convicted of capital murder had ever been sentenced to death. The other capital offenses included kidnapping involving injury to the victim or where ransom was involved (a capital offense since the law was passed in 1939); "causing a death while claim jumping (1874); causing a death while violating the state's anarchy laws (1919); and a second conviction for selling narcotics to someone twenty-five or under (1963)."[117] Two crimes on the books carried a mandatory death sentence, although again, no one was ever sentenced under these provisions: "Armed assault by a life-term prisoner during an escape (1954), and perjury in a capital case leading to the execution of an innocent person," a law dating back to 1861.[118]

Governor Love also pledged not to authorize any executions until the voters spoke. So when the Colorado Supreme Court, in November 1965, upheld the death sentences for three men—Luis José Monge, Michael John Bell, and Sylvester Lee Garrison—Coloradoans knew that the executions would not occur, at least until after the referendum was conducted.[119]

---

114. Leonard Larsen, *House Votes to Put Death Penalty on Ballot*, DENVER POST, Apr. 10, 1965, at 20.

115. The referendum was approved by an 18–12 margin. Martin Moran, *Senate Wants Voters To Weigh Death Law*, ROCKY MTN. NEWS, Apr. 20, 1965, at 5; Charles Roos, *Senate Okays Death Penalty Vote Bill*, DENVER POST, Apr. 20, 1965, at 13.

116. *Death Penalty Bill is Signed*, DENVER POST, May 6, 1965, at 34; *Love Signs Law Permitting Vote on Capital Punishment*, ROCKY MTN. NEWS, May 7, 1965, at 65.

117. Cary Stiff, *Thousands Watched Executions in Early Colorado*, DENVER POST, Oct. 31, 1966, at 36.

118. *Id.*

119. Rendall Ayers, *State Supreme Court Orders 3 Executions*, DENVER POST, Nov. 1, 1965, at 23.

In a move that would be unthinkable today, the Colorado District Attorneys Association was one of the first groups to publicly support the abolition of the death penalty in 1965. Just a month after Governor Love signed the legislation authorizing a referendum, the group passed a resolution calling for the abolition of the death penalty by a "decisive" and "overwhelming" margin.[120] According to the *Rocky Mountain News*,

> Dist. Atty. Rex Scott of Boulder said, "As far as district attorneys are concerned, the death penalty makes our job tougher, increases trial costs and increases the number of insanity pleas."
>
> He claimed capital punishment is not a deterrent to murder, carries over from the Dark Ages concept of eye for an eye, and creates the danger of executing an innocent person. He said the penalty is discriminatory in that under the same set of circumstances one jury would sentence a man to die and another would give him life imprisonment. Race and financial positions also enter into juries' verdicts he said.[121]

Other members of law enforcement professions were less supportive of abolishing the death penalty. Although no reliable polls were taken, evidence indicates that police officers did not share the prosecutors' stand against the death penalty. For example, a crude poll of one hundred Colorado law enforcement officers in September 1966 reportedly found "unanimous" support for the death penalty. On the other hand, in 1974 members of the Colorado Correctional Association voted to oppose the death penalty by an "overwhelming" margin.[122]

The prosecutors and prison employees of the 1960s were not the first of their respective professions to harbor anti–death penalty attitudes. Several wardens who supervised executions in Colorado stood opposed to the death penalty, at least privately. Warden J. A. Lamping first exhibited this sentiment when he opposed moving the site of executions to Cañon City in the late 1880s.[123] Later, the death penalty so offended Warden Thomas J. Tynan that he refused to enter the death chamber during

---

120. *State DAs Condemn Death Law*, DENVER POST, June 20, 1965, at 20.

121. William Logan, *Colorado DAs Ask Death Penalty End*, ROCKY MTN. NEWS, June 20, 1965, at 12.

122. *Correctional Group Opposes Death Penalty*, ROCKY MTN. NEWS, Oct. 5, 1974, at 27.

123. *See* discussion of Lamping in chapter 2, *infra*.

at least two executions.[124] Warden Tynan's successor, F. E. Crawford, who served from 1927 to 1931, also opposed the death penalty.[125] Roy Best shared similar opinions when, during his twenty-two-year tenure as warden, he supervised twenty-six executions (more than any other warden in the state's history) and the construction of Colorado's first gas chamber.[126] Harry C. Tinsley, who served as warden from 1955 to 1965 and supervised eight executions, also opposed the death penalty.[127] In 1965 Tinsley became both the chief of the Colorado Department of Corrections as well as the honorary chairman of a new statewide anti–death penalty group.[128] In that position, he stood at the forefront of the efforts to scrap the death penalty in the 1966 referendum.[129]

Those supporting the 1966 referendum noted that several former Colorado governors had voiced opposition to the death penalty. Gov. Davis H. Waite, in office in the late nineteenth century, was an early

---

124. *See* appendix 1, case nos. 45 and 47.

125. *What About Executions Before 1890?*, ROCKY MTN. NEWS, July 6, 1965, at 76.

126. Pasquale Marranzino, *No Sponge from Roy's Closet*, ROCKY MTN. NEWS, May 31, 1954, at 23.

127. *What About Executions Before 1890?*.

128. Rendall Ayers, *Tinsley Honed For Challenges,* DENVER POST, Sept. 12, 1965, at 35 (stating he would support the death penalty only in cases in which police officers were murdered); *Anti-Capital Punishment Council Will Incorporate*, ROCKY MTN. NEWS, Dec. 1, 1965, at 73. Warden Tinsley was later among those who filed amicus briefs in Furman v. Georgia. *See* Furman v. Georgia, 408 U.S. 238, 287, n.35 (1971).

129. Later wardens not only opposed the death penalty but also followed Tinsley's lead by taking an active role in speaking out against capital punishment. Wayne K. Patterson, who served as warden from 1965 to 1972 and pulled the lever releasing the cyanide pellets that killed Luis Monge in 1967, remained a staunch opponent of the death penalty until his death in 2003. Glenn Troelstrup, *Ex-Warden Still Opposes Death Penalty*, DENVER POST, Dec. 19, 1976, at 52; Karen Bailey, *Ex Warden Against Capital Punishment,* ROCKY MTN. NEWS, July 2, 1985, at 14. *See also* appendix 1, case no. 102. Alex Wilson, warden in 1974, also opposed the death penalty and pledged that he would never personally carry one out. He took the position that executions should not take place at the prison because "it is an extremely derogative thing to do." Joan Zyda, *Warden Personally Against Executions,* DENVER POST, June 9, 1974, at 36. In 1974 Wilson allegedly told an audience that "[p]eople who are in favor of capital punishment are nuts." John Boslough, *Warden Rakes Death Penalty*, DENVER POST, Sept. 27, 1974, at 2. However, when this quote was printed in the *Denver Post,* he denied the statement, pointing out that many people he admired were in favor of the death penalty. *"Nuts" Quote Is Denied by Warden*, DENVER POST, Sept. 29, 1974, at 2.

foe.[130] Gov. Alva Adams signed the 1897 bill that temporarily abolished the death penalty.[131] In 1901 Gov. James Orman refused to sign the bill reinstating the death penalty but allowed it to become law without his signature.[132] In the early twentieth century, Gov. John F. Shafroth also opposed the death penalty, although executions did occur while he was in office.[133] Similarly, Gov. William Adams, in office between 1927 and 1933, did not allow his personal opposition to the death penalty to cause him to stop executions during his tenure.[134] In the middle of Edwin C. Johnson's term as governor, from 1955 to 1957, he published an opinion piece in the *Rocky Mountain News* titled "I Hate Capital Punishment but a Governor Must Do His Job." At the same time, however, Governor Johnson pledged to carry out the law and enforce the death penalty in cases that warranted it.[135] Two days before the article's publication in 1956, Johnson proved his point by not intervening to delay or stop the execution of Besalirez Martinez.[136]

The religious community became increasingly involved in organizing against the death penalty during the 1960s and led the fight to outlaw capital punishment in the 1966 referendum. Charles Milligan, a professor of Christian ethics at the Iliff School of Theology in Denver, provided one of the first calls for abolition in 1961.[137] By 1965, a *Denver Post* poll

---

130. *The Condemned*, ROCKY MTN. NEWS, May 12, 1895, at 9. Governor Waite's term lasted from 1893 until 1895.

131. *No Work for Hangman*, ROCKY MTN. NEWS, Mar. 1, 1895, at 8.

132. *Kills Two Bills: Capital Punishment Becomes a Law Through Lapse of Time*, ROCKY MTN. NEWS, May 1, 1901, at 12.

133. *See* appendix 1, case no. 45. Governor Shafroth served between 1909 and 1913.

134. *See* appendix 1, case nos. 54 and 55.

135. Edwin C. Johnson, *I Hate Capital Punishment but a Governor Must Do His Job*, ROCKY MTN. NEWS, Sept. 9, 1956, at 5.

136. *See* appendix 1, case no. 95. Other governors, although apparently not opposed to the death penalty, did visit condemned inmates before executions to better inform their clemency decisions. Gov. Albert W. McIntire (1895–1897) visited Thomas Jordan. *See* appendix 1, case no. 31. Gov. Ralph L. Carr (1939–1943) visited Joe Coates and Martin Sukle. *See* appendix 1, case nos. 81 and 83.

137. *End to Death Penalty Envisaged in Colorado*, DENVER POST, Dec. 16, 1961, at 6. Relevant scholarship published by Professor Milligan includes *A Protestant's View of the Death Penalty*, in THE DEATH PENALTY IN AMERICA: AN ANTHOLOGY 175, ed. Hugo Adam Bedau (1964); *Reflections on the Gas Chamber*, ILIFF REV. 23 (1966): 3–13; *The Effect of Cruelty on Those Who Inflict It, With Special Reference to the Eighth Amendment*, CONTEMPORARY PHILOSOPHY 12 (1991): 24–26; *The "Cruel and*

of Colorado religious leaders found that a majority opposed the death penalty.[138]

By this time, the debate included several other groups. In early 1965, the Colorado branch of the American Civil Liberties Union, which had never adopted a stance on capital punishment, began to reconsider its silence.[139] Later that year, the Colorado Council to Abolish Capital Punishment was formed, headed by Denver attorney Edward H. Sherman.[140] The council also named Harry C. Tinsley, chief of corrections for the State of Colorado and former warden of Colorado State Prison, as honorary chairman.[141] In April 1966, Hugo Adam Bedau, then at Princeton and later to become the leading academic authority on the death penalty in the United States, traveled to Colorado to lend his voice to the new group's organizing efforts.[142] In October, the group sponsored an eight-day speaking tour of the state by former San Quentin Prison warden Clinton Duffy[143] and Adams County public defender John L. Kane, Jr. (who later became a district court judge) published a stinging opinion piece in the *Denver Post* calling for abolition.[144] The Colorado Young Democrats[145] also publicly opposed the death penalty. The pres-

---

Unusual" Proscription in the Eighth Amendment, in THE BILL OF RIGHTS: BICENTENNIAL REFLECTIONS 103–13, ed. Yeager Hudson & Creighton Peden (1993). By any measure, Milligan stands among the top death penalty abolitionists in the history of the state.

138. Eva Hodges, *Clergymen Oppose Capital Punishment in Poll*, DENVER POST, Mar. 20, 1965, Religion section, at 1.

139. Morgan Lawhon, *State's ACLU Mulls Death Penalty*, DENVER POST, Jan. 31, 1965, at 14.

140. Rendall Ayers, *Colo. Anti-Death Penalty Unit Formed*, DENVER POST, Nov. 29, 1965, at 3.

141. *Anti-Capital Punishment Council Will Incorporate*, ROCKY MTN. NEWS, Dec. 1, 1965, at 73.

142. Cary Stiff, *Death Penalty Debate Begins*, DENVER POST, May 8, 1966, at 35.

143. Cary Stiff, *Chessman Views Given by Ex-Warden Duffy*, DENVER POST, Oct. 3, 1966, at 48. Warden Duffy was a dogged opponent of the death penalty. *See generally*, CLINTON T. DUFFY, 88 MEN AND 2 WOMEN: ABSORBING ACCOUNTS OF NINETY EXECUTIONS WITNESSED BY THE FORMER WARDEN OF SAN QUENTIN (1962).

144. John L. Kane, Jr., *Public Defender on Capital Punishment*, DENVER POST, Oct. 3, 1966, at 12.

145. The Colorado Young Democrats first took a stand against the death penalty in 1958, when a resolution supporting abolition passed by a narrow margin (661–620) at their state convention. Roberta McIntyre, *End Capital Punishment, Dems Urge*, ROCKY MTN. NEWS, June 2, 1958, at 5.

ident of the group's Denver branch promised "to go door-to-door" to convince voters to abolish the death penalty.[146]

Yet, a series of unrelated, unusually brutal murders, which shook Colorado and the nation in the four months before the 1966 referendum, arguably affected the vote more than any statement for or against the death penalty by any person or organization. On July 9, 1966, University of Colorado student Elaura Jaquette was raped and bludgeoned to death in a room in Macky Auditorium on the Boulder campus.[147] Three months later, Jaquette's mother "very sincerely and prayerfully" called for voters to retain the death penalty.[148] Four days after Jaquette's murder, eight student nurses were found slain in their Chicago apartment, crimes that soon led to the arrest of Richard Speck.[149] On August 1, Charles Joseph Whitman killed sixteen people and wounded thirty-two others by firing from the top of the University of Texas Tower in Austin before police shot and killed him.[150] Then, less than a week before the referendum, the bullet-ridden bodies of an Arizona couple were found stuffed in an outhouse in a US. Forest Service campground forty miles north of Durango, Colorado.[151]

Against this backdrop, the November 1966 referendum to abolish the death penalty (Measure 7) failed by nearly a 2–1 margin, with Coloradans voting 389,707 to 193,245 to retain capital punishment.[152] Coincidentally, the vote was held exactly seventy-six years after the first execution was

---

146. *Denver Young Dems Push Drive to End Death Penalty,* DENVER POST, Aug. 16, 1966, at 28.

147. Clark Secrest, *Girl Found Slain in CU Auditorium*, DENVER POST, July 10, 1966, at 1.

148. *Slain Coed's Mom Backs Death Penalty*, ROCKY MTN. NEWS, Oct. 14, 1966, at 5.

149. *Eight Nurses Massacred*, DENVER POST, July 14, 1966, at 1; obituary, *Richard Speck, 49, Chicago Killer of 8 Student Nurses 25 Years Ago*, N.Y. TIMES, Dec. 6, 1991, at 21.

150. *Texas Toll: 16 Dead, 31 Shot*, DENVER POST, Aug. 2, 1966, at 1.

151. The victims' names were Milton and Mildred Moeller. Harry Gessing, *Missing Pair Found Slain in Colo. Camp*, DENVER POST, Nov. 3, 1966, at 1. One month later, Thomas Julius Sergent was arrested for the murders. Robert Kistler, *Slay-Suspect Sergent Facing Early Return*, DENVER POST, Dec. 14, 1966, at 3. Sergent was subsequently convicted of first-degree murder. Sergent v. People, 177 Colo. 354; 497 P.2d 983, 984 (Colo. 1972).

152. Roxane J. Perruso, *And Then There Were Three: Colorado's New Death Penalty Sentencing Statute*, 68 U. COLO. L. REV. 198 (1997).

held inside the prison gates in Cañon City and sixty-six years after the murder of Louise Frost, whose death resulted in the burning at the stake of John Preston Porter and led directly to the reimposition of the death penalty in Colorado.

Governor Love wasted little time in ending the moratorium. After waiting for the end of the Christmas season, on January 4, 1967, he lifted the stays that he had granted to Monge, Bell, and Garrison, as well as the stays that he had given to two other condemned inmates, John Major Young and Joe Albert Segura.[153] His action allowed the Colorado Supreme Court to schedule Garrison's execution for late April, Bell's for mid-May,[154] Monge's in early June, and Segura's soon thereafter. Because Young's direct appeal was still pending, the court did not set an execution date for him,[155] but nonetheless, at the time it looked like 1967 was going to be a busy year in the Colorado gas chamber. By the time Garrison was scheduled to die, he had already spent more than seven years on death row in Cañon City, earning nothing but respect from the warden.[156] On the day before Garrison's May 1967 execution date, however, Governor Love issued a five-week stay to allow the defense attorneys to take their appeal to federal court. Despite the stay, Warden Wayne Patterson allowed Garrison to eat the "last meal" that had already been prepared in anticipation of his death.[157] A federal judge eventually reduced the sentences of both Garrison and Segura to life in June 1971.[158] Garrison spent over eleven years on death row, had four-

153. *Gov. Love Lifts Execution Stays*, DENVER POST, Jan. 5, 1967, at 18.

154. Bell and another death row inmate, Ernest Alsip, were killed by guards in an escape attempt on May 1, 1971. Alan Cunningham, *2 Inmates Die in Escape Try in View of Students*, ROCKY MTN. NEWS, May 2, 1971, at 5.

155. Cary Stiff, *Joe Segura Execution Date Due*, DENVER POST, Feb. 19, 1967, at 31.

156. PATTERSON & ALT, KEEPER OF THE KEYS, at 135–37.

157. Fred Brown, *Governor Grants Garrison 5-Week Stay of Execution*, DENVER POST, May 4, 1967, at 1.

158. The death sentences were set aside because of the improper removal of jurors who had reservations about the death penalty from the trial juries. Segura v. Patterson, 402 F.2d 249, 251–252 (1968). Carol McMurrough, *Court Decisions Move 2 Men Off Death Row*, DENVER POST, June 29, 1971, at 3; Carol McMurrough, *Garrison Leaves Prison Death Row*, DENVER POST, June 30, 1971, at 21.

teen execution dates, and ate three "last meals" before he was ultimately paroled in 1978.[159]

Garrison had been convicted and sentenced to death for the murder of a seventy-nine-year-old man named Mort Freelander, a retired salesman, whose head was hit repeatedly with a pistol during a robbery. Garrison, an African American who steadfastly maintained his innocence, recalled, "I had 16 strikes against me—13 jurors, two prosecutors and the judge. They were all white."[160] After his parole, he lived with his mother in Denver, had an eight-year marriage, and worked as a janitor for the City of Denver until retiring in 1998.[161] His only legal problems were two traffic tickets. He died at age seventy-two in 2005.[162]

In hindsight, we can see that the political opposition to the death penalty in Colorado in the 1960s directly and indirectly resulted in fewer executions. Directly, the political opposition delayed executions and bought more time for death row inmates to obtain relief from the courts. Indirectly, the political opposition impacted public opinion to an extent that likely caused fewer prosecutors to seek death sentences and fewer juries to impose them. In the end, however, the movement failed to achieve its goal of persuading Colorado politicians or voters to remove the death penalty from the statute books.

But at the same time, there was also a nationwide legal assault on the death penalty. As in Colorado, the pace of executions throughout the United States steadily declined between the 1930s and the 1960s. The nation averaged 166 executions per year in the 1930s, 128 in the 1940s, and 72 in the 1950s. Public support for the death penalty also began to

---

159. Bill McBean, *Slayer Cheated Death and Won*, DENVER POST, Apr. 26, 1978, at 3. A few months after his release—on Thanksgiving Day 1978—Lt. Gov. George L. Brown granted Garrison a pardon while Gov. Richard Lamm was traveling out of state. Lamm immediately rescinded the pardon upon his return. Dick Foster, *Top State Jobs Have Heated History; Lieutenant Governors Not Always Loyal to Governors*, ROCKY MTN. NEWS, Oct. 10, 1999, at 5A. Garrison's suit to have the pardon restored failed. Dick Foster, *Governors Hold Solemn Power, Face Public's Wrath in Deciding Pardons*, ROCKY MTN. NEWS, Feb. 25, 2001, at 4A.

160. Ann Carnahan, *Survivor of Colorado's Death Row Now Spends His Time Forgetting*, ROCKY MTN. NEWS, Nov. 22, 2003, at 1.

161. Greg Lopez, *Politicians "Forget About the Person," Death Row Survivor Says*, ROCKY MTN. NEWS, Mar. 16, 1994, at 4.

162. Kevin Simpson, *From Death Row to a Life Devoted to Family, Normalcy*, DENVER POST, June 5, 2005, at 1.

decline in the 1950s, partly because of three especially controversial executions: Ethel and Julius Rosenberg, for espionage in New York in June 1953 under federal authority,[163] and Caryl Chessman in California in May 1960.[164] The prosecution of Dr. Sam Sheppard in Ohio in 1954, perceived by many as unfair because of questions about his guilt, also eroded support for the death penalty in the 1950s.[165] By 1966, only 47 percent of the American public voiced support for the death penalty. Between 1960 and 1966, the average number of executions in the United States fell to twenty-seven per year. After Luis José Monge's execution in Colorado in June 1967, no executions occurred anywhere in the United States for nearly a decade because of successful litigation in front of various state and federal courts.[166]

In the decade before 1967, Colorado was not the only state moving in the direction of abolition. Delaware briefly abolished the death penalty in 1958[167] and the abolitionist jurisdictions of Alaska and Hawaii became states in 1959.[168] In 1964 a large majority of Oregon voters threw out the death penalty through a public referendum[169] and in 1965 New York and Vermont greatly restricted the availability of death sentences in their

163. The Rosenbergs' guilt remains controversial, with many today proclaiming their innocence. *See, e.g.*, WALTER SCHNEIR & MIRIAM SCHNEIR, INVITATION TO AN INQUEST: A NEW LOOK AT THE ROSENBERG-SOBEL CASE (1968).

164. Chessman had attained worldwide notoriety for several well-received books that he wrote while on death row. *See, e.g.*, CARYL CHESSMAN, CELL 2455, DEATH ROW (1960). He was executed for kidnapping for the purpose of robbery, which many felt should not have been a capital offense. *See* EDMUND G. (PAT) BROWN, PUBLIC JUSTICE, PRIVATE MERCY: A GOVERNOR'S EDUCATION ON DEATH ROW 20–52 (1989).

165. This case later became the basis for the popular television show *The Fugitive*. The state sought the death penalty for Sheppard for the murder of his wife, but in a compromise verdict, he was convicted of second-degree murder and sentenced to life imprisonment. In 1966 a retrial was ordered on the grounds that massive, pervasive, and prejudicial publicity had attended his prosecution. Sheppard v. Maxwell, 384 U.S. 333 (1966). At retrial, he was acquitted when bloodstain evidence indicated that he was not the killer.

166. This litigation was ultimately ended by the US Supreme Court. Furman v. Georgia, 408 U.S. 238 (1972).

167. HUGO ADAM BEDAU, THE DEATH PENALTY IN AMERICA, 3rd ed., 22–23 (1982).

168. *See id.*

169. Hugo Adam Bedau, *The 1964 Death Penalty Referendum in Oregon: Some Notes from a Participant-Observer*, CRIME & DELINQUENCY 26 (1980): 528, 534–535.

jurisdictions.[170] Governors such as Edmund ("Pat") Brown in California, Endicott Peabody in Massachusetts, Michael DiSalle in Ohio, Milton Shapp in Pennsylvania, and Winthrop Rockefeller in Arkansas lent their voices to the abolitionists' chorus.[171] Scholars began to outline strategies to abolish capital punishment,[172] and Supreme Court Justices William J. Brennan, William O. Douglas, Abe Fortas,[173] and Arthur Goldberg[174] began to invite challenges to the constitutionality of the death penalty.

Meanwhile, in 1963 University of Pennsylvania law professor Anthony Amsterdam began to consult with the New York–based NAACP Legal Defense Fund to develop strategies to fight death sentences in state and federal courts throughout the country. These efforts would profoundly and permanently affect the administration of the death penalty from coast to coast, including in Colorado. Some victories in the courts, as well as narrow losses that left room for new challenges, gave rise to a new hope that energized these efforts. For example, in 1968 the US Supreme Court's ruling that attorneys could exclude only the most unyielding opponents of the death penalty from jury service in capital cases added many citizens with general concerns about the death penalty to those eligible to serve.[175] When that case was decided in 1968, many observers believed that another execution would never occur in the United States.[176] Furthermore, an increasing recognition of the role of race in the administration of the death penalty,[177] especially for those convicted of rape, fueled hope that the Supreme Court would invalidate the death penalty on grounds of arbitrariness and racial disparities. Nonetheless,

---

170. MICHAEL MELTSNER, CRUEL AND UNUSUAL: The Supreme Court and Capital Punishment 52 (1973) (hereinafter MELTSNER, CRUEL AND UNUSUAL).

171. *Id.* at 222, 255.

172. *See, e.g.*, Gerald H. Gottlieb, *Testing the Death Penalty*, S. CAL. L. REV. 34 (1961): 268.

173. Fortas later published his views in Abe Fortas, *The Case Against Capital Punishment*, N.Y. TIMES MAG., Jan. 23, 1977, at 9.

174. Justice Goldberg, joined by Justices Brennan and Douglas, invited a challenge to the death penalty for rape in his dissent in Rudolph v. Alabama, 375 U.S. 889 (1963). His clerk at the time was (now) Harvard law professor Alan Dershowitz. *See* Arthur J. Goldberg & Alan M. Dershowitz, *Declaring the Death Penalty Unconstitutional*, 83 HARV. L. REV. 1773, 1773 (1970).

175. Witherspoon v. Illinois, 391 U.S. 510, 520–522 (1968).

176. *See* MELTSNER, CRUEL AND UNUSUAL, at 123–24.

177. *Id.* at 27–31.

even after extensive research by University of Pennsylvania criminologist Marvin Wolfgang documented widespread racial bias in the death penalty for rape,[178] the Eighth Circuit Court of Appeals, in *Maxwell v. Bishop*, refused to intervene.[179] Nine years later, the Supreme Court abolished the death penalty for nonhomicidal rape, not based on blatant racial bias but because "a sentence of death is grossly disproportionate and excessive punishment for the crime of rape and is therefore forbidden by the Eighth Amendment as cruel and unusual punishment."[180] Current Supreme Court Justice Ruth Bader Ginsburg, then with the American Civil Liberties Union, wrote an important amicus brief in the case in support of what became the majority's decision.[181]

In addition to arguments related to evolving standards of decency and race, death penalty opponents attacked capital punishment because of pure arbitrariness in its application. On appeal to the Supreme Court, the petitioners in *Maxwell* argued for mandatory standards on which jurors should frame their life-and-death decisions in capital cases and a bifurcated trial system to allow jurors to hear testimony relating to their penalty decision in a separate proceeding following the trial.[182] Given the very real possibility that the Court would decide these issues, governors or various state and federal courts suspended all executions in the nation pending the Court's decision.[183] The Court's 1970 ruling, however, disposed of the case on narrow grounds pertaining to jury selection and sidestepped the constitutional questions. Almost immediately, however, the Court announced that existing stays of execution would remain in effect until it addressed these broader issues in other cases.[184] Thus, the

---

178. Some 405 of the 455 men executed for rape (89 percent) between 1930 and 1967 were African American. *See* Marvin E. Wolfgang & Marc Riedel, *Rape, Racial Discrimination, and the Death Penalty*, in CAPITAL PUNISHMENT IN THE UNITED STATES, ed. Hugo Adam Bedau & Chester M. Pierce (1976), 99–121. Colorado never authorized the death penalty for those convicted solely for rape.

179. The decision was written by future Supreme Court justice (and future death penalty opponent) Judge Harry Blackmun. Maxwell v. Bishop, 398 F.2d 138 (1968).

180. Coker v. Georgia, 433 U.S. 584, 592 (1977).

181. *See Coker v. Georgia—Ginsburg Revisits Her Brief*, accessed July 15, 2016, http://law.jrank.org/pages/23555/Coker-v-Georgia-Ginsburg-Revisits-Her-Brief.html.

182. Maxwell v. Bishop, 398 U.S. 262 (1970).

183. MELTSNER, CRUEL AND UNUSUAL, at 148.

184. MELTSNER, CRUEL AND UNUSUAL, at 227–28.

status of the death penalty in Colorado in the late 1960s and early 1970s was influenced by events far beyond the state's borders.

In May 1971, on identical 6–3 votes, the Supreme Court dealt two setbacks to the abolitionist strategy in *McGautha v. California* and *Crampton v. Ohio*, ruling that states were free to give juries unguided discretion in sentencing decisions[185] and that the Constitution did not require separate guilt and punishment proceedings in capital trials.[186] Despite these decisions, the following month the Court announced that it would hear a series of cases to determine whether the death penalty itself constituted "cruel and unusual punishment," in violation of the Eighth and Fourteenth Amendments. With this, the stays of execution continued and the case of *Furman v. Georgia* moved to center stage.

Early in 1972, the California Supreme Court, by a 6–1 vote, abolished the death penalty in that state, holding that it violated the "cruel or unusual" clause in the California Constitution.[187] That ruling reduced the death sentences for 102 men and five women to life imprisonment.[188] Furthermore, because the decision interpreted the state constitution, it could not be appealed to federal courts. Clearly, the abolitionist position had gained strength.

The US Supreme Court finally decided *Furman v. Georgia* in June 1972 and handed the foes of capital punishment a monumental victory. By a 5–4 vote, with each justice writing a separate opinion, the Court held that the death penalty statutes under review—and, by implication, all others in the country—constituted cruel and unusual punishment, in violation of the Eighth and Fourteenth Amendments.[189] Justices Douglas, Marshall, Brennan, Stewart, and White voted with the majority while Justices Powell, Blackmun, Rehnquist, and Chief

---

185. McGautha v. California, 402 U.S. 183, 196 (1971). This holding was opposite to what the Supreme Court was to hold the next year in *Furman*. *McGautha* involved a due process challenge, whereas *Furman* challenged the death penalty under the Eighth Amendment.

186. Crampton v. Ohio, 402 U.S. 183, 221–22 (1971).

187. People v. Anderson, 6 Cal. 3d 628 (Cal. 1972); 493 P.2d 880, 898 (1972).

188. MELTSNER, CRUEL AND UNUSUAL, at 282. The most famous men removed from death row by this decision were Charles Manson, leader of the so-called Manson Family, and Sirhan Sirhan, convicted of the murder of Sen. Robert Kennedy in Los Angeles in 1968. Both remained in prison at the time of this writing (2015).

189. Furman v. Georgia, 408 U.S. 238, 239–240 (1972).

Justice Burger dissented.[190] At the time, most observers agreed with Jack Greenberg, the executive director of the NAACP Legal Defense Fund, who stated, "There will no longer be any more capital punishment in the United States."[191] *Furman* and its related cases led to death sentences being commuted to prison terms for some 631 men and two women then on death rows in thirty-two states. Two Colorado inmates were among those who received commuted sentences: John Major Young, Jr.,[192] and James D. Mainer.[193]

Colorado, like other states, had a golden opportunity to permanently send its executioner to the unemployment office.

---

190. Ironically, in later years, two of the dissenters, Powell and Blackmun, would announce their unequivocal opposition to the death penalty. In 1991 then-retired Justice Lewis Powell told his biographer, "I have come to think that capital punishment should be abolished . . . [because it] serves no useful purpose." JOHN C. JEFFRIES, JR., JUSTICE LEWIS F. POWELL, JR. 451–52 (1994). In 1994, while still on the Court, Justice Blackmun (who, while a federal circuit judge, wrote the decision in *Maxwell v. Bishop*, denying the claim that the death penalty for rape was racially tainted) wrote, "From this day forward, I no longer shall tinker with the machinery of death. For more than 20 years I have endeavored . . . along with a majority of this Court, to develop procedural and substantive rules that would lend more than the mere appearance of fairness to the death penalty endeavor. Rather than continue to coddle the Court's delusion that the desired level of fairness has been achieved . . . I feel morally and intellectually obligated simply to concede that the death penalty experiment has failed" Callins v. Collins, 510 U.S. 1141, 1145 (1994) (citation omitted).

191. MELTSNER, CRUEL AND UNUSUAL, at 291.

192. Young (black) was sentenced to death for the 1965 murder of a Colorado Springs service station attendant. Jack Olsen, *2 in Colo. Death Row Spared by Court Ruling,* DENVER POST, June 29, 1972, at 3.

193. Mainer (white) was sentenced to death for killing his former wife in January 1970. *Id.*

CHAPTER 4

THE THIRTY-YEAR STRUGGLE TO OBTAIN EXECUTION NO. 103

TINKERING WITH THE "MACHINERY OF DEATH"

In 1994 US Supreme Court Justice Harry Blackmun issued a lengthy dissent in the Court's decision to deny a hearing requested by a Texas death row inmate, Bruce Edwin Callins. In his opinion, Blackmun maintained that the modern death penalty "remains fraught with arbitrariness, discrimination, caprice and mistake."[1] He famously asserted that he would no longer spend time trying to make the death penalty work: "From this day forward, I no longer shall tinker with the machinery of death . . . I feel morally and intellectually obligated simply to concede that the death penalty experiment has failed."[2]

Others, however, were happy to continue the tinkering.

In response to Justice Blackmun, Justice Antonin Scalia pointed to the case of two mentally disabled half-brothers from North Carolina, Henry Lee McCollum and Leon Brown. McCollum was on death row and Brown was serving a life sentence. Scalia wrote that death by lethal injection

1. Callins v. Collins, 510 U.S. 1141, 1144 (1994).
2. *Id.* at 1145.

DOI: 10.5876/9781607325123.c004

> looks even better next to some of the other cases currently before us which Justice Blackmun did not select as the vehicle for his announcement that the death penalty is always unconstitutional—for example, the case of the 11-year-old girl raped by four men and then killed by stuffing her panties down her throat. How enviable a quiet death by lethal injection compared with that![3]

Ironically, in September 2014—twenty years after Scalia's admonition, and after spending thirty years in prison—both McCollum and Brown were exonerated and freed when DNA established their innocence.[4] In June 2015, both were awarded full pardons by North Carolina governor Pat McCrory.[5]

The cases of Henry Lee McCollum and Leon Brown exemplify all too well the skirmishes that have taken place on a daily basis since the 1972 *Furman* decision and might help explain why so much tinkering was and is necessary if the United States is going to insist on keeping the death penalty. The tinkering began right after *Furman* was announced on June 29, 1972. At the time, Colorado was among the thirty-two states that housed inmates under a sentence of death.[6] While *Furman* emptied America's death rows, it was decided on a 5–4 vote,[7] and numerous legislators throughout the country held out hope that the Court would approve new death penalty laws if they could be more narrowly crafted than the laws that predated 1972. Today, these "post-*Furman*" years constitute the "modern era" of the death penalty in the United States.[8]

---

3. Callins v. Collins, 510 U.S. 1141, 1143 (1994).

4. Jonathan M. Katz and Erik Eckholm, *DNA Evidence Clears Two Men in 1983 Murder*, N. Y. TIMES, Sept. 3, 2014, at A1.

5. Daniel Bier, *Scalia's Defense of the Death Penalty Is in Tatters*, NEWSWEEK, June 14, 2015, accessed July 15, 2016, http://www.newsweek.com/scalias-defense-death-penalty-tatters-342329.

6. MICHAEL MELTSNER, CRUEL AND UNUSUAL: THE SUPREME COURT AND CAPITAL PUNISHMENT 293 (1973). The *Furman* decision led to the reversal of two death sentences in Colorado. Jack Olsen, *2 in Colo. Death Row Spared by Court Ruling*, DENVER POST, June 29, 1972, at 3.

7. Furman v. Georgia, 408 U.S. 238 (1972).

8. By the end of 1975, "30 states had enacted new or revised death penalty statutes since *Furman*." U.S. DEP'T OF JUSTICE, NATIONAL PRISONER STATISTICS BULLETIN SD-NPS-CP-4, CAPITAL PUNISHMENT 1975 at 5 (1976).

Nationwide, this effort to bring back the death penalty was led by Florida, where a new post-*Furman* death penalty statute was signed into law on December 8, 1972.[9] Colorado soon followed. In 1974 state lawmakers in Denver drafted a bill reinstating the death penalty and placed it on the ballot for voter consideration.[10] On November 5, 1974, the measure passed with 61 percent of the vote (451,403 to 286,805),[11] thereby again authorizing the death penalty in the state. Soon thereafter, in a trial in November 1975, Dean Lewis Wildermuth (a.k.a. Shane McKnight) was convicted of stabbing to death a woman he had met at a bar in Northglenn (Adams County) and became Colorado's first post-*Furman* death row inmate.[12] Within a week, Gov. Richard Lamm announced that he did not plan to commute the sentence to a prison term, even though he "personally opposed" the death penalty and had voted against putting the death penalty on the 1974 ballot while a member of the General Assembly.[13]

In 1976 those who worked to restore the death penalty won an additional victory when, in a set of five cases led by *Gregg v. Georgia*,[14] the Supreme Court struck down mandatory death penalty statutes but

---

9. Charles S. Ehrhardt and L. Harold Levinson, *Florida's Legislative Response to Furman: An Exercise in Futility?*, JOUR. OF CRIM. L. & CRIMINOLOGY 64 (1973): 10, 15.

10. *See* Act of Mar. 19, 1974, ch. 52, sec. 4, 1974 Colo. Sess. Laws 251, 252 (codified as amended at COLO. REV. STAT. § 16-11-103 (Supp. 1975)). The language of the resolution was phrased as follows, "Shall the death penalty be imposed upon persons convicted of class 1 felonies where certain mitigating circumstances are not present and certain aggravating circumstances are present?" Thus, the law approved by the voters provided that if the jury found even a single mitigating factor, the judge was required to impose a sentence of life imprisonment. This remained the law until 1984, when the legislature amended the law to allow a sentence of death even if the jury found a mitigating factor. *See* HB 1310, sec. 1–6 (1984). This is the model, *with language not approved directly by the voters*—that persists today.

11. Carol Kasel, *History of the Death Penalty Law in Colorado*, ROCKY MTN. NEWS, Feb. 25, 2003, at 10A.

12. *See* appendix 3, case no. 1.

13. *Lamm Will Refuse to Commute Death Sentence He Opposes*, ROCKY MTN. NEWS, Nov. 14, 1974, at 46.

14. Gregg v. Georgia, 438 U.S. 153 (1976). In other decisions announced the same day, the new death penalty statutes in Florida and Texas were approved. Proffitt v. Florida, 428 U.S. 242 (1976); Jurek v. Texas, 428 U.S. 262 (1976). However, mandatory death penalty statutes in North Carolina and Louisiana were not. Woodson v. North Carolina, 428 U.S. 280 (1976); Roberts v. Louisiana, 428 U.S. 325 (1976).

upheld sentencing formulas that allowed death sentences in some cases in which aggravating circumstances were determined to be present. By implication, the Colorado scheme was among those approved by the Court. Executions resumed the following year in Utah, and at the time, it appeared that Colorado would soon follow suit.

Appendix 3 provides information on the twenty-three men sentenced to death in Colorado from 1972 to 2015. Unlike appendix 1, which includes only executions, appendix 3 provides information on all post-*Furman* death sentences imposed in Colorado. Only one man, Gary Lee Davis, appears on both lists.[15]

Between 1975 and 1978, seven men were sentenced to death in Colorado, including Dean Wildermuth.[16] One noteworthy case involved Freddie Glenn, who killed three people while serving in the army and stationed at Fort Carson, near Colorado Springs.[17] He was eventually sentenced to death for the kidnapping, rape, and murder of eighteen-year-old Karen Grammer, the sister of actor Kelsey Grammer, who later had starring roles in the television series *Cheers* and *Frasier*.[18] The Colorado Supreme Court eventually vacated Glenn's death sentence, but as of year-end 2015, he remained incarcerated at the Buena Vista Correctional Complex.[19]

It is interesting to note that only one case from the 1970s involved a white defendant who was sentenced to death for killing an African American—the only time that this has happened in the state's history.[20] Scott Raymer was sentenced to death in 1977 for the murder of gas station

---

15. *See* appendix 1, case no. 103 and appendix 3, case no. 13.

16. *See* appendix 3, case nos. 1–7.

17. *See* appendix 3, case no. 3.

18. In July 2009, Grammer attended a parole hearing for Glenn, and in 2014 he spoke via video link at a subsequent parole hearing, stating that he had forgiven Glenn for the murder, adding that he still wanted Glenn to remain behind bars. Kirk Mitchell, *Actor Doesn't Want Sister's Killer Released*, DENVER POST, July 30, 2014, at 7A.

19. The Glenn case had a significant impact on the career of John Suthers, who served as the Colorado attorney general from 2005 to 2015. While finishing law school at the University of Colorado, Suthers completed an internship with the Colorado Springs district attorney's office, and he did research for this and another death penalty case. During that work, he decided he wanted to become a prosecutor.

20. In 1891 William Davis was executed for the murder of both white and black victims. *See* appendix 1, case no. 28.

attendant Doris Hargrove.[21] A 1989 study examined the records of some 16,000 executions in the United States and identified only thirty cases in which white people were executed for killing blacks.[22] Our searches of the *Denver Post* and *Rocky Mountain News* (the two principal Denver-based newspapers) for dates around the time of the homicide and the trial revealed no articles that mentioned the race of either Raymer or Hargrove and no pictures of either. We learned about Hargrove's race only when we tracked down one of Raymer's defense attorneys and confirmed Hargrove's race by purchasing a copy of her death certificate. Yet, it turns out that even though the defendant was white and the victim was black, the death sentence was not especially unusual: Raymer also killed a second gas station attendant, who was white. Although he was permitted to plead guilty to this murder in exchange for a life sentence, undoubtedly the reason why the death sentence was given for the killing of Hargrove is because Raymer also killed another person.[23]

1978–1991: MORE AND MORE TINKERING AND MORE AND MORE DEATH SENTENCING

After the seven death sentences that were imposed between 1975 and 1978, the Colorado Supreme Court forced the legislature go back to the drawing board. On October 23, 1978, it unanimously ruled that the state's 1974 death penalty statute was unconstitutional because it failed to allow juries to consider the full range of mitigating factors related to the circumstances of the offense or the offender in their sentencing decisions.[24] Not

21. *See* appendix 3, case no. 6.

22. Michael L. Radelet, *Executions of Whites for Crimes Against Blacks: Exceptions to the Rule?*, SOCIOLOGICAL QUARTERLY 30 (1989): 529, 532.

23. Similarly, in 1984 James Dupree Henry (black) was executed in Florida for the murder of an African American victim. Because defendants are rarely executed for killing blacks, this was an anomaly. However, analysis of the newspaper coverage in the case showed that far more attention was given to a white police officer who was slightly wounded when Henry was apprehended than to the black murder victim. *See* Michael L. Radelet and Michael Mello, *Executing Those Who Kill Blacks: An Unusual Case Study*, MERCER L. REV. 37 (1986): 911.

24. *See* People v. Dist. Court, 586 P.2d 31, 34–35 (Colo. 1978).

only did the ruling empty Colorado's death row,[25] but it stopped death penalty prosecutions against three other men, including serial murderer Ted Bundy (who was ultimately executed for other murders in Florida in 1989).[26] And so further tinkering ensued, and in 1979 the legislature amended the statute to create a four-step process.[27] The new legislation required juries to decide (1) if at least one statutorily specified aggravating factor existed, (2) if any mitigating factors existed, (3) whether or not the mitigating factors outweighed aggravating factors, and (4) if the defendant should be sentenced to death or life in prison.

After the bill passed, protestors began a daily vigil outside the governor's mansion urging him to veto the bill.[28] Lamm did not support the bill because of his general opposition to capital punishment but decided to let it become law without his signature. The new law took effect on August 7, 1979.[29]

The first person sentenced to death under the revised 1979 statute was Edgar Durre,[30] who was convicted of killing Gary Statler, a member of the family that owned the Statler Hotel chain, a popular hotel brand throughout the United States in the mid-twentieth century.[31] Statler had (apparently) been befriended by Durre and others and, after engaging in consensual sex, was blackmailed with threats to reveal the secret. After the death sentence was imposed, five of the original trial jurors announced their support for a life sentence, and the Colorado Supreme

---

25. The ruling affected six of the seven men sentenced to death between 1975 and 1978. It did not affect Dean Wildermuth, whose death sentence by then had been vacated for other reasons. *See* appendix 3, case no. 1.

26. Carol Green, *Colorado Death Penalty Ruled Void by Top Court*, DENVER POST, Oct. 23, 1978, at 1.

27. *See* Act of Aug. 7, 1979, ch. 158, sec. 1, 1979 Colo. Sess. Laws 673, 673–75 (codified as amended at COLO. REV. STAT. § 16-11-103 (Supp. 1979)) (current version at COLO. REV. STAT. § 18-1.3-1201 (2013)).

28. *Vigil Held to Urge Lamm's Veto of Death Penalty*, ROCKY MTN. NEWS, July 6, 1979, at 50.

29. *Death Penalty Takes Effect Tuesday*, ROCKY MTN. NEWS, Aug. 5, 1979, at 4.

30. *See* appendix 3, case no. 8.

31. *See* Mark Byrnes, *The Rise and Fall of One of America's Most Innovative Hotel Chains*, CITYLAB, Feb. 15, 2013, accessed July 15, 2016, http://citylab.com/design/2013/02/hotel-chain-grew-americas-cities/4723/.

Court reduced the sentence to life because of the lack of unanimity among the jurors.[32]

The next major change in Colorado's death penalty statute occurred in 1988, when, among other modifications, the legislature voted to change the method of execution from lethal gas to lethal injection.[33] This turned the state's gas chamber into a museum piece. It is now on display in the front yard of the prison museum in Cañon City.

The statute managed to survive judicial scrutiny[34] until it was again struck down in July 1991.[35] The Colorado Supreme Court found the 1988 law unconstitutional because it eliminated the last step in jury sentencing, which required juries to return a sentence of death if mitigating factors did not outweigh aggravating factors.[36] The court ruled that death sentences could never be mandatory; a prison sentence must always be an option.

This led the General Assembly to meet in a special session in September 1991 to repeal the 1988 law and to enact a similar statute that added a final step that allowed for unbridled juror discretion in deciding between death and life sentences.[37] During this session, life in prison was defined as "life imprisonment without the possibility of parole,"

32. People v. Durre, 690 P.2d 165 (Colo. 1984).

33. *See* Act of Apr. 11, 1988, ch. 114, sec. 1–3, 1988 Colo. Sess. Laws 673, 673–75 (codified as amended at COLO. REV. STAT. § 16-11-103 (Supp. 1988)) (current version at COLO. REV. STAT. § 18-1.3-1201 (2013)); Roxane J. Perruso, *And Then There Were Three: Colorado's New Death Penalty Sentencing Statute*, 68 U. COLO. L. REV. 190, 200 (1997) (hereinafter Perruso).

34. Perruso, at 199.

35. People v. Young, 814 P.2d 834, 846–47 (Colo. 1991); Perruso, at 200; Carol Kasel, *History of the Death Penalty Law in Colorado*, ROCKY MTN. NEWS, Feb. 25, 2003, at 10A.

36. *See* Perruso, at 200 (citing *Young*, 814 P.2d 834, 846, 1991). The 1988 statute allowed for the imposition of the death penalty when the aggravating and mitigating circumstances were of equal balance. The Court found, "The fourth step required by the pre-1988 statute—a jury determination that death is the appropriate sentence beyond a reasonable doubt—is no longer part of the process" and that this defect needed to be repaired.

37. *See* Act of Sept. 20, 1991, 1991 Colo. Sess. Laws (second extraordinary session) 8–13 (codified as amended at COLO. REV. STAT. § 16-11-103 (Supp. 1992)) (current version at COLO. REV. STAT. § 18-1.3-1201 (2013)). *See also* Perruso, at 200.

(LWOP), thereby ending the possibility of release from prison for those convicted of first-degree murder but spared the death penalty.[38]

The LWOP legislation significantly changed the nature of the death penalty question faced by Colorado citizens. Before July 1, 1985, life imprisonment meant that the inmate would need to serve at least twenty years in prison before being considered for parole. Between then and September 20, 1991, "life" meant a minimum of forty years in prison. Thereafter, all those convicted of first-degree murder but not sentenced to death would, absent judicial relief or executive clemency, still die in prison. The question presented by the death penalty therefore shifted; the question was no longer *if* the inmate would die in prison but *when* and *how*.

Indeed, the availability of the LWOP provisions does have an appreciable effect on support for the death penalty. In June 2014, an ABC/Washington Post national poll found that support for the death penalty outdistanced opposition by a 60–37 percent margin. However, when respondents were asked if they would support the death penalty over life without parole, 42 percent chose death while 52 percent supported life without parole.[39] Many other polls have echoed these findings: given the alternative of lifelong imprisonment, support for the death penalty drops precipitously.[40]

With the 1991 modifications, the basic structure of how a death sentence can today be imposed in Colorado was in place. In the sentencing phase of the trial, any evidence about the nature of the crime and "the character, background, and history of the defendant" can be presented, and, as in most death penalty jurisdictions, the jurors look at a range of aggravating and mitigating circumstances to decide who among those convicted of first-degree murder should be sentenced to death. After the defendant is convicted, the jury must deliberate three more times before a death sentence can be imposed. First, it must decide (unani-

---

38. 1991 Colo. Sess. Laws 9.

39. Reid Wilson, *Support for the Death Penalty Still High, but Down*, WASH. POST, June 5, 2014, accessed July 15, 2016, http://www.washingtonpost.com/blogs/govbeat/wp/2014/06/05/support-for-death-penalty-still-high-but-down/.

40. For summaries, *see* Death Penalty Information Center, *Public Opinion about the Death Penalty*, accessed July 15, 2016, http://www.deathpenaltyinfo.org/public-opinion-about-death-penalty.

mously) whether at least one aggravating factor has been proved beyond a reasonable doubt. Second, it must unanimously find that any mitigating factors that may exist do not outweigh the aggravating factors. If they find that the mitigation does not outweigh the aggravation, a third stage of the sentencing phase is held. In that stage, jurors can hear from victims' families, and even the defendant himself, before deciding the appropriate punishment. Then, the jury must unanimously find, beyond a reasonable doubt, that death is the appropriate punishment.[41]

After each phase, the jury needs to deliberate and agree to move forward. But if at the final stage any juror sees any reason to vote for life rather than death, his or her vote does not need to be explained. The decision to choose life is a personal, moral decision, and if made by just one juror, it ends the sentencing phase of the trial. The defendant is sentenced to life imprisonment without parole.

At the penalty phase, any information "relevant to the nature of the crime, and the character, background, and history of the defendant, including any evidence presented in the guilt phase of the trial" and "any matters relating to the personal characteristics of the victim and the impact of the crimes on the victim's family," is admissible. Aggravating circumstances must be proved "beyond a reasonable doubt," but "[t]here shall be no burden of proof as to proving or disproving mitigating factors."

In arguing for death, the prosecution can use only aggravating factors listed in the statue—for example, if the offense was "especially heinous, cruel, or depraved," "the defendant knowingly created a grave risk of death to another person" (in addition to the homicide victim/s), the homicide included multiple victims, or the murder was committed for pecuniary gain.

The Colorado statute has a long list of aggravating factors, leading some scholars to argue that there are few first-degree murders that are *not* eligible for the death penalty. As will be further explained below, University of Denver law professor Justin Marceau and his colleagues count seventeen aggravating factors in the Colorado statute.[42] Mitigating

---

41. *See* CRS § 18-1.4-102 (2013); People v. Tenneson, 788 P.2d 786, 791–792 (Colo. 1990); People v. Dunlap, 975 P.2d 723 (Colo. 1999).

42. Justin Marceau, Sam Kamin, and Wanda Foglia, *Death Eligibility in Colorado: Many Are Called, Few Are Chosen*, UNIV. OF COLO. L. REV. 84 (2013): 1069–115, at 1088.

factors can include such factors as the age of the defendant, an absence of prior criminal convictions, the defendant's capacity to appreciate the wrongfulness of his conduct, or limitations by the defendant to conform his conduct to the requirements of law.[43] The statute does list some mitigating factors, but unlike aggravators, mitigation is not limited to those enumerated in the statute. Any information about the character, background, and history of the defendant, as well as the nature of the crime, can be introduced as evidence of mitigation. Information about the nature of the death penalty itself—for example, lack of deterrence, racial bias, or religious views—cannot be brought up in court. Instead, these are issues that the legislature might consider if it ever revisits the appropriateness of allowing death sentences in the state.

THE EXPERIMENT WITH THREE-JUDGE PANELS

By the early 1990s, there was growing concern among Colorado legislators that too many defendants were being improperly sentenced to prison terms rather than death, and it was thought that if three-judge panels determined sentences, more inmates would find themselves on death row and there would be greater consistency in the way that death sentences were imposed.[44] Proponents of the change included Denver district attorney (and future Colorado governor) Bill Ritter, who told the Senate Judiciary Committee considering the legislation that he believed three-judge panels would probably deliver more death sentences than juries. Jurors, he explained, could easily be "awed" or "overwhelmed," and, unlike judges, they had little or no expertise or experience in determining which homicide cases were the most deserving of death.[45] Ritter expressed agreement with one of his assistants, Nathan Ben Coats (who would later join the Colorado Supreme Court), in the belief that getting

43. *See* COLO. REV. STAT. § 18-1.4-102 (2013).

44. Perruso, at 206.

45. Hearings before the Senate Judiciary Committee on SB 54, CD 3&4, Jan. 16, 1995 (Ritter's testimony begins at about the forty-minute mark). He repeated many of his points in his testimony eighteen days later to the Senate Appropriations Committee, February 3, 1995. Audio recordings of the hearings are available through the Colorado State Archive, accessed July 15, 2016, https://www.colorado.gov/pacific/archives/legislative-records.

a death sentence from a Denver jury would be the "functional equivalent" of "having lightning strike the defendant."[46] Added Ritter, "that's not reliability, that's not consistency, that's not measurability."

In the end, on June 5, 1995, the legislature decided to remove the life-or-death decision from jurors and put it into the hands of judges, who theoretically could be not retained by the voters if their decisions in death penalty cases were unpopular.[47] This ended Colorado's 135-year history of allowing juries to determine which defendants should be sentenced to life and which should be sentenced to death.[48] Under the new system, a three-judge panel would decide whether to impose a sentence of life or death, and any death sentence required a unanimous vote.[49] The panel would be made up of the trial judge and two additional judges designated by the chief justice of the Colorado Supreme Court. In theory, any two judges could be asked to serve, but a preference was given to judges from the same or neighboring judicial districts to the district where the case was tried. Shortly thereafter, the Colorado Supreme Court decided to group Colorado's judicial districts into four regional groups and pick two judges at random from the group representing the region where the trial was held to join the trial judge in determining sentence.[50] The new law took effect July 1, 1995.[51]

The new sentencing scheme won the approval of all twenty-two district attorneys in the state. Critics feared that the three-judge panels would greatly increase the number of people sentenced to death. Denver defense attorney David Lane, for example, issued a pessimistic forecast to fellow abolitionists by stating, "Once they see it is like getting candy from a baby to get a death verdict, prosecutors will crank up the death

---

46. *Id.* CD 4, at 4:20.

47. *See* COLO. REV. STAT. § 16-11-103(1)(a) (Supp. 1996) (current version at COLO. REV. STAT. § 18-1.3-1201 (2013)). *See also* Perruso, at 200.

48. *See* Perruso, at 201.

49. *See id.*

50. *See* Robin Lutz [now Robin Lutz Beattie], *Experimenting with Death: An Examination of Colorado's Use of the Three-Judge Panel in Capital Sentencing*, U. COLO. L. REV. 73 (2002): 227, 231 (hereinafter LUTZ).

51. Two men—Robert Harlan and Nathan Dunlap—whose trials were already underway when the new law took effect, were sentenced to death by juries after July 1, 1995.

machine."[52] Another concern was that putting the decision into the hands of judges, who must stand in front of the voters for retention every six years, might unnecessarily politicize judicial retention decisions. As we shall see in the next chapter, Lane got it wrong and Denver defense attorney Craig Truman got it right: "The legislature has given us on the defense a wonderful tool by goofing around with the law for political expediency. They have given us new life to attack the [death penalty] law as unconstitutional."[53]

CASES WHERE DEATH PENALTY SOUGHT, 1980–1999

Meanwhile, while the death penalty statute was almost constantly being tweaked, Colorado prosecutors continued to regularly seek death sentences. In a paper published in 2006, Stephanie Hindson and her colleagues looked at 3,933 Colorado homicides that were committed in the twenty-year span between January 1, 1980 and December 31, 1999 (an average of two hundred homicides per year).[54] The death penalty was sought in 110 cases[55] for an annual average of 5.5 death penalty prosecutions. Of the 110 cases where death was pursued, a death sentence was actually imposed in thirteen cases.[56] In twenty-four other cases, the case went to a "penalty phase," and life was imposed by the jury or by the panels of three judges.[57] Of the 110 cases where death was pursued, the defendant was not convicted of first-degree murder in thirty cases.[58] Juries acquitted eleven of these thirty of first-degree murder and three were acquitted of all charges.[59] Of the thirteen men sentenced to death,

52. Perruso, at 209–10.

53. Perruso, at 210. In her article, Perruso concluded, "current case law, from both the United States Supreme Court and several state supreme courts, clearly indicates that Colorado's new judicial sentencing statute will withstand constitutional scrutiny" (at 227). As we shall see in the next chapter, Perruso's prediction was incorrect.

54. Stephanie Hindson, Hillary Potter, & Michael L. Radelet, *Race, Gender, Region and Death Sentencing in Colorado, 1980–1999*, U. OF COLO. L. REV. 77 (2006): 549–94 (hereinafter Hindson et al.).

55. Hindson et al., at 592–94, appendix B.

56. *See* appendix 3, case nos. 8–20; Hindson et al., at 571, table 2.

57. Hindson et al., at 574, table 4.

58. Hindson et al., at 572.

59. *Id.*

one was executed in Colorado[60] and another was executed in Texas.[61] Only one remains on death row.[62]

The authors found strong regional disparities in death sentencing in Colorado for death penalty prosecutions for the homicides from the 1980s and 1990s. Overall, in counties with more than one hundred homicides during the study period (1980–1999), the death penalty was sought in 2.8 percent of the cases. Rates were highest in Jefferson (7.9 percent), Adams (6.9 percent), Arapahoe (4.5 percent), Pueblo (3.9 percent), and Weld (3.2 percent) Counties.[63] And while white victims (non-Hispanic) accounted for 54 percent of all homicide victims, they accounted for 81.8 percent of victims in cases where the death penalty was sought.[64] The authors concluded that the probability the death penalty would be sought for a Colorado homicide was 4.2 times higher for those who kill whites than for those who kill blacks.[65]

While this analysis is instructive, it is also limited. It simply compared the race and gender of defendants and victims in cases where death was sought with the race and gender characteristics of all Colorado homicides. The higher rates of seeking death in cases with white and/or female victims may be a function of the possibility that those cases are more aggravated (e.g., they may be more likely to include felony circumstances). And with the death penalty being sought in fewer and fewer cases, obtaining statistical significance after controlling for aggravation becomes more and more difficult.

Looking at more recent cases, Professor Justin Marceau and his colleagues concluded that the Colorado death penalty statute and its long list of aggravating factors make 90 percent of Colorado homicides eligible for the death penalty. Using a database that included all Colorado homicides over a twelve-year period, from 1999 to 2010, the authors "discovered that while the death penalty was an option in over 90% of all first-degree murders, it was sought by the prosecution initially in only 3% of those killings, pursued all the way through sentencing in only 1%

60. *See* appendix 1, case no. 103.

61. *See* appendix 3, case no. 9.

62. *See* appendix 3, case no. 16.

63. Hindson et al., at 576, table 6.

64. Hindson et al., at 578.

65. Hindson et al., at 579.

of those killings, and obtained in only 0.6% of all cases."[66] As the authors see it, this failure to statutorily narrow the class of all first-degree murders to a smaller subset of cases for which the death penalty is suitable renders the Colorado statute—as well as those in other death penalty states with similar problems—unconstitutional.[67] These data had been introduced in the last three capital prosecutions in Colorado by the end of 2015. In the first case, the state hired experts to try to discredit the study, but the experts concluded that the study was sound and found patterns almost identical to those that Marceau and his colleagues had documented. Instead, the state was left to argue that the fact that so few death penalty prosecutions result from the high number of death-eligible cases was perfectly okay.[68]

THE CASE OF GARY LEE DAVIS

While the death penalty statute in Colorado was being tweaked and revised, only one inmate was executed: Gary Lee Davis. On July 21, 1986, Davis and his (third) wife, Rebecca Fincham, kidnapped, beat, raped, and shot Virginia "Ginny" May in a rural area in Adams County, approximately forty-five miles east of Denver. The crime was easily solved. May's husband, Gary, was not at home at the time, but when he returned a half hour after the abduction, their two children, ages seven and four, told him that they had witnessed the kidnapping and implicated their next-door neighbors, Gary Davis and Becky Fincham Davis.[69] Once taken into custody, only seventeen hours after the crimes, Davis confessed. He and his public defender worked out a deal with prosecu-

---

66. Marceau, Kamin, & Foglia, *Death Eligibility*, at 1070.

67. Sam Kamin & Justin Marceau, *Waking the* Furman *Giant*, UC Davis L. Rev. 48 (2015): 981–1042.

68. People v. Montour, *Order [2013-05-02] D-181* (Douglas County District Court No. 02CR782 May 2, 2013), at 2 ("The prosecution found that the aggravating-factor rate was 88.49%, and the death-sentence rate was 0.57%.") and *id.* at 2 n.5 ("The Court will use the defense's statistics . . . to resolve this motion on the merits, because the parties' statistics are similar, and because the prosecution stipulated to the defense's numbers for purposes of this motion.").

69. The couple divorced within a year. Hereinafter Becky Davis will be referred to as Becky Fincham, although the Colorado Department of Corrections referred to her as Rebecca F. Davis.

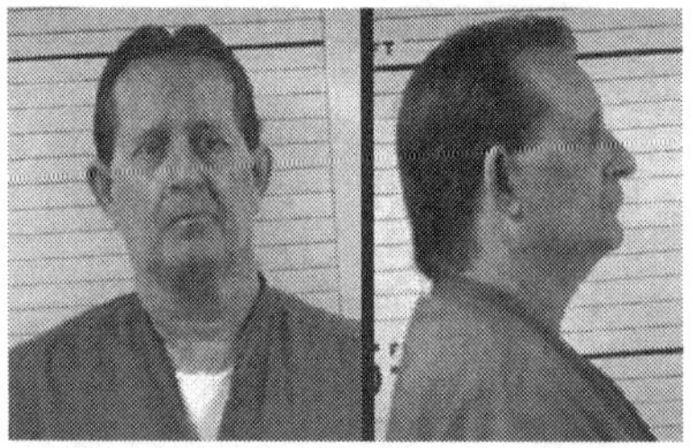

FIGURE 4.1. *Gary Lee Davis, executed October 13, 1997—the only person executed in Colorado since 1967. Photo courtesy of the Colorado State Archives.*

tors. Hoping (or pretending) that May was still alive, Davis agreed to tell the authorities where she could be found and given medical assistance. In return, prosecutors agreed that they would not seek the death penalty if she later died. But when her body was found two days after the abduction and it was clear that she had suffered an immediate death, the deal was voided and the public defender's office asked to be removed from the case.[70] Thereafter, court-appointed private attorneys handled Davis's and Fincham's cases.

Both suspects were well known to the police. Davis had lifelong problems with alcohol, and his addiction was related to previous convictions for burglary and the rape of a fifteen-year-old child at knifepoint. On another occasion he pointed a gun at the head of one of his ex-wives. Inexplicably, he served only three-and-a-half years on the rape conviction. While serving that sentence he obtained an address for Fincham, and after exchanging several letters—some quite salacious—they decided to get married (via telephone) while Davis was still incarcerated. Fincham, in turn, was convicted of sending lewd pictures of her thirteen-year-old daughter to Davis so he could pass them on to another inmate.[71] Although newspaper accounts written around the time of the crime can be sensational and inaccurate, and probably no one (not even Davis) knew what he was thinking at the time, apparently the motive for kidnapping Ms. May was that the couple thought they could turn her into their "sex slave." After the kidnapping, "[w]hile Becky . . . drove, the defendant held Virginia May down in the back seat of the car, removed

70. Kit Miniclier, *Abducted Byers Woman Beaten Before Dying*, DENVER POST, July 25, 1986, at B1; Kit Miniclier, *Male Suspect Told Police Where to Find Body in Kidnapping*, DENVER POST, July 26, 1986, at C1.

71. Kevin Simpson, *Wife Seen as Killer's Equal*, DENVER POST, Oct. 14, 1997, at A17.

her clothing, and sexually assaulted her."[72] Later, the couple tied a rope around May's neck and forced her to perform oral sex on Fincham.[73] She was then shot fourteen times, suggesting that when Davis made the initial plea bargain with the authorities, he knew full well that she was dead, or else he was so drunk at the time of the murder that he could not remember what happened.

Fincham was tried first, and on June 20, 1987, she was convicted of first-degree murder, kidnapping, and conspiracy. Her sentencing was deferred until after Davis's trial, apparently leading him to think that if he took the brunt of the responsibility, she would receive a more lenient sentence. On August 13 of that year she was sentenced to life imprisonment plus thirty years for her role in the crimes.[74]

Davis's trial was held in July 1987 in Brighton before Judge Harlan Bockman and an Adams County jury. Through his lawyer, veteran death penalty defense attorney Craig Truman, Davis initially attempted to waive the jury and have both the guilt and sentencing phases conducted solely before the judge, but the prosecutor objected, and the objection was sustained. At trial, Truman argued that Davis was equally or even less involved in the crimes than Fincham, but that defense was sabotaged when Davis got on the stand and took sole responsibility for masterminding and carrying out the crimes. Because Truman was confident—justifiably so, in the minds of several other death penalty attorneys—that the argument of comparative culpability would win at least one vote among the jurors and thereby spare Davis from the gurney, he had spent almost all his time preparing for a penalty phase that focused on that issue. So Davis's testimony, which was in all likelihood aggrandized—and may have been outright false, in an effort to win a lighter sentence for Fincham—pulled the rug out from under Truman and left him with no solid alternate defense strategy. Later, this decision to put all the eggs in one basket became a central component of the (failed) argument in the appellate courts that Truman had provided ineffective assistance of counsel.

---

72. People v. Davis, 794 P.2d 159, 168 (1990).

73. People v. Davis, 794 P.2d 159 (Colo. 1990). The US Supreme Court declined the request to hear an appeal of this ruling. Davis v. Colorado, 498 U.S. 1018 (1991).

74. People v. Fincham, 799 P.2d 419 (Colo. App. 1990).

Davis was a difficult client, even for an experienced and dedicated trial attorney. Truman, obviously frustrated and even angry with his client, told the jury in closing arguments, "There are times in this case that I hate Gary Davis, I am going to tell you that, and I think you know it. There are times I hate the things he has done, and I have told him, and I tell you, there's no excuse for it. There's no excuse for it whatsoever."[75] This comment later became another prong of Davis's contention that Truman had provided ineffective legal assistance to him.

On July 22, 1987, as the Colorado Supreme Court later wrote, "The jury found Mr. Davis guilty of murder in the first degree after deliberation; felony murder; conspiracy to commit murder in the first degree; second degree kidnaping; and conspiracy to commit second degree kidnaping."[76] The next day, exactly one year after May's murder, the same jury voted unanimously to sentence him to death.[77] Soon thereafter, Davis wrote to Gov. Roy Romer and asked for his immediate execution.[78]

Davis later changed his mind, and Shelley Gilman, an attorney in private practice (and now a district court judge) in Denver, handled his initial appeal. This appeal, and all subsequent appeals, failed. In 1990 the Colorado Supreme Court upheld the conviction (and the state's death penalty statute). As we have often seen (to varying degrees) among the voters and political leaders in Colorado throughout the state's history, the vote was split, 4–3.[79] Davis did prevail on one point: the Supreme Court agreed that Judge Bockman had improperly allowed the jury to consider the "heinous, cruel or depraved" aggravating circumstance, although they held that the error was harmless. Soon thereafter, Davis wrote to the trial court and renewed his demand for an immediate execution.[80] Nonetheless, appellate attorney Gilman vowed to continue to

---

75. Davis v. People, 871 P.2d 769, 776 (1994).

76. Davis v. Executive Director of the Department of Corrections, 100 F.3d 750 (1996).

77. For a case timeline, *see* Steve Garnass, *Governor to Decide Davis' Fate; Death-Row Inmate to Quit Appeals Route*, DENVER POST, June 27, 1997, at B1.

78. Bill McBean, *Lawyers Fight to Keep Alive Inmate Who Covets Execution*, DENVER POST, July 6, 1990, at 2B.

79. People v. Davis, 794 P.2d 159 (Colo. 1990); John Sanko, *Supreme Court Upholds State Death Penalty*, ROCKY MTN. NEWS, May 15, 1990, at 6.

80. McBean, *Lawyers Fight*; Mark Brown, *Slayer is Eager to Die, and It Could Happen This Year*, ROCKY MTN. NEWS, Aug. 10, 1990, at 6.

fight the conviction,[81] and soon Davis changed his mind again and (more or less) gave her the green light to proceed.

At this point, Colorado Springs attorney Dennis Hartley took over the defense. In the next round of appeals, he and Davis argued that Truman had provided ineffective legal assistance at trial. At a hearing on this motion back at the original trial court in Brighton, Truman conceded that parts of his work had indeed been ineffective. But the trial judge found otherwise, and he refused to grant relief. On appeal in 1992, the Colorado Court of Criminal Appeals declined to overturn the trial court's decision, this time by a 2–1 vote.[82] Hartley appealed the ruling to the Colorado Supreme Court, and the defense again lost—and this time the decision was unanimous.[83]

Meanwhile, former governor Richard Lamm (1975–1987) was eager to get Colorado's executioner back to work, and some of what he wrote shows how nasty the death penalty fight had gotten. Lamm, a Democrat who originally opposed the death penalty, had by then become a strong death penalty supporter. "I'm in favor of the death penalty. I think in the young Democrat days, I was probably against the death penalty, but that was before life started getting so cheap. We need the death penalty to uphold the sanctity of life."[84] In 1994 he published an op-ed in the *Denver Post* that focused on the case of Frank Rodriguez, who was convicted for a 1984 murder that sent him to death row (where he died of natural causes in 2002).[85] Lamm was livid at Rodriguez's public defenders—especially attorney Michael Heher, who Lamm accused of adopting a strategy "to delay and stall whenever possible." He attacked Denver district court judge Harold Reed for giving Rodriguez "an extraordinarily lenient single-digit term in prison" for offenses that predated the murder. Most curiously, he also attacked two justices on the Colorado Supreme Court, who at one time or another found in favor of some of the arguments that Rodriguez's defense team advanced. "I regret more than words can convey appointing Judge Reed and Justices George Lohr and Howard Kirshbaum. They are not following the constitution, but

81. McBean, *Lawyers Fight*.
82. People v. Davis, 849 P.2d 857 (1992).
83. Davis v. People, 871 P.2d 769 (1994).
84. Poll, DENVER POST, Mar. 13, 1994, at 17A.
85. *See* appendix 3, case no. 12.

their own anti-death-penalty agenda. We will get a chance to correct this mistake by voting not to retain these judges."[86] Lamm had not only completely changed his opinion on the death penalty, but his newfound support was passionate.

This was one of several skirmishes between Lamm and Judge Reed. Reed was later appointed (by Gov. Roy Romer) to the Colorado Court of Appeals, where his years of service were highly respected by friend and foe alike.[87]

In addition to what can only be described as Lamm's grandstanding, other skirmishes occurred on the sidelines as the Davis case grabbed the headlines. Denver district attorney Bill Ritter, Jr., defended the decisions made by his office not to seek the death penalty in two of its recent homicide cases.[88] At the same time, the *Denver Post* renewed its editorial stand against the death penalty.[89]

In 1994 the Davis case headed into federal court, and assistant federal public defender Vicki Mandell-King, a tenacious advocate who was handling her first federal death penalty appeal,[90] joined Hartley on the defense team. Robert M. Petrusak, senior assistant attorney general from Denver, and trial co-counsel Steven Bernard represented the state. In 1995 Davis's petition for a writ of habeas corpus was denied in federal district court,[91] and the Tenth Circuit Court of Appeals affirmed this order in 1996.[92] On May 12, 1997, the US Supreme Court announced that it would not review this decision.[93]

Six weeks thereafter, Hartley appeared in the trial court in Brighton and announced that Davis would not pursue any additional appeals.

---

86. Richard D. Lamm, *Judiciary Has Sabotaged the State's Death Penalty*, DENVER POST, Mar. 13, 1994, at 1F.

87. Mike McPhee, *Appellate Judge Reed Dies at 77*, DENVER POST, May 9, 2000, at C15.

88. Bill Ritter, Jr., *Death Penalty Decisions are Based on Legal Concerns*, DENVER POST, Mar. 13, 1994, at 5F.

89. Editorial, *Death Penalty Ineffective and Should Be Abolished*, DENVER POST, Mar. 13, 1994, at 2F.

90. Sarah K. Duran, *Lawyer to Witness Death of a Client*, BOULDER DAILY CAMERA, Oct. 13, 1997, at 1.

91. Davis v. Executive Director of Dept. of Corrections, 891 F.Supp. 1459 (1995).

92. Davis v. Executive Director of Dept. of Corrections, 100 F.3d 750, 10th Cir. (1996); rehearing denied Dec 23, 1996.

93. Davis v. Zavaras, 520 U.S. 1215 (1997) (*certiorari denied*).

This decision was, no doubt, influenced by Davis's own ambivalence about wanting to live in prison, the low probability that any further appeals would succeed, and the wish by the defense team to allow Davis the dignity of having some control over his own fate. On the other hand, Hartley and Mandell-King did receive Davis's permission to present a petition for clemency to Romer, knowing full well that the odds for success were low.[94] Trial judge Harlan Bockman then announced that the execution would be scheduled for any time over an eight-day period, between October 11 and October 18, 1997.

Some four hundred people wrote to Governor Romer in support of commuting the sentence to life imprisonment. Among those was Pope John Paul II, who wrote at the request of Davis's aunt, a Catholic nun in Wichita, Kansas.[95] On September 15, Romer met with both the prosecutors and defense attorneys, but everyone knew that the meetings were perfunctory and there was little chance that Romer would block the execution. Just two hours after those meetings, Romer announced that he had decided to deny executive clemency.[96] This was a relief to Davis, who made it clear that he thought life imprisonment was a worse punishment than execution.[97]

There were no further delays, and at 8:30 p.m. on October 13, 1997—the day after famed Colorado musician John Denver died in a plane crash in California—Davis was executed by lethal injection in Cañon City.[98] District Attorney Bob Grant and Vicki Mandell-King were among the witnesses.[99] Davis thus became the 103rd person executed in Colorado and, at least as of the end of 2015, the most recent.

---

94. Garnass, *Governor to Decide Davis' Fate*. Romer, a Democrat, served as Colorado's governor from 1987 to 1999.

95. Genevieve Anton, *Pope Sends Letter Asking for Mercy from Romer; Davis' Aunt Calls for Intervention*, COLORADO SPRINGS GAZ., Sept. 18, 1997, at 1.

96. Kevin Simpson, *Romer Denies Davis Clemency: Ginny May's Killer to be Executed in Oct.*, DENVER POST, Sept. 16, 1997, at 1.

97. Kevin Simpson, *Davis' Death Row Interview Released: Killer Glad He's Not Serving Life*, DENVER POST, Sept. 19, 1997, at B1.

98. Kevin Simpson, *Davis Dies at 8:33 pm; Ginny May's Killer Fulfills Sentence after 11 Years*, DENVER POST, Oct. 14, 1997, at 1; Lisa Levitt Ryckman, *Davis Pays Final Price*, ROCKY MTN. NEWS, Oct. 14, 1997, at 1. During the week of Davis's execution, a long and relatively unsympathetic biography of Davis was published in Denver's *Westword* Magazine. Alan Prendergast, *The Killer Inside Him*, WESTWORD, Oct. 16, 1997, at 1.

99. Duran, *Lawyer to Witness Death*.

Davis was also the first person executed in the new Colorado State Penitentiary, located just east of Cañon City, which opened in 1993 and still houses Colorado's execution gurney. The original penitentiary, where all executions from 1890 through 1967 had been held, was renamed the Colorado Territorial Correctional Facility in 1979. Part of the territorial prison is now home to the Museum of Colorado Prisons, where the state's old gas chamber is on display.[100] When the new penitentiary opened, all death row inmates were housed there until 2011, when the state's death row was moved to the Sterling Correctional Facility (in Sterling, 125 miles northeast of Denver) because the penitentiary did not have adequate areas for outside exercise.[101] In 2015 the issue was resolved and inmates were moved back to Cañon City.[102]

Davis was one of seventy-four people executed in the United States in 1997—that year was the third busiest for American executioners since the *Furman* decision (as of 2015), topped only by ninety-eight in 1999 and eighty-five in 2000.[103] Davis's length of time on death row was normal; he was executed 135 months after the murder and 122 months (ten years, two months) after he was sentenced to death.[104] The average time on death row for the seventy-four US inmates put to death in 1997 was 133 months (eleven years), so Davis was executed just a bit more quickly than average.[105] After Davis's death, four men remained on Colorado's death row: Ronald White,[106] Frank Rodriguez,[107] Nathan Dunlap,[108] and Robert Harlan.[109]

---

100. MUSEUM OF COLORADO PRISONS, http://www.prisonmuseum.org/.

101. Kirk Mitchell, *Change on Death Row, Dunlap, Others Can Stay at Sterling, Exercise Outdoors*, DENVER POST, July 28, 2011, at A1.

102. Kieran Nicholson, *Colorado Death Sentence Inmates Moved to State Penitentiary*, DENVER POST, Nov. 2, 2015, accessed July 15, 2016, http://denverpost.com/2015/11/02/colorado-death-sentence-inmates-moved-to-state-penitentiary/.

103. *Executions by Year*, DEATH PENALTY INFORMATION CENTER, http://www.deathpenaltyinfo.org/executions-year.

104. *See* table 1.1, *infra*.

105. Office of Justice Programs, *Capital Punishment, 2007—Statistical Tables*, table 11, BUREAU OF JUSTICE STATISTICS, accessed July 15, 2016, http://www.bjs.gov/content/pub/html/cp/2007/tables/cp07st11.cfm.

106. *See* appendix 3, case no. 15.

107. *See* appendix 3, case no. 12.

108. *See* appendix 3, case no. 16.

109. *See* appendix 3, case no. 17.

Meanwhile, Fincham sat in her cell in the Colorado Women's Prison Facility in East Denver, convicted of first-degree murder and kidnapping and eligible for parole in 2038 (in 1991 the legislature made life without parole automatic for those convicted of first-degree murder, but this was several years after she and Davis were tried). Prosecutor Bob Grant believed that she too deserved to be executed, but because he did not believe that he could get a unanimous jury to agree, he did not seek the death penalty in her case. But roughly consistent with the argument that Craig Truman had planned to advance at trial, "despite the different sentences, Grant [saw] them as equal partners in one of the state's most perverse and notorious crimes."[110] On September 12, 2008, eleven years after Davis was executed, Fincham died in obscurity while still in custody. An extensive search of newspaper archives in 2015 failed to uncover any mention of her death.

To this day, Mandell-King, who knew Davis in the last three years of his life better than anyone, maintains that the image of Davis as an unremorseful sex fiend and unapologetic killer is inaccurate. Writing in the Buddhist magazine *Shambhala Sun* in 1998, Mandell-King described Davis as shy and reticent and a person who had rehabilitated and redeemed himself.[111] Buttressed by opinions from various experts, she held to the theory that Fincham, not Davis, was the instigator of the crime. She reported that Davis was thoroughly remorseful. She also reported that Gov. Roy Romer agreed that Davis had changed while in prison, but that his changes were not enough to merit clemency.

Nonetheless, the Davis case proved that the death penalty in Colorado was a serious weapon in the prosecutorial quivers. The question therefore shifted from if convicted murderers *could be* executed to the question of how often they *should be*.

---

110. Kevin Simpson, *Wife Seen as Killer's Equal*, DENVER POST, Oct. 14, 1997, at A17.

111. Vicki Mandell-King, *Sympathy for the Devil*, SHAMBHALA SUN, Sept. 1, 1998, http://www.lionsroar.com/sympathy-for-the-devil/ (the title of this article was chosen by the magazine, not by Mandell-King).

CHAPTER 5

THE DEATH PENALTY IN COLORADO IN THE EARLY TWENTY-FIRST CENTURY

THE SPEEDY DEMISE OF THREE-JUDGE PANELS

In October 2015, Colorado marked the eighteenth year since the execution of Gary Lee Davis, and thus, its eighteenth year with no executions. During those years, Colorado prosecutors spent massive amounts of energy and funds trying to get execution No. 104 under their belts, and defense attorneys spent just as much time and money trying to block those efforts. While many legislators hoped that putting the sentencing authority in the hands of judges rather than jurors would do the trick, this 1995 change in the statue proved to have little effect in increasing the number of death row residents and, in fact, ended up sparing the lives of some defendants who might otherwise have been sentenced to death by juries. In the seven-year period with three-judge panels, from mid-1995 through mid-2002, only three defendants (George Woldt, Francisco Martinez, and William "Cody" Neal) were sentenced to death,[1]

1. *See* appendix 3, cases 18–20. For murders during the twenty years between 1975 and 1995, seventeen people were sentenced to death, an average of .85 per year. In the seven-year period from mid-1995 to mid-2002, when the three-judge panels were used, there were three death sentences, an average of .42 per year. In other words, the death sentencing rate with three-judge panels dropped in half, although it is impossible to state exactly how much of the decline can be attributed to the change in the sentencing authorities.

DOI: 10.5876/9781607325123.c005

while five others had their three-judge panels return life sentences.[2] Had Colorado retained jury sentencing, more of these defendants might have been sentenced to death, and today those sentenced to death during this span might still be on death row or even have been executed.

At the same time, death was sought twenty-four times against defendants who were accused of homicides committed between July 1, 1995 through 1999, a discernable uptick in the number of cases threatened by the death penalty.[3] The three-judge panels may have given prosecutors more hope, inspiring them to make more initial decisions to seek death, but it did not pay off with more inmates being sent to death row, much less being executed.

The end of three-judge panels came on June 24, 2002, when, in *Ring v. Arizona*, the US Supreme Court ruled that juries, not judges, must be responsible for finding the statutory aggravators needed to justify death sentences.[4] *Ring* made it clear that the Colorado General Assembly would again need to modify the state's death penalty statute if it wanted the state's executioner to remain in business. Colorado governor Bill Owens, disappointed by the fact that *Ring* promised to leave Colorado without a functioning death penalty law, quickly called the General Assembly into special session without even waiting for the Colorado Supreme Court to rule in hopes that the lawmakers would enact a new death penalty statute that would put sentencing authority back into the hands of juries. The legislators met in Denver in early July 2002 (just two weeks after *Ring* was announced) to enact the changes. When Governor Owens signed the bill on July 12, 2002, Colorado became the first state to pass

---

2. These defendants are Robert Riggan, Danny Martinez, Jacques Richardson, Lucas Salmon, and Donta Page. *See* Robin Lutz, Comment, *Experimenting with Death: An Examination of Colorado's Use of the Three-Judge Panel in Capital Sentencing*, UNIVERSITY OF COLORADO LAW REVIEW 73 (2002): 227–87, at 250–62 (hereinafter Lutz). Coincidentally, shortly after Lutz's paper was published, Colorado returned to jury sentencing, so her work now constitutes a relatively comprehensive history of the era of three-judge panels in the state.

3. Stephanie Hindson, Hillary Potter, and Michael L. Radelet, *Race, Gender, Region and Death Sentencing in Colorado, 1980–1999*, UNIVERSITY OF COLORADO LAW REVIEW 77 (2006): 549–94. To supplement the information presented in this article, table 5.1 presents information on Colorado murders that occurred on or after January 1, 2000, for which the death penalty was sought (as of December 31, 2015).

4. 536 U.S. 584, 618 (2002).

a law that most legislators hoped would bring the state into compliance with *Ring*.[5]

Subsequent history showed that Governor Owens was correct in his belief that *Ring* would invalidate the Colorado death sentencing statute, but the urgency and expense of a special session was not needed. In the three-and-a-half years following the special session, only one person was sentenced to death in Colorado, and then only after waiving his right to a jury and entering a guilty plea.[6]

Meanwhile, in light of *Ring*, and after the amended sentencing statute had already returned sentencing authority to jurors, on February 24, 2003, the Colorado Supreme Court declared Colorado's three-judge sentencing system unconstitutional and ordered life prison terms for Martinez and Woldt:

> We declare Colorado's three-judge capital sentencing statute, under which Woldt and Martinez received the death penalty, to be unconstitutional on its face under *Ring*. The three-judge capital sentencing statute required the judges to make factual findings as a prerequisite to imposition of the death penalty, in violation of defendants' Sixth Amendment right to have a jury make such findings. We also conclude that Woldt and Martinez are entitled to be re-sentenced to life imprisonment without the possibility of parole.[7]

Later, Neal's death sentence was vacated and a district court judge imposed a life sentence.[8] Two other defendants—Abe Hagos and Randy Canister—were spared penalty-phase proceedings by *Ring* because the

---

5. *See* Carol Kasel, *History of the Death Penalty Law in Colorado,* ROCKY MTN. NEWS, Feb. 25, 2003, at 10A; Julia C. Martinez, *Death-penalty Changes Now Law; Owens Signs Bill, but Fate of 3 Still in Doubt*, DENVER POST, July 14, 2002, at B1.

6. As will be discussed in more detail in the next chapter, in February 2003, Edward Montour was sentenced to death for the murder of a prison guard, but the conviction and death sentence were later vacated; in 2014 he was sentenced to life imprisonment after a guilty plea. *See* appendix 3, case no. 21.

7. Woldt v. People, 64 P.3d 256, 259 (Colo. 2003); Howard Pankratz, *Justices Take Two Off Death Row: Colorado Court Voids Sentencing by Judges; Life Terms Ordered*, DENVER POST, Feb. 25, 2003, at A1.

8. *See '99 Death Sentence Commuted for Neal*, DENVER POST, Dec. 14, 2003, at B2.

decision was announced after their convictions but before the penalty phases of their trials had begun.[9]

And so it was clear: the 1995 effort to put more inmates on death row by eliminating the role of jurors in the decision was a colossal flop.

THE EFFORTS TO ABOLISH THE DEATH PENALTY IN 2009

In and around 2005, anti–death penalty efforts in Colorado began to be led by an unusual alliance of activists and families of homicide victims. They were united by a concern for unsolved homicides. In 1961 the proportion of homicides cleared by arrests in the United States stood at 94 percent.[10] In 1976, 79 percent of homicides were cleared by arrest. By 2005, this figure had fallen to 62 percent.[11] In other words, almost four out of every ten murders committed in the United States in recent years has not resulted in the apprehension of a suspect. This proportion of unsolved homicides has doubled since 1976, when the US Supreme Court gave the green light to states to resume executions after the temporary moratorium established by the *Furman* decision in 1972.[12] The families and friends of the homicide victims in these cases are left to cope not only with the after-effects of the murder, but without any solid information about who committed the murder, much less why.

This raises a crucial question: If the death penalty is meant to help families of homicide victims, are there other more cost-effective ways to help these families? If one listens to the families of the victims, many would argue that arresting more perpetrators should be given higher priority than occasionally imposing a super-expensive death sentence on a small number of them, especially when those death sentences have little chance of being carried out.

---

9. People v. Hagos, 110 P.3d 1290, 1290–91 (Colo. 2005); People v. Canister, 110 P.3d 380, 381 (Colo. 2005); Howard Pankratz, *2 Killers Spared in High Court's Ruling on '02 Sentencing Law*, DENVER POST, Apr. 19, 2005, at B1.

10. Charles Wellford & James Cornin, *Clearing Up Homicide Clearance Rates*, NATIONAL INST. OF JUSTICE JOUR. (June 2000): 3–7.

11. James Alan Fox and Marianne W. Zawitz, *Homicide Trends in the United States*, BUREAU OF JUSTICE STATISTICS, July 1, 2007, at 165–67, http://www.bjs.gov/content/pub/pdf/htius.pdf.

12. Gregg v. Georgia, 408 U.S. 153 (1976).

This story necessarily becomes a bit autobiographical. In 2001, after twenty-two years at the University of Florida, I joined the faculty at the University of Colorado Boulder. In Florida I had worked with both death row inmates and families of homicide victims, and when my wife and I left Gainesville we were presented with a Special Service Award by the Gainesville chapter of Parents of Murdered Children to recognize our work with the group.

Soon after I accepted the position in Colorado, the seventeen-year-old daughter of a close friend was murdered in Westminster, about twenty miles from campus. In 2002 this friend invited me to speak to the Denver chapter of Parents of Murdered Children. At that meeting, I met a remarkable man named Howard Morton, whose oldest son was murdered in Arizona in 1975 by an unknown assailant.

Howard and I hit it off immediately, and I invited him to speak to my senior-level Criminology class in Boulder. In the class, Howard explained that he and a handful of other family members of homicide victims wanted to start a group called Families of Homicide Victims and Missing Persons, or FOHVAMP, that focused on unresolved homicide cases in the state.[13] He said that they were attempting to identify unsolved homicides in Colorado and identify family members of the victims.

So many students volunteered to help that in spring 2003, Howard and I co-taught a class on homicide victimization. The dozen students enrolled identified well over 100 relevant Colorado cases with unsolved homicides. Soon thereafter, I was invited to join FOHVAMP's board of directors and the students, now working as volunteers, continued to work on identifying cases. By 2015, FOHVAMP had identified over 1,750 unsolved homicides, either in Colorado or in other states where the victim had a family member who is a Colorado resident.

In 2004 FOHVAMP members began to write Colorado politicians, asking for their help in doing something about these unsolved homicides. Letters to Governor Owens met with no response, but some legislators responded with short letters that basically said, "I am sorry for your loss" without any commitment to act. However, the letters caught the attention of Rep. Paul Weissmann, a foe of the death penalty who had been trying for several years to abolish it. He and Howard Morton—without

13. *See* http://unresolvedhomicides.org/.

my involvement—began to work on a plan to eliminate the death penalty and use the money saved to establish statewide cold case squads, specially trained to reinvestigate old homicides. To be sure, many FOHVAMP members still supported the death penalty in theory, but they had come to realize that it drained too many resources from the state's coffers, leaving far less to help families of other homicide victims—especially in cases where the murder was unsolved.[14]

The bill to eliminate the death penalty and use any monetary savings to reinvestigate cold cases was introduced by Representative Weissmann in the 2007 General Assembly. It won a lot more support than anyone would have predicted, passing through the House Judiciary Committee on a 7–4 vote but ultimately failing before the full House, 35–30.

By 2008, Weissmann was the House minority leader. No bill relating to the death penalty was introduced, but Weissmann did attempt to amend the state budget by deleting $380,000 that was allocated to the Attorney General's office to help prosecute capital crimes and instead direct the money to establish a cold case team within the Colorado Bureau of Investigation. That effort narrowly failed before the full House, 33–31.

Earlier that year, FOHVAMP won a $5,000 grant to conduct statewide polling on its idea to find resources to help solve some of the unsolved homicides. The poll, funded by Sheilah's Fund of the Tides Foundation in San Francisco,[15] was conducted by a well-respected Denver polling organization, RBI Strategies and Research.[16] They polled five hundred "likely voters" in Colorado.

The results indicated that public opinion in Colorado, like the rest of the country,[17] was evenly split, with 45 percent somewhat or strongly

14. Indeed, after discussing the emergence of the argument that "we need the death penalty to help families of homicide victims"—a relatively recent justification for executions—noted legal scholar Franklin E. Zimring has argued that capital punishment today has been transformed from a government function to a victim services program. He argues, "The evocative term 'closure' was a public relations godsend" for death penalty supporters. THE CONTRADICTIONS OF AMERICAN CAPITAL PUNISHMENT (2003), at 58.

15. *Tides*, http://www.tides.org/.

16. *RBI Strategies & Research*, http://www.rbistrategies.com/.

17. The Colorado poll mirrors the results of national polls taken at about the same time. A May 2006 Gallup Poll, surveying a national sample, found that 47 percent

favoring the death penalty and 45 percent opposed. On the other hand, 70 percent of the respondents supported the idea of allocating an additional $3 million per year toward unsolved Colorado murders. In the end, 63 percent supported scrapping the death penalty and using the savings to help resolve more unsolved murders.[18]

To say the least, many politicians and the general public found the polling results to be stunning. With additional financial support from Tides, FOHVAMP organized a series of seven forums around the state in 2008 for politicians, law enforcement officials, and the general public to meet with families of the victims of unresolved homicides and discuss the polls and the larger issue of unsolved homicides. Clearly, the public was becoming more informed about the huge number of unsolved homicides, and most seemed ready to give up the death penalty to find the cash to address the problem.

In 2009 Representative Weissmann introduced HB09-1274, a bill that would abolish the death penalty and use the cost savings to investigate unsolved homicides. FOHVAMP titled their efforts to support the bill "The Cold Case Squad: Trade Vengeance for Justice." When the bill was heard before the House Judiciary Committee, over one hundred FOHVAMP members showed up—many holding pictures of their murdered loved ones—so many that the hearing had to be moved into the old Supreme Court chambers.[19] In the end, the repeal bill passed on a 7–4 party-line vote.[20] Despite vigorous opposition from many of the state's district attorneys, on April 21, 2009, the bill passed in the full House (with only one supporting vote from a Republican), 33–32.

---

of the respondents favored the death penalty and 48 percent favored life imprisonment without parole (LWOP). Jeffrey M. Jones, *Two in Three Favor Death Penalty for Convicted Murderers: Public Divided over Death Penalty or Life Imprisonment as Better Punishment*, GALLUP NEWS SERVICE, June 1, 2006, http://www.gallup.com/poll/23167/two-three-favor-death-penalty-convicted-murderers.aspx.

18. *RBI Strategies & Research*, February 2008, http://www.deathpenaltyinfo.org/COpoll08.pdf.

19. Not all the family members spoke in support of the bill. Rhonda Fields, a future state representative whose son was murdered by two men (one of whom was already on death row and the second of whom would later be sentenced to death), spoke in opposition. *See* appendix 3, case nos. 22 and 23.

20. Tim Hoover, *Execution Repeal Gains: House Panel Backs Bill Banning Death Penalty in Colorado*, DENVER POST, Feb. 25, 2009, at B2.

In the Senate, several legislators powerfully fought the bill, and the families of the victims found some (not all) of their comments insulting. For example:

Senator Shawn Mitchell (R) said the FOHVAMP bill "cruelly plays on the emotions of families" and called the portion of the bill that funds the cold case Team at the Colorado Bureau of Investigation "a gimmick."

Senator Dave Schultheis (R) referred to the Senate State Affairs Committee hearing, where FOHVAMP members showed pictures of their murdered loved ones, and asked, "How can anyone use people like that?" He said the bill "creates false hope."

Senator Bill Cadman (R) said "a state agency can't be effective because these murders happened across Colorado." He opined that the killers, if caught, "should not be excused from the death penalty." He spoke of needing the death penalty for the most horrendous murderers.

Senator Lois Tochtrop (D) said the FOHVAMP bill was "disingenuous" and presented a "false choice."

Despite these and other opponents, a week later the bill passed by one vote in the Senate State Affairs Committee and later, in the Senate Appropriations Committee. But when it reached the full Senate, it failed on an 18–17 vote. Despite the loss, it was a startling achievement. The General Assembly had come within one vote of putting a bill to abolish the death penalty on the governor's desk.

It is likely that the failure of the bill in the Senate was a relief to Colorado governor Bill Ritter, Jr., who himself had authorized his office to seek or threaten to seek eight (by my count) death penalty prosecutions while serving as the Denver district attorney from 1993 to January 2005.[21] Ritter, who served as governor from 2007 to 2011 and did not seek reelection in 2010, is a self-described "pro-life" Catholic and a former seminarian, and it is possible that he personally dislikes the death

21. The defendants included Jon Morris, Jacques Richardson, Nathan Thill, Cong Van Than, Abraham Hagos, Sammang Prim, Omar Ramirez, and Donta Page. None were sentenced to death. *See* Hindson et al., at 594-84; Natasha Gardner & Patrick Doyle, *The Politics of Killing*, 5280, Dec. 2008, http://www.5280.com/magazine/2008/12/politics-killing?page=full.

penalty. But he did not take a public position on the bill, and no one knows—perhaps not even Governor Ritter himself—if he would or would not have signed it.

FOHVAMP's efforts to abolish the death penalty alienated it from several district attorneys, and Howard Morton estimates that FOHVAMP lost close to $15,000 in grants that they had been getting from law enforcement agencies to support their work. After the narrow defeat in 2009 and Morton's pending retirement, FOHVAMP ceased to be a player in the efforts to abolish the death penalty in Colorado. But Morton's dedicated work in bringing attention to the problems of unsolved homicides will live on in Colorado for decades.

THE DECLINING NUMBER OF DEATH PENALTY PROSECUTIONS

Since 1980 or so, the number of homicides and the homicide rate per 100,000 residents in Colorado has fallen precipitously, and this trend has continued into the twenty-first century. In the last chapter, I noted that the state averaged 200 homicides per year in the twenty years between 1980 and 1999. Over the next fourteen years (2000–2013), there were 2,270 additional murders in Colorado, an annual average of 162.[22] Per 100,000 inhabitants, the homicide *rate* has also shrunk. In fact, the homicide rate today is half of what it was during 1972–1979:

TABLE 5.0. Colorado homicides per 100,000 residents

Span	*Years*	*Average*
1972–1979	8	7.0
1980–1989	10	6.2
1990–1999	10	5.1
2000–2013	14	3.4

The number of cases in which the death penalty is sought has also dropped dramatically since the 1980s and 1990s. Again, in the last chapter, I determined that for homicides in those two decades, the death

22. *Colorado Crime Rates 1960–2013*, http://www.disastercenter.com/crime/cocrime.htm.

penalty was sought, on average, in 5.5 cases per year. Table 5.1 gives information on the twenty defendants against whom the death penalty was sought, as of December 31, 2015, for homicides that occurred after January 1, 2000.[23] In those sixteen years, the death penalty was sought against nineteen defendants (one on two occasions for the same murder), or, on average, 1.2 times per year. When adjusted for the number of homicides, a death sentence was sought once for every 36.3 murders committed between 1980 and 1999, but once for every 131.4 murders committed from 2000 to 2013. In other words, from 1980 to 1999, a death sentence was sought in 2.75 percent of the homicides; for homicides between January 1, 2000, and December 31, 2013, it was sought in three-quarters of one percent (0.75) of the homicides.[24] Clearly, since the dawn of the twenty-first century, death penalty cases have become increasingly scarce.

By any measure, one of the main reasons that Colorado has seen so few executions since 1972 is that it has an exceptionally strong public defender system and private criminal defense bar. One public defender, David Wymore (now retired), was involved in many of the death penalty cases in the 1980s and 1990s and is widely regarded as one of the very top criminal defense attorneys in the United States. Other public defenders who have won dramatic victories include Doug Wilson (who has served as the head of the state's public defender's office since 2006), often assisted by Terri Brake, Kathleen Lord, and Michael Heher. David Lane, an attorney in private practice who headed the defense team for Edward Montour, has also been involved in several death penalty battles. The district attorneys who are most experienced with capital litigation include former Adams County DA Bob Grant and his chief assistant (now a member of the Colorado Court of Appeals), Steven Bernard; Mike Little in Denver; and Jim Peters and (most recently) George Brauchler in Arapahoe County.[25]

---

23. As of December 2015, official data on 2014 homicides in Colorado are not yet available. Table 5.1 includes two cases in which the death penalty was sought for murders committed in 2014. I do not include these two defendants in this analysis.

24. From 2000 to 2013, there were 2,092 homicides in Colorado; the death penalty was sought in seventeen of these cases.

25. I acknowledge that reasonable people will differ on who should be included on lists such as these; these names are offered only as examples.

Led by Wymore, the capital defense attorneys in Colorado have gained national notoriety by developing a method of voir dire—the questioning of prospective jurors—that has come to be called The Colorado Method. This entails ranking prospective jurors on a scale of one to seven based on perceptions of how likely they are to vote for the death penalty and how rigid they would be at efforts to change that initial vote. Prospective jurors who are resolutely in favor of the death penalty (or opposed to it) can be excused from jury service for cause, while others are quizzed about their ability to respect and accept the views of jurors who might vote for life. Each prospective juror must be informed and fully understand that if seated on the jury, she or he will have the power, acting alone, to reject the death penalty and ensure that the defendant is sentenced to life in prison.[26]

By the end of 2015, despite twenty cases in which the death penalty was threatened or sought for homicides that occurred after January 1, 2000, only two men were on death row in Colorado for murders committed in the twenty-first century—Sir Mario Owens and Robert Ray—who, at the time of their sentences, joined Nathan Dunlap on Colorado's death row. Both were convicted for the June 2005 murders of Javad Marshall Fields and Fields's fiancée, Vivian Wolfe. At the time of his death, Fields had been scheduled to testify in an accessory to murder case against Ray (the death of Gregory Vann) for which Ray was later convicted.[27] Thus, the alleged motive for the murders of Fields and Wolfe was witness elimination.

By year's end 2015, their convictions and sentences were still being litigated, and the formal appeals in the cases had not yet been filed. One major issue is Colorado's unitary review statute (or URS), which

---

26. Matthew Rubenstein, *Overview of the Colorado Method of Capital Voir Dire*, CHAMPION [National Association of Criminal Defense Lawyers] 34 (Nov. 2010): 18–28.

27. After trial in November 2006, Ray was acquitted of Vann's murder, but he was convicted of accessory to murder and other charges connected to the crime. Carlos Illescas, *Man Convicted in Aurora '04 Killing*, DENVER POST, Nov. 5, 2006, at C4. In February 2007, he was sentenced to 108 years for the convictions. In January 2007, Owens was convicted of first-degree murder in the case and sentenced to life imprisonment without parole. Carlos Illescas, *Guilty Verdict Brings Comfort A Jury Convicts Sir Mario Owens in the 2004 Murder of Gregory Vann*, DENVER POST, Jan. 31, 2007, at A1.

the General Assembly passed in 1997 in an effort to speed up death penalty appeals.[28] This law mandated that all claims in both the direct appeal and post-conviction appeal be combined into a single gigantic appeal, theoretically streamlining the case. As with Colorado's earlier unconstitutional elimination of the final step of the capital juror's decision-making and its disastrous experiment with abolition of capital juries altogether, the URS may face a dubious fate as well. By the end of 2015, the first Colorado death penalty URS case (Owens) has spawned no less than three interlocutory appeals, two federal court cases, and many thousands of hours of attorney litigation time.[29] Complex ethical rules have prompted the district court to declare numerous conflicts-of-interest among various attorneys representing the inmate, causing multiple substitutions of entire teams of attorneys, guaranteeing delays as each new team of attorneys gets up to speed on literally hundreds of thousands of pages of material. While getting a death sentence for Owens took only forty-two months—a relatively short time as modern Colorado death penalty cases go—the URS quagmire has taken some seven years so far in district (trial) court. And so, by mid-2016, a formal appeal has not even begun. By all indications from the first URS case, the Colorado URS has increased exponentially the projected time from imposition of a death sentence to the point of finding out if the conviction and/or sentence will even withstand an appeal, or if, as is the case with so many other Colorado death penalty cases, the mind-numbing complexity of modern capital cases will result in yet another reversal on appeal.

In addition to cases in state court, the death penalty has been sought in federal court against four defendants accused of Colorado crimes from 2000 to 2015. In 2001 prosecutors announced that they would seek death for two cousins—William and Rudy Sablan—accused of the 1999 murder of a cellmate at the Supermax federal prison in Florence, Colorado. Both hailed from Saipan, in the Northern Mariana Islands (a US territory), some 3,750 miles west of Hawaii. William was tried first

28. §§ 16-12-201 to -210, C.R.S. 2008 (adopted in ch. 268, sec. 1, 1997 Colo. Sess. Laws 1573–82).

29. *See, e.g.*, People v. Sir Mario Owens, 228 P.3d 379 (Colo. App. 2009); People v. Owens, 228 P.3d 969 (Colo. 2010); People v. Owens, 330 P.3d 1027 (2014).

and found guilty in March 2007, but after three weeks of deliberation, his jury returned a life sentence.[30] Nonetheless, prosecutors continued to pursue the death penalty against Rudy. He was found guilty in May 2008, but his jury voted 7–5 for a life term, far short of a unanimous vote needed in federal courts for a death sentence.[31] The federal prosecutors surely thought that the cousins would be sentenced to death, but they spent nearly nine years—requiring thousands of hours of time from attorneys, judges, court personnel, and other associated participants—and ended up with sentences that could have been obtained with a few hours' work through plea bargains.

Another federal death penalty case also originated in the federal prison in Florence. In 2008 an inmate serving a life term on a murder charge—Gary Douglas Watland—stabbed to death inmate Mark James Baker. At the time, Watland was serving a sentence for a murder that occurred in 2004 in Maine. In March 2011, federal prosecutors announced that they would seek the death penalty for Watland.[32] However, on February 5, 2014, just before the trial began,[33] an agreement was struck, and Watland was sentenced to life imprisonment without parole.

A 2005 death penalty case from the Florence prison was still pending eleven years after the homicide. In April 2005, Richard Santiago and Silvestre Mayorqui Rivera allegedly beat to death a sixty-five-year-old prisoner named Manuel Torrez in the prison yard in Florence. On March 28, 2011, federal prosecutors announced that they would seek a death sentence for Santiago, who already was serving a term for a previous murder while in custody in a prison in Fresno, California.[34] Denver attorney Patrick Burke, who was also the lead defense attorney for William Sablan and Gary Douglas Watland, initially worked on the Rivera case. But when prosecutors announced that they would seek a death sentence for Santiago and not Rivera, Burke took over the defense in the Santiago

30. Bruce Finlay, *Jail Death Nets Life Term*, DENVER POST, Apr. 8, 2007, at C1.

31. Felisa Cardona, *Prisoner Gets Life Sentence in Attack: Rudy Sablan Was Spared Death but Has No Chance at Parole after the Killing of a Cellmate*, DENVER POST, June 22, 2008, at B1.

32. Sara Burnett, *Death Penalty Sought in Supermax Cases*, DENVER POST, Mar. 29, 2011, at B1.

33. Tom McGhee, *Inmate's Trial over Prison Slaying Nears*, DENVER POST, Jan. 12, 2014, at B6.

34. Burnett, *Death Penalty Sought*.

case. Whether he remains on the case remains to be seen; but if the case does proceed to trial, federal prosecutors will face formidable opposition.

The only case known to me in which a defendant was accused of a crime in Colorado and sentenced to death under federal jurisdiction comes from the 1940s and involved an Army private named Dale H. Maple. Maple was a Harvard alumnus who was stationed at Camp Hale, near Leadville.[35] Maple helped two German POWs escape from the camp and cross the Mexico border. He was charged with aiding the enemy and desertion—both capital crimes that today are subsumed under the crime of treason. After a trial at Fort Leavenworth, Kansas, Maple was sentenced to death on April 24, 1944. However, in December 1944, President Roosevelt commuted the death sentence to life imprisonment.[36]

INNOCENCE AND THE POSTHUMOUS PARDON OF JOE ARRIDY

Governor Ritter did not have a chance to make history by signing a bill that would have abolished the death penalty. However, as mentioned in chapter 3, in January 2011, he made death penalty history of another sort: he acknowledged that in 1939, the state had executed an innocent man named Joe Arridy and granted him a full posthumous pardon. It was an astounding act, unprecedented in Colorado and nearly unprecedented nationwide.

Absent DNA (which, to date, has never resulted in the exoneration of an executed defendant anywhere in the world) or an assumed murder victim who later turns up alive,[37] almost any claim of innocence by one convicted of murder (or any other crime) is controversial. In the end, claims of innocence are best viewed as probability statements, suggesting, for example, that a given defendant "may have been" or "probably was" innocent. After conviction, the burden of proof shifts from the

35. Timothy McVeigh was sentenced to death after his trial in Denver for killing 167 people in the bombing of the Alfred P. Murrah Federal Building in 1995, but that bombing occurred in Oklahoma, not Colorado.

36. *See* Fred L. Borch, *Tried for Treason: The Amazing Case of Dale Maple*, LITIGATION 38 (Spring 2012): 1–2.

37. For examples, *see* ROB WARDEN, WILKIE COLLINS'S THE DEAD ALIVE: THE NOVEL, THE CASE, AND WRONGFUL CONVICTIONS (2005).

state having to prove guilt to the defendant having to prove innocence. American history, however, is replete with examples of inmates convicted of murder who, despite the initial judgments of the prosecutors, jurors, and judges involved, actually were innocent.[38] Often, these exonerations resulted from pure luck.[39]

Like other death row inmates throughout the world, some Colorado inmates facing execution steadfastly maintained their innocence.[40] Some admitted that they actually killed the victim but claimed that they did so in self-defense[41] or by accident.[42] Others claimed that they had committed second-degree or lesser types of criminal homicide but not capital murder.[43] Others claimed (or their lawyers claimed) that because of mental illness or developmental disabilities they could not form the criminal intent necessary to sustain a conviction for capital murder. Still others claimed they were both legally and physically uninvolved in any behavior that led to another person's death.

While it can be reasonably concluded that many or most of these claims of innocence are not supported by the evidence, we certainly do

---

38. Michael L. Radelet, Hugo Adam Bedau, & Constance E. Putnam, In Spite of Innocence 5–10 (1992). By far, the most comprehensive listing of erroneous convictions today is maintained by Northwestern University's Rob Warden and Sam Gross, professor at the University of Michigan. As of mid-2016, they had documented over 1,800 cases of erroneous convictions in the United States since 1989. *See* University of Michigan Law School, National Registry of Exonerations, accessed July 15, 2016, http://www.law.umich.edu/special/exoneration/Pages/about.aspx.

39. For a discussion of the role of Lady Luck in exonerating convicted defendants, *see, e.g.*, Michael L. Radelet & Hugo Adam Bedau, *The Execution of the Innocent*, L. & Cont. Prob. 61 (Autumn 1998): 105–24, at 117–18. Examples of cases where an innocent death row inmate owes his or her vindication to luck include cases in which previously silent eyewitnesses step forward, the inmate or his friends are able to convince a journalist or journalism class to take an interest in the case, and cases where biological material that can be used for DNA analysis is left at the crime scene.

40. *See* appendix 1, case no. 8 (Henry Stone); case no. 12 (Victor Nunez); case no. 14 (W. H. Salisbury); case no. 44 (James Lynn); case no. 48 (Oscar Cook); case no. 56 (Edward Ives); case no. 71 (William Cody Kelley); and case no. 99 (Harold David Wooley).

41. *See* appendix 1, case no. 10 (Theodore Myers); case no. 18 (George N. Woods); case no. 24 (Nicolai Femenella); case no. 62 (William Moya); and case no. 81 (Joe Coates).

42. *See* appendix 1, case no. 23 (Andrew Green) and case no. 80 (Harry Leopold).

43. *See* appendix 1, case no. 68.

not know with absolute certainty which claims, few though they may be, are legitimate. We can say, however, that in some cases, in addition to a defendant's claims of innocence, some very reasonable people had very reasonable doubts about a defendant's guilt. Merrick Rosengrants was executed in Leadville despite no prior record of criminality, an alibi witness who did not testify at trial, and the belief of several Leadville citizens that his innocence claim was indeed true.[44] Five years later, Cyrus Minich[45] was also hanged in Leadville despite scant evidence against him and his steadfast insistence on his innocence from the moment of his arrest until the moment he dropped from the gallows.[46] When the Colorado General Assembly reenacted the death penalty in 1901, it banned executions of defendants "convicted on circumstantial evidence alone."[47] This led three Colorado Supreme Court justices to dissent when the court sustained John Berger's conviction and death sentence,[48] arguing, "The whole record is sufficiently satisfying to sustain the verdict of guilty of murder, but not to warrant the infliction of the death penalty."[49] Looking at these cases individually, in hindsight, some chance exists that the defendants may have been guilty. But combining the probabilities, there is a high probability that at least one was not guilty of capital murder. The problem is, we do not know which one.

When the modern era of innocence scholarship began in 1987, Hugo Adam Bedau and I pointed to twenty-three cases in which we felt that "most people" would today conclude that the executed inmate was "probably" innocent.[50] Those who supported the death penalty hotly contested this claim.[51] Indeed, at the time, no one could point to any case

---

44. *See* appendix 1, case no. 15.

45. *See* appendix 1, case no. 22.

46. Minich v. People, 9 P. 4, 14 (Colo. 1885).

47. Act of May 2, 1901, ch. 64, § 2, 1901 Colo. Sess. Laws 153, 154.

48. *See* appendix 1, case no. 94.

49. Berger v. People, 122 Colo. 367; 224 P.2d 228, 246 (Colo. 1950), *cert. denied*, 342 U.S. 837 (1951).

50. Hugo Adam Bedau & Michael L. Radelet, *Miscarriages of Justice in Potentially Capital Cases*, STANFORD L. REV. 40 (1987): 21–179 (hereinafter Bedau and Radelet).

51. *See* Stephen J. Markman & Paul G. Cassell, *Protecting the Innocent: A Response to the Bedau-Radelet Study*, STANFORD L. REV. 41 (1988): 121–60. For a response to these criticisms, *see* Hugo Adam Bedau & Michael L. Radelet, *The Myth of Infallibility: A Reply to Markman and Cassell*, STANFORD L. REV. 41 (1988): 161–70.

in the twentieth century in which the state acknowledged that a person who had been executed turned out to be innocent. The 1927 hangings of Nicola Sacco and Bartolomeo Vanzetti come close; on the fiftieth anniversary of their executions in 1977, Massachusetts governor Michael Dukakis apologized for the massive due process errors in the case but did not concede their innocence.[52] By 1999, the last people to be executed and later exonerated had been hanged in the 1880s.[53]

Between 2000 and 2015, however, five inmates who were executed in the twentieth century outside of Colorado were exonerated.

In Maryland in 2001, Gov. Parris Glendening issued a pardon to John Snowden, a black man who was hanged in 1919 for the rape and murder of the wife of a prominent white businessman. Two key trial witnesses had recanted their testimony and before the hanging, eleven of the twelve jurors had pled for mercy.[54]

In 2005 Georgia pardoned Lena Baker, who in 1945 became the only woman to have died in that state's electric chair. Baker, who was black, was convicted of killing a white man for whom she worked as a caretaker. Authorities who reviewed the case concluded that he was extremely abusive and was killed in self-defense, and therefore Baker should have been convicted of involuntary homicide (at most).[55] But even so, it was clear that Baker still killed the man.[56]

In 2009 South Carolina pardoned two African American brothers—Thomas and Meeks Griffin—who had been electrocuted in 1915 for mur-

---

52. Bedau and Radelet (1987), at 74, note 274.

53. In Illinois in 1893, Gov. Peter Altgeld pardoned three of the Haymarket defendants six years after four of their codefendants had been hanged. An eighth defendant had taken his own life on the eve of his scheduled execution. Altgeld issued the pardons because all eight "had been wrongfully convicted and were innocent of the crime." PAUL AVRICH, THE HAYMARKET TRAGEDY 423 (1984).

And, in recent years, there have been other pardons issued for prisoners executed in the nineteenth century. For example, in 1987 Nebraska governor Bob Kerry issued a pardon to William Jackson Marion, who had been hanged exactly one hundred years earlier in Beatrice for the murder of a man who later turned up alive. WARDEN, WILKIE COLLINS'S THE DEAD ALIVE, 157–58.

54. Jay Apperson & Andrea F. Siegel, *Glendening Pardons Black in 1919 Murder: Governor Attempts "To Correct Inequity"*, BALTIMORE SUN, June 1, 2001.

55. *Briefly: State Officials to Pardon Executed Black Woman*, N.Y. TIMES, Aug. 17, 2005.

56. LELA BOND PHILLIPS, THE LENA BAKER STORY (2001).

dering a white Confederate War veteran. They were convicted on the perjured testimony of the actual murderer, who falsely fingered the men to save himself from the executioner.[57]

On December 17, 2014, a judge in South Carolina, citing "fundamental, constitutional violations of due process," vacated the conviction of George Stinney, who was executed at age fourteen in 1944.[58] He was the youngest person to be put to death in the United States in the twentieth century. His innocence was not definitively proved, but other reasonable suspects were identified, and all parties today agree that Stinney was executed without anything resembling a fair trial.

And so when the case of Joe Arridy began to attract new attention in the early years of the twenty-first century, few thought there was much chance of officially clearing his name. Arridy was executed in January 1939 for sexually assaulting and murdering fifteen-year-old Dorothy Drain in her Pueblo home and seriously wounding her twelve-year-old sister, Barbara, with a hatchet.[59] The girls were the grandchildren of a former state legislator, which, no doubt, heightened the pressure on the police to find the culprit(s).

The murder proved relatively easy to solve. Five days after the crimes, during Drain's funeral, police arrested Frank Aguilar, a Mexican national, and found the murder weapon in his home. His guilt was never seriously questioned. But authorities persisted and soon tried to argue that Arridy was also involved. At first, Aguilar said he had never met Arridy, then he said that they had both killed the girl, and later he retracted that admission. At Aguilar's trial, Barbara Drain identified Aguilar as the assailant and never mentioned the presence of a second man. The jury took only twenty-eight minutes to find Aguilar guilty and sentence him to death, and Aguilar later admitted killing another woman

---

57. Christina Sterbenz, *These Are the Only 7 People In The US Pardoned AFTER They Were Executed*, BUSINESS INSIDER, May 19, 2014, http://www.businessinsider.com/people-pardoned-after-their-executions-2014-5 and Alex Spillius, *Black Pair's Justice—After 94 Years*, DAILY TELEGRAPH (London), Oct. 19, 2009, at 22.

58. DAVID STOUT, CAROLINA SKELETONS (2011); Campbell Robertson, *South Carolina Judge Vacates Conviction of George Stinney in 1944 Execution,* N.Y. TIMES, Dec. 17, 2014; David Zucchino, *"I Never Saw My Brother Alive Again": The Exoneration of George Stinney Jr., Executed in 1944 at Age 14, Eases his Family*, L.A. TIMES, Dec. 19, 2014, at A10.

59. *See* appendix 1, case nos. 76 and 77.

in Pueblo just two weeks before the Drain murder. On August 13, 1937, Frank Aguilar became the fifth person to die in Roy's Penthouse.[60] The only unusual aspect to the case was that during the execution, one of the official witnesses—Adlai S. "Ad" Hamilton—a Pueblo resident and conductor for the Missouri Pacific Railroad, had a heart attack and died.[61]

Arridy entered the picture four days after Aguilar was arrested. With an IQ of 46, the Pueblo native had spent much of the previous seven years in what was then called the Colorado State Home and Training School for Mental Defectives, located in Grand Junction, three hundred miles west of Pueblo. At the time of the Drain murder, Arridy had run away from the hospital and hopped on a freight train, only to be discovered a few days later in Cheyenne, Wyoming. County sheriff George Carroll knew about the Drain murder (although not about Aguilar's arrest), and when he learned that Arridy was also from Pueblo, he saw an opportunity for fame and fortune in solving the case.

What followed was a series of purported confessions. No one knows for sure what they contained since only Sheriff Carroll witnessed them, and he never wrote down what Arridy allegedly said. Back in Pueblo, there wasn't a shred of evidence that Arridy had even met Aguilar, much less Dorothy Drain. Nonetheless, Arridy's insanity defense failed (even though three psychiatrists testified that Arridy had the mind of a five- or six-year-old child) and, based exclusively on Carroll's statements, he soon followed Aguilar to death row.

On appeal, Arridy's case was handled by Gail Ireland, a first-rate litigator who later served as Colorado's attorney general. There were no legal barriers to executing inmates who were developmentally disabled, so Ireland had to argue that Arridy was insane. His multiple attempts to raise the issue of Arridy's sanity—which was first raised prior to the trial—failed in the Colorado Supreme Court (by 4–3 votes), and Gov. Teller Ammons refused to intervene. Warden Roy Best, for whom the gas chamber was named and who had earned a reputation as a tough and even brutal warden, virtually adopted Arridy as a member of his

---

60. After the execution, one of Aguilar's children was killed in a house fire, and the other two were abandoned by his widow, placed in an orphanage, and eventually taken by their grandmother to live in Mexico. *See* appendix 1, case no. 76.

61. *Puebloan Witness Dies at Execution*, PUEBLO CHIEFTAIN, Aug. 11, 1937, at 1.

FIGURE 5.1. *Joe Arridy (right), giving his toy train to fellow death row inmate Angelo Agnes, January 6, 1939. Arridy was executed later that day. Photo courtesy of the Royal Gorge Regional Museum & History Center, Cañon City.*

family. In fact, it was at Best's urging that Ireland became involved in the case.[62] Best rather famously told reporters that Arridy "is the happiest man who ever lived on death row."[63] But that living stopped on January 6, 1939. After a day of eating ice cream and playing with a toy train that Best had given him, Arridy was taken to the gas chamber.

It is an amazing story. This is not a case that slipped through the cracks without any authorities knowing about the many questions that surrounded it. Ireland made sure that the justices on the state Supreme Court and Governor Ammons knew about Arridy's mental disabilities and the strong questions about his guilt. The tragedy is not only that

62. TERRI BRANDT & GAIL IRELAND: COLO. CITIZEN LAWYER 38–56, at 42 (2010).

63. ROBERT PERSKE, DEADLY INNOCENCE? 126 (1995). For a later (and shorter) overview of the case, *see* Alan Prendergast, *Joe Arridy Was the Happiest Man on Death Row*, WESTWORD, Sept. 20, 2012, at 1.

Arridy was wrongfully convicted and executed but that the authorities at the time knew exactly what the problems were and how unreliable the conviction was. Yet, they stood silent and did nothing.

Luckily, a poem was written about the case,[64] and in 1992 it fell into the hands of Robert Perske, a Connecticut resident who had spent his life working with children with mental disabilities. Perske contacted death penalty historian Watt Espy,[65] whose work formed much of the basis for the list of executions in this book, and Espy identified the subject as Joe Arridy. Perske had been raised in Denver and immediately tracked down every detail of the case that he could find. In 1995 he published his manuscript about the case under the title *Deadly Innocence?*

The book soon attracted a small circle of dedicated followers. A journalist in Trinidad, Colorado, Daniel Leonetti, wrote a screenplay about Ireland's efforts to save Arridy from death. Perske's book also fell into the hands of Craig Severa, an advocate for people with developmental

64. The warden wept before the lethal beans
Were dropped that night in the airless room,
Fifty faces peering against glassed screens,
A clinic crowd outside the tomb.
In the corridor a toy train pursued
Its tracks past countryside and painted station
Of tinny folk. The doomed man's eyes were glued
On these, he was the tearless one.
Who waited unknowing why the warden wept
And watched the toy train with the prisoners
Who watched the train, or ate, or simply slept.
The warden wrote a sorry letter.
"The man you kill tonight is six years old,
He has no idea why he dies,"
Yet he must die in the room the state has walled
Transparent to its glassy eyes.
What warden weeps in the stony corridor
What mournful eyes are peering through the glass,
Who will ever shut a final door
And watch the fume upon his face?

Marguerite Young, *The Clinic*, in MODERATE FABLE (1944).

65. The original copy of Perske's letter to Espy is today in the Watt Espy Papers, Grenander Department of Special Collections and Archives, University at Albany–SUNY.

FIGURE 5.2. *Headstone marking the grave of Joe Arridy, executed in 1939 and pardoned in 2011, Woodpecker Hill, Greenwood Cemetery, Cañon City. The Friends of Joe Arridy purchased this headstone in 2007 to replace the rusted license plate marking his grave. The inscription "Pardoned on Jan. 7, 2011" was added later. Photo by author.*

disabilities from The Arc in Colorado Springs.[66] In 2007 Severa, Leonetti, myself, and four dozen or so others formed a group called Friends of Joe Arridy and purchased a granite tombstone (with a picture of Arridy on it, playing with his toy train) to replace the metal license plate that the prison used to denote graves of those who died in prison and had no family to claim their body.[67] A ceremony to dedicate the new tombstone was held at Woodpecker Hill, the section of Greenwood Cemetery in Cañon City holding the bodies of prisoners who have died in custody with no other resting place.[68] Denver attorney David Martinez also

66. "ARC" refers to the Association of Retarded Citizens, although the term *retarded* is no longer used.

67. The group still exists. *See* http://www.friendsofjoearridy.com/index.html. The most recent gathering of the Friends of Joe Arridy was at Arridy's grave on June 7, 2014. *See* http://www.friendsofjoearridy.com/index.html.

68. Kirk Mitchell, *Inmates' Thorny Histories Call Out from the Graves*, DENVER POST, Apr. 11, 2011, at B1.

FIGURE 5.3. *Greenwood Cemetery's Woodpecker Hill, in Cañon City, where many unclaimed bodies of prisoners are buried. The oldest marker is over the grave of William Kelley, the first person put to death in Colorado's gas chamber on June 22, 1934. Photo by author.*

attended that gathering.[69] He was so moved by the story of the case that he prepared a four-hundred-page summary of it and presented it as a clemency petition to Gov. Bill Ritter.

On January 11, 2011, seventy-two years after his death, Joe Arridy was issued a "full and unconditional posthumous pardon" by Governor Ritter.[70] The new granite headstone was redone to note that event.

By December 2015, the National Registry of Exonerations at the University of Michigan Law School listed four people from Colorado who had been exonerated since 1989 after being convicted of homicide: Robert Dewey (convicted in 1996 and exonerated in 2012), Alarico

---

69. Michael de Yoanna, *"Sorry, Joe," Calls to Pardon Joe Arridy, Executed in the Gas Chamber, Come Amid Renewed Interest in 68-year-old Case*, COLO. INDEPENDENT (Colorado Springs), June 7, 2007.

70. *Gov. Ritter Grants Posthumous Pardon in Case Dating Back to 1930s*, Jan. 7, 2011, http://www.deathpenaltyinfo.org/documents/ArridyPardon.pdf.

Joe Medina (1991–1995), Lorenzo Montoya (2000–2014), and Timothy Masters (1999–2008).[71] Masters, the most widely known defendant, later reached out-of-court settlements with the City of Fort Collins and Larimer County for his erroneous convictions, winning $10 million in settlements.[72]

Overall, by the end of 2015, the Death Penalty Information Center counted 156 death row inmates from across the United States who had been released from death rows since 1970 because of doubts about their guilt. Whatever benefits the death penalty may have, the possibility of erroneous executions remains a significant risk.

And so, in the early twenty-first century, the death penalty in Colorado continued its slow demise. By the end of 2015, Coloradans could look back over a full fifty-one years—since the execution of John Bizup in September 1964—and evaluate the fruits that the millions of dollars spent on the death penalty had produced. Those fifty-one years had witnessed only two executions (and Luis José Monge's execution in 1967 would have never occurred had he pursued his appeals), one posthumous pardon, and three people on death row. The death penalty that began with speedy trials and speedier executions in the second half of the nineteenth century had evolved into a penalty that is today virtually irrelevant.

Still, a lot of people in Colorado, including many politicians and prosecutors, think they can make the system work—and they keep trying.

71. The website for the National Registry of Exonerations is http://www.law.umich.edu/special/exoneration/Pages/about.aspx.

72. *See* TIMOTHY MASTERS & STEVE LEHTO, DRAWN TO INJUSTICE: THE WRONGFUL CONVICTION OF TIMOTHY MASTERS (2012).

TABLE 5.1. Cases where death penalty sought in Colorado for murders committed after January 1, 2000
(**Bold** designates death sentence imposed through December 31, 2015)

		Date of offense	*County*	*Defendant*	*Victim*	*Outcome*
1.	Anthony Jimenez	08/24/00	Teller	HM	WF	Mistrial in trial 1, then death dropped
2.	Cruz Palomo	October 2000	Morgan	HM	HF	Pled to second-degree murder
3.	Edward Robert Brown	June 2001	Arapahoe	BM	BM	Pled to attempted murder and second-degree murder*
4.	Allen Bergerud	04/07/02	Weld	WM	WF WM	First guilt phase mistried, then death dropped; jury convicted Bergerud of first-degree murder and second-degree murder sentenced to life plus 48 years
5.	Jimmy J. Vasquez	09/03/02	Adams	HM	HF	Death dropped—developmental disability; LWOP.
6–7.	**Edward Montour**	10/19/02	Lincoln	HM	WM	Sentenced to death, sentence vacated; pled to life 3/6/14
8.	David Bueno and	03/28/04	Lincoln	HM	WM	Sentenced to life, conviction vacated†
9.	Alejandro Perez			HM	WM	Acquitted
10.	Michael Medina	05/21/05	Alamosa	HM	HM	48 years—child abuse causing death
11.	**Sir Mario Owens and**	06/20/05	Arapahoe	BM	BM and AF	Death 12/8/08
12.	**Robert Ray**	06/20/05	Arapahoe	BM		Death 5/5/10
13.	Jose Luis Rubi-Nava	09/17/06	Douglas	HM	HF	LWOP 2/19/09
14.	Marco Lee	12/04/06	El Paso	BM	WM	LWOP 12/19/08

continued on next page

TABLE 5.1.—*continued*

		Date of offense	*County*	*Defendant*	*Victim*	*Outcome*
15.	Josiah Sher	02/23/11	Douglas	WM	WM WF	LWOP
16.	James Holmes	07/20/12	Arapahoe	WM	12 victims 58 injured	LWOP by jury at penalty phase
17.	Dexter Lewis	10/17/12	Denver	BM	AF, WM, 3WF	LWOP by jury at penalty phase
18.	Brendan Lee Johnson and	May 2014	Sterling	WM	WM and WF	LWOP
19.	Cassandra Ann Rieb			WF	WM and WF	Pled to second-degree murder, sentenced to 80 years
20.	Miguel Contreras-Perez	09/24/12	Ordway‡	HF	WF	Pending

Codes of defendants' and victims' race/ethnicity and gender: W = white; B = black; A = Asian; H = Hispanic; M = male; F = female

* The death sentence in Arapahoe County was originally sought for the murder of Lamont Monroe. In Denver Brown pled guilty to the murders of Felix Sharp and Demarco Taylor, and in Adams County he was acquitted for the murder of Jeremy Green. Death was not sought in any of the latter three cases.

† The state appealed this order to the Colorado Court of Appeals, which upheld the lower court's ruling in November 2013. Carlos Illescas, *Colorado Inmate May Get New Trial in Prison Slaying*, Denver Post, Nov. 22, 2013, at A6. The state then appealed to the Colorado Supreme Court, which on November 24, 2014, agreed to hear the case. As of December 2015, the final disposition is still pending.

‡ Crowley County.

CHAPTER 6

THE HICKENLOOPER YEARS

By the end of 2015, a wide range of international, national, and statewide developments made the immediate future of the death penalty in Colorado virtually impossible to predict. At the same time, however, the long-term trend is clear. Whether one goes back 139 years to when Colorado attained statehood in 1876, the 114 years since Colorado's brief experiment with abolition ended in 1901, or the 18 years since the execution of Gary Lee Davis in 1997, it is easy to spot strong indicators that the death penalty in Colorado is in steep decline. In the 51 years since the execution of John Bizup in 1964, Colorado has seen only two executions, and at least one of them—that of Luis José Monge in 1967—would not have occurred had the inmate not preferred it to a sentence of life imprisonment.[1] It is unlikely, although certainly not impossible, that Colorado will see many more executions in the next fifty years.

To understand what is happening in Colorado, we need to first briefly examine the international and national context.

1. As discussed in chapter 4, Gary Lee Davis also forfeited some opportunities to further appeal his case.

DOI: 10.5876/9781607325123.c006

THE CHANGING INTERNATIONAL AND NATIONAL CONTEXT

After Monge's execution in 1967, no executions took place anywhere in the United States for nearly a decade. As we have seen, in 1972 the US Supreme Court effectively invalidated all death penalty statutes, but in July 1976, the Court gave the green light for states to resume executions under newly revised death penalty provisions.[2] The national moratorium ended in January 1977, when a drifter named Gary Gilmore refused to authorize appeals in his case and went to his death before a Utah firing squad. Through December 2015, just over 1,400 additional men and 16 women were put to death in the United States since Gilmore's death and just over 3,000 inmates were housed on America's death rows.[3]

Those same years witnessed a remarkable turn away from the death penalty throughout the world. When Gilmore faced the firing squad in 1977, only 16 countries worldwide had abolished the death penalty.[4] By the end of 2015, 140 countries had abolished the death penalty in law or in practice, and just 58 countries actively employed executioners.[5] Indeed, the number of countries that can be described as "active retentionists" (i.e., those that have hosted at least one execution in the preceding ten years that have not enacted a moratorium) decreased from 51 in December 2007 to only 39 at the end of April 2014.[6] In 2012, 2013, and

---

2. Gregg v. Georgia, 428 U.S. 153 (1976).

3. As of April 1, 2015, the largest death rows were in California (746 condemned prisoners), Florida (401), Texas (271), Alabama (201), and Pennsylvania (184). *Death Row, USA*, NAACP Legal Defense and Educational Fund, Inc., Apr. 1, 2015, http://www.naacpldf.org/death-row-usa. The best source for current figures on the death penalty in the United States is maintained by the Death Penalty Information Center, http://www.deathpenaltyinfo.org/.

4. *Death Penalty*, Amnesty International, accessed July 15, 2016, http://www.amnesty.org/en/death-penalty/numbers. In early 1965, there were 11 countries that had completely abolished the death penalty, and 14 others that had abolished it for ordinary crimes during peacetime. Roger Hood & Carolyn Hoyle, The Death Penalty: A Worldwide Perspective, 5th ed., 14 (2015) (hereinafter Hood & Hoyle).

5. *See* https://www.amnesty.org/en/what-we-do/death-penalty/. *See also* Hood & Hoyle, at 16.

6. Hood & Hoyle, at 5.

2014, the countries that executed the most prisoners were China, Iran, Iraq, Saudi Arabia, and the United States.[7]

In December 2014, the majority of countries in the United Nations voted (for the fifth time since 2007) to support a resolution calling for a global moratorium on the death penalty, with an eye toward abolition. A record 117 countries voted in favor of the resolution, with 34 abstentions and 38 countries (including the United States) that opposed it. With the exception of Belarus, all European countries have outlawed executions, and the only other industrialized democracy that retains the death penalty is Japan.

Of special note is Asia, where upwards of 90 percent of the world's executions occur. Sixteen of the twenty-nine countries in Asia do not use capital punishment. Only one country (China) has an annual execution rate higher than one per 1 million citizens, although, on a per capita basis, Pakistan, Vietnam, and Singapore still show a warm regard for their executioners. On the other hand, there are commonalities. Chief among them is an overall gradual decline in the use of the death penalty (albeit in several countries the path toward abolition is crooked or reverses directions); even in the most staunchly retentionist countries, which tend to have authoritarian governments, many express a growing ambivalence about its appropriateness.[8]

Overall, there is no question that, with a global view, we can see that the United States has become increasingly isolated in terms of its relatively liberal execution policies.

Fueled in part by what is arguably the most important death penalty book in recent decades—*Dead Man Walking*—the leadership of the Catholic Church, along with the leaders of virtually every other mainstream religious denomination in the United States, have solidified their stands opposing the death penalty. As *Washington Post* political commentator E. J. Dionne puts it, "I think the religious community has played an enormous role in having people question their consciences

---

7. *Death Sentences and Executions 2014*, AMNESTY INTERNATIONAL, March 31, 2015, http://www.amnestyusa.org/research/reports/death-sentences-and-executions-2014. Pakistan, with over 300 executions, will join this list in 2015.

8. DAVID T. JOHNSON & FRANKLIN E. ZIMRING, THE NEXT FRONTIER: NATIONAL DEVELOPMENT, POLITICAL CHANGE, AND THE DEATH PENALTY IN ASIA (2009).

about where they stand on the death penalty."[9] In an October 2014 speech to the International Association of Penal Law, Pope Francis not only reiterated his call for an end to the death penalty but also called for an end to sentences of life imprisonment without parole.[10] As will be discussed in the following chapter, his stand seems to be strengthening.

In the United States, 2014 saw the lowest number of executions in twenty years (N = 35), and the lowest number of new death sentences in forty years (N = 72).[11] In 2015 the total number of executions fell further, to twenty-eight, as did the number of new death sentences, to an estimated 266.[12] Eight states abolished the death penalty between 1972 and the end of 2015: Massachusetts (1984), New York (2004), New Jersey (2007), New Mexico (2009), Illinois (2011), Connecticut (2012), Maryland (2013), and Nebraska (2015). Because the bills were not always retroactive, there are still two people on death row in New Mexico, but in August 2015, the Connecticut Supreme Court found its death penalty statute to be unconstitutional,[13] thereby removing twelve people under a sentence of death for sentences imposed before the state's legislature approved prospective abolition. On December 31, 2014, Gov. Martin O'Malley commuted the sentences of the last four death row inmates in Maryland.[14] The governors of Colorado, Oregon, and Washington have stated that there will be no executions in their states as long as they are in office, and in early 2015, the incoming governor of Pennsylvania, Tom Wolf, announced that there would be no executions in that state until a study on their fairness is completed.

---

9. Again, the Death Penalty Information Center is the best single source for information on religion and the death penalty (and this quote). *See Religion and the Death Penalty*, accessed July 15, 2016, http://www.deathpenaltyinfo.org/article.php%3Fdid%3D2249.

10. *Pope Francis Blasts Life Sentences as "Hidden Death Penalty"*, GUARDIAN, Oct. 23, 2014.

11. *The Death Penalty in 2014: Year End Report*, DEATH PENALTY INFORMATION CENTER, accessed July 15, 2016, http://www.deathpenaltyinfo.org/documents/2014YrEnd.pdf.

12. *The Death Penalty in 2015: Year End Report*, DEATH PENALTY INFORMATION CENTER, accessed July 15, 2016, http://deathpenaltyinfo.org/documents/2015YrEnd.pdf.

13. State v. Eduardo Santiago, SC 17413 (Aug. 13, 2015).

14. *Maryland Governor Commutes Sentences for Remaining Death Row Inmates*, N.Y. TIMES, Dec. 31, 2014.

In 2014 seven former death row inmates were exonerated of all charges. Three of these seven each spent thirty-nine years behind bars for their wrongful convictions, and three others spent thirty years.[15] In 2015 another six were exonerated and released, having served an average of nineteen years on death row after their erroneous convictions. This brought the total number of people released from death row between 1972 and the end of 2015 because of likely innocence to 156.[16]

Anyone who would have predicted these developments a couple decades ago would have been ignored, if not ridiculed. Changes like this were not on anyone's radar.

Not coincidentally, support for the death penalty has also sharply declined in the United States. In a 1994 Gallup poll, some 80 percent of Americans expressed support for capital punishment. In 2014 only 63 percent did so.[17] More importantly, in the 2014 Gallup poll, supporters of the death penalty outnumbered those who preferred the option of life imprisonment without parole by a slim 50–45 percent margin. As recently as 2006, a slight plurality supported the life-without-parole (LWOP) option in the Gallup polls.[18] Similarly, a poll by the *Washington Post* and ABC News released in June 2014 found that 61 percent of the respondents favored the death penalty and that more Americans now support life without parole (52 percent) than the death penalty (42 per-

---

15. *The Innocence List*, DEATH PENALTY INFORMATION CENTER, accessed July 15, 2016, http://www.deathpenaltyinfo.org/innocence-list-those-freed-death-row?scid=6&did=110.

16. *See Innocence and the Death Penalty*, DEATH PENALTY INFORMATION CENTER, last modified Oct. 13, 2015, http://www.deathpenaltyinfo.org/innocence-and-death-penalty. The list of innocent people released from death row in the modern era was begun by Hugo Adam Bedau and Michael L. Radelet. *See* Hugo Adam Bedau & Michael L. Radelet, *Miscarriages of Justice in Potentially Capital Cases*, STANFORD L. REV. 40 (1987): 21–179, note 40 and Michael L. Radelet, William S. Lofquist, & Hugo Adam Bedau, *Prisoners Released from Death Rows since 1970 Because of Doubts About Their Guilt*, COOLEY L. REV. 13 (1996): 907–66. Since the late 1990s, the list has been maintained and updated by the Death Penalty Information Center.

17. *Death Penalty*, GALLUP, INC., accessed July 15, 2016, http://www.gallup.com/poll/1606/death-penalty.aspx. Additional information on public support for the death penalty in recent years will be presented in the next chapter.

18. Jones, *Two in Three Favor Death Penalty for Convicted Murderers: Public Divided Over Death Penalty or Life Imprisonment as Better Punishment*, GALLUP NEWS SERVICE, June 1, 2006, available at http://www.gallup.com/poll/23167/two-three-favor-death-penalty-convicted-murderers.aspx.

cent).[19] This finding was echoed in a June 2015 Quinnipiac poll, which found 43 percent supported the death penalty and 48 percent supported life without parole.[20] In other words, politicians today who want to follow public opinion have a solid argument for scrapping the execution gurneys. By any measure, the death penalty does not receive the strong support that it did just two decades ago. And, with the exception of attitudes toward same-sex relationships and maybe recreational marijuana, it is difficult to name another issue that has seen such dramatic attitudinal shifts in America in the young twenty-first century.

Trends are only trends, and like the stockbrokers say, "past performance does not guarantee future results." Every student of the death penalty in America quickly learns that predicting the future is a precarious hobby.

In early 2015, Americans were presented with yet another opportunity to study and debate the death penalty. On the national scene, the most visible death penalty case involved Dzhokhar A. Tsarnaev, who stood accused of placing a bomb at the finish line of the 2013 Boston Marathon, killing four people, blowing the legs off sixteen others, and injuring 260 more.[21] Tsarnaev's guilt was never in question. Massachusetts itself abolished the death penalty in 1984,[22] so only with a federal prosecution could Tsarnaev end up on death row.

Not everyone was enthusiastic about seeing Tsarnaev put on death row. Tsarnaev was nineteen years old at the time of the offense and had no prior criminal record. The US attorney general who authorized his subordinates to seek death in the case was Eric H. Holder, Jr., an opponent of the death penalty. A September 2013 poll by the *Boston Globe* found that only 33 percent of the residents of Boston (one of the most liberal, Democratic, Catholic cities in the country) supported a death sentence in the case, with a very strong 57 percent of respondents favor-

---

19. Reid Wilson, *Support for the Death Penalty Still High, But Down*, WASH. POST (BLOG), June 5, 2014, http://www.washingtonpost.com/blogs/govbeat/wp/2014/06/05/support-for-death-penalty-still-high-but-down/.

20. *U.S. Voters Back Supreme Court Ok For Gay Marriage, Quinnipiac University National Poll Finds; Less Support For Death Penalty—Except For Terrorism*, QUINNIPIAC UNIVERSITY, June 1, 2015, http://www.quinnipiac.edu/news-and-events/quinnipiac-university-poll/national/release-detail?ReleaseID=2229.

21. Katharine Q. Seelye, *Boston is Eager to Begin Marathon Bombing Trial, and To End It*, N.Y. TIMES, Jan. 2, 2015, at A12.

22. Commonwealth v. Colon-Cruz, 470 N.E.2d 116 (1984).

ing life imprisonment without parole.[23] By the time that the trial began in March 2015, one poll found that support for the death penalty for Tsarnaev among Bostonians had dropped to 15 percent.[24] Even some of the victims' families spoke out against the death penalty.

Tsarnaev had a "dream team" of attorneys and investigators working on the case. Famed death penalty attorneys Judy Clarke and David Bruck took the lead, and Scharlette Holdman, arguably the very best defense investigator in death penalty cases in the modern era, assisted.[25] Sister Helen Prejean, who had befriended Tsarnaev after his arrest, was among the defense witnesses. Clearly, there was little chance that the jury's verdict would be overturned because of ineffective assistance of counsel.

To no one's surprise, on April 8, Tsarnaev was found guilty on all charges.[26] Soon thereafter, the parents of Martin Richard, the youngest victim in the case, published a letter on the front page of the *Boston Globe* asking the Justice Department to stop seeking the death penalty.[27] But then, in May 2015, with death penalty opponents excluded for cause from the Boston jury (as they are in all death penalty jurisdictions throughout the United States), a unanimous jury sentenced Tsarnaev to death.[28] In June he was transferred to the US Penitentiary in Florence, Colorado, to await the outcome of his appeals. In August the only juror to date who has spoken publicly about the case, Kevin Fagan, said he "probably" would have voted for life had he known that some of the

---

23. Brian MacQuarrie, *In Globe Poll, Most Favor Life Term for Dzhokhar Tsarnaev*, BOSTON GLOBE, Sept. 16, 2013, http://www.bostonglobe.com/metro/2013/09/15/most-boston-residents-favor-life-without-parole-for-tsarnaev-convicted-poll-shows/Ur6ivWIUiYCpEZLXBApHDL/story.html?event=event12.

24. Evan Allen, *Few Favor Death for Dzhokhar Tsarnaev, Poll Finds*, BOSTON GLOBE, Apr. 26, 2015.

25. Patrick Radden Keefe, *The Worst of the Worst*, NEW YORKER, Sept. 15, 2015, http://www.newyorker.com/magazine/2015/09/14/the-worst-of-the-worst.

26. Katharine Q. Seelye, *Boston Verdict Is a Conviction on All Counts*, N.Y. TIMES, April 9, 2015, at A1.

27. Katharine Q. Seelye, *Parents of Youngest Boston Victim Oppose Death Penalty for Bomber*, N.Y. TIMES, Apr. 18, 2015, at A11.

28. Katharine Q. Seelye, Abby Goodnough, & Jess Bidgood, *Death Sentence for Boston Bomber, Dzhokhar Tsarnaev, Unsettles City He Tore Apart*, N.Y. TIMES, May 17, 2015, at A1.

victims' families wanted a life sentence.[29] Clearly, the case has a long way to go before its final outcome is determined.

COLORADO: THE ELECTION AND RE-ELECTION OF GOV. JOHN HICKENLOOPER

It was in this context of declining support for the death penalty around the world in the early twenty-first century that on January 11, 2011, John Hickenlooper was sworn in as Colorado's forty-second governor. As discussed in the previous chapter, he took office at a time when homicide rates in both the nation and the state were on the decline.[30] No doubt this falling homicide rate was one factor that contributed to a decline in calls to ramp up the execution machinery.

A Pennsylvania native, Hickenlooper attended Wesleyan University in Connecticut, eventually graduating with a master's degree in geology in 1980. He then worked in the Colorado oil and gas industry for several years before starting a successful brewpub in Denver in 1988. In 2003 he was elected Denver's mayor and held that post until taking over as governor.

When he arrived at the Capitol, three men sat on Colorado's death row: Nathan Dunlap, sentenced to death for four 1993 murders, and codefendants Sir Mario Owens and Robert Ray, convicted (in separate trials) of a 2005 double murder. All were tried and sentenced to death in the Eighteenth Judicial District (by population, the largest judicial district in the state), which covers Arapahoe, Douglas, Elbert, and Lincoln Counties. All went to Overland High School in Aurora and all are African American.

Upon taking office, no one predicted that the death penalty in Colorado would consume so much of Hickenlooper's mental and political energy during his first term in office. Still, the number of people on Colorado's death row did not change during Hickenlooper's first term—after those four years ended, the state ended up with no additions or removals from its death row cells.

---

29. Associated Press, *Boston Marathon Trial Juror Addresses Death Penalty Decision*, N.Y. TIMES, Aug. 25, 2015.

30. *Colorado Crime Rates 1960–2014*, http://www.disastercenter.com/crime/cocrime.htm.

Renewed Abolition Efforts in 2013

No serious efforts were made to abolish the death penalty during Hickenlooper's first two years in office, but that changed in 2013. The near-victory of the abolitionists in 2009 had attracted national interest, and private foundations—led by the Atlantic Philanthropies in New York City[31]—contributed funding for buttressing Colorado's abolition efforts. While some in Colorado were eager to push for a bill to scrap the death penalty, others had two major concerns: (1) winning Hickenlooper's support (at the time, he was poised to run for reelection in 2014) and (2) dealing with state representative Rhonda Fields, a strong and articulate supporter of the death penalty whose son was murdered by two of the three men on Colorado's death row. The latter concern was especially important, since in 2013, Fields threatened to introduce a bill that would put the question of abolition to a popular vote. To do so, the bill would have needed support from two-thirds of the members of both legislative chambers.[32] But if it was on the ballot, either by action of the legislature or through gathering voters' signatures, it would be an initiative that abolitionists would likely lose and thereby impede their efforts for years to come.[33] Thus, abolition promised little gain (given the small size of Colorado's death row and the hopes for gubernatorial commutations or reprieves) but posed much risk. Some Colorado abolitionists felt pulled in both directions. Still, the effort to abolish the death penalty in 2013 went forward.

While it is sometimes difficult to separate what politicians say they think from what they *really* think, Hickenlooper eventually made the

---

31. *See Atlantic Philanthropies*, http://www.atlanticphilanthropies.org/. Atlantic Philanthropies was formed by Chuck Feeney, who made his fortune running duty-free shops. His remarkable story is found in CONER O'CLERY, THE BILLIONAIRE WHO WASN'T: HOW CHUCK FEENEY MADE AND GAVE AWAY A FORTUNE (2007).

32. *See Laws Governing the Initiative Process in Colorado*, BALLOTPEDIA, accessed July 15, 2016, http://ballotpedia.org/Laws_governing_the_initiative_process_in_Colorado. If passed, the legislation authorizing the initiative would not need the governor's approval.

33. Arizona abolished the death penalty by referendum in 1914, and Oregon did likewise in 1916. STUART BANNER, THE DEATH PENALTY 222. In 1964 Oregon did so again. Hugo Adam Bedau, *Capital Punishment in Oregon, 1903–1964*, OREGON L. REV. 45 (1965): 1, 2; Hugo Adam Bedau, *The 1964 Death Penalty Referendum in Oregon: Some Notes from a Participant-Observer*, CRIME AND DELINQUENCY 26 (1980): 528–36.

referendum bill superfluous, thereby avoiding the possibilities of both a ballot initiative and the potential backlash of the voters in the 2014 election. At a luncheon with House members on March 19, 2013, the governor took the wind out of the abolition sails by indicating that if the bill passed and got to his desk, he might veto it.[34] Within a week, the House Judiciary Committee killed the abolition bill on a 6–4 vote. Rep. Claire Levy, who with Rep. Jovan Melton had sponsored the measure, stated, "I think had the governor not signaled so strongly he wouldn't sign the bill, I think we would have had those votes."[35]

While some abolitionists were disappointed with the news, others believed that Hickenlooper's failure to support the bill saved the day—at least in the long run—for death penalty opponents. Hickenlooper's concerns resulted in Fields quickly dropping her effort to put the measure on the 2014 ballot.[36] Had she not withdrawn the bill, some legislators who otherwise may have supported repeal would likely have taken cover behind the ballot initiative, saying something like "I support abolition but I think the voters should decide." Still, it is unlikely that a referendum bill ever would have gotten the requisite two-thirds vote in both the House and the Senate needed to put it on the ballot.[37]

What would happen if the question of death penalty abolition were left to voters? Some opinion polls suggest there was a chance that voters would reject capital punishment in favor of LWOP, although most observers saw this chance as slim.[38] Voters unfamiliar with traditional criticisms of the death penalty—its cost, arbitrariness, and the inevitability of sending innocent people to death row, for example—may "vote their gut" and enthusiastically choose to retain the gurney. Undoubtedly, voters would be pummeled by commercials featuring police officers, dis-

---

34. Kurtis Lee & Lynn Bartels, *Governor Hints at a Veto*, DENVER POST, Mar. 21, 2013, at 4A.

35. Kurtis Lee & Lynn Bartels, *Sponsor Blames Governor's Remarks*, DENVER POST, Mar. 27, 2013, at 10A.

36. Fields's legislation was House Bill 1270. Lynn Bartels, *Rep. Fields Kills Her Own Death-Penalty Bill*, DENVER POST, Mar. 28, 2013, at 6A.

37. The governor cannot veto any measure initiated or referred to the people. *See* Colorado Constitution, article 5, section 1 (4).

38. A June 2014 ABC/Washington Post poll found that only 42 percent of Americans supported the death penalty and 52 percent supported life imprisonment without parole. Wilson, *Support for Death Penalty Still High, But Down.*

trict attorneys, and crime victims expressing their heartfelt support for the executioner. Where would the money come from to mount a campaign that could successfully neutralize or counter those messages? Even in California, with the country's largest death row and an execution gurney that had only been used a dozen times since 1972, voters in 2012 rejected an effort to wipe its death penalty statute off the books. The vote was close—only 52 percent of the voters favored retention[39]—but those favoring abolition spent over $7 million in the losing effort. Ballot initiatives are not cheap.

What if the death penalty had been abolished and the legislature did not vote to put the question on the ballot? It is likely that the question would still not have gone away. Death penalty supporters would no doubt push for a citizen-initiated ballot initiative, and if that vote was held shortly after a well-publicized heinous murder or murders (as in 1966), a measure reinstating the death penalty could easily garner enough signatures to end up on the ballot. Getting initiatives on the ballot in Colorado is relatively inexpensive and easy: "To be placed on the ballot, a proposal must receive five percent of the total votes cast for all candidates for the Office of Secretary of State at the previous general election."[40] To achieve that number, in 2015 only 98,492 valid signatures were needed, which, one would think, could be obtained relatively quickly at a few Broncos and/or Air Force Academy football games.

Instead of focusing on formal abolition, which would be a fragile victory given the opportunities for voters to reinstate it with a ballot initiative, some Colorado abolitionists favored an alternative strategy that would prioritize efforts to continue to stop executions. With only three men on death row, commuting their sentences by executive power would give Colorado at least twenty years before the next prisoner—whoever that may be—was facing imminent execution. Even a full commutation

39. *California Proposition 34, the End the Death Penalty Initiative (2012)*, BALLOTPEDIA, accessed July 15, 2016, http://ballotpedia.org/California_Proposition_34,_the_End_the_Death_Penalty_Initiative_%282012%29.

40. *See Placing an Initiated Proposal on the Statewide Ballot*, COLORADO LEGISLATIVE COUNCIL, accessed July 15, 2016, https://www.colorado.gov/pacific/cga-legislativecouncil/how-file and *Signature Requirement for Statewide Initiative Petitions*, COLORADO SECRETARY OF STATE, Dec. 5, 2014, http://www.sos.state.co.us/pubs/elections/Initiatives/signatureRequirements.html.

for only one condemned inmate—Nathan Dunlap—would mean that Hickenlooper's successor, who takes office in early 2019, would not have the chance to preside over any executions, since the appeals for Ray and Owens are still many years from resolution. If current trends continue, those years could very well see the continued evolution of a political climate (nationally and statewide) where abolition may actually stick. But predicting future abolitionist strategy, both in the near and far term, is impossible because of so many political unknowns.[41]

Nathan Dunlap's "Temporary Reprieve"

In 2013 Governor Hickenlooper exercised executive branch leadership—or foolishness, in the minds of his critics—when he blocked the execution of Dunlap, Colorado's longest-serving death row inmate. In December 1993, Dunlap (nineteen at the time of the crimes) killed four employees (including three teenagers) and seriously wounded a fifth in an after-hours robbery at a Chuck E. Cheese's restaurant in Aurora.[42] Dunlap had been fired from his employment at the restaurant some five months earlier. In 1996, after the trial was moved to Colorado Springs, he was convicted and sentenced to death. His appeals were unsuccessful and once they were exhausted, his execution date was set for the week of August 18, 2013.

Unlike some other states, where commuting a death sentence to a prison term requires approval from a State Board of Pardons or a similar entity, in Colorado, the governor alone has the power to make the final life-and-death decisions. Two defense attorneys, Phil Cherner from Denver and Madeline Cohen from the federal public defender's office in Denver oversaw the preparation of a petition for executive clemency and submitted it to Governor Hickenlooper on May 6. They presented evidence on several issues, such as documentation of Dunlap's long-standing mental problems that were not properly diagnosed and treated until he went to prison, his remorse and satisfactory adjustment

41. It is also likely that abolitionist strategies in Colorado will be influenced by what happens in Nebraska. As will be discussed in the next chapter, in 2015 the death penalty was abolished in that state, but enough signatures were quickly gathered to put the issue before the voters in November 2016.

42. *See* appendix 3, case no. 16.

to prison after his mental conditions were treated, and information about other Colorado murder cases that were just as heinous in which the defendants were not facing the death penalty. The request for executive clemency did not at all suggest that Dunlap should ever be released from prison; this was a request to allow him to serve a sentence of life imprisonment without parole.

The governor also met with the prosecutors in the case, the families of the victims, ministers, law enforcement officials, and numerous others who had an opinion in the case. It was clear that whatever he decided, a lot of people would be disappointed.

On May 22, 2013, Hickenlooper surprised all observers by announcing that he had decided neither to grant a commutation nor to allow the execution to move forward. Instead, he granted a temporary reprieve, which meant that Dunlap would not be executed until the governor either changed his mind (by commutation or simply removing the temporary reprieve) or left office.[43]

While death penalty opponents obviously would have preferred a commutation, they were pleased to hear that the execution was no longer imminent. On the other hand, some supporters of the death penalty were outraged. This reaction was led by the district attorney for the Eighteenth Judicial District, George Brauchler, whose office (under prior district attorneys) had prosecuted the cases of all three men on death row and who was handling the (then) pending prosecutions of Edward Montour and James Holmes. Both of these cases will be discussed below, as will Brauchler's reaction to the reprieve.

A month after the reprieve was announced, a statewide poll taken by Quinnipiac University found that 69 percent of Coloradans supported the death penalty and 67 percent disagreed with the decision to grant the reprieve.[44] Coloradans were not asked if they would still support the death penalty given the option of life imprisonment without parole, so this and similar polls overstate death penalty support. And while measures of public opinion that so closely follow a front-page story on the

---

43. *See* Executive Order D 2013-006 (May 22, 2013), accessed July 15, 2016, https://www.colorado.gov/governor/2013-executive-orders.

44. Kurtis Lee, *Poll: Coloradans Say Death Penalty a Key Governor Issue*, DENVER POST, June 14, 2013, at 6A; editorial, *What Poll Means for Death Penalty*, DENVER POST, June 14, 2013, at 28A.

relevant topic are unreliable,[45] it was clear at the time that Dunlap's reprieve could become an issue in the 2014 election.

Edward Montour: Yet Another Setback for Prosecutors

The case of Edward Montour provides a telling example of just how bizarre modern death penalty cases have become. In 1997 Montour was arrested for the murder of his three-month-old daughter in Colorado Springs. Despite his claim that he had accidentally dropped the baby, jurors believed that Montour had beaten the child to death. He was convicted of first-degree murder and, in August 1998, given a mandatory sentence of life imprisonment without parole.

Then, in October 2002, while working in the kitchen at the state's maximum security prison in Limon, Montour killed a prison guard, Eric Autobee.[46] Officer Autobee was the first corrections officer killed in a Colorado prison since the 1929 prison riot in Cañon City discussed in chapter 3. And his murder occurred just seventeen days after the sentencing authority in Colorado capital cases was returned to juries.

However, the newly restored juries had nothing to do with the case: Montour waived his right to a jury trial and pled guilty, thereby putting his fate in the hands of a single trial judge. He acted as his own attorney, called no witnesses, and presented no evidence or testimony in his defense. To the surprise of no one, just four months after the murder, he became the first person sentenced to death in Colorado since the demise of the three-judge panels.

Among those welcoming the death sentence were Colorado governor Bill Owens and Delores (Lola) Autobee, Eric's mother, who told the

---

45. For example, a February 2015 national poll found that only 55 percent of Americans supported the death penalty for James Holmes, then pending trial for the 2012 murders of twelve people in an Aurora movie theater. This was down 11 points from responses to a similar question posed shortly after the murders. *See Most Still Favor Death Sentence for Colorado Theater Shooter*, RASMUSSEN REPORTS, Feb. 5, 2015, http://www.rasmussenreports.com/public_content/lifestyle/general_lifestyle/february_2015/most_still_favor_death_sentence_for_colorado_theater_shooter.

46. The murder weapon was an industrial soup ladle. Michael BeDan & Charley Able, *Limon Prison Kitchen Boss Slain*, ROCKY MTN. NEWS, Oct. 19, 2002, at 3A; Kieran Nicholson, *Inmate Kills Corrections Worker, State Says Officer is 1st Killed by Prisoner Since '29*, DENVER POST, Oct. 20, 2002, at B1.

Denver Post that "the right decision was made."[47] Eric's father, Bob—a former prison guard—told the *Rocky Mountain News*, "Justice will not be served until that man's heart stops beating. He laughed through the whole [trial]. He makes Charles Manson look like an altar boy."[48] The parents' opinions, as we shall see, were soon to change.

After four years of litigation, the Colorado Supreme Court vacated the death sentence, finding that even in cases where the defendant pleads guilty, she or he retains the right to have a jury determine the sentence.[49] During this period, Montour's lead defense attorney, Denver-based Judy Lucero, worked tirelessly to help him recognize that his life was worth living and who, in the end, stands as the unsung hero (for Montour) in the case. After the death sentence was vacated, six more years of fighting ensued. By then, Montour's defense had been taken over by David Lane, a gifted defense attorney whose take-no-enemies style left many foes with trembling knees. Finally, in April 2013, the trial court allowed Montour to withdraw his guilty plea, the conviction was vacated, and he case went back to square one.[50]

The fight was far from over. George Brauchler, the district attorney for the region that included Limon, rejected the offer (first made to Brauchler's predecessor in 2007) for Montour to plead guilty in exchange for a life sentence and moved quickly to schedule a new trial. But the second trial would be very different from the initial proceeding that sent Montour to death row in 2003. Montour was now fighting, and he had an outstanding legal team led by David Lane to help him out. And not only had Montour changed, so had the parents of the victim. Bob and Lola Autobee had completely switched their positions on the death penalty and began to do everything in their power to make sure that Montour would not be sentenced to death for the murder of their son.[51]

---

47. Howard Pankratz, *Prison Slaying Brings Death Sentence: Convict Faces Execution for Murder of Worker*, DENVER POST, Feb. 28, 2003, at B1.

48. Mike Patty, *Inmate Gets Death for Murder; Man Was in Prison for Slaying Daughter before Killing Officer*, ROCKY MTN. NEWS, Feb. 28, 2003, at 5A.

49. People v. Montour, 157 P.3d 489 (2007).

50. Karen Augé, *Prison-Killing Case Goes Back to Court,* DENVER POST, Apr. 10, 2013, at 5A.

51. Bob Autobee, *A Terrible Burden to Victims' Families*, PUEBLO CHIEFTAIN, Feb. 10, 2013. In 2015 Autobee received the Abolitionist of the Year Award from Coloradans for Alternatives to the Death Penalty.

By the time that jury selection began in early 2014, the defense team announced that it would introduce evidence that would challenge Montour's prior conviction for killing his daughter, which had been used as an aggravating circumstance to justify the initial death sentence. In addition, Montour's attorney also announced that he would plead not guilty by reason of insanity for the Autobee murder. Against that backdrop, as 2014 began, some 2,100 potential jurors were summoned for jury service. After two months of formal jury selection, a final panel of twelve jurors and six alternates was selected. Bob Autobee regularly traveled to the courthouse, moving up and down the line where potential jurors were queuing, carrying a picture of his son and a large sign asking them to spare Montour's life.[52] This trial was clearly going to be a judicial version of a heavyweight boxing match.

And then, two days after opening statements began, the case came to an abrupt end. For whatever reason, Brauchler saw the writing on the wall and decided to accept the deal that Montour had been asking for since 2007: a life sentence in exchange for a guilty plea.[53]

Now it was up to Montour to make the final decision. Lane told him that there was a chance that the 1998 conviction for killing his daughter could be vacated, and a chance that he would indeed be found not guilty by reason of insanity for the Autobee murder. That meant that there was a chance that someday he would be released and would again be free. But according to Lane, in large part because Montour did not want to put the Autobee family through the pain of further litigation, he took the deal and was promptly given a sentence of LWOP. After eleven-and-a-half years of litigation, most of it avoidable, the case was over.[54]

---

52. He was joined by Tim Ricard, whose wife was murdered by an inmate at Arkansas Valley Correctional Institution in Ordway in 2012. As will be discussed in the next chapter, in December 2015, the state announced that despite the wishes of the Ricard family, it would seek the death penalty against the suspect, Miguel Alonso Contreras-Perez.

53. The plea offer came in a telephone call to defense attorneys on the evening of the very first day of the trial. On day two, the jury was sent home and the plea was entered. And on day three, the jurors returned, were informed of what had happened, and were discharged.

54. Jordan Steffen, *Emotional End: No Death Penalty*, DENVER POST, Mar. 7, 2014, at 4.

Interestingly, from all indications, Brauchler did not suffer any political backlash for spending so much money and time—that of his own staff, the defense team, the court personnel, the jail staff, and the prospective and chosen jurors—in the aborted pursuit of a death penalty in the case. In fact, it is likely that in certain circles, he received political benefits from doing all he could to send Montour back to death row. As we shall see, Brauchler was certainly not deterred by his experience with Montour from vigorously pursuing a death sentence in 2015 against James Holmes.

The Death Penalty in the 2014 Gubernatorial Election

After Governor Hickenlooper announced the temporary reprieve for Nathan Dunlap in May 2013, reactions across the state fell along a long continuum. Some thought he made the right call, others wanted to see Dunlap executed immediately, and still others criticized the governor for not commuting the sentence to life imprisonment without parole. Brauchler led the criticism, sparking the backlash within minutes of Hickenlooper's announcement. Standing on the steps of the State Capitol in Denver, Brauchler said the execution of Dunlap should be a "no-brainer."[55] He attacked Hickenlooper for what he called his "refusal to make any hard decision today," adding, "This is inaction. This is shrugging. This is not justice." Republican attorney general John Suthers agreed: "The governor, by refusing to make any hard decisions today—whether in carrying out Dunlap's sentence or conclusively granting clemency—has only guaranteed suffering and delayed justice for the victims' loved ones for years to come."[56] Bob Crowell, whose daughter was one of Dunlap's victims, was similarly angered. "We have a chicken governor, making us a chicken state, inviting all would-be murderers to come to Colorado." On the other hand, Jodie McNally-Damore, whose daughter, Colleen O'Connor, was also killed by Dunlap, said, "I would

---

55. Karen Augé & Lynn Bartels, *Governor Gives Killer "Temporary Reprieve,"* DENVER POST, May 23, 2013, at 1A.

56. *Id.*

not want to be in [Hickenlooper's] shoes for anything in the world. What an incredible decision he has to make."[57]

Within a few days, former US congressman Tom Tancredo, famous for his anti-immigration platform when he ran for the Republican presidential nomination in 2008, threw his hat into the race for governor. "This Dunlap thing is the last straw," said Tancredo in a message to the *Denver Post*.[58] Nonetheless, in June 2014, Tancredo was defeated by a large margin in the Republican primary for governor by former Congressman Bob Beauprez.

Despite facing reelection in 2014, Hickenlooper did not back down or try to sidestep his decision. Consequentially, Republicans tried to make the temporary reprieve and Hickenlooper's stand on the death penalty an issue. In May 2014, speaking to an audience at Colorado Christian University, Republican gubernatorial candidate Beauprez made it clear that "[w]hen I'm governor, Nathan Dunlap will be executed." The remark was met with loud applause. But in August—just three months before the election—instead of backing down, Hickenlooper announced that by then he had become a firm opponent of the death penalty.[59] A week later, Hickenlooper told CNN that he might consider commuting Dunlap's sentence to life imprisonment before leaving office.[60] Beauprez quickly responded:

> John Hickenlooper's "temporary reprieve" for Nathan Dunlap is one of [the] clearest examples of his indecision and weak leadership . . . It's outrageous that now John Hickenlooper is threatening to give a convicted mass-murderer full clemency if people vote against him.

---

57. *What They Are Saying*, DENVER POST, May 23, 2013, at 7A.

58. Kurtis Lee, *Tom Tancredo Formally Announces Run for Governor Thursday on Conservative Radio*, DENVER POST (BLOG), May 22, 2013, http://blogs.denverpost.com/thespot/2013/05/22/tom-tancredo-says-he-will-formally-announce-run-for-governor-thursday-on-conservative-talk-radio/96737/.

59. Joey Bunch, *John Hickenlooper Opposes Death Penalty, But Nathan Dunlap Could Still Die*, DENVER POST (BLOG), Aug. 18, 2014, http://blogs.denverpost.com/thespot/2014/08/18/john-hickenlooper-now-opposes-death-penalty-killer-nathan-dunlap-still-die/111535/.

60. Jesse Paul, *Gov. Suggests Killer Could Get Full Reprieve*, DENVER POST, Aug. 26, 2014, at 1A; *Show on Dunlap Stirs Death Penalty Debate*, DENVER POST, Sept. 8, 2014, at 4A.

> There are plenty of good moral arguments for and against the death penalty, but the law in Colorado is very, very clear. Nathan Dunlap has gone through twenty years exhausting every option available to him under Colorado law. His execution date was set. John Hickenlooper took an oath to enforce the laws of the state of Colorado, but when it was up to him to simply make the decision, he said "I can't decide, so I'll just leave it to the next guy.
>
> That day justice was stolen from the families of the victims of that convicted murderer. On my watch, justice will be carried out, the laws of the state of Colorado will be enforced, and I will never turn my back on the victims.[61]

This quote, of course, misses the point that the Colorado Constitution[62] also charges the governor with considering executive clemency in capital cases and commuting the sentence if he or she deems it appropriate. This is a crucial point. In Colorado, a trial jury's decision to impose a death sentence is basically a *recommendation* to the governor—who has absolute power to take it or leave it.

Despite this political rhetoric, in September 2014, the *Denver Post*'s editorial board published an editorial that strongly condemned the death penalty, concluding, "The death penalty may be a winner politically, but it's a loser in terms of fair and reasonable public policy."[63] The next day, a Rasmussen Poll showed Beauprez with a one-point lead in the race.[64] A *Denver Post* poll released on September 11 found that 18 percent of Colorado voters found the death penalty to be a major issue in the gubernatorial race.[65] Respondents supporting the death penalty numbered 63 percent, with 28 percent opposed and 10 percent undecided. The poll did not measure support for the death penalty given the alternative of life without parole.

---

61. Eli Stokols, *Beauprez Hits Hickenlooper on Dunlap Decision after Clemency Comment*, KDVR, Aug. 25, 2014, http://kdvr.com/2014/08/25/beauprez-hits-hickenlooper-on-dunlap-decision-after-clemency-comment/.

62. Colorado Constitution, article 4, section 7.

63. Editorial, *The Enemy of Speedy Justice*, DENVER POST, Sept. 7, 2014, at D3.

64. Joey Bunch, *Rasmussen Poll Gives Bob Beauprez First Lead in Governor's Race*, DENVER POST (BLOG), Sept. 8, 2014, http://www.denverpost.com/News/ci_26493885/Rasmussen-poll-gives-Bob-Beauprez-first-lead-in-governors-race.

65. Jon Murray, *Voters Run a Tight Race*, DENVER POST, Sept. 12, 2014, at A1.

Beauprez continued to voice his support for the death penalty as the election approached. Critics pointed out that Beauprez was Catholic and that the Catholic Church stood in opposition to the death penalty. But none of the Catholic bishops publicly challenged Beauprez for his comments. Beauprez claimed that the former archbishop of Denver—conservative cleric Charles Chaput—had told him that while he personally opposed executions, it was permissible for Catholic politicians to support the death penalty since the issue was not as important as opposing abortion, gay marriage, or pornography.[66] Throughout the campaign, Beauprez's strong support for the death penalty was met (at least in public) by silence from Catholic Church officials. Their private conversations, if any, with Beauprez or with people in the governor's office about the Dunlap reprieve remain just that—private.

One more item further illustrates the prominence of the death penalty in the 2014 gubernatorial race. In October the Republican Governors Association ran a TV ad featuring the father of one of Dunlap's victims calling Hickenlooper a "coward" for halting the execution. The father then claimed that Hickenlooper would give "full clemency" to Dunlap and "set him free," even though if Hickenlooper commuted the sentence, Dunlap would still spend the rest of his life in prison. Beauprez apparently had nothing to do with the ad, but the editorial board of the *Denver Post* said that calling it a "whopper" would be too kind—"more like a malicious falsehood."[67] The reality is that only a formal pardon or commutation to a non-life sentence could free Dunlap, and a pardon or commutation to non-life was never on the table (or even contemplated) for him.

On election night, Hickenlooper prevailed by a 49–46 percent margin. While his internal polling remains confidential, it looks like Hickenlooper may have lost some votes because of his decision on Dunlap or his limited efforts to explain or defend it, making the race closer than most would have predicted just a few months earlier. If so, had he not poured

---

66. William Saletan, *Archbishop, Confess! Does Archbishop Charles Chaput Give Catholic Republicans Wiggle Room on the Death Penalty?*, SLATE.COM, Oct. 14, 2014, http://www.slate.com/articles/news_and_politics/politics/2014/10/archbishop_charles_chaput_bob_beauprez_and_the_death_penalty_does_the_archbishop.html.

67. Editorial, *Dunlap Attack Ad Abandons Reality*, DENVER POST, Oct. 29, 2014, at 23A.

cold water on the abolition bill in 2013, it is plausible that he (and an unknowable number of Democratic legislators) would have lost in 2014.

Former Denver district attorney and Colorado governor Bill Ritter, Jr., posed what may be the best death penalty question that Colorado voters could now ponder. In an interview on a CNN program called *Death Row Stories* in September 2014, Ritter asked, "Is executing someone 20 years later really the kind of retribution that is making us a better society?"[68]

THE 2015 DEATH PENALTY CASES

As 2015 began, four defendants in three separate cases were being threatened with the death penalty in Colorado. By year's end, all four had ended without any new death sentences.

1–2. BRANDON LEE JOHNSON AND CHRISTINA RIEB. The first case, with two defendants, ended with plea bargains, with both defendants sentenced to long prison terms. It was unusual on proportionality grounds: although the crime was horrendous, dozens of defendants with more serious records of criminal convictions have been convicted of more heinous murders in recent decades in Colorado without facing the death penalty. However, in September 2014, prosecutors in Sterling 125 miles northeast of Denver, announced that they would seek the death penalty against Brendan Lee Johnson (nineteen at the time of the crime) and his then-girlfriend, Cassandra Ann Rieb (eighteen at the time of the crime), for the gruesome murders of Johnson's seventy-year-old grandparents, Charles and Shirley Severance. The alleged motive, striking for its stupidity, was that Johnson and Rieb wanted to inherit the victims' house and money.[69] Johnson's mother, Jill, was both the daughter of the victims and the mother of the defendant, and she very strongly opposed the death penalty in the case.[70]

In an ending that virtually all observers expected, in March the death penalty was dropped against Johnson after he agreed to plead guilty

68. Nathan Dunlap, *Death Row Stories*, CNN.COM, Sept. 7, 2014, http://transcripts.cnn.com/TRANSCRIPTS/1409/07/drow.02.html.

69. *Death Penalty Sought*, DENVER POST, Sept. 6, 2014, at 4A.

70. Michael Roberts, *Mom Tries to Save Son from Death Penalty Even Though He Killed Her Parents*, WESTWORD, Feb. 18, 2015.

to first-degree murder for the death of Shirley Severance.[71] In May the threat of a death sentence for Rieb was removed after she was permitted to plead guilty to second-degree murder and first-degree assault in exchange for an eighty-year prison term.[72]

3. JAMES EAGAN HOLMES. By any measure, the biggest death penalty case of recent decades in Colorado was that of James Eagan Holmes. On July 20, 2012, the twenty-four-year-old entered the Century Aurora 16 theater (just eleven miles east of the Colorado Capitol in Denver), killed twelve people, and injured seventy others. Aurora is in Arapahoe County, in the heart of Colorado's Eighteenth Judicial District, where almost all of the recent death penalty cases in the state originated. As mentioned above, all three inmates on Colorado's death row in 2015 were from Arapahoe County, and their district attorney, George Brauchler, is a strong supporter of the death penalty. His predecessor, Carol Chambers, had authorized several death penalty prosecutions in her years in office, from 2005 to 2013. People may disagree with Brauchler's pro–death penalty stand, but no one doubts that he is an extremely talented litigator.

With his steadfast effort to put Edward Montour back on death row, his outspoken criticism of Governor Hickenlooper for the temporary reprieve of Nathan Dunlap, and his dogged efforts in 2015 to obtain a death sentence for James Holmes, Brauchler (age forty-five in 2015) was by any measure the leading proponent of the death penalty in Colorado at the time of Holmes's trial. As the trial drew near, it was widely speculated that he hoped to eventually run for the US Senate or the Colorado governor's office, and no one underestimated his political skills.[73] Whether or not his pursuits of the death penalty were successful in the courtrooms, the prosecutions were a sure way to keep his name in the headlines. In some circles, the amount of money that would be

---

71. Sara Waite, *Brendan Johnson Pleads Guilty to Grandmother's Murder; Will Get Life*, STERLING JOURNAL-ADVOCATE, Mar. 12, 2015.

72. Sara Waite, *Updated: Rieb to Serve 80 Years in Severance Murder Case*, STERLING JOURNAL-ADVOCATE, May 1, 2015.

73. Sadie Gurman & Nicholas Riccardi, *Political Questions Swirl Around Theater Shooting Prosecutor*, DURANGO HERALD, Jan. 18, 2015, http://durangoherald.com/article/20150118/NEWS02/150119547/Political-questions-swirl-around-theater-shooting-prosecutor-.

expended on the Holmes case in order to seek death was nothing less than an indirect contribution to Brauchler's future political campaigns. No survey data is available, but already, in the three years after he took office in early 2013, no other prosecutor in Colorado could match his name recognition.

In March 2013, Holmes, through his attorneys—public defenders Daniel King, Tamara Brady, and Kristen Nelson—offered to plead guilty in exchange for consecutive sentences of life imprisonment.[74] Prosecutors rejected that deal, and four days later, Brauchler announced that his office would seek the death penalty.[75] Three months later, Holmes formally entered a plea of not guilty by reason of insanity.

Holmes was born and raised in San Diego. His father, a mathematician, has degrees from Stanford University, UCLA, and the University of California, Berkeley. His mother is a registered nurse. He has one sister and no record of prior criminal convictions. Holmes graduated from the University of California, Riverside, in the upper 1 percent of his class, with a degree in neuroscience, the highest honors, membership in Phi Beta Kappa, and a GPA of 3.95. Like Ted Kaczynski, the so-called Unabomber, who was sentenced to life in prison in 1998 for sending bombs through the mail that killed three people and injured two dozen others, there was no question that Holmes was exceptionally smart. He was an atypical death penalty defendant in terms of class, race, and intelligence, but (arguably) not especially atypical in his mental status.

In 2011, Holmes entered the PhD program in neuroscience at the University of Colorado Anschutz Medical Campus in Aurora. There his psychological condition deteriorated. He struggled, and in spring 2012,

74. For their perspective on the case, *see* Kristen Nelson, Tamara Brady & Daniel King, *The 'Evil' Defendant and the 'Holdout' Juror: Unpacking the Myths of the Aurora Theater Shooting Case As We Ponder the Future of Capital Punishment in Colorado*, DENVER L. REV. 93 (2016): 595–633.

75. Apparently, the majority of the families of the victims were opposed to the decision to go through a trial and seek the death penalty. On August 10, 2015, Brauchler spoke on Colorado Public Radio's Colorado Matters and disclosed that a "significant number" of victims did not want the death penalty sought. In fact, he said that "greater than a majority were in favor of ending the case with a plea." Michael De Yoanna, *Theater Trial Prosecutor Would "Seriously Consider" Pursuing Death Penalty Again*, COLO. PUBLIC RADIO, Aug. 10, 2015, https://www.cpr.org/news/story/theater-trial-prosecutor-would-seriously-consider-pursuing-death-penalty-again.

he did poorly on his comprehensive exams and began the process of withdrawing from school. At the time he was seeing multiple mental health professionals through the university's health center. Indeed, a month before the shootings, one of the psychiatrists who had seen him, Dr. Lynne Fenton, alerted campus police that he might be dangerous. Nonetheless, in the two months before the shooting, Holmes passed background checks and was permitted to purchase several guns, a semi-automatic rifle, and somewhere in the neighborhood of six thousand rounds of ammunition from local gun dealers.

In August 2013, after formal charges were filed, Holmes was transferred to the Colorado Mental Health Institute in Pueblo, where he stayed for about a month. The examination was conducted by University of Colorado forensic psychiatrist Jeffrey Metzner, who was appointed by the court to conduct a sanity exam. His report found Holmes competent to stand trial and sane at the time of the crimes but with "schizoaffective disorder," which is a severe mental illness. Soon after this report was delivered, prosecutor Karen Pearson, apparently disagreeing with the conclusion that Holmes was mentally ill, charged that Metzner was biased.[76] According to news reports, Metzner refused to meet with prosecutors to discuss the report, although he did meet with defense attorneys on three occasions.[77] As a result, the judge in the case, Carlos Samour, ordered a second psychiatrist to evaluate Holmes. That moved the trial date back to October 2014, and when the psychiatrist and defense attorneys asked for more time, the trial was postponed to December 8 and then to January 20, 2015.

One short vignette will give some insight into the intensity of the feelings on both sides of the fight. In December 2014, defense attorneys asked for another delay, citing medical emergencies suffered by an attorney and an investigator. This request was blasted by *Denver Post* columnist Rick Tosches, who basically charged that the medical emergencies were fake.[78] A week later, the investigator in the case, John Gonglach,

---

76. John Ingold, *Mental Exam Contested: Prosecutors Accuse Psychiatrist of an "Unfair Bias" in Evaluation of Holmes*, DENVER POST, Dec. 27, 2013, at A4.

77. John Ingold, *James Holmes Insanity Case Shapes Up as a Battle of Mental Health Experts* DENVER POST, Feb. 24, 2014, at A1.

78. Rich Tosches, *Giving Lawyers a Worse Name*, DENVER POST, Dec. 14, 2014, at 3D.

wrote to the *Post* to explain that his daughter, born November 6, had been diagnosed with cystic fibrosis ("a rare and deadly genetic disease").[79] On the same day, defense attorney Tamara Brady wrote to publicly explain that her father had died on December 5.[80]

And so, these emergencies were not fake. To his credit, Tosches devoted his December 30 column to an apology.[81] But the exchanges show just a tiny bit of the nastiness in the fight for the life of James Holmes. Even a letter from Holmes's parents pleading for the life of their son to be spared was met by numerous hateful reactions in the newspaper.[82]

Unpersuaded by the medical emergencies, in mid-December Judge Samour denied the request for a postponement, announced that he would deny any similar requests in the future, and scheduled jury selection to begin on January 20,[83] thirty months after the murders. As an indicator of how much the death penalty in Colorado has changed over the years, only 8 of the 103 men executed in Colorado's history have survived longer than thirty months after the date of the crime.[84]

Meanwhile, the costs for seeking the death penalty in the case were growing exponentially. In a story buried in the *Post* on a slow news day on the Saturday after Christmas, prosecutors announced that they

---

79. John K. Gonglach, *Holmes Investigator: Here's My Emergency*, Denver Post, Dec. 21, 2014, at 2D.

80. Tamara Brady, *Holmes Attorney: Writer Was Heartless*, Denver Post, Dec. 21, 2014, at 2D. Brady took the high road, ending her comments with this: "Mr. Tosches, in honor of my gentle and kind father, I hope you and your loved ones have a healthy and happy holiday season. Peace." For profiles of Brady and Brauchler, *see* John Ingold, *Theater Shooting Defense Attorney Tamara Brady Prepares for Case of a Lifetime*, Denver Post, Apr. 26, 2015, at A1; *Greeley's Tamara Brady Has Spent Her Career, and Much of Her Life, Defending against the Death Penalty, Including for James Holmes*, Greeley Trib., Oct. 25, 2015, at 1; John Ingold, *Theater Shooting Trial Could be Defining Case for DA George Brauchler*, Denver Post, Apr. 26, 2015, at A1; Robert Sanchez, *Life After Death: How District Attorney George Brauchler became Colorado's Most Visible Proponent of Capital Punishment*, 5280, December 2015.

81. Rich Tosches, *One I Wish I Had Back*, Denver Post, Dec. 28, 2014, at 3D.

82. John Ingold, *Holmes' Parents Say: "He is not a Monster"*, Denver Post, Dec. 19, 2014, at 11A. Holmes's mother later wrote a book about the guilt that she felt for not being able to predict the shootings. Arlene Holmes, When the Focus Shifts: The Prayer Book of Arlene Holmes (2015).

83. John Ingold, *Holmes Judge Won't Delay Trial*, Denver Post, Dec. 11, 2014, at A4.

84. See table 1.1, *infra*.

would not even present the testimony from two of their mental health experts at trial—neither of whom had personally examined Holmes—even though they had billed the state $300 and $400 per hour for their work. One had already billed the state $45,000.[85]

In February 2015, Yahoo News estimated (conservatively) that Colorado had already spent $5.5 million on the Holmes case, even though the Arapahoe County District Attorney's Office claimed that only one prosecutor had been assigned full time to the case.[86] Another estimate put the pretrial costs at $2.2 million—and that did not include defense costs.[87] In an effort to find twelve jurors and twelve alternates, 9,000 summonses were mailed to potential jurors just before Christmas, by far the most for any case in the history of the state.[88] The postage alone cost $3,500. By the end of the trial, three journalists gave a preliminary estimate that Colorado had spent $4.5 million for prosecution and defense costs, most of which would have been avoided had Holmes been permitted to enter a guilty plea.[89]

This is only part of the larger issue that promises to play a role in Colorado's future with the death penalty: voters may still support it—at least in theory—but with a growing recognition of its monumental fiscal costs, they may ultimately decide that this is a luxury we can do without. In the only detailed published study of the costs of the death

---

85. John Ingold, *Two Experts Won't Be Called*, DENVER POST, Dec. 27, 2014, at 2A. Later, the Arapahoe District Attorney's Office put estimates of their expenditures on the Internet. *See* http://www.da18.org/DAsOffice/Finance/ArapahoeCountyCase2012CR1522.aspx. The listed costs are confusing and almost certainly underestimated; they do not include the costs to law enforcement or court personnel. Colorado public defenders are prohibited by the Attorney Regulation Counsel, Colorado Supreme Court, from releasing any case-related information about their individual clients. Thus, what the public defenders spend on any given death penalty case is confidential.

86. Jason Sickles, *Cost of Colorado Theater Shooting Case Exceeds $5 Million Months before Opening Arguments*, YAHOO NEWS, Feb. 5, 2015, https://www.yahoo.com/news/cost-of-colorado-theater-shooting-exceeds-5-million-months-before-opening-arguments-185259025.html?ref=gs.

87. Dan Elliott, *Holmes Pre-Trial Bill Climbing*, DENVER POST, Apr. 2, 2015.

88. John Ingold, *Jury Summonses Mailed for Aurora Shooting Trial*, DENVER POST, Dec. 12, 2014, at A4.

89. Carol McKinley, Lo Snelgrove, & Peri Duncan, *Aurora Theater Shooting Case Cost Colorado $4.5 Million—and Counting*, WESTWORD, Dec. 23, 2015.

penalty in Colorado, Justin F. Marceau and Hollis A. Whitson found that cases in which the death penalty is sought require substantially more court days and take a much longer time to resolve than cases with similar facts in which the death penalty is not pursued.[90] Again, with these efforts resulting in only two executions in the past fifty years, there will undoubtedly be an ongoing conversation about whether any benefits of the death penalty over life without parole are worth the expense, especially given the low probability that the monies will result in eventual execution. Of course, others will continue to argue that even though the chances of ultimate execution are slim, the effort to execute those convicted of Colorado's most heinous murders is worth every cent.

Cost issues aside, jury selection began on schedule on January 20, 2015, and opening arguments were held on April 27. The trial lasted ten weeks. There was no question that Holmes—or "that guy," as Brauchler regularly referred to him—had committed the murders. The only question during the guilt phase of the trial was whether he was sane at the time of the crimes. At trial, two court-appointed psychiatrists said he was (although both agreed that he had a severe mental illness) and two defense psychiatrists said he was not. On July 16, after twelve hours of deliberation, the jury rejected the insanity defense and returned 165 guilty verdicts on charges related to the shootings.[91]

Thereafter, the jury went through the three stages of sentencing. They first found that aggravating factors existed. Next, they found, by a unanimous vote, that the mitigation did not outweigh the aggravation. But on the final vote—should James Holmes be sentenced to death—three jurors were unconvinced, with one saying that her opposition was so firm that she would not change her mind.[92] With a nonunanimous jury,

---

90. Justin F. Marceau & Hollis A. Whitson, *The Cost of Colorado's Death Penalty*, UNIV. OF DENVER CRIM. L. REV. 3 (2013): 145–63.

91. Jack Healy & Julie Turkewitz, *Verdict Is Guilty in Aurora Attack*, N.Y. TIMES, July 17, 2015, at A1.

92. Originally, Brauchler insisted that only one juror thought Holmes should get life and the eleven others wanted a death sentence. Sadie Gurman, *DA: Holmes' Life Sentence Came Down to 1 Juror*, DUBUQUE (IA) TELEGRAPH-HERALD, Aug. 15, 2015, at B6. Three months after the verdict, an anonymous juror revealed that three of the jurors were solidly for life imprisonment in the case. Jordan Steffen, *Juror in Aurora Theater Trial Says Three Wanted Life Sentence*, DENVER POST, Oct. 4, 2015, at A1.

the trial was over.[93] At formal sentencing on August 26, Holmes was given the maximum punishment for each of his convictions: twelve consecutive sentences of life imprisonment without parole and 3,318 additional years in prison. Judge Samour then, according to the *Denver Post*, "looked toward the killer with a scowl uncharacteristic of the normally even-tempered judge," and exclaimed, "Sheriff, get the defendant out of my courtroom, please."[94]

Two days later, Brauchler announced that he was definitely considering running for the US Senate in 2016.[95]

4. DEXTER LEWIS, JR. The fourth defendant who faced the death penalty in 2015 was Dexter Lewis, and again, the brutality of the crimes was unfathomable. Before Lewis, the most recent Denver homicide for which the death penalty was sought occurred in February 1999 and involved defendant Donta Page. The last time the death penalty was imposed in a Denver case was in December 1986, against Frank Rodriguez, who was convicted of a murder committed in November 1984.[96]

On October 17, 2012, twenty-year-old Lewis, brothers Joseph and Lynell Hill, and Demarea Harris entered Fero's Bar in Denver and, in the course of a robbery, fatally stabbed four women and one man who were inside, and then set the bar afire.[97] Four of the victims were white and one Asian, and all the assailants were African American. On July 25, 2013, Denver district attorney Mitch Morrisey announced that his office would seek the death penalty.[98]

---

93. John Ingold & Jordan Steffen, *Life in Prison*, DENVER POST, Aug. 8, 2015, at 1.

94. John Ingold & Elizabeth Hernandez, *"Get the Defendant Out of My Courtroom,"* DENVER POST, Aug. 27, 2015, at 1.

95. John Frank, *DA Mulls Senate Run*, DENVER POST, Aug. 29, 2015, at A1. A month later, Brauchler decided not to run. Instead, in 2016 he will run for a second four-year term as DA. John Frank, *No Senate Bid for Brauchler*, DENVER POST, Oct. 1, 2015, at 2A.

96. *See* case of Frank Rodriguez, appendix 3, case no. 12.

97. Killed in the robbery were the bar's owner, Young Suk Fero, fifty-three, and customers Daria M. Pohl, twenty-one; Kellene Fallon, forty-four; Tereasa Beesley, forty-five; and Ross Richter (the only male victim), twenty-nine.

98. Prior to the Lewis case, the most recent homicide for which the Denver DA sought the death penalty involved defendant Donta Paige, who was ultimately convicted of a murder that occurred on February 24, 1999. The last Denver case that

Lewis had a long history of troubles. He had first entered a juvenile detention facility when he was thirteen, and while in various jails and detention facilities, he had been charged with assaulting another prisoner and two guards. At the time of these offenses, he was diagnosed with bipolar disorder and post-traumatic stress disorder. His father (Dexter Lewis, Sr.), a leader in the Denver Crips gang, was murdered in 1994, shortly before his son's fourth birthday.[99]

Jury selection began in May 2015, with a pool of six hundred potential jurors summoned for possible service. By that time, the Hills had agreed to settle their cases with prosecutors, with Lynell Hill sentenced to seventy years and Joseph Hill to LWOP in exchange for their guilty pleas and testimony against Lewis. The fourth man, Demarea Harris, an informant for the US Bureau of Alcohol, Tobacco, Firearms and Explosives, was never charged in the case.[100]

The trial started in late July.[101] Leading the prosecution were chief deputy district attorneys Joe Morales and Matt Wenig, while the defense team was led by public defenders Chris Baumann (head of the Denver public defender's office), David Kraut, and Jon Grevillius. Lynell Hill and Demarea Harris both testified for the prosecution, claiming that Lewis had stabbed four of the victims, while Joseph Hill had stabbed the owner of the bar, Ms. Young Suk Fero.[102] In addition, one of Lewis's post-arrest cellmates, Robert Desersa, testified that Lewis tried to get him to kill several witnesses in the case, including Lewis's wife.[103] Joseph Hill, violating the terms of his plea agreement, refused to testify against Lewis, but there was little that prosecutors could do short of throwing out his

---

resulted in a death sentence involved Frank Rodriguez, who was convicted of the November 1984 murder of Lorraine Martelli.

99. Matthew Nussbaum, *Lewis Had a Troubled Upbringing*, DENVER POST, Aug. 10, 2015, at A1.

100. Jordan Steffen, *Trial Delayed in Fero Deaths*, DENVER POST, Dec. 13, 2014, at 8A and Kieran Nicholson, *Jury Selection in 5 Deaths at Denver Bar Underway*, DENVER POST, May 27, 2015, at A4.

101. Jordan Steffen & Matthew Nussbaum, *Trial Opens in Deaths of 5 at Bar*, DENVER POST, July 21, 2015, at A2.

102. Matthew Nussbaum, *Witness Recalls Carnage*, DENVER POST, July 29, 2015, at A8.

103. Matthew Nussbaum, *Lewis Wanted Others Killed*, DENVER POST, July 31, 2015, at A2.

guilty plea and starting anew, this time seeking his execution. His guilty plea stood, and he did not face any further sanction for not living up to his part of the deal.

On August 10, Lewis was found guilty on all charges: ten counts of first-degree murder,[104] four counts of attempted aggravated robbery, one count of aggravated robbery,[105] and one count of arson.[106] The penalty phase began the next day.

During the penalty phase, the defense emphasized Lewis's life of abuse and how he grew up surrounded by violence, assaults, gangs, and rapes. Lewis's father regularly assaulted his mother, and Dexter was regularly beaten—first by both of his parents and then solely by his mom after his dad was murdered.[107] His aunt recalled Lewis's mother, Tammesa Jones, "punching him like he was a grown man" when he was a toddler: "He would be bleeding. It would be, like, closed fist to the face . . . Something a kid his age shouldn't have experienced."[108] Jones herself testified, recalling for the jurors how she drank heavily and regularly punched her own stomach while pregnant with the boy. The beatings became worse after Lewis was born.[109]

In the end, the jurors could not unanimously agree that the aggravating circumstances outweighed these mitigating circumstances (the second of three questions posed during the sentencing portions of Colorado death penalty trials). This avoided the final stage of the sentencing pro-

---

104. There were two counts of first-degree murder for each victim: one, that the defendant "unlawfully, feloniously, after deliberation and with the intent to cause the death of a person other than himself," and two, that the murder was done during the course of a robbery.

105. Jurors convicted Lewis on the lesser charge of attempted aggravated robbery for four victims and on the charge of aggravated robbery in the case of Fero.

106. Matthew Nussbaum & Noelle Phillips, *Lewis Found Guilty: Death Sentence Testimony Starts Tuesday, Only Days after Aurora Theater Gunman Was Given Life*, DENVER POST, Aug. 11, 2015, at A6.

107. Matthew Nussbaum, *Lewis Faced Life of Abuse*, DENVER POST, Aug. 18, 2015, at A1.

108. Matthew Nussbaum & Kirk Mitchell, *Tales of Pain and Grace*, DENVER POST, Aug. 19, 2015, at A6.

109. Matthew Nussbaum & Kirk Mitchell, *Mother of Killer Testifies*, DENVER POST, Aug. 20, 2015, at A5.

cess and brought the penalty phase in the Lewis case to a close.[110] At least one member of the jury—the exact number was not publicly revealed—apparently believed that the abuse and neglect that Lewis suffered as a youngster outweighed the depravity of the crime. Because the jury did not reach the third and ultimate question of whether Lewis should be sentenced to life or death, we only know that he would not be sentenced to death because at least one juror believed that the aggravating circumstances did not outweigh the mitigators.

The next day, an editorial in the *Denver Post* observed, "The death penalty in Colorado has effectively expired. And it didn't happen because of bleeding-heart lawmakers or activist judges. It happened because juries themselves wanted no part of it."[111]

On September 30, after Lewis was found to be a habitual offender, eight friends and family members of the victims were permitted to address Judge John Madden and talk about their murdered loved ones. It was clear that words alone could not adequately describe the horror and pain experienced by these co-victims. When they were finished, Lewis was formally sentenced to five life sentences without parole and 180 years in prison, all to be served consecutively.[112] The sentence was handed down just two weeks shy of the third anniversary of the crimes.

And so ended death penalty litigation in trial courts in Colorado in 2015. By any measure, Lewis and Holmes were convicted of two of the most aggravated multiple murders in the state since the 1957 murders by airplane bomber John Gilbert Graham.[113] Yet, both cases were added to the list of failed death penalty prosecutions. Undoubtedly, even the strongest death penalty supporters in the state were wondering if Colorado would ever see another execution.

---

110. Jordan Steffen & Matthew Nussbaum, *Dexter Lewis Gets Life Sentence for Fero's Bar Massacre*, DENVER POST, Aug. 28, 2015, at A1.

111. Editorial, *The Lewis Verdict Sends a Message*, DENVER POST, Aug. 28, 2015, at A21.

112. Jordan Steffen, *Killer Lewis Gets Life*, DENVER POST, Oct. 1, 2015, at 8.

113. *See* appendix 1, case no. 96.

EPILOGUE

SUMMARY, TRENDS, AND SOME FUTURE POSSIBILITIES

In the business world, the rearview mirror is always clearer than the windshield.
—Warren Buffett

In chapter 6, I wrote, "Every student of the death penalty in America quickly learns that predicting the future is a precarious hobby." Nonetheless, our look at the history of the death penalty in Colorado has identified several themes and trends, and sometimes the future is best predicted by looking, as Warren Buffett would advise, in the rearview mirror. The history of Colorado's death penalty, inexorably linked with the history of the death penalty in the United States as a whole, is one characterized by three main themes: ambivalence, inconsistencies, and expense.

AMBIVALENCE

As the previous chapters have demonstrated, Coloradans have always been ambivalent about the death penalty. We can see this beginning in the late 1880s—when administrators at the Colorado State Penitentiary resisted efforts to move hangings to Cañon City—through the massive efforts of the 1890s to find a more "humane" method of execution (i.e., the twitch-up gallows). Also in the 1890s, several prison officials refused to participate in executions, a hydraulic hanging machine eliminated the need for an executioner, and the state briefly experimented with abolition (1897–1901). Throughout the twentieth century, regular

DOI: 10.5876/9781607325123.c007

efforts were made to abolish the death penalty and the number of executions fell steadily after World War II. In the fifty-three years since the execution of John Bizup in May 1962, Colorado had only two executions.

Public opinion polls on the death penalty in Colorado are often too superficial to accurately monitor prevailing attitudes. As mentioned in chapter 6, a June 2013 poll found that 69 percent of Coloradans favored the death penalty,[1] and in September 2014, support outpolled opposition by a 63–28 margin.[2] Overall, these polls mean very little, since they usually do not measure support for the death penalty given the alternative of life without parole and/or they have rather obvious methodological limitations. The only fairly reliable polls measure support for the death penalty *given the option of life imprisonment without parole* (LWOP)—the only two sentences available for those convicted of first-degree murder in the state. RBI Strategies and Research conducted one such poll in 2008, and it found that the public was evenly split, with 45 percent favoring death and 45 percent favoring LWOP (see chapter 5).[3] Similarly, a September 2015 poll found that support for the death penalty exceeded support for LWOP by a slim 47–43.[4] Colorado usually mirrors national attitudes about capital punishment, and the June 2015 Quinnipiac poll (national) found that support for LWOP, at 48 percent, exceeded support for the death penalty, which measured 43 percent.[5]

Some observers might argue that the waning support for the executioner reflects "evolving standards of decency," which are often invoked to determine what "cruel and unusual punishments" are under an Eighth Amendment analysis.[6] These evolving standards of decency caused the US Supreme Court, in 2002, to ban the death penalty for

---

1. Editorial, *What Poll Means for Death Penalty*, DENVER POST, June 14, 2013, at 28A.

2. Jon Murray, *Poll: Death Penalty Not Major Factor for Colorado Voters*, DENVER POST, Sept. 11, 2014, http://www.denverpost.com/News/ci_26515352/Poll:-Death-penalty-not-major-factor-for-Colorado-voters.

3. http://www.deathpenaltyinfo.org/COpoll08.pdf.

4. John Frank, *Colorado Voters Split on Death Penalty, Life in Prison*, DENVER POST, Sept. 15, 2015, at A6.

5. http://www.quinnipiac.edu/news-and-events/quinnipiac-university-poll/national/release-detail?ReleaseID=2229.

6. *See, e.g.*, HUGO ADAM BEDAU, THE DEATH PENALTY IN AMERICA: CURRENT CONTROVERSIES 189, 198–99 (1997).

those with developmental disabilities,[7] and, later, for those convicted of crimes committed at age seventeen or younger.[8] It may be that evolving standards of decency in Colorado are moving away from the death penalty, but these concerns have always been present, so it may be a stretch to argue that opposition to the death penalty is evolving. Perhaps what is changing or evolving instead is the public's knowledge about the alleged benefits (retribution) and drawbacks of the death penalty (e.g., arbitrariness, innocence, cost), and (since 1991) the availability of life imprisonment without parole as the only possible sentence in first-degree murder cases in which the defendant is not sentenced to death.

INCONSISTENCIES

At the end of 2015, Colorado had three men on death row. All were prosecuted in the same judicial district, all the cases came from Aurora, all are young black men, and indeed all attended the same high school. This raises the question of whether the death penalty in Colorado may be correlated with race and geography.

It is. However, to say that death penalty decisions are correlated with race does not necessarily mean that prosecutors and other decision makers are acting with discriminatory intent. The bias can be unintentional.

One study, discussed in chapter 4, found that the race of the victim was more important than the race of the defendant in determining whether the death penalty was sought. In their analysis of all homicides and all death penalty cases in Colorado, from 1980 to 1999, Hindson et al. concluded that "the probability the death sentence will be sought for a Colorado homicide is 4.2 times higher . . . for those who kill whites than for those who kill blacks."[9] The authors also found that the odds that the death penalty is sought are 1.8 times higher for cases with female victims than with male victims.[10] In addition, there are regional disparities in the probability that the death penalty was sought. In counties with

---

7. Atkins v. Virginia, 536 U.S. 304 (2002).

8. Roper v. Simmons, 543 U.S. 551 (2005).

9. Stephanie Hindson, Hillary Potter, and Michael L. Radelet, *Race, Gender, Region and Death Sentencing in Colorado, 1980–1999*, UNIVERSITY OF COLORADO LAW REVIEW 77 (2006): 549–94, at 579 (hereinafter HINDSON ET AL.).

10. *Id.* at 580.

over 180 homicides during the twenty-year study period, the death penalty was most likely to be sought in Jefferson (7.9 percent), Adams (6.9 percent), and Arapahoe (4.5 percent) Counties, and least likely in El Paso (Colorado Springs) (2.8 percent) and Denver (1.1 percent) Counties.[11]

In a project that used more recent data, Meg Beardsley and colleagues looked at all murder cases filed in Colorado district courts in a twelve-year period, from January 1, 1999, through December 31, 2010.[12] The data included information on 546 cases that were eligible for the death penalty by Colorado statute, although death was actually sought in only 22. The authors found huge regional disparities in seeking the death penalty in Colorado. Capital sentences were sought in 11.7 percent of the cases from the Eighteenth Judicial District (Arapahoe, Douglas, Lincoln, and Elbert Counties) and 3.1 percent of the cases from all other counties in the state. The Eighteenth Judicial District is home to all three of Colorado's death row inmates.

In addition, the authors found significant effects due to the defendant's race; the death penalty was sought against 1.1 percent of eligible white defendants but against 5.6 percent of eligible minority defendants. Unfortunately, however, the researchers did not have data on the race of the victim, which in most contemporary research has been shown to correlate more strongly with death penalty decisions than the race of the defendant.[13] Clearly, more research on these disparities is needed.

Racial and geographic disparities are part of the larger question of whether the death penalty is reserved for "the worst of the worst." While Gary Lee Davis was executed in 1997 for the murder of one person—horrible though that murder was—there are numerous examples of people convicted of two or more murders where the death penalty

11. *Id.* at 575.

12. Meg Beardsley, Sam Kamin, Justin Marceau, & Scott Phillips, *Disquieting Discretion: Race, Geography & the Colorado Death Penalty in the First Decade of the Twenty-First Century*, DENVER UNIV. L. REV. 92 (2015): 431–52.

13. Catherine M. Grosso, Barbara O'Brien, Abijah Taylor, & George Woodworth, *Race Discrimination and the Death Penalty: An Empirical and Legal Overview*, in AMERICA'S EXPERIMENT WITH CAPITAL PUNISHMENT, 3rd ed., ed. James R. Acker, Robert M. Bohm, & Charles S. Lanier, 525–76 (2014).

was not pursued, or pursued and not imposed, or imposed and (for a variety of reasons) not carried out.[14] Just a few examples:

EDWARD HERRERA. DENVER. AUGUST 2003. Herrera plead guilty to four murders and was sentenced to four life sentences. He also pled guilty to two counts of attempted murder (one victim was rendered paralyzed for life). Each victim was bound with duct tape and shot in the head while the three-year-old daughter of one of the victims watched. All four victims were Hispanic.[15]

JAACOB [*SIC*] HARDING VANWINKLE. CAÑON CITY. MARCH 9, 2014. Vanwinkle, thirty-one, a convicted sex offender, was convicted of killing thirty-five-year-old Mandy Folsom; her nine-year-old daughter, Marissa; and her five-year-old son, Mason, in March 2014. He also sexually assaulted the woman's teenage daughter. On June 30, 2014, he pled guilty to all the offenses. On September 29, 2014, he was sentenced to three consecutive life sentences for the murders and was also sentenced to three indeterminate life terms for sexually assaulting Folsom, Marissa, and Folsom's sixteen-year daughter (who survived the attacks). Folsom's mother, Dawn Wassal, of Salida, said, "Whatever I say won't make a difference, but as long as he is locked away and cannot hurt another family like he hurt mine, it's fine with me."[16] Folsom's father, Jim Stoler, supported the death penalty in the case, but added, "He makes all the other murderers on death row in Colorado look not so bad."[17]

RICHARD PAUL WHITE. DENVER AND ARAPAHOE COUNTIES. 2002. White was sentenced to LWOP in 2004 for two murders and three counts of sexual assault, in a deal in which he agreed to help authorities find the bodies of three other women who he confessed to killing. Later

---

14. A plausible (albeit academic) argument could be made that if the murder committed by Davis and his codefendant had occurred in 2016 rather than 1986 he would not have faced the death penalty.

15. Howard Pankratz, *DA Won't Seek Death Term in Slaying of 4 at Duplex*, DENVER POST, Mar. 30, 2004.

16. Tracy Harmon, *Canon* [*sic*] *City Killer Gets 3 Life Sentences, No Parole*, PUEBLO CHIEFTAIN, Sept. 29, 2014.

17. *Id.*

that year, he was given a third life sentence for fatally shooting Jason Reichardt.[18] "He had a childhood riddled with sexual and physical abuse," said DA Bill Ritter, in explaining the plea bargain.[19] Five of the victims were prostitutes.

Given these and literally dozens of other cases since 1972[20] where people convicted of multiple murders were never executed, it would be preposterous to argue that the death penalty in Colorado is reserved for "the worst of the worst."

EXPENSE

If there is one aspect of the contemporary death penalty debate in the United States that all informed parties agree on, it is that the costs of a criminal justice system in which the death penalty is available far exceed the costs of a system in which the maximum penalty is life imprisonment without parole. Calculating the cost for each defendant who ends up on the gurney is meaningless, however, since an accurate figure would need to include the costs of pursuing death in cases in which the death penalty is sought but not imposed and those in which it is imposed and not carried out. Whether the study has been done by journalists, state legislatures, state supreme courts, or academic scholars, the results are consistent: the costs of a death penalty case are roughly four to six times the cost of life imprisonment.[21]

In Colorado this would involve calculating the costs for each of the 110 cases in which the death penalty was sought for murders from 1980 through 1999,[22] plus the costs of the 20 additional cases in which the

---

18. Kirk Mitchell, *Serial Killer Given Third Life Sentence*, DENVER POST, Dec. 3, 2004.

19. Kirk Mitchell, *Serial Killer Won't Face Death*, DENVER POST, Sept. 17, 2004.

20. Furman v. Georgia, 408 U.S. 238 (1972)—the case that signaled the beginning of the "modern" era of the death penalty in the United States.

21. The best single place for summaries and overviews of these studies is the Death Penalty Information Center, *Costs of the Death Penalty*, accessed July 15, 2016, http://www.deathpenaltyinfo.org/costs-death-penalty. *See also* Richard C. Dieter, *The Issue of Costs in the Death Penalty Debate*, in AMERICA'S EXPERIMENT WITH CAPITAL PUNISHMENT, 3RD ED., ed. James R. Acker, Robert M. Bohm, and Charles S. Lanier (2014), 595–609.

22. *See* table 5.1, *infra*. *See also* Hindson et al.

death penalty was sought for murders committed between January 1, 2000 and the end of 2015. This expense has resulted in one execution, three men on death row, and one pending death penalty case (as of December 31, 2015).[23] As three legal scholars recently noted, in Colorado death penalty cases, many are called but few are chosen.[24]

One recent study examined the added time it takes to prosecute a death penalty case in Colorado over and above the time it takes in cases where life imprisonment is the maximum punishment.[25] The study looked at thirteen Colorado death penalty prosecutions for cases initiated in the twelve years following January 1, 1999, and compared them to 148 first-degree murder trials that ended with a sentence of LWOP. The authors found that both the number of court days and the length of time from charge to sentence were significantly longer in death penalty prosecutions.

Supporters of the death penalty argue that the huge fiscal outlays are justified. In part, this is because the death penalty brings "justice": the offender has caused immeasurable pain to the victim and the victims' family, friends, and community, and he or she deserves to suffer as much as possible in return. A dwindling minority also point to the death penalty's supposed value over long imprisonment in reducing homicide rates, although a 2012 study by the National Academy of Sciences effectively ended the debate (for those who base their opinions on empirical data) when it found no credible evidence to support this argument.[26]

On the other hand, a sizeable proportion of Coloradans take the position that whatever benefits the death penalty may offer over LWOP,

---

23. The pending case involves Miguel Contreras-Perez, who stands accused of killing corrections officer Mary Ricard at the Arkansas Valley Correctional Facility in Ordway in 2012. Despite pleas from Ricard's family not to pursue the death penalty, in December 2015, the district attorney of the Sixteenth Judicial District, Jim Bullock, announced that his office would seek the death penalty in the case. The case is further complicated by the fact that Contreras-Perez has fired his attorneys twice and currently (as of December 2015) has no legal representation. Alan Prendergast, *DA Pursues Death Penalty in Mary Ricard Murder over Daughter's Objections*, WESTWORD, Dec. 16, 2015.

24. Justin Marceau, Sam Kamin, & Wanda Foglia, *Death Eligibility in Colorado: Many Are Called, Few Are Chosen*, UNIV. OF COLO. L. REV. 84 (2013): 1069–115, at 1088.

25. Marceau & Whitson, *Costs of Colorado's Death Penalty*.

26. DANIEL S. NAGIN AND JOHN V. PEPPER, DETERRENCE AND THE DEATH PENALTY (2012).

they are not worth the cost. A prime example is the Colorado-based group Families of Homicide Victims and Missing Persons, which led the effort in 2009 to scrap the death penalty and use the cost savings to solve more of the unsolved homicides in the state. As we saw in chapter 5, roughly 40 percent of homicides are not solved, and decreasing this figure would not only bring peace to more families but it also might add to the deterrent effect of criminal law, which depends to a large extent on the certainty of apprehension. In short, even if the death penalty can be justified in some cases, there are those who would argue that it is a "luxury" that we can do without.

WHERE WE'RE AT

Although the historical trend is unquestionably in the direction of reducing executions, if not outright abolition, obviously no one knows if or when the death penalty in Colorado will finally come to an end and no one knows how many people will be executed before the last one takes place (if it has not already taken place). When Governor Hickenlooper granted the temporary reprieve to Nathan Dunlap in May 2013, he expressed the hope that his decision would "continue the intense conversation that Coloradans are having about the death penalty."[27] Since then, we have seen death penalty cases that have raised important issues about executing the mentally ill, the role of child abuse in the development of criminality, the relatively easy access to handguns and other weapons, and a wide array of related issues, giving even more fodder for the state's current and future conversations.

Clearly, Colorado does not operate in a vacuum; what happens in Colorado relates to what is happening internationally and nationally, and vice versa. Innumerable variables can and will affect the future of the death penalty, both across the country and in Colorado. And even though Colorado has a small death row and an informal moratorium on executions, continuing its nineteen-year history of no executions is important because it adds to the argument that there is a long-term trend, nationwide and worldwide, away from the death penalty.

---

27. *See* Executive Order D 2013-006, May 22, 2013, https://www.colorado.gov/governor/2013-executive-orders.

The effect of future presidential elections on the types of Supreme Court justices appointed is one important factor. After the 1972 *Furman* decision, Justices Thurgood Marshall and William Brennan remained staunch abolitionists throughout their tenure on the Court, and Justices Harry Blackmun, Lewis Powell, and John Paul Stevens joined them—although late in their careers or after their retirements. Few foresee a day when political authorities in Texas, Oklahoma, Virginia, or Florida vote to abolish the death penalty; but changing demographics make that a possibility. If the current trend of fewer death sentences, fewer executions, more states abolishing the death penalty, and dwindling public support for it continues, a future Supreme Court may very well impose a national ban on the death penalty, just as it has in recent years for executions of juveniles and the developmentally disabled.

Given the right case, even the current Supreme Court may soon take another look at the constitutionality of the death penalty writ large. In June 2015, the Court, led by Justice Samuel Alito, gave its approval (by a 5–4 margin) to Oklahoma's use of a controversial drug for lethal injections—midazolam—that Justice Sonia Sotomayor and three other justices characterized as resulting in executions that were "the chemical equivalent of being burned at the stake." In a second dissenting opinion, Justices Stephen G. Breyer and Ruth Bader Ginsburg opined that they now believed the death penalty in the United States today constitutes cruel and unusual punishment and, therefore, that it was "highly likely that the death penalty violates the Eighth Amendment." Not only did Oklahoma's use of the drug result in a "cruel" punishment, but the decline in executions over the past forty years makes the punishment highly unusual. They also criticized the arbitrary imposition of the death penalty, citing research that documented major disparities in geography and the race of the victim as well as the lack of any significant deterrent effect.[28]

In a separate concurring opinion, Justices Antonin Scalia and Clarence Thomas threw cold water on Justice Breyer's observations, calling them "gobbledy-gook." So, while the future may bring more justices to endorse Breyer's position, one can also easily imagine a future conservative president appointing justices who (like Scalia and Thomas) seemingly rubber-stamp any death sentence and refuse to intervene in any case,

28. Glossip v. Gross, 136 S. Ct. 2726 (2015).

period. For this and many other reasons, Scalia's death in February 2016 has ignited a fierce battle over whether President Obama or his successor should have the right to nominate a replacement.

Even an attorney general who opposes the death penalty does not seem to have much clout. Eric Holder, Jr., who served as attorney general from February 3, 2009 until April 21, 2015, has stated on several occasions that he stands opposed to the death penalty. Nonetheless, he regularly authorized the Justice Department to seek death sentences (most notoriously, for the defendant in the Boston Marathon bombing, Dzhokhar Tsarnaev).[29] In February 2015, Holder stated his belief that a moratorium on executions "would be appropriate" until the Supreme Court resolves questions surrounding the drugs and procedures involved, but that statement has had little or no effect.[30]

The Catholic Church may have an increasing role in the death penalty debate, both in Colorado and nationwide. Approximately 38 percent of the 5.2 million Colorado residents describe themselves as "religious," which is below the national average of 49 percent. Of the 38 percent who are religious, 16 percent are members of the Catholic faith, which makes Catholicism the largest religious denomination in the state.[31] Virtually all church leaders today stand opposed to the death penalty, and the official position of the Catholic Church—since tightened by less official statements from recent popes—is that cases in which the death

---

29. During his term as attorney general, Holder authorized forty-one federal death penalty prosecutions. In July 2015, he told the *National Law Journal*, "When you look at our system of justice, it is the best in the world, but it's imperfect. I think that at some point in our history we have probably executed an innocent person, and that's irreversible. And as wonderful as our system is, it is still made up of men and women who are imperfect and I worry about that, especially when you look at the levels of representation at the state level. I just think we can do better as a nation." Tony Mauro & Katelyn Polantz, *Q&A: Eric Holder, Jr., Returns to Private Practice*, NAT'L L. JOUR., July 5, 2015, at 11.

30. Mollie Reilly, *Moratorium on Death Penalty "Would Be Appropriate" Pending Supreme Court Decision*, Feb. 2, 2015, http://www.huffingtonpost.com/2015/02/17/eric-holder-death-penalty_n_6701062.html. That decision, which gave the green light for executions to proceed, was handed down in June 2015. Glossip v. Gross, (decided June 29, 2015).

31. World Population Statistics, *Colorado Population 2013*, August 25, 2013, http://www.worldpopulationstatistics.com/colorado-population-2013/.

penalty is necessary "are very rare, if not practically nonexistent."[32] To date, Catholic Church leadership in Colorado has been relatively silent in working against the death penalty (although regularly mentioning it in the church's "pro-life" work), but more work may be occurring behind the scenes than from the pulpits. This may change.

Nonetheless—and not unexpectedly—not all Catholics have the same view of the death penalty. In fact, some Catholic politicians in Colorado—such as former attorney general John Suthers, 2014 gubernatorial candidate Bob Beauprez, and District Attorney George Brauchler—are among the most vocal death penalty supporters in the state and claim that their support is consistent with Catholic doctrine. Furthermore, six of the current Supreme Court justices in 2015—Alito, Kennedy, Roberts, Scalia, Sotomayor, and Thomas—were also Catholics but (quite properly) do not allow their religious affiliation to dictate their judicial opinions.

It is perfectly plausible to predict that in future years, with more vocal leadership from the Catholic hierarchy,[33] the support for the death pen-

---

32. This phrase comes from section 56 of Pope John Paul II's *Evangelium Vitae*, Mar. 25, 1995. Now known as Saint John Paul II or Pope Saint John Paul II, he served as pope from 1978–2005.

The official position of the Catholic Church on the death penalty is elaborated in section 2267 of the *Catechism of the Catholic Church*, including Pope John Paul II's words as its last line, which reads, "Assuming that the guilty party's identity and responsibility have been fully determined, the traditional teaching of the Church does not exclude recourse to the death penalty, if this is the only possible way of effectively defending human lives against the unjust aggressor.

If, however, non-lethal means are sufficient to defend and protect people's safety from the aggressor, authority will limit itself to such means, as these are more in keeping with the concrete conditions of the common good and more in conformity to the dignity of the human person.

Today, in fact, as a consequence of the possibilities which the state has for effectively preventing crime, by rendering one who has committed an offense incapable of doing harm—without definitely taking away from him the possibility of redeeming himself—the cases in which the execution of the offender is an absolute necessity 'are very rare, if not practically nonexistent.'"

See CATECHISM OF THE CATHOLIC CHURCH, accessed July 15, 2016, http://www.vatican.va/archive/ccc_css/archive/catechism/p3s2c2a5.htm.

33. Archbishop Samuel Aquila of Denver, who individually stands opposed to the death penalty, has made no specific public statements about the last three death penalty prosecutions in Colorado (Montour, Holmes, and Lewis), even though the prosecutor in the first two, George Brauchler, is Catholic.

alty among Catholics will continue to dwindle.[34] In May 1987, Mother Teresa[35] visited death row inmates in San Quentin; if Pope Francis followed her footsteps today, it could have seismic effects on death penalty debates.[36] In a March 2015 letter to the International Commission against the Death Penalty, Pope Francis made his position crystal clear: "Today capital punishment is unacceptable, however serious the condemned's crime may have been."[37] Lest there be any doubt about his personal opinion, in a speech before a joint session of Congress in Washington in September, the pontiff made a direct appeal to end the death penalty. "Every life is sacred, every human person is endowed with an inalienable dignity, and society can only benefit from the rehabilitation of those convicted of crimes," he said.[38]

Meanwhile, in early 2015, unpredictable events continued to occur around the country with predictable regularity. On February 12, just three weeks after taking office, Pennsylvania governor Tom Wolf announced a moratorium on executions in his state, which houses the nation's fifth largest death row. At the time, the state had held only three executions since 1972 (the last in 1999), and all three inmates were executed only because they dropped their appeals, preferring death to life imprisonment. Predictably, Governor Wolf was loudly criticized by groups of prosecutors and crime victims,[39] but large numbers of religious

---

34. Mark Oppenheimer, *Catholics on Left and Right Find Common Ground Opposing Death Penalty*, N.Y. TIMES, Mar. 28, 2015, at A15.

35. It is expected that Mother Teresa will be named a saint in the near future. Sewell Chan, *Francis Moves Mother Teresa Closer to Sainthood*, N.Y. TIMES, Dec. 19, 2015, at A4.

36. Indeed, in March 2015, the four most visible Catholic magazines and newspapers—the *National Catholic Reporter*, *America Magazine*, the *National Catholic Register*, and *Our Sunday Visitor*—published a joint editorial calling for an end to the death penalty. *See, e.g.*, Caitlin Hendel, *Standing Together to Bring an End to the Death Penalty*, NAT'L. CATH. REP., Mar. 5, 2015.

37. International Commission against the Death Penalty, *ICDP President Meets with Pope Francis*, Mar. 23, 2015, http://www.icomdp.org/2015/03/icdp-president-meets-with-pope-francis/.

38. Peter Baker & Jim Yardley, *Pope Francis, in Congress, Pleads for Unity on World's Woes*, N.Y. TIMES, Sept. 24, 2015, at A1.

39. Jan Murphy, *Gov. Tom Wolf's Death Penalty Moratorium Not Sitting Well with Crime Victims, Others*, PENN LIVE.COM, Mar. 4, 2015, http://www.pennlive.com/politics/index.ssf/2015/03/gov_tom_wolfs_death_penalty_mo.html; Kim Bellware, *Pennsylvania Governor's Death Penalty Moratorium Under Fire*, Mar. 5, 2015, http://

leaders and civil rights activists supported him. With the support of the majority of the Pennsylvania State Board of Pardons, Wolf could also commute the death sentences for all 182 men and women living under a death sentence in his state to sentences of LWOP.

Most of Colorado's neighboring states are also moving away from the death penalty. New Mexico abolished it in 2009. The last execution in Kansas was in 1965.[40] At the end of 2015, Wyoming's death row stood empty. Even more unusual is Nebraska, which is one of the most conservative states in the country.[41] In 2015 its legislature not only voted to abolish the death penalty, but after Gov. Pete Ricketts vetoed that effort, it overrode the veto on a strong 30–19 vote.[42] Back in Colorado, the *Denver Post* applauded the Nebraska legislature and called for Colorado to follow its leadership.[43]

But in the near future, Nebraska will teach a lesson that Colorado abolitionists will need to study. Governor Ricketts was outraged that the abolitionist legislation was passed, and especially that it was passed over his veto. His father, Joe Ricketts, is the founder of the brokerage firm TD Ameritrade, and the family has ample supplies of money. Governor Ricketts reportedly donated $200,000 from his personal funds, and his father contributed another $100,000, to mount an effort to put the issue on the ballot in November 2016.[44] By October they had collected 143,000 signatures, far more than the 58,000 needed to put the issue on the ballot.[45] If the referendum restores the death penalty,

---

www.huffingtonpost.com/2015/03/05/pennsylvania-death-penalty-supreme-court_n_6804722.html.

40. Attempts to reinstate the death penalty in Kansas were vetoed by Gov. John W. Carlin in 1979, 1980, 1981, and 1985. In 1994 Gov. Joan Finney allowed a reinstatement bill to become law without her signature. Of the states that currently authorize the death penalty, Kansas was the most recent to put it on its books. As of this writing, nine inmates were on death row in Kansas.

41. Julie Bosman, *Conservative Support Aids Bid in Nebraska to Ban Death Penalty*, N.Y. TIMES, May 18, 2015, at A10.

42. Julie Bosman, *Nebraska Bans Death Penalty, Defying a Veto*, N.Y. TIMES, May 28, 2015, at A1.

43. Editorial, *Follow Nebraska on Death Penalty*, DENVER POST, May 29, 2015, at A19.

44. The family also owns 95 percent of the Chicago Cubs baseball team.

45. Julie Bosman, *Petition Drive in Nebraska Forces Vote on Abolishing Death Penalty*, N.Y. TIMES, Oct. 17, 2015, at A12.

it is likely the death penalty in Nebraska will be cemented in for many years to come.[46]

Gov. John Kitzhaber of Oregon announced in November 2011 that he would not allow any executions as long as he was in office.[47] As it turned out, he was forced to resign from office in February 2015 (for reasons unrelated to his stand on capital punishment), just one month after being sworn in for his fourth term. His successor, Kate Brown (who received her BA from the University of Colorado Boulder in 1981), quickly pledged to continue the indefinite moratorium on executions. Nonetheless, the events in Oregon again illustrate that death penalty politics can change quickly and unpredictably. Reprieves like those issued by governors such as Hickenlooper, Wolf, Jay Inslee in Washington,[48] Kitzhaber, and Brown are, after all, temporary.

Similarly, there are too many unknowns in Colorado to make reliable predictions. The failed efforts to secure death sentences for James Holmes and Dexter Lewis in 2015 may have contagious effects, perhaps amplifying discussion about executing the mentally ill (and not just those who are found not guilty by reason of insanity, a much narrower criterion). The cases are bound to fuel debates about whether seeking the death sentence is worth all the time and expense. From initial appearances, prosecutor George Brauchler's political standing was not at all undermined by his dogged pursuit of a death sentence for Edward Montour before suddenly capitulating and agreeing to Montour's offer to plead guilty in exchange for a life sentence. And it is possible that he believes that his political standing will not be hurt because of his

---

46. Julie Bosman, *Petition Drive Threatens to Undo Nebraska Legislature's Death Penalty Repeal*, N.Y. TIMES, July 19, 2015, at 13A. The fate of the ten men currently on death row in Nebraska is very much up in the air. The power to grant executive clemency is in the hands of the executive branch, not the legislature, and in Nebraska a three-person committee (governor, secretary of state, and attorney general) makes up the clemency board. Even if the repeal bill fails, the men currently on death row might not have their sentences commuted to life imprisonment. On the other hand, the repeal bill also repealed all methods of execution. So, if the repeal bill stands, those on death row will effectively be resentenced to life imprisonment because there will be no way to kill them.

47. William Yardley, *Oregon Governor Says He Will Not Allow Executions*, N.Y. TIMES, Nov. 23, 2011, at A14.

48. Ian Lovett, *Executions Are Suspended by Governor in Washington*, N.Y. TIMES, Feb. 13, 2014, at A12.

failure to get a death sentence in the Holmes case. Indeed, his political star may rise because of all the publicity that he received in the case. Although elected as DA relatively recently (2012), at the end of 2015, he was unquestionably the most well-known prosecutor in the state.[49]

There are other political unknowns. We can be certain that we will regularly see especially atrocious murders in Colorado in the future, any one of which could increase death penalty support. Nonetheless, since the murders by Montour, Lewis, and Holmes—among the very worst in the history of the state—failed to result in even one death sentence, prosecutors may be even more reluctant to seek it in future cases.[50] One can also imagine the possibility that Rep. Rhonda Fields will change her position on the death penalty, giving Governor Hickenlooper the green light to commute the death sentences of the two men who killed her son. If Hickenlooper does decide to commute the death sentences of the three men currently on death row before leaving office, the decision would instantaneously put Colorado's executioner on the unemployment line for at least a generation.

Colorado death penalty opponents certainly have more resources than ever before to further their cause. In 2014 several national foundations

---

49. Brauchler will stand for reelection as DA in 2016, and there are widespread rumors that he is considering a run for governor in 2018. John Frank, *No Senate Bid for Brauchler*, DENVER POST, Oct. 1, 2015, at 2A.

50. However, as mentioned above, after the life sentences were given to both Holmes and Lewis, prosecutors announced their intention to seek a death sentence against Miguel Contreras-Perez for the 2012 murder of a corrections officer.

In another case that might have implications for the future of the death penalty in Colorado, Robert L. Dear, Jr., age fifty-seven, stands accused of the murder of three people at a Planned Parenthood clinic in Colorado Springs on November 27, 2015. The victims include a University of Colorado Colorado Springs police officer Garret Swasey; an Iraq war veteran, Ke'Arre Stewart; and Jennifer Markovsky, a mother of two. The murders are thought to result from Dear's stand against abortion. At an initial hearing, where prosecutors accused Dear of 179 charges, he proclaimed, "I am guilty, there is no trial, I am a warrior for the babies." Dear has also refused to cooperate with Dan King, his defense attorney. (King also served as the lead attorney for James Holmes and is an expert in dealing with mentally ill clients.) Jordan Steffen, *Planned Parenthood Shooter: I am Guilty . . . A Warrior for Babies*, DENVER POST, Dec. 10, 2015, at A1. At a later hearing, Dear repeated his vows not to cooperate with his attorneys or with a court-ordered exam to determine if he was competent for trial. The evaluation could take up to nine months. Jordan Steffen, *Judge: Is He Fit for Trial?* DENVER POST, Dec. 24, 2015, at 1A.

committed several hundreds of thousands of dollars to further the abolitionist cause by funding a campaign—known as the Better Priorities Initiative—in Colorado through the state chapter of the American Civil Liberties Union. Much of this funding is channeled through a national group of funders that supports the Massachusetts nonprofit "The Proteus Action League,"[51] which has pooled money from several sources in what is called The Themis Fund[52] and set up a group called the Eighth Amendment Project[53] to support and coordinate abolitionist efforts nationwide. Better Priorities in Colorado has operated primarily with a goal of developing support in some future General Assembly for an abolition bill (if not the ballot initiative that would probably follow).

Of increasing centrality in death penalty debates are growing calls from political conservatives to scrap it. The movement by anti–death penalty activists to reach out to conservatives began in the early 1990s when Virginia Sloan, then a counsel to the US House Judiciary Committee, formed the Emergency Committee to Save Habeas Corpus, and continued when Ms. Sloan created The Constitution Project (TCP) in 1997.[54] TCP works with capital punishment supporters and opponents—conservatives and progressives alike—all of whom believe the system is profoundly broken. The seeds sewn by TCP have only recently begun to bear fruit—and Nebraska is a prime example.

The conservative critique of the death penalty has several incarnations today, but in general, it consists of three major prongs. The first is fiscal austerity. Conservatives have always applauded fiscal restraint, but, as we have seen, the death penalty means giving blank checks to enable prosecutors, defense attorneys, courts, and their teams to leave no stone unturned, thereby eliminating the goal of closure that the death penalty is supposed to attain.

---

51. Proteus Fund, http://www.proteusfund.org/.

52. Proteus Fund, *The Time Is Now*, http://www.proteusfund.org/themis/about.

53. Proteus Fund, *The 8th Amendment Project*, http://www.proteusfund.org/themis/8th-amendment-project.

54. *See* The Constitution Project, accessed July 15, 2016, http://www.constitutionproject.org/. For an earlier discussion of the importance of the conservative critique of the death penalty, *see* Michael L. Radelet, *The Executioner's Waning Defenses*, in THE ROAD TO ABOLITION? THE FUTURE OF CAPITAL PUNISHMENT IN THE UNITED STATES, ed. Charles J. Ogletree, Jr. and Austin Sarat 19, 25–30 (2009).

Second, conservatives often cite religious principles, arguing that such principles should play a larger role in public policy than they do today. Without a doubt, any vote by American religious leaders on the death penalty today would overwhelmingly support abolition.

But it is the third prong of the conservative perspective that seems to be especially important in modern death penalty discourse. As political commentator George F. Will reminds us, "[c]apital punishment, like the rest of the criminal justice system, is a government program, so skepticism is in order."[55] One might question if the same government that takes too long to deliver the mail or fill potholes is a government that can be trusted to make life and death decisions. Indeed, as mentioned in chapter 5, since 1990, there have been four defendants convicted of murder in Colorado who were later vindicated.[56]

This argument rests on several smaller points that are regularly made in death penalty debates: botched executions, erroneous convictions, racial bias and arbitrariness, and the general question of whether the death penalty is reserved for the worst of the worst. More and more Americans seem to agree that we are making godlike decisions without godlike skills—although it remains to be seen just how these imperfections will impact future public opinion and legislation in Colorado. Today's problems in the administration of the death penalty, both in Colorado and nationally, seem to be shifting the relevant question from "Who deserves to die" to "Who deserves to kill?"[57]

---

55. George F. Will, *Innocent on Death Row*, WASH. POST, Apr. 23, 2000, at A23. For a more recent critique of the death penalty by this columnist, *see* George F. Will, *A Slow Death for Capital Punishment*, WASH. POST, May 21, 2015, at A17. Libertarians also tend to oppose the death penalty. *See* Ron Paul, *Death Penalty: The Ultimate Corrupt, Big Government Program*, June 14, 2015, http://www.ronpaulinstitute.org/archives/featured-articles/2015/june/14/death-penalty-the-ultimate-corrupt-big-government-program/.

56. They include Alarico Medina, Denver (convicted in 1991, released in 1995); Robert Dewey, Mesa County (convicted in 1996, released in 2012); Tim Masters, Larimer County (convicted in 1999, released in 2008); and Lorenzo Montoya, Denver (convicted in 2009, released in 2012). Dewey and Masters were exonerated by DNA evidence. For more information on these and other erroneous convictions, see the website for the National Registry of Exonerations, http://www.law.umich.edu/special/exoneration/Pages/about.aspx.

57. *See* Marvin E. Wolfgang, *We Do Not Deserve to Kill*, COOLEY L. REV. 13 (1996): 977–90.

APPENDIX 1

Catalog of Colorado Executions, 1859–Present (N = 103) (ordered by date of execution)

1. JOHN STOEFEL (a.k.a. Stofel, Stuffle). April 9, 1859. Denver. W-W. Hanging. For committing the first murder ever to be recorded in the new settlement of Denver, Stoefel became the first of five men executed under orders by Denver's People's Courts. Stoefel "confessed to shooting a fellow prospector for his gold dust."[1] The victim was Stoefel's brother-in-law, Thomas Biencroff. A party of three Germans that included an elderly man and his two sons (one of whom was Biencroff) and a son-in-law (Stoefel, who was Hungarian) had left their camp looking for cattle, and Biencroff was shot during the trip. The hanging occurred less than forty-eight hours after the murder. At the time, Denver was part of Arapahoe County, Kansas Territory, and had been settled by Euro-Americans for only six months. Some one thousand spectators attended the execution. A fortnight later, the hanging was mentioned in the inaugural issue of the Denver newspaper, the *Rocky Mountain News*.[2]

1. WAYNE GARD, FRONTIER JUSTICE 206 (1949) (hereinafter GARD).
2. *Murder and Execution*, ROCKY MTN. NEWS, Apr. 23, 1859, at 3; Francis S. Williams, *Trials and Judgments of the People's Courts of Denver*, COLO. MAG. 27 (1950): 294, 294–95 (hereinafter WILLIAMS); Olga Curtis, *Denver's First Murderer*, DENVER POST (Empire Magazine), May 7, 1978, at 66, 70, 71; JEROME C. SMILEY, HISTORY OF DENVER 339 (1901) (hereinafter SMILEY); STEPHEN J. LEONARD, LYNCHING IN COLORADO, 1859–1919, at 16–18 (2002) (hereinafter LEONARD).

DOI: 10.5876/9781607325123.c008

2. MOSES YOUNG. March 15, 1860. Denver. W-W. Hanging. Convicted by Denver's People's Court of killing William West with a shotgun. Both men hailed from Leavenworth, Kansas Territory, and were "old acquaintances, if not friends."[3] Within forty-eight hours, Young was tried before a jury of twelve men and hundreds of spectators. A scaffold was erected near the site of the murder (the slain man's house) and amid the roar of drums, Young was marched to the gallows and hanged.[4]

3. MARCUS GREDLER. June 15, 1860. Denver. W-W. Hanging. Convicted of killing Jacob Rodler, a friend and traveling companion, while passing though Denver, by chopping off his head with an ax. Gredler, a thirty-one-year-old brewer by trade, was born in Germany and had lived in the United States for six years before the crime. Rodler often quarreled with others, and even his wife (a member of the traveling party) said that her life was better with Rodler dead. Gredler claimed that Rodler's wife had asked him to kill Rodler. Between three and four thousand people attended the hanging.[5]

4. JAMES A. GORDON. October 6, 1860. Denver. W-W. Hanging. By age twenty-three, Gordon's "reputation as a desperado accredited him with having killed three or four men before he came here."[6] He was educated as an engineer and owned a saloon in Denver. While intoxicated in a Denver bar on July 20, 1860, Gordon shot and killed an unarmed stranger, a German named John Gantz. He escaped to Kansas Territory but was apprehended and taken to Leavenworth. He was nearly lynched after being freed briefly on a writ of habeas corpus. He was returned to Denver on the morning of September 28, tried that afternoon before an

---

3. SMILEY, at 342.

4. SMILEY, at 342; Williams, at 295–96; B. Richard Burg, *Administration of Justice in the Denver People's Courts, 1859–1861*, JOUR. OF THE WEST 7 (Oct. 1968): 510–21, at 514; *The Murder of William West*, ROCKY MTN. NEWS, Mar. 21, 1860, at 2 (transcript at http://freepages.genealogy.rootsweb.ancestry.com/~wynkoop/webdocs/3211860.htm).

5. SMILEY, at 342; Williams, at 296; *Execution of Marcus Gredler*, WESTERN MOUNTAINEER (Golden), June 28, 1860, at 8.

6. SMILEY, at 343.

audience of one thousand, and hanged the next week in front of a crowd of several thousand.[7]

5. PATRICK WATERS (a.k.a. Watters). December 21, 1860. Denver. W-W. Hanging/Broken Neck. Waters, a farmhand born in Ireland, shot and killed Thomas R. Freeman, his employer, near Fort Lupton, where the two had journeyed to pick up a load of hay. The motive was robbery of the money that Freeman carried with him to purchase the hay. Once arrested (in Nebraska, two weeks after the homicide) and returned to Denver, Waters was threatened with immediate lynching if he did not disclose the location of the body, and so he did—as the rope was being placed over his head. Waters had no prior arrest record and had a reputation of peaceableness and honesty. He gave a full confession before his death.[8]

6. WILLIAM S. VAN HORN. December 18, 1863. Central City. W-W. Hanging. Convicted of killing Josiah Copeland, who was allegedly lured to the scene of the murder by Van Horn's mistress (who was never charged with the crime), where Van Horn lay in wait to kill him.[9] Hundreds attended the trial; to avoid a lynching, Van Horn was taken to Denver and lodged in the Arapahoe County jail. Thousands attended the execution, which was the first carried out under territorial law in Colorado.[10]

7–8. FRANKLIN FOSTER and **HENRY STONE.** May 24, 1866. Denver. W-W. Hanging. The two defendants, both former Union soldiers with no prior criminal records, were convicted of killing two men—Isaac H. Augustus

---

7. GARD, at 206; WILLIAMS, at 298–300; ALICE POLK HILL, TALES OF THE COLORADO PIONEERS 57–61 (1884); William MacLeod Raine, *The Gordon Case*, in DENVER MURDERS 13, ed. Lee Casey (1946); LEONARD, at 24–25.

8. GARD, at 207; SMILEY, at 348; WILLIAMS, at 300–2; *Murder of Thomas Freeman*, ROCKY MTN. NEWS, Dec. 6, 1860, at 2; *The Waters Trial*, ROCKY MTN. NEWS, Dec. 19, 1860, at 2; *Trial of Patrick Waters for the Murder of Thomas R. Freeman Before a Court of the People*, ROCKY MTN. NEWS, Dec. 20, 1860, at 2; *The Execution of Waters*, ROCKY MTN. NEWS, Dec. 21, 1860, at 2.

9. *The Van Horn Case*, ROCKY MTN. NEWS, Dec. 2, 1863, at 2; *William S. Van Horn*, ROCKY MTN. NEWS, Dec. 23, 1863, at 1.

10. Stephen J. Leonard, *Judge Lynch in Colorado, 1859–1919*, COLO. HERITAGE 3 (Autumn 2000): 3; FRANK HALL, HISTORY OF THE STATE OF COLORADO, VOL. 2, 150–54 (1890) (hereinafter HALL).

and F. H. Sluman—and stealing some $8,000 in gold.[11] The murders occurred while Foster and Stone were soldiers stationed near the present site of Fort Morgan and took place approximately one hundred miles east of Denver.[12] Foster was twenty and Stone was twenty-four at the time of the crime.[13] "Foster confessed to the crime and implicated Stone, who denied all connection with the murder for which he was executed, but admitted the commission of four other murders of men in the states."[14] "There was probably not less than 3,000 present."[15] "Although we hope never to witness another scene like that presented yesterday, it is an extremely gratifying thought that the majesty of the law is upheld by a people who are evidently looked upon by the 'all-civilized' people of the east as little better than barbarians."[16]

9. GEORGE SMITH. February 18, 1870. Central City. B-W. Convicted of beating and strangling to death William Hamblin, a milkman. The murder occurred in February 1868; the motive was to obtain the victim's money. After the murder, Hamblin's body was thrown down a mine shaft. Suspicion immediately fell on Smith and another African American, Bob Reynolds. Both were soon apprehended—and both confessed—with the evidence showing that Smith beat the victim and Reynolds strangled him to death.[17] Reynolds, however, escaped from custody and a week later was wounded while being apprehended. He died in prison before trial. After Smith was convicted and sentenced to death, several unsuccessful efforts were made to save him from the gallows, including an appeal to the Supreme Court of Colorado Territory[18] and a plea for

---

11. *Robbing and Murder!*, ROCKY MTN. NEWS, Jan. 6, 1866, at 1; *Justice Appeased*, ROCKY MTN. NEWS, May 25, 1866, at 1; *The Execution*, ROCKY MTN. NEWS, May 25, 1866, at 4.

12. HALL, at 154.

13. *Prisoners Sentenced*, ROCKY MTN. NEWS, Apr. 28, 1866, at 4.

14. *The Penalty Paid: Miears, The Murderer of Bonacina, Hanged*, ROCKY MTN. NEWS, Jan. 25, 1873, at 1.

15. *Execution of Franklin Foster and Henry Stone for the Murder of Isaac H. Augustus and Sluman*, ROCKY MTN. NEWS, May 24, 1866, at 1.

16. *The Execution*. *See generally* JENNIFER PATTEN, IN VIEW OF THE MOUNTAINS: A HISTORY OF FORT MORGAN, COLORADO 199–203 (2011).

17. ROCKY MTN. NEWS, Feb. 19, 1868, at 4; ROCKY MTN. NEWS, Feb. 20, 1868, at 4.

18. Smith v. People, 1 Colo. 121 (1869).

clemency to the governor.[19] Approximately two thousand people witnessed the hanging.[20]

10. THEODORE MYERS. January 24, 1873. Denver. W-W. Hanging/Broken Neck. A German immigrant and farmhand, Myers, age twenty-six, was convicted of killing his employer, George Bonacina, and wounding a female companion of the employer's, who was variously described as the employer's mistress or sister. The murder occurred in August 1871. Myers had loaned the employer $25, and the murder resulted from an argument when the employer failed to return the money. The defense claimed both lack of premeditation and self-defense. After a trial court vacated Myers's initial conviction,[21] his second trial began on October 28, 1872. "Two of the jurors are well-known men of color, the first of their race in the territory."[22] He was sentenced to death on December 30. Appeals for relief to the state Supreme Court (supported by a petition signed by four hundred citizens) and the governor failed. Because the governor was out of state, the acting governor, who later wrote his reflections on the case, made the decision to deny clemency.[23] In addition, the defense attorney, N. Harrison, later published his criticism of the refusal of any member of the State Supreme Court to issue a writ of error and regarding the statute under which Myers was executed.[24] Three thousand people attended the execution.[25]

11. JAMES MILLER. February 2, 1877. West Las Animas (Bent County). B-W. Hanging/Strangulation. This was the first execution in Colorado after the territory achieved statehood. Miller, a twenty-three-year-old "mulatto," had been a soldier with the US Colored Troops for the previous five years.

---

19. ROCKY MTN. NEWS, Feb. 19, 1870, at 4.

20. *The Scaffold—Execution of George Smith—Two Thousand People Present*, COLO. TRIB. (Golden), Feb. 24, 1870, at 2.

21. *The Grand Jury and the District Court*, ROCKY MTN. NEWS, Apr. 10, 1872, at 2. *See also* People v. Myers, 1 Colo. 508 (1872).

22. *Dock and Docket*, ROCKY MTN. NEWS, Oct. 22, 1872, at 4.

23. HALL, at 147–50.

24. N. HARRISON, A REVIEW OF THE TRIAL OF THEODORE MYERS FOR THE MURDER OF GEORGE M. BONACINA (1873), Special Collections & Archives, Norlin Library, University of Colorado Boulder.

25. *Penalty Paid.*

He entered a dance hall, which (that night) was reserved for whites, and an inebriated white customer forced him at gunpoint to leave. Another white customer, John Sutherland, told the thug to leave Miller alone. Miller and a friend, Benjamin Smith, later returned and shot into the bar, missing the thug but killing Sutherland. Both men were sentenced to death, but the governor commuted Smith's sentence. At the hanging (delayed two weeks by the governor so Miller could be married and join a church), the trapdoor at first would not open, and when it did, it fell to the ground. Miller dropped through the opening in the platform, but the rope was too long and his feet came to rest on the trapdoor that had fallen below him. The trapdoor was quickly removed so Miller could swing unimpeded. He did so for twenty-five minutes before expiring. Later, the sheriff, distraught over the bungled hanging, resigned his position and left the community.[26]

12. VICTOR NUNEZ. March 14, 1879. Pueblo. H-H. Despite consistent protestations of innocence, Nunez, a fifty-seven-year-old ranch hand born in Mexico, was executed for the murder of an affluent Mexican rancher. The alleged motive was that Nunez "entertained an unlawful passion" for the victim's wife, who served as a prosecution witness. No one immediately suspected that the victim, Luis Rascone, had been murdered—they thought he had simply left town—while Nunez spent the winter with the victim's wife in Pueblo. Eventually, a young Indian girl who had witnessed the murder came forward and revealed the story. Between twelve and fifteen hundred people witnessed the execution. "Among them we were astonished and pained to see many females and a horde of children, from five years old upward. The morbid curiosity that prompts such desires ought not to be gratified and we hope that the next execution that occurs in Pueblo will be a private one.[27]

13. CICERO C. SIMMS (a.k.a. Sims). July 23, 1880. Fairplay (Park County). W-W. Hanging/Broken Neck. Aged twenty-two, Simms, a prospector

---

26. WILLIAM M. KING, GOING TO MEET A MAN 163 (1990) (hereinafter KING); *The Gallows*, PUEBLO CHIEFTAIN, Feb. 3, 1877, at 1; *The Execution*, ROCKY MTN. NEWS, Feb. 6, 1877, at 2.

27. Nunez Hanged for the Murder of Luis Rascone, PUEBLO CHIEFTAIN, Mar. 15, 1879, at 4.

and miner, was convicted of shooting and killing a friend, John Johnson (a.k.a. Jansen), in Alma, after some horseplay resulted in an angry rage.[28] Johnson, a Dane by birth, was well respected in the community and had provided housing and food for Simms in exchange for cooking and household duties.[29] On at least three occasions prior to the murder, Simms had inappropriately brandished a pistol during various quarrels. He had been arrested several times for crimes of varying degrees of violence and was suspected of a previous murder. Simms's attorney protested that Simms had an unfair trial because on the night before it started, another prisoner, John Hoover, had been abducted from the Fairplay jail and lynched after being spared the death penalty.[30] This caused the trial judge and district attorney, in fear for their own lives if they tried other murder defendants, to leave town immediately after the Simms trial. After the execution, an editorial in the *Rocky Mountain News* questioned capital punishment, especially in such cases where the crime was committed in the "spasm of passion."[31] Approximately eight hundred people attended the hanging.[32] The local newspaper saw the execution as a deterrent: "The record of the past two years has indeed been a bloody one, but we believe that the execution of Simms will have a salutary influence upon the minds of evil-doers."[33]

---

28. *Sentenced to Hang*, ROCKY MTN. NEWS, Apr. 30, 1880, at 5.

29. *Shot by His Friend*, FAIRPLAY FLUME, Jan. 29, 1880, at 4. In an article after the hanging, the local newspaper reported that at the time of the murder, it had "denominated it as the most useless expenditure of human life that was ever chronicled in the west." *The Fatal Trap: How It Engulfed Cicero Simms*, FAIRPLAY FLUME, July 29, 1880, at 1.

30. *Doomed: Sims [sic], the Alma Murderer, to Hang To-Morrow*, ROCKY MTN. NEWS, July 22, 1880, at 4; *The Gallows: Cicero C. Simms, the Alma Murderer, Suffers the Penalty of His Dastardly Crime*, ROCKY MTN. NEWS, July 24, 1880, at 1.

31. Editorial, *The Plea of the State*, ROCKY MTN. NEWS, July 25, 1880, at 4.

32. *The Fatal Drop: How It Opened to Engulf Cicero Simms*, FAIRPLAY FLUME, July 29, 1880, at 1. Additional information about the case can be found in LINDA BJORKLUND, DOIN' TIME IN FAIRPLAY 26–29 (2003); LINDA BJORKLUND, A BRIEF HISTORY OF FAIRPLAY 89–90 (2013); Christie Wright, SOUTH PARK PERILS: SHORT ROPES & TRUE TALES OF HISTORIC PARK COUNTY COLORADO 182–197 (2013). I am indebted to Wright not only for her book but also for sharing her transcriptions of several newspaper articles about this case.

33. *Other Murders*, FAIRPLAY FLUME, July 29, 1880, at 1.

14. W. H. SALISBURY (a.k.a. William H. Canty). Buena Vista (Chaffee County). W-W. Hanging/Broken Neck. June 17, 1881. After a change of venue to Colorado Springs, Salisbury, age thirty-four, was convicted (after the jury deliberated for four hours) of the murder of a Buena Vista police officer, Thomas L. Perkins. Officer Perkins was shot four times as he attempted to arrest a friend of Salisbury's. Several eyewitnesses identified Salisbury; his defense was that the friend, not he, was the triggerman. The execution was held in the jail yard of the El Paso County Jail in Colorado Springs, with only ticketed spectators present, but over one thousand people assembled in an open square surrounding the jail to try to get a glimpse of the hanging. On the scaffold, Salisbury made a tearful speech reiterating his innocence. When the trapdoor opened, the rope broke from the hook holding it to the scaffold, allowing Salisbury's body to fall to the ground. The rope was quickly reattached, and physicians later claimed that Salisbury's neck had been broken by the original fall and the broken rope caused no additional agony.[34]

15. MERRICK ROSENGRANTS. July 29, 1881. Leadville (Lake County). W-W. Hanging. Convicted on the deathbed declaration of John Langmeyer, who claimed Rosengrants shot him when he found Rosengrants inside his cabin ransacking his trunk. Rosengrants had an excellent reputation, and those who knew him thought he would never rob another person's property, much less shoot someone. He also had an alibi witness, who did not testify at trial because the defense attorney thought that, because of alcohol abuse, this witness was not credible. Rosengrants steadfastly maintained his innocence until his death, as did a number of Leadville citizens. He was hanged on a two-rope gallows simultaneously with Franklin Gilbert.[35]

---

34. *Beginning the Trial of Canty, the Alleged Murderer of Tom Perkins*, COLO. SPRINGS DAILY GAZ., Apr. 19, 1881, at 4; *Continuation of the Trial of Canty—The Case Under Argument*, COLO. SPRINGS DAILY GAZ., Apr. 20, 1881, at 4; *The Jury Finds Canty Guilty of Premeditated Murder*, COLO. SPRINGS DAILY GAZ., Apr. 21, 1881, at 4; *Life for a Life. Law Vindicated and Life More Secure. W. H. Salisbury, Alias W. H. Canty, Expiates His Crime*, COLO. SPRINGS DAILY GAZETTE, June 18, 1881, at 1.

35. SHERRILL WARFORD, VERDICT, GUILTY AS CHARGED: LEADVILLE JUSTICE, 1879–1886 16–29 (1977). *See* case no. 16, *infra*.

FIGURE A.1. *The execution of Tomas Coleman in Gunnison, December 16, 1881. Photo by Bruce Hartman, from Duane Vandenbusche, The Gunnison Country (1980). Photo courtesy of Duane Vandenbusche.*

16. FRANKLIN GILBERT. July 29, 1881. Leadville (Lake County). W-W. Hanging/Broken Neck. A charcoal salesman, approximately thirty years of age, Gilbert was convicted of shooting and stabbing James McCollom, allegedly because McCollom owed him money. He was hanged with Merrick Rosengrants[36] in front of some five thousand spectators.[37]

17. THOMAS COLEMAN. December 16, 1881. Gunnison (Gunnison County). B-B. Hanging/Broken Neck. A railroad worker and foreman of a grading

36. *See* case no. 15, *infra.*

37. *Id.*

crew, Coleman, aged twenty-seven, was convicted of killing another African American, a teamster named Albert Smith. The two had quarreled several months before the murder about $5 that Coleman had lost in a card game. Coleman felt Smith had cheated him, and on July 5, 1881, he shot Smith when Smith refused to return the money. The execution took place before a "large crowd" in the yard of the Gunnison jail. Coleman was intoxicated and had to be carried to the gallows.[38] When the signal was given to proceed with the hanging, the trapdoor failed to open, and Coleman was removed from the gallows while the mechanism was repaired. Once adjustments were made, it worked properly. The *Pitkin Independent*'s headline after the hanging read, "Jerked to Jesus. The Negro Coleman Bids Adieu To All Earthly Sights and Takes a Flying Trip Over the River Jordan."[39] Later, Coleman's body was left to freeze, and bits of it were chipped off for souvenirs.[40]

18. GEORGE N. WOODS. June 23, 1882. Durango (La Plata County). W-W. Hanging/Strangulation. Executed less than one month after he shot and murdered M. G. Buchanan. Both Woods (age thirty-four) and Buchanan were members of the Stockton Gang, and its leader, Ike Stockton, had recently died. Both Woods and Buchanan were friends with Stockton's widow (who by the time of the murder had already married another suitor). Woods and Buchanan frequently quarreled about her, apparently because Woods was attracted to her, and Buchanan (who was also friends with the widow's new husband) tried to discourage the romance. The murder occurred in a Durango saloon, where both brandished weapons before Buchanan was killed. Woods argued self-defense and said that his only regret was that he did not also kill the woman's new husband, Joel Estes.[41]

---

38. *Paid in Full*, GUNN. DAILY NEWS DEMO., Dec. 17, 1881, at 1; *Sent Heavenward*, PUEBLO CHIEFTAIN, Dec. 18, 1881, at 1.

39. Duane Vandenbusche, THE GUNNISON COUNTRY 181–2 (1980).

40. *Id.* at 182.

41. *Murder!*, DURANGO DAILY NEWS, May 25, 1882, at 1; *Home Stretch: Woods Does Not Weaken as He Approaches the Same*, DURANGO DAILY HERALD, June 20, 1882, at 4; *Woods Willing*, DURANGO DAILY NEWS, June 22, 1882, at 4; *Wild Woods, Fails to Shuffle Off the Sheriff's Coil; He Died the Death Due His Dark Deed At Durango*, ROCKY MTN. NEWS, June 24, 1882, at 1; Duane A. Smith, ROCKY MOUNTAIN BOOM TOWN: A HISTORY OF DURANGO 51 (1980). Clever headlines were not uncommon in stories about hangings. *Press Pointers: George N. Woods Dances on Air*

FIGURE A.2. *Execution of George Woods in Durango, June 23, 1882. As the headline in the Rocky Mountain News put it, "He Died the Death Due His Dark Deed at Durango." General Photograph Collection, file number P001-10920. Photo courtesy of Center for Southwest Studies, Fort Lewis College, Durango.*

19. MIGUEL GARCIA. December 20, 1884. Pueblo. H-W. Hanging/Broken Neck. A native of Mexico, Garcia, aged fifty-four, did not speak English. He was employed gathering old rags, bones, iron, etc. After three trials and a change of venue to Pueblo, he was convicted—three different times—of killing his employer, Dennis Wilkes, near Las Animas (Bent County).[42] Wilkes's head was crushed while he lay in bed sleeping; the alleged motive was robbery. The murder occurred after Wilkes employed Garcia for two weeks. Garcia abruptly left town before the body was discovered and pawned a watch that had belonged to the victim. A crowd estimated at four thousand attended the execution, which, like the trial, was also held in Pueblo.[43]

---

for the Amusement of the Good People of Durango, LEADVILLE DAILY HERALD, June 24, 1882, at 1.

42. *Garcia Convicted*, PUEBLO CHIEFTAIN, Nov. 27, 1884, at 4.

43. *Sentence Passed*, PUEBLO CHIEFTAIN, Dec. 2, 1884, at 5; *Gone Glimmering: The Soul of Miguel Garcia Takes Its Flight to a Higher Court for A Hearing*, PUEBLO CHIEFTAIN, Dec. 21, 1884, at 4; *Garcia's Adios*, ROCKY MTN. NEWS, Dec. 21, 1884, at 8.

20. CHARLES HIBBARD. April 24, 1885. Trinidad (Las Animas County). W-W. Hanging/Broken Neck. Convicted of the murder of William Knowles in Stonewall, approximately forty miles north of Trinidad. Hibbard was living at his uncle's ranch in Stonewall when Knowles (an elderly man who had a large sum of money) came to visit. When the uncle left for a trip to Illinois, Hibbard and Knowles stayed behind to care for the ranch. Neighbors soon realized that Knowles was missing, and their inquiries caused Hibbard to leave town. When the uncle returned, Knowles's body was discovered. When Hibbard was apprehended in Kansas, he confessed to the murder and to a long history of other crimes (including murder and horse and cattle theft).[44]

21. MARSHALL CLEMENTS. December 3, 1885. Saguache (Saguache County). W-W. Hanging. Convicted of killing his brother, Thomas H. Clements, and sister-in-law, Susie Y. Clements. In his written confession, Clements accused the victims of mistreating his father and sister (who had raised the two boys and four other siblings after their mother's death), living off them, calling his sisters prostitutes, and causing his father's death through physical and psychological abuse. The family had emigrated from Ireland two years before the murders.[45] At the execution, because the sheriff "had no stomach," the trapdoor was sprung by an anonymous person using a rope strung from the hanging scaffold to the nearby county clerk's office."[46] Some five thousand spectators were in attendance.[47]

22. CYRUS MINICH. February 5, 1886. Leadville (Lake County). W-W. Hanging. Convicted of killing Samuel Baldwin, a miner who was widely rumored to hold all his money on his person because he distrusted the banking system. Baldwin had been beaten to death, allegedly by four robbers, and the only evidence connecting Minich with the crime was

---

44. *Hibbard Hanged*, ROCKY MTN. NEWS, Apr. 25, 1885, at 1.

45. *Four Fiends; The Clements Murder at Saguache a Deed of Atrocity Unparalleled in Colorado*, ROCKY MTN. NEWS, Oct. 2, 1885, at 8.

46. *That Fatal Drop*, ROCKY MTN. NEWS, Dec. 4, 1885, at 1.

47. Patrea Jensen, *Colorado's 86 Legal Executions*, COLO. SHERIFF AND PEACE OFFICER 14 (Oct.–Nov. 1966): 14–15.

that he deposited $360 in a bank on the day after Baldwin's death.[48] One self-confessed participant fingered Minich, but he later jumped bail and, like a third suspect, was never heard from again. The fourth man initially implicated in the murder had an alibi. Meanwhile, Minich, aged thirty-seven, steadfastly maintained his innocence from the time of his arrest until the time of his death. Even the Colorado Supreme Court acknowledged the case against Minich was totally circumstantial, "Yet there is woven about the defendant a web of circumstances which, coupled with his attempted explanation thereof, point irresistibly to him as one of the guilty parties."[49] On the gallows before some seven thousand observers,[50] Minich again proclaimed his innocence and then said, "Good bye to all. Good bye." As the local newspaper put it, "The crowd then responded with one voice . . . Good bye, Cy, Good bye, Cy."[51]

23. ANDREW GREEN. July 27, 1886. Denver. B-W. Hanging/Suffocation. Convicted of the robbery-murder of Joseph C. Whitnah, a driver for the Denver City Railway Company. Green, twenty-five, and an accomplice were overheard in a saloon talking about the murder, and within a few days, Green had been arrested for vagrancy, drunkenness, and carrying a concealed weapon—charges that were soon upgraded to murder. He had been imprisoned previously in both Colorado and Missouri for thefts and at age twelve had shot and wounded his father. Green claimed that he simply wanted to rob Whitnah, he had no intent to commit murder, and his gun had discharged accidentally. Nonetheless, he was convicted under the felony-murder doctrine, which holds that if a person is killed when the perpetrator is committing another felony (e.g., rape, robbery), the question of intent to kill is not relevant. He was sentenced to death. The accomplice, after entering a guilty plea to second-degree murder, was sentenced to life imprisonment at hard labor. Thereafter, in

---

48. *Network of the Baldwin Murder—A Poor Chance for Gillespie*, ROCKY MTN. NEWS, Oct. 19, 1884, at 2.

49. Minich v. People, 9 P. 4, 14 (Colo. 1885).

50. *Paid the Penalty: Cyrus Minich Is Sent to the Other World*, ASPEN DAILY TIMES, Feb. 6, 1886, at 1.

51. Warford, *Verdict*, 30–43 (1977); DON L. GRISWOLD & JEAN HARVEY GRISWOLD, HISTORY OF LEADVILLE AND LAKE COUNTY, COLORADO, VOL. 2, 1772–83 (1996); *Minich—His Terrible Crime and Awful Punishment, A Full History of the Murder, Arrest, and Trial*, LEADVILLE HERALD DEMO., Feb. 6, 1886, at 1.

the twenty-five days between the verdict and the execution, the Denver newspapers had a lengthy debate about whether the hanging should be public. This debate continued after Green's death, eventually culminating in legislation signed in 1889 that relegated all future Colorado executions to the state prison in Cañon City. Some fifteen to twenty thousand people attended the execution, many of whom were repulsed while they watched, for twenty-two-and-a-half minutes, as Green twisted and slowly suffocated to death. A century later, University of Colorado historian William M. King authored a book about the crime and execution and late nineteenth-century race relations in Denver.[52]

24. NICOLAI FEMENELLA (a.k.a. Mike George, Nocolo Fiminello). August 23, 1888. Buena Vista (Chaffee County). W-W. Hanging/Broken Neck. An Italian immigrant, Femenella was convicted of killing William (Pat) Casey (Irish), who, like Femenella, was employed as a railroad section hand in the city of Granite. The murder resulted from a quarrel between several Irish and Italian immigrants about the men's different ethnic heritages. After his conviction, Femenella began to claim self-defense, a plea that, had it originally been used, would probably have saved him from the gallows.[53] Gov. Alva Adams deferred the execution on three occasions. "According to prevalent opinion here Femenella has received more consideration than would be accorded to the majority of life-long citizens in this commu-

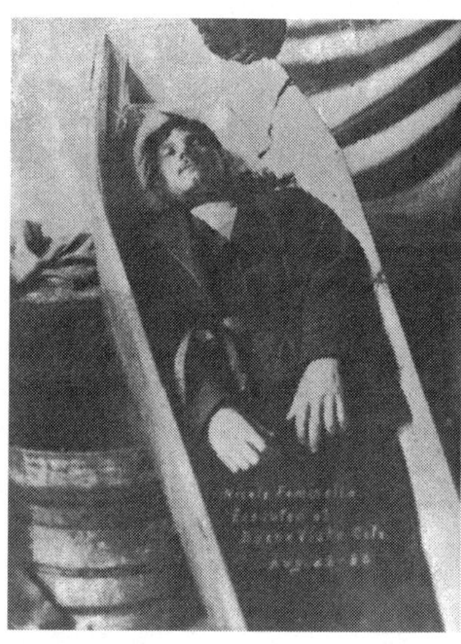

FIGURE A.3. *The execution of Nicolai Femenella, Buena Vista, May 17, 1888. Femenella in his coffin, with the rope still around his neck. Photo courtesy of Suzy Kelly, Buena Vista Heritage.*

52. KING.

53. *Justice Satisfied at Last*, SALIDA MAIL, Aug. 24, 1888, at 2.

FIGURE A.4. *The execution of Nicolai Femenella, Buena Vista, May 17, 1888. Femenella on the gallows. Photo courtesy of Suzy Kelly, Buena Vista Heritage.*

nity."[54] One report estimated that 1,500 people witnessed the execution, which was carried out in the yard of the Buena Vista jail.[55] Femenella was hanged with rope left over from an order placed with a St. Louis company that was used to hang Andrew Green.[56]

54. *Femenella Is Hanged*, ROCKY MTN. NEWS, Aug. 24, 1888, at 1. *See also Hanged!*, BUENA VISTA DEMO., Aug. 23, 1888, at 3.

55. ELEANOR FRY, SALIDA: THE EARLY YEARS 210–211 (2011).

56. KING, at 117. *See* case no. 23, *infra*.

25. JOSE ORTIZ (a.k.a. James Abram Ortiz). July 16, 1889. Antonito (Conejos County). H-W. Hanging/Broken Neck. Convicted of the murder of O. E. LeDuc, a miner. "The murder was one of a peculiarly revolting character."[57] LeDuc, on a short business trip, disappeared after stopping to spend the night at Ortiz's cabin. His friends spent several weeks searching for him. After tracking him to Ortiz's home, a search party found the home abandoned and smeared with blood, and they soon found LeDuc's body on the property. The evidence indicated that he had been killed with a heavy instrument—probably an ax—while in bed. When Ortiz was found, he was wearing LeDuc's watch. The jury, which included six Mexicans, deliberated for a full day before returning its verdict. The execution took place three months after Gov. Job A. Cooper signed a bill prohibiting public executions.[58] However, the ban did not take effect until July 19, three days after Ortiz's scheduled execution. Thereafter, all Colorado executions took place at the state prison in Cañon City. The *Rocky Mountain News* wrote, "Ortiz was small and stunted, and a typical Mexican, stunted naturally and morally as well as physically."[59]

26. NOVERTO GRIEGO. November 8, 1890. Trinidad (Las Animas County). H-W. Hanging/Broken Neck. Griego (Mexican) was convicted of killing W. L. Underwood, a merchant who ran a grocery store that catered to the Hispanic community. Underwood was hit on the back of his head with a hammer while working at the store. Clutched in his hand was a piece of paper, which indicated that his last sale had been to someone named "Griego." When his body was discovered the next morning, the authorities also found that Underwood's jewelry, as well as all the cash in the store, had been stolen. A second participant in the crimes, George Upton (a.k.a. John Jones) (African American), was sentenced to life imprisonment rather than death, in exchange for testifying against Griego. Both men admitted their crimes. This was the first execution under state authority at the prison in Cañon City. The exact time of his

57. *Judicially Hanged.*

58. KING, at 158.

59. *Judicially Hanged: Ortiz, the Mexican Murderer, Suffers the Penalty of Law for His Crime*, ROCKY MTN. NEWS, July 17, 1889, at 1.

execution was not announced in advance, the name of the executioner was kept secret, and no representatives from the press were permitted to witness it.[60]

27. JAMES T. JOYCE. January 17, 1891. Denver (Arapahoe County). W-W. Hanging/Broken Neck. Convicted of "one of the coldest blooded murders in Colorado's history." Both Joyce (age thirty-three) and the victim, twenty-year-old John Snooks, worked at a Denver slaughterhouse. The murder occurred on July 4, 1890, when many of the employees had been drinking all day (in celebration of Independence Day), first at work and then in a neighborhood saloon. Snooks was accused of drinking more than his share of beer and was thrown out of the bar, and he returned a few minutes later with an empty musket and threatened Joyce with it. Later that day, back at work, Joyce was skinning a sheep when Snooks walked by, and Joyce attacked him with the knife, killing him. Joyce was believed to have committed an earlier murder in Kentucky and had also been involved in a prior assault. No journalists were permitted to witness the execution.[61] "The neck was instantly broken, and, according to the surgeons present, the most successful and painless execution that has ever been performed in America."[62]

28. WILLIAM H. DAVIS. Sept. 22, 1891. Pueblo. W-B&W. Hanging/Broken Neck. Convicted, at age twenty-five or twenty-six, of murdering his foster mother, Carrie Armsby ("a light mulatto"), and her alleged paramour, James Arnold (white), because they refused to give him money to continue a drinking binge. The time of the execution was not announced before the hanging, and no journalists were invited to attend.[63]

---

60. *Unknown Assassins*, ROCKY MTN. NEWS, June 5, 1890, at 1; *Three Mexicans Arrested*, ROCKY MTN. NEWS, June 6, 1890, at 1; *Hung for Murder: The Brute Who Slugged Poor Underwood Stretches Hemp*, PUEBLO CHIEFTAIN, Nov. 9, 1890, at 1.

61. *Joyce Hanged*, PUEBLO CHIEFTAIN, Jan. 18, 1891, at 1.

62. *Without A Tremor*, ROCKY MTN. NEWS, Jan. 18, 1891, at 1.

63. *Hanged in Prison*, ROCKY MTN. NEWS, Sept. 23, 1891, at 1; *The End of His Rope: W. H. Davis, The Pueblo Murderer, Hung at Cañon City*, PUEBLO CHIEFTAIN, Sept. 23, 1891, at 1.

29. CHARLES SMITH. December 14, 1891. Walsenburg (Huerfano County). B-B. Hanging. A thirty-year-old coal miner, Smith was convicted of killing (Mr.) Taylor Sillman, a neighbor whose wife was having relations with Smith. The affair resulted in "bad blood" and physical altercations between the two men. Eventually, after receiving a hefty beating by Sillman, Smith returned home, got his shotgun, and used it to shoot Sillman off his horse.[64]

30. THOMAS LAWTON. May 6, 1892. Colorado Springs (El Paso County). W-W. Hanging. Convicted of the murder of a streetcar conductor, John Hemming, during an attempted robbery. An accomplice, Albert Russell, admitted his role in the crime to friends, implicating Lawton. Russell was convicted of second-degree murder and sentenced to life imprisonment. Lawton (an assumed name) was twenty-four; he refused to tell anyone his real name or anything about his background or family.[65] He spent the four hours before his death moaning and wailing, although by the time he was executed, he had become calm.[66]

31. THOMAS A. JORDAN. May 11, 1895. Littleton (Arapahoe County). W-W. Hanging/Strangulation. Jordan (a native of Ireland, age twenty-nine at his death) was employed at a Denver-area smelter but was fired after drinking heavily and being tardy for work. The next day (while continuing to drink heavily) he purchased a pistol and went to the smelter to kill the foreman who had fired him. That person was not at the factory when Jordan arrived, but Jordan's presence at the smelter caused a disturbance. He instead shot a friend named August (Gus) Sisin, a smelter watchman who had come to quell the ruckus.[67] On death row, his sanity was questioned, and a panel of physicians was appointed to evaluate him. The found him to be sane. Gov. Albert W. McIntire visited Jordan in prison but denied executive clemency. At the execution, Jordan's neck was not broken, and he strangled to death. The *Rocky Mountain News*

---

64. *Met Death Bravely: Charles Smith, the Walsenburg Murderer, Hanged at the State Penitentiary Last Night*, ROCKY MTN. NEWS, Dec. 15, 1891, at 1.

65. *Lawton is Executed*, DENVER REPUB., May 7, 1892, at 1.

66. *Crying Like a Baby, a Man Who Shot Down a Fellow Creature Begs for Mercy*, PUEBLO CHIEFTAIN, May 7, 1892, at 1.

67. Jordan v. People, 36 P. 218 (Colo. 1894).

asserted that Jordan and Peter Augusta (hanged that same night) had "the most remarkable records of any persons ever sentenced to execution at Cañon City. Through the law's delays and executive clemency their lives were prolonged by two years."[68]

32. PETER AUGUSTA. May 11, 1895. Littleton (Arapahoe County). W-W. Hanging/Broken Neck. Convicted of killing Harry Sullivan (a.k.a. David McClennigan) in a jealous rage, under the belief that Sullivan was having an affair with the woman with whom Augusta was living. In a statement made as he was dying, Sullivan fingered Augusta as the man who assaulted him, saying he was stabbed while sleeping in the woman's house. Augusta was a forty-seven-year-old immigrant from Italy, and the Italian consulate was among those petitioning for a commutation.[69]

33. ABE TAYLOR. December 13, 1895. Alamosa (Conejos County). W-W. Hanging/Broken Neck. Taylor (a thirty-two-year-old ranchman) and an accessory, William Thompson (age sixteen), were charged with the murder of Charles H. Emerson. The two men had stolen a wagonload of oats and Taylor shot Emerson with a gun given to him by Thompson. Emerson was the town marshal and constable of Alamosa, and he was shot while apprehending the two men for theft. In his final statement, Taylor told the fourteen witnesses that the murder was not premeditated and that he had never held any malice toward the victim.[70]

34. BENJAMIN RATCLIFF (a.k.a. Radcliff). February 7, 1896. Salida (Chaffee County). W-W. Hanging/Broken Neck. A farmer, Ratcliff was convicted of killing three members of the Michigan Creek School Board—George Douglas Wyatt, Samuel Taylor, and L. F. McCurdy. The murders occurred near Bordenville, about fifteen miles northeast of Fairplay. Ratcliff believed that one of the members (McCurdy) had slandered Ratcliff's

---

68. *The Condemned*, ROCKY MTN. NEWS, May 12, 1895, at 1.

69. *Id.*

70. Taylor v. People, 42 P. 652 (Colo. 1895); *Shot the Marshal*, ROCKY MTN. NEWS, Jan. 20, 1895, at 4; *Marshal Emerson Dead*, ROCKY MTN. NEWS, Jan. 22, 1895, at 2; *Abe Taylor Executed*, ROCKY MTN. NEWS, Dec. 14, 1895, at 1; *The Suicide Machine: Abe Taylor Tried the Automatic Gallows; Death Sudden and Sure*, PUEBLO CHIEFTAIN, Dec. 14, 1895, at 1.

daughter by claiming she was pregnant after an incestuous relationship with Ratcliff. The murders occurred at a school board meeting. Ratcliff had gone to the meeting to demand a retraction and apology and shot wildly when no retraction was offered.[71] He later turned himself in to authorities, who housed him in several jails before trial to avoid lynching.[72] The trial, in July 1895, was moved to Salida to thwart another possible lynching. The Colorado Supreme Court affirmed his conviction in January 1896.[73]

35–37. WILLIAM HOLT, ALBERT NOBLE, and DEONICIO ROMERO. June 26, 1896. Trinidad (Las Animas County). W-W. Hanging/Broken Necks. This case involved three codefendants convicted of the felony murder of a Trinidad police officer, John Solomon. In July 1895, Romero and Noble became acquainted with Leonardo Martinez and Pedro Baca, who were being held in the Las Animas County Jail awaiting trial for murder. Romero was serving a jail sentence for assault (having served several previous sentences for petty offenses) and Noble had been arrested for a robbery in New Mexico (he had previously served a seven-year sentence for robbing a post office).[74] After being released from jail, Romero and Noble, along with William Holt (age twenty-one), conspired to rob the Horse Shoe Gambling Club in Trinidad in order to secure funds for Martinez and Baca's defense. Several others, including Martinez's mother, assisted with the scheme. The robbery was foiled when discovered by Officer Solomon, who struggled with Holt and then was shot in the back by Noble. Holt was the first person arrested; he was tied to the crime by a gun left at the scene that had been sold to him a few days earlier by a local pawnbroker. Upon interrogation, Holt confessed, and Romero quickly confirmed his story. Noble was tried first, followed by a joint

---

71. Ratcliff v. People, 43 P. 553 (Colo. 1896); *Ratcliff Must Hang*, DENVER POST, Jan. 15, 1896, at 2; *Would See Him Die*, DENVER POST, Feb. 7, 1896, at 2.

72. *Radcliff Was Executed Last Night*, ROCKY MTN. NEWS, Feb. 8, 1896, at 1; *His Life a Forfeit*, DENVER POST, Feb. 8, 1896, at 2.

73. LAURA VAN DUSEN, HISTORIC TALES FROM PARK COUNTY 127–34 (2013). For a comprehensive overview of the case and the lives of Ratcliff's descendants, *see* CHRIS O. ANDREW, THE LEGEND OF BENJAMIN RATCLIFF: FROM FAMILY TRAGEDY TO A LEGACY OF RESILIENCE (2010).

74. *Noble's Record*, ROCKY MTN. NEWS, Dec. 2, 1895, at 8.

trial for Holt and Romero. The convictions were affirmed on appeal.[75] The three were executed in the first triple execution in Colorado's history (the only other one was in 1931). The men were executed in alphabetical order, in private, with all details prior to the executions kept secret. Originally, the men were supposed to be hanged in the order of their culpability (Noble, Romero, and then Holt), but Holt was so distressed that he "was called first" (and had to be carried to the death chamber).[76]

38. AZEL D. GALBRAITH. March 6, 1905. Central City (Gilpin County). W-W. Hanging/Broken Neck. Convicted of murdering his wife and eight-year-old son, "one of the most shocking in the criminal annals of the state."[77] Shortly before the murders, Galbraith had been dismissed from his position as a mine manager. After the murders, he lived in Denver for one month before being arrested for forgery for signing his employer's name to checks worth $1,000. Two days thereafter, the bodies were discovered. Galbraith confessed to the murders, detailing how he shot his unsuspecting wife as they lay in bed together and how he then brought his eight year-old son into the bed and shot him. Galbraith blamed his crimes on drinking and gambling and a desire to be with his paramour.[78] He was thirty-four at the time of his death, had no prior convictions (and attended two years of college), and worked as a timekeeper in a mine.[79] He faced his death stoically, with witnesses reportedly in agreement that he was "the bravest man that ever stepped on a scaffold in Colorado."[80]

---

75. Holt et al. v. People, 45 P. 374 (Colo. 1896); Noble v. People, 45 P. 376 (Colo. 1896).

76. *Shot A Police Officer*, ROCKY MTN. NEWS, Nov. 21, 1895, at 1; *Officer Solomon Dead*, ROCKY MTN. NEWS, Nov. 22, 1895, at 6; *Confessed The Murder*, ROCKY MTN. NEWS, Nov. 30, 1895, at 6; *Three Men Executed at Cañon City*, ROCKY MTN. NEWS, June 27, 1896, at 1.

77. *Story of One of Most Horrible Crimes in History of Colorado*, ROCKY MTN. NEWS, Mar. 7, 1905, at 3.

78. *Azel Galbraith Is Hanged for His Crime*, ROCKY MTN. NEWS, Mar. 7, 1905, at 3.

79. *His Last Hope Gone, Azel D. Galbraith Must Hang Tonight*, DENVER POST, Mar. 6, 1905, at 1.

80. Azel Galbraith Is Hanged.

39–40. J. NEWTON ANDREWS and FRED ARNOLD. June 16, 1905. Denver. W-W. Hanging/Broken Necks. Convicted, in separate trials, of the murder of sixty-three-year-old Amanda E. Youngblood during an attempted robbery at her home (which also served as a small neighborhood grocery store). Her husband had responded to a knock at the door at 11:30 p.m. on New Year's Eve 1903 and found three men who requested to use his telephone. Thinking nothing of it, he invited them inside, where they immediately announced a hold-up. Youngblood resisted. His wife was murdered and their son was shot in the jaw when, awakened by the commotion, they entered the room where the confrontation was taking place. While both defendants confessed to their involvement in the crimes (saying they were drunk), each blamed the other for firing the fatal shot. The third intruder, Charles Peters, age twenty-five, was also sentenced to death for the murders, but his sanity was questioned and he was never executed. Arnold, a laborer, was nineteen years old at the time of the execution; Andrews, who worked for the railroads, was two years older and had a prior arrest for burglarizing telephone boxes.[81] Before their executions, the Colorado Supreme Court upheld a new death penalty statute passed by the Colorado Legislature in 1901, ending a four-year period of abolition.[82]

41. JOSEPH JOHNSON. September 13, 1905. Trinidad (Las Animas County). W-W. Hanging/Broken Neck. Convicted of killing John H. Fox, "ex-county treasurer, and one of the most prominent Democratic politicians in the county and state."[83] Johnson was a deputy sheriff and worked as a bodyguard for a state senator. The trouble began when a

---

81. *Robbers Kill Mother and Wound Her Son*, ROCKY MTN. NEWS, Jan. 1, 1904, sect. 2, at 1; *Boys Confess to Wanton Murder of Aged Woman*, ROCKY MTN. NEWS, Jan. 2, 1904, at 1; *Boy Murderers to Hang Today*, DENVER POST, June 16, 1905, at 1; *Arnold's Brutal Nature Displayed in Last Hours*, ROCKY MTN. NEWS, June 16, 1905, at 1; *Mother's Love Grows in Face of Inevitable*, ROCKY MTN. NEWS, June 16, 1905, at 1; *Quiet and Successful Execution Occurs Inside Walls of State Penitentiary*, DENVER REPUB., June 17, 1905, at 1; *Andrews and Arnold Pay the Penalty of Their Crime*, ROCKY MTN. NEWS, June 17, 1905, at 1.

82. *Capital Punishment Law Is Upheld by Supreme Court*, DENVER POST, Feb. 6, 1905, at 1; Andrews et al. v. People, 79 P. 1031 (Colo. 1905).

83. *Shot from Behind: John H. Fox Is Killed by a Deputy Sheriff Who Escapes the Mob*, DENVER POST, Apr. 9, 1905, at 1.

former clerk of Fox's was arrested in California for misappropriating Las Animas County funds, and Johnson wanted the job of going to California to retrieve the prisoner. Fox refused the appointment, a quarrel ensued, and Johnson shot Fox with a revolver. Johnson was immediately apprehended and admitted his guilt.[84]

42. JOHN McGARVEY. January 12, 1907. W-W. Grand Junction (Mesa County). Hanging/Broken Neck. A native of Scotland, McGarvey was in jail awaiting trial for attempting to assault a twelve-year-old girl when he crushed the skull of the jailer, Edward Innes, with a piece of firewood. He then stabbed the unconscious Innes—who died a few days later—stole his pistol, and escaped.[85] He was quickly apprehended, tried, and (at age twenty-three) convicted.[86]

43. GIUSEPPE ALIA. July 15, 1908. Denver. W-W. Hanging/Strangulation. Alia shot and killed a Catholic priest, Fr. Leo Heinrich, as Heinrich distributed Communion to Alia and other congregants during Mass at St. Elizabeth's Church in Denver on February 23, 1908. Alia, fifty-one at the time of his death, spent his first thirty-eight years in Italy and did not speak English. After leaving Italy, he worked as a shoemaker in Argentina for twelve years. He hated the Catholic Church and believed that Father Leo had somehow mistreated him in Portugal some years before the murder. The jury, however, rejected his insanity plea. Pleas for clemency by the Italian government and the Franciscan order—to which Father Leo belonged—to the acting governor were unsuccessful. At the time of his death (less than five months after the crime), Alia shouted "Viva Italia" and "Viva Protestant" and implored God to destroy the Roman Catholic priesthood. Because the rope slipped or was purposely put around his neck improperly, it took nineteen minutes for Alia to strangle to death.[87]

---

84. *Joseph Johnson Will Be Hanged Tonight for the Murder of John H. Fox*, DENVER POST, Sept. 13, 1905, at 6; *Met Death Stoically*, DENVER POST, Sept. 14, 1905, at 1.

85. *M'Garvey Must Surrender or Die in Boots*, DENVER POST, Sept. 30, 1906, at 1.

86. *M'Garvey Jerked to Eternity*, DENVER POST, January 13, 1907, at 1; *M'Garvey Pays Death Penalty*, DENVER REPUB., Jan. 13, 1907, at 1.

87. *Alia Will Be Hanged Tonight*, DENVER POST, July 15, 1908, at 1; *Slayer of Priest, With Curses on His Tongue, Died of Strangulation*, TRINIDAD DAILY NEWS, July 16, 1908, at 1.

44. JAMES LYNN. October 8, 1908. Pueblo. B-W. Hanging/Broken Neck. On May 14, 1908, Pueblo residents were shocked by the front-page headlines in the local newspaper: "Negro Drives Two White Women From Their Home and Shoots Them Down in the Street."[88] The article went on to identify a neighbor, James Lynn (a Pueblo resident for twenty-two years), as the shooter. Sarah James, sixteen, died and her mother, Julia—a widow with six children—was wounded ("expected to die at any moment"). Julia later recovered. She and her daughter had fled their home when Lynn burst into it at 1:00 a.m. Sarah supported the entire family of seven by working as a "servant" to a local physician. Lynn, a day laborer, was infatuated with Sarah and became jealous when another man (who left by the rear door as Lynn entered through the front) came to spend the night with her. Lynn had a prior arrest for assaulting a man with a poker.[89] After his arrest, Lynn was kept in Colorado Springs to prevent a lynching. At trial, exactly one month after the murder, he maintained his innocence. However, the jury returned a guilty verdict after only fifteen minutes of deliberation.[90]

45. LEWIS J. WECHTER. August 31, 1912. Denver. W-W. Hanging/Strangulation. Convicted of the murder of W. Clifford Burrowes, a hardware store salesman, during the attempted robbery of a cafe. Burrowes had just finished eating at the cafe when a masked robber entered and ordered everyone to move behind the counter. He refused and was shot. Two women (mother and daughter) who owned the cafe quickly overpowered Wechter, disarmed him, and held him until the authorities arrived. Burrowes died the next day. Wechter, twenty-nine, had served in the navy for twelve years and at the time of the crime was employed in a mattress factory.[91] He was wanted by Utah authorities for killing a

88. *Negro Drives Two White Women From Their Home and Shoots Them Down in the Street*, PUEBLO CHIEFTAIN, May 14, 1908, at 1.

89. *Officers Discover Motive Which Actuated Negro in Murder of Young White Girl*, PUEBLO CHIEFTAIN, May 15, 1908, at 1; *Negro Murderer Lynn Caught*, PUEBLO CHIEFTAIN, May 18, 1908, at 1.

90. *Lynn Is Hanged as He Protests His Innocence*, ROCKY MTN. NEWS, Oct. 9, 1908, at 1.

91. *Women Catch Bandit; Man Shot in Cafe*, ROCKY MTN. NEWS, Feb. 12, 1911, at 1; *Bandit's Victim Dies; Slayer in His Cell Merely Smiles*, ROCKY MTN. NEWS, Feb. 13, 1911, at 2.

man a few months prior to the Burrowes murder.[92] The jury deliberated for only fifteen minutes before returning a guilty verdict and a recommendation of a death sentence.[93] On appeal, the state Supreme Court affirmed the conviction.[94] Despite being personally opposed to capital punishment, Gov. John Shafroth declined to commute the sentence.[95] The prison warden, Thomas Tynan, also opposed the death penalty and refused to participate in the execution.[96] Because the time of the execution was supposed to be kept secret, Wechter's execution was postponed for twenty-four hours after the newspapers learned the time when it was originally scheduled. Death was by strangulation; "For 23 minutes the black-capped form dangled to and fro in the shadows cast by a great arc lamp."[97]

46. HARRY EDGAR HILLEN (a.k.a. James Nelson, Frank Allen). June 24, 1915. Denver. W-W. Hanging/Broken Neck. Convicted of the murder of real estate agent Thomas J. Chase during the commission of a robbery. A number of other robberies occurred in Denver in the time period surrounding the murder.[98] When arrested (for brandishing weapons while drunk), Hillen confessed to nine of the robberies.[99] The next day he confessed to killing Chase "because he snarled at me. I can't stand snarls."[100] "The lawyer who would defend the confessed slayer of my husband is a

---

92. *Wechter to Meet Murderer's Doom at Nine Tonight*, DENVER POST, Aug. 30, 1912, at 2.

93. *Noose Urged for Wechter By Jury*, ROCKY MTN. NEWS, Mar. 23, 1911, at 1.

94. Wechter v. People, 124 P. 183 (Colo. 1912).

95. *Wechter to Live Until Week's End, General Opinion*, DENVER POST, Aug. 26, 1912, at 3.

96. *Id.*

97. *Wechter Hangs After Torture from Suspense*, ROCKY MTN. NEWS, Sept. 1, 1912, at 1.

98. *1 Man Slain, Another Shot; Bandit Suspect Captured in Pistol Duel with Police*, ROCKY MTN. NEWS, Oct. 24, 1913, at 1; *Bandit Pair Hold Denver in Grip of Fear; Bullets Fly as Victim Fights Back*, ROCKY MTN. NEWS, Oct. 25, 1891, at 1; *Lone Bandit Loots Grocer, Flees in Rain of Lead; One New Suspect in Dragnet*, ROCKY MTN. NEWS, Oct. 26, 1913, at 1.

99. *Terror of Denver Caught; Confesses Nine Holdups; Woman Flees with Loot*, ROCKY MTN. NEWS, Oct. 27, 1913, at 1.

100. *Shot Chase Dead When He Snarled, Bandit Confesses*, ROCKY MTN. NEWS, Oct. 28, 1913, at 1.

far worse criminal than [Hillen]," said the widow.[101] His conviction was affirmed on appeal.[102] Hillen, twenty-four at the time of the murder, was suspected of over fifty forgeries and armed robberies throughout the United States, including approximately twenty robberies in Denver during the week of the murder.[103]

47. GEORGE QUINN. January 28, 1916. Denver. W-W. Hanging/Broken Neck. Convicted of killing the husband of the woman with whom he was having an affair and who was carrying his unborn child. The victim was William Herbertson, age thirty-six, a contractor; the weapon was a sawed-off shotgun that had been fired from close range. Quinn, thirty-two at the time, was employed as a teamster. After killing Herbertson, Quinn threatened his mistress and her twenty-month-old baby. She became the chief prosecution witness, but while Quinn was in jail, she recanted her testimony and married him "so that the babe might be given a name." She also became very active in attempting to convince the governor to commute the sentence. Nonetheless, the conviction was affirmed on appeal and no commutation was granted.[104] At the execution, warden Thomas Tynan, who opposed capital punishment, refused to enter the death chamber and instead remained in his office until Quinn was executed.[105]

48. OSCAR COOK. February 26, 1916. Denver. W-W. Hanging/Broken Neck. Convicted of the murders of patrolman William McPherson and saloonkeeper Andrew J. Loyd in an exchange of gunshots during the robbery of a Denver saloon. Two men entered the saloon announcing a holdup, and the shooting commenced when McPherson (who was visiting the saloon and in uniform) reached for his revolver, and a shoot-out

101. *I'd Kill Bandit, Cries Mrs. Chase*, ROCKY MTN. NEWS, Oct. 28, 1913, at 2.

102. Hillen v. People, 149 P. 250 (Colo. 1915).

103. W. L. Morrissey, *Hillen Goes to Death Asserting Innocence and Forgiving Enemies*, DENVER POST, June 25, 1915, at 1; *Hillen Dies on Gallows Maintaining His Innocence to End*, ROCKY MTN. NEWS, June 25, 1915, at 1.

104. Quinn v. People, 152 P. 148 (Colo. 1915).

105. *Quinn Dies On Gallows, Calm to End*, ROCKY MTN. NEWS, Jan. 29, 1916, at 1; *Tell Them I Died Game, Says Quinn, as He Goes to Death upon Gallows*, DENVER POST, Jan. 29, 1916, at 1; *Quinn Goes to Trap for Herbertson's Death*, DENVER POST, Jan. 29, 1916, at 1.

ensued.[106] In an ante-mortem statement, Officer McPherson implicated two other men as the gunmen; these men were arrested but released soon thereafter when Cook and an accomplice were arrested. Cook's arrest occurred after he requested medical care for a bullet wound, which the state argued he received in the crossfire and Cook said was received when he was trespassing in a lumberyard. A more complete confession came from a partner, Edward Seiwald (age nineteen), who was tried with Cook for the murders. Seiwald implicated Cook as the gunman; he claimed that he shot Cook after he realized that their robbery plans had—because of Cook—ended in murder. At trial, Cook argued insanity[107] but was sentenced to death; Seiwald was convicted of second-degree murder and sentenced to twelve years in prison. On appeal, Cook's conviction was vacated because of a failure to grant a severance.[108] At retrial, Cook was again convicted and sentenced to death; this conviction and sentence were affirmed on appeal.[109] In his last words before being hanged, Cook continued to maintain that he had not fired the fatal shots. As was the custom at the time, the warden allowed Cook to name the exact hour of his execution.[110]

49. GEORGE R. BOSKO (a.k.a. Bosco). December 10, 1920. Pueblo. W-W. Hanging/Broken Neck. Executed for the murders of William T. Hunter and Elton C. Parks. Bosko's brother and accomplice, Tom, was under eighteen at the time of the crimes,[111] and because of his young age, he was sentenced to life imprisonment rather than death for his role in the crimes. Parks was a car salesman demonstrating a new car to Hunter, a ranch owner, when they picked up the two brothers. The victims were shot and their car was stolen. Bosko, age twenty-eight, was employed as

106. *Policeman and Barkeeper Fatally Shot by Assassins*, ROCKY MTN. NEWS, Mar. 10, 1912, at 1; Arthur M'Lenan, *Policeman M'Pherson [(sic]) and Saloon Owner Die of Wounds; Boy Bandit's Confession Clears Double Murder Mystery*, DENVER POST, Mar. 11, 1912, at 1.

107. *Death Penalty for Oscar Cook*, ROCKY MTN. NEWS, Oct. 25, 1914, at 1.

108. Cook v. People, 138 P. 756 (Colo. 1914).

109. Cook v. People, 153 P. 214 (Colo. 1915).

110. *Cook, in Last Second of Life, Protests Innocence*, ROCKY MTN. NEWS, Feb. 27, 1916, at 1; *Oscar Cook Pays Penalty of Murder Just Before Dawn Creeps into Prison*, DENVER POST, Feb. 26, 1916, at 1.

111. Bosko v. People, 188 P. 743 (Colo. 1920).

a ranch hand, had no prior arrests, and had served in the army for three years. Upon his arrest, he gave a full confession and at trial pleaded guilty. The convictions were affirmed on appeal.[112] The lieutenant governor delayed the execution for five months so physicians could evaluate Bosko's sanity. At the time of the execution, Bosko's mother "is said to have suffered a collapse . . . and was not expected to live thru [*sic*] the night."[113]

50. DANIEL BORICH. August 18, 1922. Oak Creek (Routt County). W-W. Hanging. Executed for the murders of his wife, Milla, to whom he had been married for twenty-six years, and Joseph Kezele, who had tried to protect Milla when her husband began to stab her. Prior to the murder, Milla had filed for divorce, and the couple had been fighting. Borich, a fifty-one-year-old coal miner, was a "Mohammedan," born to Turkish parents in Serbia, and did not speak English very well. No appeal was taken. He was executed in the prison boiler room on a hastily built hanging machine. Prior hangings in Cañon City had taken place in a separate "execution house."[114]

51. JOE McGONIGAL (a.k.a. M'Gonnigal, McGonigle). April 26, 1924. Trinidad (Las Animas County). W-W. Hanging. Convicted of killing Wilbur N. Ferguson, a student at the Colorado School of Mines, and Ella Centers, the daughter of the owner of a rooming house where both Ferguson and McGonigal lived. McGonigal, forty-two, was employed as a watchman at a mine, and at one time had been prominent in the affairs of the United Mine Workers of America. He shot Ferguson inside the house and Centers fled in terror. McGonigal chased her and killed her with a shotgun as she pleaded for her life. Several nearby workmen witnessed

---

112. *Id.*

113. *George Bosko Pays Penalty for Crime*, PUEBLO CHIEFTAIN, Dec. 11, 1920, at 1; *Bosco* [*sic*] *Hanged at Cañon City, Aged Mother is Near Death*, ROCKY MTN. NEWS, Dec. 11, 1920, at 1.

114. *Borich Hanged at Cañon City for Double Oak Creek Killing*, DENVER POST, Aug. 19, 1922, at 1; *Wife Slayer Hanged in State Prison; Was Routt County Miner*, ROCKY MTN. NEWS, Aug. 20, 1922, at 8. Several articles about the case from the local newspaper, the *Oak Creek Times*, were transcribed by historian Peter "Mike" Yurich, from the Tracks and Trails Museum in Oak Creek. They are available in the booklet *South Routt County Homicides, 1910–1933*, distributed by the museum.

the murder. McGonigal then returned to the house and, allegedly to create a self-defense claim, shot himself in the foot (which later had to be amputated). The state alleged that the murders were committed while McGonigal was drunk and that he was jealous of the relationship between Ferguson and Centers. The sole defense was insanity, although only jail prisoners—and no experts—were proffered to support that claim. On the other hand, three psychiatrists testified that the defendant was sane.[115] On appeal, the defense attorney defaulted on the case by failing to file an abstract of the record and brief. However, after being reprimanded and cited for contempt, the attorney was permitted to continue on the case.[116] Thereafter, the conviction was affirmed.[117] After the governor granted a one-month stay of execution so McGonigal's sanity could be evaluated, he was hanged with the "old water type" gallows.[118]

52. RAY F. SHANK. September 18, 1926. Denver. W-W. Hanging. After being served with divorce papers, Shank, age fifty-two, shot and killed his wife, Marion, and their nineteen-year-old son, Paul (as he was sleeping). He then beat and tried to kill their twenty-one-year-old daughter, Ruth, but her life was saved when a neighbor disarmed Shank. Shank, a machinist, had a history of domestic abuse but no prior arrests. At trial, his insanity defense failed, and he was sentenced to death for the murder of his wife. The conviction was affirmed on appeal.[119] On the eve of his execution, Shank was quoted as saying, "This is the happiest night for me since the tragedy. I know it will soon be over."[120]

---

115. *Slayer of Student to Plead Insanity*, ROCKY MTN. NEWS, Oct. 13, 1922, at 11; *Slayer of Student and Girl Convicted; Penalty Is Death*, ROCKY MTN. NEWS, Oct. 14, 1922, at 14; *Convicted Slayer Sentenced to Hang*, ROCKY MTN. NEWS, Nov. 19, 1922, at 14.

116. *M'Gonnigal Is Hanged at Dawn Saturday at Penitentiary for Double Murder*, DENVER POST, Apr. 26, 1924, at 1.

117. McGonigal v. People, 220 P. 1003 (Colo. 1923).

118. *Girl Slain by Jealous Admirer After He Kills Mines Student*, DENVER POST, June 2, 1922, at 1; *M'Gonnigal Is Hanged at Dawn*; *M'Gonnigal Dies on Gallows as Last Pardon Hope Fails*, ROCKY MTN. NEWS, Apr. 26, 1924, at 1.

119. Shank v. People, 247 P. 559 (Colo. 1926).

120. *Shank's Body Sent Here after He Pays Supreme Penalty*, ROCKY MTN. NEWS, Sept. 19, 1926, at 1.

53. ANTONIO CASIAS. November 12, 1926. Del Norte (Rio Grande County). H-H. Hanging/Broken Neck. Convicted of stabbing to death Carmen Barela (a.k.a. Barilla) on the main street of Monte Vista. Barela, a widow, was the mother of four children, and her death quickly led to lynching threats.[121] She and Casias, a laborer, had been friends. Both were of Mexican ethnicity. Casias pleaded guilty and said that the motive was jealousy. He did not speak English, and some officials thought him to be "unbalanced" because for many years he "suffered from a loathsome [unnamed] disease. There is nothing pretty about the case of Antonio Casias."[122] A newspaper reported, "He went to his death with the singular distinction of being the only prisoner ever executed in Colorado over whom no one displayed the slightest concern."[123]

54-55. RAYMOND JASPER NOAKES and ARTHUR ALONZO OSBORN. March 30, 1928. Hot Sulfur Springs (Grand County). W-W. Hanging. Convicted of robbing Fred N. Selak (a hermit, aged sixty-five) and hanging him from a tree on his property. The murder resulted from a robbery and feud between the parties over a road owned by Selak that Osborn and Noakes needed to use to remove lumber from a nearby property owned by Osborn's father. Selak had forbidden his road to be used. Osborn had been arrested previously and fined for assaulting Selak. Osborn (a lumberjack, twenty-two at the time of the crime) and his cousin, Noakes (also a lumberjack, aged twenty at the time of the crime) were very close, having been raised as brothers for the previous fifteen years. Upon their arrests three weeks after the murder (for purchasing items with coins proved to have been owned by Selak), the men confessed and directed authorities to where the body was still hanging.[124] At trial, they pleaded not guilty by reason of insanity, and after this failed, their convictions and death sentences were affirmed on appeal.[125] Gov. William H. Adams,

---

121. *Lynching Near as Monte Vista Woman Is Slain*, DENVER POST, June 20, 1926, at 1.

122. *Murderer of Woman Pays Death Penalty on Cañon City Gallows*, DENVER POST, Nov. 12, 1926, at 1.

123. *Id.*

124. *Youth Admits Hanging Grand Lake Hermit*, ROCKY MTN. NEWS, Aug. 17, 1926, at 1; *Second Confession Is Made by Osborne* [sic] *in Selak Slaying*, ROCKY MTN. NEWS, Aug. 20, 1926, at 1.

125. Osborn et al. v. People, 262 P.2d 892 (Colo. 1927).

while a strong foe of the death penalty, nonetheless did not find grounds for commutation,[126] even though warden Francis E. Crawford (among others) traveled to Denver to plead the case.[127]

56. EDWARD IVES. January 10, 1930. Denver. W-W. Hanging/Strangulation. A career criminal who had served five prior prison terms and was suspected in over one hundred Denver burglaries,[128] Ives, forty-six at the time of his hanging, was sentenced to death for the murder of Denver police officer Harry R. Ohle. Ives (who was white) and an African American friend, Henry Hill, had gone to a "Negro Party House" in Denver where black customers (primarily) were offered liquor and the services of prostitutes. While there, the police raided the house. The customers scattered, and Ohle was shot as he searched under a bed for anyone hiding there. Mrs. Reese, the proprietor, was also shot and killed that night, but no one was ever tried for that murder. Another officer was wounded.[129] While no one witnessed Ohle's murder, the gun used in the crime was in Ives's possession when he was arrested. Ives maintained his innocence, blaming the murder on Hill, and appealed his conviction to the Colorado Supreme Court under a law that prohibited the execution of anyone convicted solely on circumstantial evidence. However, the Supreme Court found the evidence sufficient to sustain the conviction and sentence.[130] Alleging insanity, Ives was granted a short

---

126. *Executive Is Unnerved by Trying Ordeal*, DENVER POST, Mar. 30, 1928, at 2.

127. *Noakes, Osborn Hanged*, ROCKY MTN. NEWS, Mar. 30, 1928, at 1; *Face Noose Calmly*, DENVER POST, Mar. 30, 1928, at 1.

128. *Eddie Ives Ends 40 Years of Crime in Three States on Gallows at Cañon City*, ROCKY MTN. NEWS, Jan. 11, 1930, at 3. Ives "had spent all but eight of his 46 years doing time in one prison or another, including the penitentiaries of Colorado, Utah, and Oregon." Frances Melrose, *Little Eddie Ives Played Big Role in Changing Execution*, ROCKY MTN. NEWS, Jan. 17, 1977, at 8.

129. This officer was Robert Evans. When admitted to the hospital, nurse Farice King was assigned to care for him. King recognized Evans as a person with whom she had an affair a dozen years previously. She purchased a pistol, and five days after he was admitted to the hospital, she shot and killed him as he slept and then attempted to take her own life. She was eventually sentenced to life imprisonment but was pardoned by Gov. Edwin C. Johnson in 1934. *See* Melrose, *Little Eddie Ives*; BETTY L. ALT & SANDRA K. WELLS, MOUNTAIN MURDERS: HOMICIDE IN THE ROCKIES 15–35 (2009).

130. Ives v. People, 278 P. 792 (Colo. 1929).

stay of execution so psychiatrists could examine him. This motion was unsuccessful. Shortly before the execution, warden Francis E. Crawford traveled to Denver to meet with Gov. William H. Adams to support the insanity claim and appeal for clemency.[131] This, too, was unsuccessful. In his final statement, Ives continued to protest his innocence.[132] The hanging was horribly botched. When the weight was dropped to jerk Ives upward, he was accelerated skyward, but because he weighed only eighty pounds, the rope fell off the pulleys and he fell back to the ground. He was semiconscious but yelled, "you can't hang a man twice."[133] He was wrong. The second time, the machinery worked, although it failed to break his neck.[134]

57. HAROLD I. WEISS. May 28, 1930. Denver. W-W. Hanging/Strangulation. Convicted of killing his wife. Jewish Romanian by birth, Weiss and his wife were estranged, and she had been seeking alimony from him for their three children (who, shortly before the murder, had been hospitalized for malnourishment). On the night of the crime, the couple went for a drive to discuss payment, but a quarrel ensued and Mrs. Weiss jumped from the car. Weiss, age twenty-six, a proprietor of a cleaning establishment, fired five shots at her with a gun he had purchased earlier that afternoon.[135] He then picked her up and carried her into a neighboring home, where he waited until the police and medical personnel arrived. "I hated her because she wouldn't stop loving me," said Weiss upon his arrest.[136] His wife had filed for divorce three times before she

---

131. *Warden to Make Final Plea for Life of Ives*, ROCKY MTN. NEWS, Jan. 9, 1930, at 1; *Last Hope of Eddie Ives Escaping Noose Vanishes*, ROCKY MTN. NEWS, Jan. 10, 1930, at 1.

132. *Eddie Ives is Hanged at Cañon City Prison*, ROCKY MTN. NEWS, Jan. 11, 1930, at 1.

133. Melrose, *Little Eddie Ives*.

134. *Belongia Goes to Death Gladly In Gas Chamber*, DENVER POST, June 22, 1935, at 1; Alice Spencer Cook, *The Man Was Hanged Twice*, DENVER POST (Empire Magazine), Apr. 6, 1958, at 6.

135. *Shoots Down Wife On Street*, ROCKY MTN. NEWS, Feb. 14, 1929, at 1; *Denver Man Shoots His Wife in Spine After a Row in Auto*, DENVER POST, Feb. 14, 1929, at 14.

136. *Wife's Unyielding Love Spelled Death at Hand of Her Husband*, DENVER POST, Feb. 15, 1929, at 3.

was murdered, but the couple reconciled after the first two.[137] The conviction was affirmed on appeal.[138]

58–60. RALPH EMERSON FLEAGLE (July 10, 1930), HOWARD L. ROYSTON, and GEORGE J. ABSHIER (a.k.a. Bill Messick) (July 18, 1930). Lamar (Prowers County). W-W. Hanging/Broken Neck, Strangulation, Strangulation. This trio killed four men in connection with a $220,000 robbery of the First National Bank in Lamar on May 23, 1928. At the scene, bank president A. Newton Parrish and his son, cashier John F. Parrish, were murdered. E. A. Kesinger, a teller at the bank, was taken as hostage and later murdered in Kansas. In Kansas the men abducted W. W. Wineinger, a physician, and forced him to treat Royston, who had been wounded in the shoot-out in the bank. After care was rendered, Wineinger, too, was murdered with a gunshot wound to the back of his head. Rewards totaling $7,000, including $1,000 from the *Denver Post*, were immediately offered, and stories about the murders dominated newspapers.[139] On appeal, Fleagle claimed that the state promised he would be sentenced to life imprisonment in exchange for his confession and guilty plea for the murder of the bank president. The court agreed but stated that the district attorney did not explicitly *ask* the jury for death and that the district attorney did not have the power to usurp the jury by promising a sentence of life.[140] Royston and Abshier also confessed, pleaded guilty, and had their convictions and sentences affirmed on appeal.[141] Fleagle was hanged a week before the other two,[142] and Abshier and Royston were permitted to decide that Abshier would be hanged before

---

137. *Weiss Will Hang Wednesday Night*, ROCKY MTN. NEWS, May 28, 1930, at 1; *Harold Weiss Is Hanged for Slaying Wife*, DENVER POST, May 29, 1930, at 1; *Weiss Hanged with Prayer on His Lips*, ROCKY MTN. NEWS, May 29, 1930, at 1.

138. Weiss v. People, 285 P. 162 (Colo. 1930).

139. *See, e.g.*, *Lamar Bandits Still at Large*, DENVER POST, May 24, 1928, at 1.

140. Fleagle v. People, 289 P. 1078 (Colo. 1930). *See also Lamar Demands Death for Ralph Despite Promise*, DENVER POST, Oct. 17, 1929, at 3; *Court Rules Lamar Gang Must Die; Declares Fleagle Not Victim of Broken Promise Made by State*, DENVER POST, June 9, 1930, at 1.

141. Royston v. People, 289 P. 1077 (Colo. 1930); Abshier v. People, 289 P. 1081 (Colo. 1930).

142. *Ralph Fleagle Dies On Gallows*, DENVER POST, July 11, 1930, at 1.

Royston.[143] At the time of the hangings, a fourth member of the gang, Jake Fleagle (Ralph's brother), had not been apprehended, but he was subsequently killed by a detective in Branson, Missouri.[144]

61. EMELIO HERRERA. August 20, 1930. Denver. H-H. Hanging/Broken Neck. A railroad section hand, Herrera, age twenty-one, was convicted of firing four shots into his wife, Maria, in the street outside their home.[145] One of the bullets entered through her back. At first, Herrera insisted that his wife had committed suicide but then admitted that he had killed her.[146] Later, he gave what the state Supreme Court labeled (in affirming the conviction) as inconsistent and self-contradictory statements.[147] Shortly before his death, Herrera told a priest that he was a full-blooded Navajo Indian,[148] although prison records, the Colorado Supreme Court, and the *Denver Post* classify him as Mexican (born in New Mexico).[149] He accepted full responsibility for the murder before his execution.[150]

62. WILLIAM MOYA. December 12, 1930. Denver. H-W. Hanging. Convicted of beating to death Joseph Zemp, his eighty-year-old landlord, allegedly in the course of a robbery. Moya, of Mexican ethnicity (born in New Mexico), argued self-defense. Zemp's body was found stuffed in an outhouse. Eight years prior to this murder, Moya had been tried and acquitted for a New Mexico murder, but he received a prison term of

143. Fred S. Warren, *Lamar Bandits Are Avenged! Bandits Strangle to Death as Rope Fails to Break Their Necks*, DENVER POST, July 19, 1930, at 1.

144. *Kansas Gets Flood of Letters Favoring Capital Punishment*, DENVER POST, Feb. 1, 1931, at 16.

145. *Denver Woman Shot to Death in Her Bedroom*, DENVER POST, June 30, 1929, at 4.

146. *Evidence Closes around the Mexican Murder Suspect*, DENVER POST, July 1, 1929, at 6; Emelio Herrera, *Wife Slayer, Says He "Wants to Die"*, DENVER POST, July 2, 1929, at 3.

147. Herrera v. People, 287 P. 643 (Colo. 1930).

148. *Wife Slayer to Hang Tonight*, ROCKY MTN. NEWS, Aug. 20, 1930, at 1.

149. *Herrera Is Hanged for Murder of Wife*, DENVER POST, Aug. 21, 1930, at 1.

150. *Emelio Herrera, 21-year-old Wife Murderer, Is Hanged*, ROCKY MTN. NEWS, Aug. 21, 1930, at 1; *Herrera Is Hanged*.

six to eight years for perjury during that trial.[151] The Colorado murder conviction was affirmed on appeal.[152] He was thirty-three at the time of his execution.[153]

63–65. CLAUDE RAY, JOHN WALKER, and ANDREW HALLIDAY. January 30, 1931. Eads (Kiowa County). W-W. Hangings/Strangulations. After robbing a bank in Manter, Kansas (giving them the nickname the "Manter bandits"), the defendants fled to Colorado, where local authorities had been warned to be on the lookout for them. While passing through Eads, the trio was stopped by Sheriff Coral A. Hickman, who was shot and murdered. The bandits continued their escape, later shooting at three men (wounding two of them), stealing a car, and fleeing back to Kansas before they were apprehended. All three gave full confessions to the murders as well as to between seven and ten bank robberies. Their convictions were affirmed on appeal.[154] Walker was forty-one; Ray, the triggerman, was twenty-three; and Halliday (who shouted to Ray, "Let him have it" at the time of the murder)[155] was twenty-two when they died. The men determined the order of the executions by flipping coins.[156] The 1,000-pound weight on the gallows failed to break the men's necks, and

151. *Recluse Slayer Goes on Trial*, ROCKY MTN. NEWS, Mar. 5, 1930, at 2; *Slayer's Wife Testifies to Save Him from the Noose*, ROCKY MTN. NEWS, Mar. 6, 1930, at 1; *Denver Recluse Slayer to Die on Gallows for Crime*, DENVER POST, Mar. 8, 1930, at 1.

152. Moya v. People, 293 P. 335 (Colo. 1930).

153. *Moya Walks Firmly to Gallows*, ROCKY MTN. NEWS, Dec. 13, 1930, at 1.

154. Walker et al. v. People, 295 P. 787 (Colo. 1931).

155. A 1991 movie titled *Let Him Have It* got its name from the words spoken by Derek Bentley to an accomplice shortly before a police officer was murdered by the accomplice in England in 1952. After Bentley spoke, the sixteen-year-old accomplice fired the fatal shot. Whether Bentley meant "Let the officer have your gun" or "Let the officer have a bullet" has been hotly debated. Bentley's trial jury asked for mercy, but he was nonetheless executed in 1953. He was nineteen when he was executed and had a low IQ. In 1993 Bentley received a limited pardon from the British government. William E. Schmidt, *Youth Hanged in Error in '53, Britain Says*, N.Y. TIMES, Aug. 1, 1993, at 10.

156. *Manter Bandits to Flip Coin to Decide Order of Hanging*, DENVER POST, Jan. 30, 1931, at 1; *State Ready to Execute 3 Bank Bandits Tonight*, ROCKY MTN. NEWS, Jan. 30, 1931, at 1; *Hanged Bandit Is Buried in Prison Plot*, ROCKY MTN. NEWS, Feb. 1, 1931, at 4.

all three died by strangulation.[157] The murders provoked strong sentiment for a return of capital punishment to Kansas, which had abolished it in 1907 and not hosted an execution since 1870.[158]

66. JAMES V. FOSTER. December 11, 1931. Greeley (Weld County). W-W. Hanging. Convicted of killing his wife and three children by dousing them with gasoline and lighting them afire. Foster, age forty-five, was a salesman with no prior criminal record. No appeal was made because Foster's attorney did not believe that any error had been committed. Before the execution, the attorney and three prison officials expressed the belief that Foster was insane, as did a psychiatrist (the head of the Colorado Psychiatric Hospital) who had examined Foster during the trial. However, Gov. William H. Adams (who never commuted a death sentence during his three terms in office) refused to intervene.[159]

67. E. J. FARMER. March 18, 1932. Craig (Moffat County). W-W. Hanging. A rancher, Farmer became involved in a dispute with two other ranchers—Earl Hopkins and Joe J. Jones—over the ownership of some hay located on Farmer's ranch. The dispute ended when Farmer shot the two men. Farmer's son-in-law witnessed the murders. Farmer first argued self-defense, but at trial, he pleaded insanity. On appeal, the conviction was affirmed.[160] While on death row, Farmer twice attempted suicide. Thirty people witnessed the hanging, including some relatives of Farmer's victims.[161]

68. JOE MAESTAS. May 27, 1932. San Luis (Costilla County). Other-W. Hanging. Convicted of the murder of Ben Addis, a cookie salesman, near

---

157. Charles T. O'Brien, *Three Manter Bandits Hanged; Noose Fails to Break Necks and Slayers Strangle to Death*, DENVER POST, Jan. 31, 1931, at 1.

158. *Kansas Gets Flood of Letters*.

159. *Preparations Are Made to Hang Greeley Torch Slayer Tonight*, DENVER POST, Dec. 9, 1931, at 1; *Adams Takes No Action in Foster Case*, DENVER POST, Dec. 10, 1931, at 13; *Adams Says Torch Slayer Must Hang*, DENVER POST, Dec. 11, 1931, at 1; *Greeley Torch Slayer Dies on Prison Gallows*, DENVER POST, Dec. 12, 1931, at 1; *Foster Is Executed for "Torch Killings"*, ROCKY MTN. NEWS, Dec. 12, 1931, at 1.

160. Farmer v. People, 7 P.2d 947 (Colo. 1932).

161. *Farmer Breaks Down as Hour of Death Nears*, DENVER POST, Mar. 18, 1932, at 1; *Farmer Dies on Gallows at Cañon City Pen*, DENVER POST, Mar. 19, 1932, at 1.

Fort Garland. Addis and his sister were sleeping in their car, parked on the roadside, when Maestas and a companion, Agipito Fernandez, awakened them. Addis and his sister tried to escape, but Addis was unable to avoid being shot by Maestas and died the next day. Fernandez's trial ended with the trial judge ordering a verdict of not guilty. Maestas, an ex-con who was inebriated that night, admitted to the shooting, initially claiming that it had been done in self-defense. On appeal, he argued that while he may have been guilty of second-degree murder, the proof of deliberate and premeditated design was not sufficient to sustain a verdict of first-degree murder because of his inebriation.[162] Maestas was twenty-five years old and half Navajo and half Mexican. At 240 pounds, he was the heaviest man ever hanged in Colorado.[163]

69. NELIVELT MOSS (a.k.a. Nelivelt Elliott). March 10, 1933. Gunnison (Gunnison County). B-W. Hanging. Aged twenty (and drunk) at the time of the crime, Moss killed an eighty-year-old white woman, Rena Schrienbeck, in retaliation for a racial slur and because she accused him of stealing $20 from her. Her body was found in a bed in the ashes of her home, which had been burned to the ground. An autopsy revealed that she had been struck with a heavy object before the fire began.[164] Moss, who confessed to the murder, had once received a ten-year sentence in Mississippi for an unknown crime but had escaped after serving only forty days. Some sixty legislators and state employees witnessed the execution.[165]

70. WALTER "SHORTY" JONES (a.k.a. John Morgan). December 1, 1933. Grand Junction (Mesa County). W-W. Hanging/Strangulation. Jones became the forty-fifth man—and the last—to be hanged in the state

---

162. Maestas v. People, 11 P.2d 227 (Colo. 1932).

163. *Joe Maestas Dies On Prison Gallows*, ROCKY MTN. NEWS, May 27, 1932, at 1; *Fort Garland Killer Hangs at Cañon City*, DENVER POST, May 28, 1932, at 6; Opening Brief of Plaintiff in Error, Maestas v. People (filed Jan. 29, 1932).

164. *Pitkin Woman Believed Slain*, ROCKY MTN. NEWS, Mar. 12, 1932, at 2; Moss v. People, 18 P.2d 316 (Colo. 1932).

165. *Negro Slayer Hanged at Pen*, ROCKY MTN. NEWS, Mar. 11, 1933, at 7; *Slayer Dies On Gallows at Colorado Pen*, DENVER POST, Mar. 11, 1933, at 11.

prison in Cañon City;[166] after he was sentenced to hang, the Colorado legislature changed its method of execution from hanging to asphyxiation.[167] He was convicted of killing Hartford Johnson, a fellow tramp. His accomplice, Montad J. Nelson, was sentenced to life imprisonment for his role in the crime. Jones and Nelson plotted to rob two fellow tramps traveling on a train. Each was armed with a heavy bolt and struck one of the men, and together they threw the victims off the train. Jones's victim, Hartford Johnson, died; the other victim lived and testified at trial. The conviction was affirmed on appeal.[168] Jones's execution was postponed one week so that he could enjoy Thanksgiving.[169] His last request was for some beer, and warden Roy Best obliged by giving him two bottles. "A blizzard howled a dirge around the gray prison walls as the 23-year-old, 200-pound slayer was jerked from his feet in the hemp noose ." It took fourteen minutes for Jones to strangle to death.[170]

71. WILLIAM CODY KELLEY. June 22, 1934. Delta (Delta County). W-W. Asphyxiation. Kelley and an accomplice, Lloyd Frady, were convicted of beating rancher Russell Downing with a pipe, binding him with barbed wire, and then burning down his house. The defendants were tried separately—both blamed the murder on the other—and both were sentenced to death. Kelley claimed that he was very drunk at the time of the murder and remembered very little, but he insisted on his innocence until the time of his death.[171] His conviction was not appealed.[172]

---

166. The forty-five hangings took place over a span of forty-three years at the Colorado State Penitentiary in Cañon City.

167. *Jones Is Brave as Hour of His Execution Approaches*, DENVER POST, Dec. 2, 1933, at 2.

168. Jones v. State, 26 P.2d 103 (Colo. 1933).

169. *Colorado Will Hang Hobo Slayer Friday*, ROCKY MTN. NEWS, Nov. 26, 1933, at 5.

170. Wallis M. Reef, *Last Victim of Gallows Strangled at Cañon City*, ROCKY MTN. NEWS, Dec. 2, 1933, at 1. *See also Killer Strangles in Fourteen Minutes on Colorado Gallows*, DENVER POST, Dec. 2, 1933, at 1.

171. *Young Wife's Plea for Mercy Fails to Save Kelley From Death Chamber*, DENVER POST, June 19, 1934, at 1.

172. His conviction was not appealed because, unlike Frady, he did not have the $200 needed to prepare a trial transcript. This may have been the only death sentence in Colorado that was not appealed to the state Supreme Court. FIELD, MAINLINER DENVER: THE BOMBING OF FLIGHT 629 at 199 (2005). When informed of

The preparations for the execution were extensive, as this was the first using lethal gas. Fifteen Colorado physicians arrived at the prison to witness the execution, anxious to learn about the effects of the gas: "The gruesome custom of 'cutting the heart out,' which has been practiced for years following hangings, to make certain of death, will be abandoned with the new method of execution."[173] A few days before the execution, the gas chamber was tested on a pig, which squealed and struggled momentarily before proving that the chamber indeed worked. The warden also tested it with a dog, a pigeon, and some canaries. After Kelley died, Warden Best pronounced the execution "the most successful and painless one ever conducted at the penitentiary."[174] Hundreds of requests were received from physicians from all over the country for copies of the autopsy report.[175] In exchange for his testimony against Kelley, the district attorney recommended a conviction for second-degree murder (with no death sentence) for Frady, but the jury nonetheless sentenced him to death. On appeal (after Kelley's execution), Frady argued that the judge should have accepted this agreement. His conviction and death sentence were affirmed, although the court recommended

---

the case on a visit to Colorado, the $200 was nearly donated by Lorena A. Hickok, a close friend of First Lady Eleanor Roosevelt, who served as the chief investigator for Harry L. Hopkins, administrator of the Federal Relief Administration. A Colorado relief worker, however, warned Hickok that her intervention might embarrass the president. Writing to Mrs. Roosevelt, Hickok explained her feelings: "This thing has nearly driven me crazy. How *can* you have any faith or hope in us if we do things like that in this supposedly enlightened age? . . . I feel as though we were living in the Dark Ages, and I *loathe* myself for not having more courage and trying to stop it, no matter what the consequences were. *You* would have *done* it. Well—I guess I'd better not think about it any more." RICHARD LOWITT & MAURINE BEASLEY, EDS., ONE THIRD OF A NATION: LORENA HICKOK REPORTS ON THE GREAT DEPRESSION 285–86 (1981) (emphasis in original). Mrs. Roosevelt tried to comfort her friend, replying, "You mustn't agonize so over things . . . your giving the $200 would have been useless." *Id.* at xiv. *See also* STEPHEN J. LEONARD, TRIALS AND TRIUMPHS: A COLORADO PORTRAIT OF THE GREAT DEPRESSION, WITH FSA PHOTOGRAPHS 215 (1993).

173. Charles T. O'Brien, *Last-Minute Fight on to Save Kelley*, DENVER POST, June 22, 1934, at 1.

174. Charles T. O'Brien, *Kelley Executed in New Gas Cell*, DENVER POST, June 23, 1934, at 1.

175. *Autopsy Will Be Performed Upon Kelley*, DENVER POST, June 24, 1934, at 5.

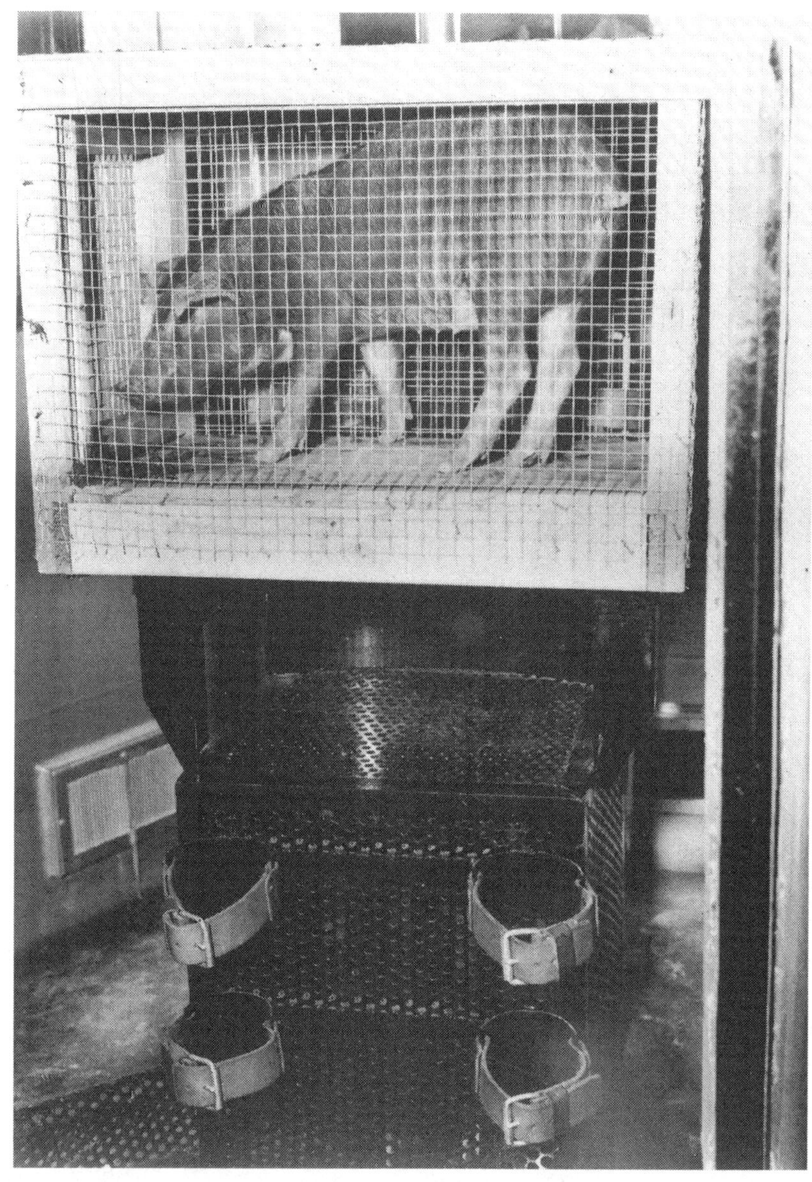

FIGURE A.5. *Pig being executed in a test of the gas chamber, probably from the 1930s. It is unknown if they offered him life if he would squeal. Photo courtesy of Tom Noel, from the Tom Noel Collection.*

to the executive branch that the sentence be commuted.[176] In 1935 his sentence was commuted, and he became wealthy in prison selling "curio goods" (leatherwork, beaded arts, and silver jewelry). With the earnings, he purchased a new home for his parents and a new car for himself, which was waiting for him at the prison gates when he was released in 1949.[177]

72-73. LOUIS PACHECO and JOHN PACHECO. May 31, 1935. Greeley (Weld County). H-W. Asphyxiation. "Two fiendish killers invaded the ranch home of Clifford Smith, 32, . . . shot Smith and Robert Griffin, 16, a ranch hand, to death, wounded Mrs. [Violet] Smith and then fled after an unsuccessful attempt to cremate all three victims."[178] Griffin was shot first as he lay in bed, and the Smiths were shot when they returned home from an outing. The suspects were brothers who at one time had worked for Smith: John Pacheco, twenty-two, and Louis Pacheco, thirty-seven (an ex-convict recently released from prison). The alleged motives were robbery (for $50 that Smith was known to have) and arguments over the rustling of a calf. While in prison in Cañon City before the murders, Louis had stabbed a deputy warden. Both men confessed to the murders, and Mrs. Smith identified them at trial; she also described an "attack upon her person" (possibly a sexual assault) after she had been shot.[179] The convictions were affirmed on appeal.[180] As the brothers sat in two of the three chairs in Colorado's gas chamber, they were "stolid as a pair of Aztec idols."[181]

74. LEONARD (LEE) BELONGIA. June 21, 1935. Greeley (Weld County). W-W. Asphyxiation. Convicted of killing a rancher, Albert E. Oesterick, and wounding the rancher's wife as they lay sleeping in their beds and

176. Frady v. People, 40 P.2d 606, 613 (Colo. 1934).

177. *Con Who Won Wealth Behind Bars Freed*, DENVER POST, Apr. 4, 1949, at 3.

178. *Burglars Murder Colorado Farmer and Schoolboy and Wound Woman; Fiends Shoot Three Then Pour Kerosene On Them and Light It*, DENVER POST, Feb. 28, 1934, at 1.

179. *Defense Suddenly Rests Case in Trial of Pacheco Brothers*, DENVER POST, Mar. 30, 1934, at 25.

180. Pacheco et al. v. People, 43 P.2d 165 (Colo. 1935).

181. Wallis M. Reef, *Two Brothers Die for Brutal Murder*, ROCKY MTN. NEWS, June 1, 1935, at 1.

beating the couple's thirteen-year-old son over the head with a rifle. Belongia, aged twenty-four at the time, worked for the rancher as a sheepherder, receiving room and board in compensation, and murdered Oesterick because he felt he was underpaid (and he needed money so he could get married). He gave a full confession when he was arrested. Shortly before the murder, Belongia had been released from a Minnesota prison, where he had served a sentence of eight years for auto theft.[182] At trial, he admitted the crimes; a physician also testified, rendering the opinion that Belongia had the mentality of a ten-year-old.[183] Belongia welcomed the death sentence and made no attempt to avoid it. His last request was for an opportunity to will his body to a medical school so scientists could examine his brain and determine what made him a murderer.[184] The offer was accepted by the medical school at the University of Colorado in Denver but then rejected because no one offered the $10 needed to ship the body to Denver.[185] After his death, the *Denver Post* published a letter he dictated explaining his own thoughts on what had caused his criminality.[186]

75. OTIS McDANIELS. February 14, 1936. Telluride (San Miguel County). W-W. Asphyxiation. McDaniels (age thirty) and his brother Herbert (age twenty) robbed and bound a Montezuma County sheep rancher, leaving him to die of exposure and starvation in his isolated cabin. Once arrested, they were held in the jail of a neighboring city (Glenwood Springs) to maximize security. Two months later, while being driven back to Montezuma County for arraignment, they overpowered the sheriff, W. W. Dunlap, and a deputy who were transporting them. The brothers grabbed a

---

182. *Rancher Slain and Wife Shot Near Greeley*, ROCKY MTN. NEWS, Dec. 17, 1934, at 1; *Ex-Convict Murders Colorado Rancher and Wounds His Wife*, DENVER POST, Dec. 17, 1934, at 14.

183. *Ex-Convict on Trial at Greeley for Killing Planned to Escape*, DENVER POST, Mar. 6, 1935, at 11; *Ex-Convict Gets Death Penalty for Killing Colorado Rancher*, DENVER POST, Mar. 7, 1935, at 19.

184. *Murderer Offers Brain to Science*, DENVER POST, June 20, 1935, at 1; *College Rejects Murderer's Brain*, DENVER POST, June 21, 1935, at 1.

185. *Belongia Goes to Death Gladly in Gas Chamber*, DENVER POST, June 22, 1935, at 1.

186. *Slayer Leaves Letter of Advice to Parents, Explaining Causes of His Life of Crime*, DENVER POST, June 22, 1935, at 1.

gun, which Otis used to murder Sheriff Dunlap.[187] Otis was sentenced to life imprisonment for the first murder and death for the second, while Herbert received life sentences for both. Otis admitted the murders but said that they were not intended. No appeal was taken. He had served previous prison terms in Utah and New Mexico. The warden allowed four other convicts to witness the execution.[188]

76–77. FRANK AGUILAR (August 13, 1937) and JOE ARRIDY (January 6, 1939). Pueblo. (H-W and O-W). Asphyxiation. Convicted of the murder of Dorothy Drain. The men were accused of breaking into the Drain home on August 16, 1936, sexually assaulting Dorothy, then killing her and seriously wounding her younger sister with a hatchet. In 1925 Arridy (who was born in Pueblo shortly after his parents immigrated from Syria) had been adjudicated as mentally incompetent and sent to the State Home and Training School for Mental Defectives in Grand Junction. At the institution his IQ was measured at 46. He was released after a nine-month stay but three years later was forced to return to the institution. In 1936 he walked away from the home and was not seen until his arrest in Wyoming sixteen days later (ten days after the Drain murder). There, he (allegedly) gave the first of many confessions to the crime, with each confession changing a bit to conform with newly discovered facts. Arridy's arrest surprised officials in Pueblo, who had already arrested Aguilar, a Mexican national, for the murder. They had discovered the murder weapon in Aguilar's home, and Aguilar ultimately confessed. The Wyoming authorities then secured a new confession from Arridy, in which he said that he had *not* acted alone in the murder. He was first given a jury trial to determine if he was sane, where three psychiatrists testified that Arridy had the mind of a five- or six-year-old child. However, law enforcement officials (and no mental health experts) disagreed and claimed that Arridy was sane, and that position prevailed. He was then convicted of murder in a separate jury proceeding, in which the defense attorney focused (again) on proving

---

187. *Posses Encircle Slayers of Sheriff in Colorado*, ROCKY MTN. NEWS, July 16, 1935, at 1; *Sheriff Slayers Caught*, ROCKY MTN. NEWS, Aug. 7, 1935, at 1.

188. Jack Carberry, *M'Daniels Shows Remorse and Fear on Execution Day*, DENVER POST, Feb. 14, 1936, at 1; *Otis McDaniels Walks Smiling to Gas Chamber to Die as Double Slayer*, ROCKY MTN. NEWS, Feb. 15, 1936, at 1.

that Arridy was insane, not on challenging the "evidence." The conviction was affirmed on appeal, and further attempts to show that Arridy was mentally incompetent for execution failed, each time by 4–3 votes in the Colorado Supreme Court.[189] Meanwhile, Aguilar was executed in 1937.[190] During the execution, one of the official witnesses, Adlai S. "Ad" Hamilton, a Pueblo resident and conductor for the Missouri Pacific Railroad, had a heart attack and died.[191] During his eighteen months on death row, Arridy became close friends with the warden, Roy Best. Best, who spoke out against the pending execution, bought him toys, picture books, and, for Christmas in 1938, a wind-up toy train that quickly became Arridy's favorite toy.[192] During this time, Arridy's attorney was Colorado's future attorney general, Gail Ireland (male). Later, the case formed the basis for a seminal book-length case study written by Robert Perske. Among other things, the book shows how the desire to please through false confessions shaped by authority figures, coupled with ineffective assistance of counsel and an environment in which there was little concern for understanding the developmentally disabled, cost an innocent person his life.[193]

As a direct result of that book, Arridy was awarded a complete posthumous pardon by Gov. Bill Ritter in 2011.

---

189. Arridy v. People, 82 P.2d 757 (Colo. 1938); People ex rel. Best v. Eldred, 86 P.2d 248 (Colo. 1938).

190. Several months after the execution, Aguilar's three-year-old daughter died when the family's Pueblo home burned. Later, Aguilar's other two children were placed in an orphanage when authorities claimed that Aguilar's widow abandoned them. Eventually, the children were returned to Aguilar's mother. However, other children constantly ridiculed them. In December 1938, with funds provided by the county welfare department, Mrs. Aguilar (aged seventy-seven) and her two grandchildren left the state to live with relatives in Mexico. *Aguilars to Start Life Anew in Mexico*, PUEBLO CHIEFTAIN, Dec. 4, 1938, at 1.

191. *Puebloan Witness Dies at Execution*, PUEBLO CHIEFTAIN, Aug. 11, 1937, at 1.

192. On the day of his execution, Arridy gave the train to a fellow death row inmate, Angelo Agnes (case no. 79).

193. ROBERT PERSKE, DEADLY INNOCENCE? (1995). In 1993 Colorado banned the death penalty for the developmentally disabled. Act of Apr. 29, 1993, Colo. Sess. Laws 543. In 2002 the US Supreme Court did the same, finding that such executions violated the Eighth Amendment's protections against cruel and unusual punishment. Atkins v. Virginia, 536 U.S. 304 (2002).

78. PETE CATALINA (a.k.a. Catalino). September 29, 1939. Salida (Chaffee County). W-H. Asphyxiation. A native of Italy,[194] Catalina, forty-one, was executed for the murder of twenty-three-year-old John Trujillo. Catalina was the part owner of a cigar store in which he allowed gambling. Trujillo, a customer, purchased some poker chips, but a quarrel erupted because he owed Catalina fifty cents more than he paid and openly accused other players of cheating. This ended when Catalina shot him.[195] The conviction was affirmed on appeal.[196] Prior to the execution, a pig was used to test the gas chamber's lethality, and the warden invited twenty inmates to watch the pig's death—mostly young men convicted of armed robbery—thinking that watching the death would deter them from future criminality. Catalina was executed in Colorado's three-seat gas chamber with Angelo Agnes,[197] with warden Roy Best serving as the executioner. "The quickest and most humane execution we ever had," said prison officials.[198] Only later was it revealed that some leakage of the fumes drove the spectators from the room.[199]

79. ANGELO AGNES. September 29, 1939. Denver. B-B. Asphyxiation. Executed for killing Malinda Agnes, his wife. He was thirty-one at the time of his death. The couple was living with Malinda's mother and brother, and Angelo left after a domestic quarrel. Two weeks later, they

---

194. One newspaper lists him as a native of Greece. *Two Murderers Will Die Together in Gas Chamber*, DENVER POST, Sept. 29, 1939, at 1. However, his prison records (available at the Colorado State Archives) state that he was born in Italy.

195. *Salida Man Held in Fatal Shooting*, DENVER POST, Mar. 16, 1938, at 10; *Alamosan Shot and Killed Here*, SALIDA DAILY MAIL, Mar. 16, 1938, at 1; *Murder Charge to be Filed against Catalino, Says D.A.*, SALIDA DAILY MAIL, Mar. 18, 1938, at 1.

196. Catalina v. People, 93 P.2d 897 (Colo. 1939).

197. *See* case no. 79, *infra*.

198. *Two Murderers Will Die Together in Gas Chamber*, DENVER POST, Sept. 29, 1939, at 1; *Agnes and Catalina Executed Together in Lethal Chamber*, DENVER POST, Sept. 30, 1939, at 1; *Men Walk Bravely to Death in State's First Double Gas Execution*, SALIDA DAILY MAIL, Sept. 30, 1939, at 1. I am indebted to Martha Quillen at the Salida Public Library for her assistance in researching this case.

199. *Death Chamber at Pen Tested*, ROCKY MTN. NEWS, Dec. 5, 1939, at 1.

met at another location and he shot her.[200] He had a prior conviction for burglary.[201]

80. HARRY LEOPOLD. December 8, 1939. Denver. W-W. Asphyxiation. Convicted of murdering a Denver tavern owner, Emil Albrecht. Leopold, age thirty at the time of his execution, had been paroled from the state penitentiary in Cañon City in September 1936, where he had served a sentence for aggravated assault. He and a prison friend, Robert Gwynne, robbed Albrecht's tavern and shot Albrecht, killing him instantly. After fleeing in a taxi, the men were confronted by the police about three hours after the murder. In a shoot-out, Gwynne was killed and Leopold was wounded. "Less than three hours after a pair of gunmen shot and killed a tavern keeper last night, one of them was a bullet-ridden corpse and the other was a badly wounded prisoner."[202] Leopold later confessed, stating that the murder was accidental. On a failed appeal, Leopold did not contest the conviction—only the sentence.[203] At Leopold's request, warden Roy Best delayed the execution for thirty minutes so Leopold could listen to a favorite radio show.[204] Leopold was put to death in "the quickest and cleanest gas execution ever held at the prison."[205]

81. JOE COATES. January 10, 1941. Denver. B-W. Asphyxiation. Employed in the commercial sex industry (as a pimp), Coates was convicted of killing Denver police detective Frank Renovato. Coates's previous convictions were for petty offenses such as vagrancy and disorderly conduct and included seven arrests in the previous four years. The murder resulted from an argument that Coates had with an old girlfriend (for

200. *Negro Woman Dies from Wounds*, ROCKY MTN. NEWS, Nov. 21, 1937, at 5; *Negro Surrenders as Wife-Slayer*, ROCKY MTN. NEWS, Nov. 23, 1937, at 16.

201. Agnes v. People, 93 P.2d 891 (Colo. 1939); *Two Murderers Will Die Together in Gas Chamber*, DENVER POST, Sept. 29, 1939, at 1; *Agnes and Catalina Executed Together in Lethal Chamber*, DENVER POST, Sept. 30, 1929, at 1.

202. *Trapped Bandits Shoot It Out with Officers*, ROCKY MTN. NEWS, Dec. 5, 1938, at 1.

203. Leopold v. People, 95 P.2d 811 (Colo. 1939).

204. W. T. Little, *Humor Not to Be Denied Even at Grim Execution Hill*, ROCKY MTN. NEWS, Nov. 18, 1951, at 34.

205. *Smiling Leopold Goes to His Death in Gas Chamber*, ROCKY MTN. NEWS, Dec. 9, 1939, at 1.

whom he had been pimping), the man she was living with, and their landlord. Coates threatened the woman's paramour and landlord with a gun, and the landlord rushed to find a police officer. He returned to the scene with Detective Renovato, whom he found on a nearby street. A shootout ensued; Renovato was killed in the crossfire.[206] Coates (a "marijuana-crazed negro") was immediately identified[207] and was arrested six days after the murder.[208] Upon arrest, he admitted firing the fatal shots (claiming self-defense), and the district attorney announced that he would demand a death sentence.[209] Within two months, "Joe Coates, 61, the shuffling, stoop-shouldered Negro known as 'the bad man of Larimar Street,' was condemned to die."[210] This was affirmed on appeal,[211] although the state Supreme Court delayed the execution at least four times.[212] After visiting with Coates, Gov. Ralph L. Carr denied clemency. The execution was described as "the easiest and quickest death of any of the fourteen men" who had succumbed in Colorado's gas chamber.[213]

82. JAMES STEPHENS (a.k.a. "Mancos Jim"). June 20, 1941. Cortez (Montezuma County). W-W. Asphyxiation. Convicted of killing Lynn Dean (male), town marshal of Mancos, Colorado. Stephens had been employed as a railroad section hand. On the night of the murder, Stephens had been drinking heavily and was belligerent, and Officer Dean told him to go home. When Stephens instead went to another tavern, Dean arrested him but did not inspect him for hidden weapons. Dean was then shot. The conviction was affirmed on appeal.[214] At the time of the execution, the warden claimed that Stephens, aged seventy-six, was the oldest person ever executed in the history of the United States. In the death chamber, Stephens wiggled his left hand out of the strap that bound it to the chair, removed the mask covering his face, loosened his right hand and

206. *City Detective Shot to Death As He Tries to Save Woman*, ROCKY MTN. NEWS, Oct. 14, 1938, at 1.

207. *Door-to-Door Hunt Seeks Police Killer*, ROCKY MTN. NEWS, Oct. 15, 1938, at 1.

208. *Renovata's Slayer Is Captured*, ROCKY MTN. NEWS, Oct. 19, 1938, at 1.

209. *Death Penalty Demanded for Coates*, ROCKY MTN. NEWS, Oct. 20, 1938, at 1.

210. *Coates Must Die as Slayer of Detective*, DENVER POST, Dec. 4, 1938, at 1.

211. Coates v. People, 106 P. 2d 354 (Colo. 1940).

212. *Denver Killer Goes to Death*, ROCKY MTN. NEWS, Jan. 11, 1941, at 1.

213. *Coates Begs for Prayer In Death Chair*, DENVER POST, Jan. 11, 1941, at 1.

214. Stephens v. People, 111 P.2d 1057 (Colo. 1941).

the waist strap holding him to the chair, sang a Navajo death chant, and waited calmly for the gas to hit his nostrils.[215]

83. MARTIN SUKLE. May 22, 1942. Colorado Springs (El Paso County). W-W. Asphyxiation. Sukle was arrested (but never tried) for killing his second wife, Marie, and convicted and sentenced to death for killing her "partner in illicit relations," Jack Russell.[216] A thirty-five-year-old janitor, Sukle had served three years in prison in Montana for attempting to murder his first wife. He killed Russell first, then killed Marie two days later. Upon his arrest, Sukle, an employee of a psychiatric hospital, gave a full confession. On appeal, the conviction for Russell's murder was reversed because during deliberations, the jury forwarded a question to the judge about whether the defendant, if sentenced to life, would be eligible for parole. The judge answered that he would be eligible, and the Colorado Supreme Court ruled that this question was not within the jury's proper concern.[217] Sukle was retried, reconvicted, and resentenced to death, and this conviction and sentence were affirmed on appeal.[218] After visiting with him in prison, Gov. Ralph L. Carr denied a request for clemency.[219]

84. DONALD H. FEARN. October 23, 1942. Pueblo. W-W. Asphyxiation. Sentenced to death for kidnapping, raping, torturing, and shooting a sixteen-year-old high school student, Alice Porter, daughter of a former Pueblo detective. Thirty-six hours before the murder, Fearn's wife gave birth to their second child. Fearn abducted the victim at gunpoint off a Pueblo street and took her to an abandoned ranch where he forced her to disrobe, bound her, and burned her (two dozen times) with wire he had heated in the fireplace. He then raped her, beat her over the head with a hammer, and shot her to make sure she was dead. Her body was

---

215. *Mancos Jim is Ready for Death Friday*, DENVER POST, June 19, 1941, at 1; *Colorado Killer Jerks from Chair, Dies Calmly "Like Indian Victim"*, ROCKY MTN. NEWS, June 21, 1941, at 1.

216. *"I Warned Him," Says Janitor; Gives Self Up*, ROCKY MTN. NEWS, Oct. 10, 1939, at 1.

217. Suckle v. People, 111 P.2d 233 (Colo. 1941).

218. Sukle v. People, 125 P.2d 151 (Colo. 1942).

219. *Sukle Almost Runs to Gas Chamber*, DENVER POST, May 23, 1942, at 2; *Murderer Sukle Pays His Penalty*, ROCKY MTN. NEWS, May 23, 1942, at 2.

later found in a cistern. During the crimes a heavy rainstorm passed over the area, sinking Fearn's car in mud, forcing him to walk several miles for assistance and get a tow truck to retrieve the car. This led to his arrest. Fearn, a twenty-six-year-old railroad brakeman, immediately confessed.[220] He had no prior arrests but, in his confession, told authorities that since childhood he had felt an uncontrollable urge to commit a crime like the one he did. Fearn believed that he deserved to die. After psychiatrists determined that he was sane at the time of the crimes, he pleaded guilty, and the conviction was not appealed. He was executed six months after the crimes. His last request, for a bottle of beer, was honored. The victim's father and two of her uncles witnessed the execution.[221]

85. JOHN SULLIVAN. September 20, 1943. Colorado Springs (El Paso County). W-W. Asphyxiation. Convicted of sexually assaulting and killing Carrie Winona Culbertson, who he believed had been mean to his employer the previous summer.[222] Sullivan went to Culbertson's home to deliver some mail and, using a letter opener he found there, stabbed her to death. Upon his arrest, Sullivan, a handyman aged forty-two, was described as a "decidedly subnormal person" by the sheriff.[223] His confession was the main evidence used against him at trial, where the experts were "practically unanimous" in their opinions that Sullivan had limited intelligence.[224] On appeal, the death sentence was challenged on the basis of Sullivan's subnormal intelligence and Colorado's restriction against executing people under age eighteen. This appeal failed, and Sullivan went to his death with little debate about the propriety of executing prisoners with developmental disabilities.[225]

---

220. *Murder of Pueblo Girl by Torture Confessed*, DENVER POST, Apr. 27, 1942, at 1.

221. *Sex Slayer Dies in Gas Chamber*, ROCKY MTN. NEWS, Oct. 24, 1942, at 5; *Pueblo's Torture Murderer Dies in Gas Chamber*, DENVER POST, Oct. 24, 1942, at 5; ALT & WELLS, MOUNTAIN MURDERS, 91–103.

222. *Woman Found Raped, Slain*, ROCKY MTN. NEWS, Jan. 12, 1942, at 1.

223. *Handyman Is Held in Slaying of Woman at Manitou Springs*, DENVER POST, Jan. 12, 1942, at 5; *Sex Murder Confessed by Handy Man*, ROCKY MTN. NEWS, Jan. 13, 1942, at 9.

224. Sullivan v. People, 139 P.2d 876, 877 (Colo. 1943).

225. *Slayer Dies in Colorado Gas Chamber*, DENVER POST, Sept. 20, 1943, at 2; *Manitou Springs Killer Executed*, ROCKY MTN. NEWS, Sept. 21, 1943, at 31.

86. GEORGE MASAYOSHI HONDA. October 8, 1943. Denver. A-A.[226] Asphyxiation. The owner of a restaurant, Honda quarreled with his wife, Mary, over her failure to design menus for the day and because, as he told authorities, he felt that she never loved him. He then stabbed her to death in the lobby of a Denver hotel where they lived.[227] Honda, thirty-seven, had no previous record of criminality. He was tried in an atmosphere of anti-Japanese sentiment in the middle of World War II. Efforts to delay the trial until after the war ended did not succeed. The conviction was affirmed on appeal.[228] In his last statement, he expressed the hope that America would win the war.[229]

87. HOWARD C. ("SONNY") POTTS (a.k.a. Metzgar). June 22, 1945. Denver. W-W. Asphyxiation. Convicted of beating and killing his wife, Mary, and burying her in the basement of their home. Neighbors, knowing that relations between the couple were precarious and that Potts had a history of spouse abuse, became suspicious when they did not see Mary for several weeks. He explained that she had gone to visit relatives in California. Police were called when Potts was seen carrying a pick and shovel into his house. When confronted by the police nearly seven weeks after the murder, Potts confessed and directed them to where he had buried the body.[230] Potts, thirty-nine at the time of the crime, had been employed by Western Electric as a shipping clerk for the previous fourteen years and had no prior arrests. The conviction was affirmed on appeal.[231] The execution was described as "routine."[232]

---

226. Honda was an American citizen, born in Honolulu. He and his family lived in Japan from the time he was three months old until he was sixteen. His wife was of Japanese descent, born and raised in Colorado.

227. *Japanese Cuts Wife to Death in Hotel Lobby*, DENVER POST, May 4, 1942, at 8.

228. Honda v. People, 141 P.2d 178 (Colo. 1943).

229. *Denver Jap [sic] Goes to Death Chamber Wishing Allies Well*, DENVER POST, Oct. 9, 1943, at 4; *Honda Dies Calmly in Lethal Cell, Hopes Allied Armies Will Win War*, ROCKY MTN. NEWS, Oct. 9, 1943, at 5.

230. *Denver Woman Found Dead in Cellar Grave*, DENVER POST, May 21, 1943, at 1; Fred Pettid, *Find Body of Denver Wife in Cellar Grave*, ROCKY MTN. NEWS, May 21, 1943, at 1; *Potts Tells Police He Stamped [sic] Wife to Death in Mad Frenzy*, DENVER POST, May 22, 1943, at 1.

231. Potts v. People, 158 P.2d 739 (Colo. 1945).

232. *Potts Pays with Life for Killing Wife*, DENVER POST, June 23, 1945, at 1. *See also Potts Prepares to Die Friday Evening*, DENVER POST, June 22, 1945, at 1.

88. CHARLES FORD SILLIMAN. November 9, 1945. Littleton (Arapahoe County). W-W. Asphyxiation. Arrested for killing his wife, Esther, and four-year-old daughter, Patricia, by poisoning them with strychnine. He was convicted of the former murder but was not tried for the latter. Silliman, thirty-four, was employed at a truck freight dock. In his confession, given shortly after his arrest, he said that he and his wife had entered into a murder-suicide pact because of indebtedness but that he lost his nerve after killing her when it was time to kill himself.[233] His insanity plea at trial failed. Shortly before the execution, two psychiatrists found him to be insane, but neither the state Supreme Court nor the governor intervened to stop the execution.[234] His execution was delayed two hours while some 550 Fremont County merchants and farmers enjoyed a previously scheduled banquet at the prison.[235]

89. FRANK MARTZ. November 23, 1945. Littleton (Arapahoe County). W-W. Asphyxiation. Convicted in the beating, strangling, and mutilation of three-year-old Kathleen Geist, whose body was found crammed under a kitchen sink. The girl had been lured away from her mother at a tavern. A Denver police officer noticed Martz walking with the girl and remembered where they went, and this led to the discovery of the victim and to Martz's arrest. When arrested (just two hours after the murder), Martz claimed he remembered abducting the girl, but because he was so drunk, he could not remember what he did with her. He stuck to this statement until the time he died. Martz, aged thirty-three at the time of the crime, was a staff sergeant stationed at Fort Logan, where he was employed as a cook. He had no prior convictions.[236] His conviction

---

233. *Girl, 4, Mom Die in Agony, Dad Quizzed*, ROCKY MTN. NEWS, Jan. 23, 1944, at 5; *Father Admits Poisoning Two*, ROCKY MTN. NEWS, Jan. 24, 1944, at 1.

234. *Supreme Court Refuses to Stay Silliman Execution Slated Tonight*, ROCKY MTN. NEWS, Nov. 9, 1945, at 5; *Silliman Calmly Waits Death Cell*, DENVER POST, Nov. 9, 1945, at 1.

235. *Prisoner Silliman Dies in Gas Chamber*, DENVER POST, Nov. 10, 1945, at 1; *Silliman Meets Death by Gas for Poisoning Wife*, ROCKY MTN. NEWS, Nov. 10, 1945, at 5.

236. *Four-Year-Old Girl Found Murdered, Soldier Arrested*, DENVER POST, Dec. 7, 1943, at 1; *Soldier Faces Murder Trial in Girl's Death*, DENVER POST, Dec. 8, 1943, at 1; *Sergeant Confesses Beating Girl Found Dead in Englewood*, DENVER POST, Dec. 9, 1943, at 1.

was affirmed on appeal.[237] A day before the scheduled execution, Martz was examined by a psychiatrist (at the order of a district court judge) to determine his competence for execution.[238] The judge ultimately found him to be sane, and he was executed on schedule.[239]

90. JOHN HENRY BROWN. May 23, 1947. Denver. B-B.[240] Asphyxiation. Convicted of the shotgun murder of Evelyn Smith, his paramour. Brown, aged fifty at the time of his death, had served six years of a ten-year sentence in Missouri for armed robbery. He and Smith had gone to a social gathering, and Brown was jealous over attentions paid to her by another man and her refusal to leave the party and return to Brown's room with him.[241] At trial, Brown pleaded insanity, but this failed and the conviction was affirmed on appeal.[242] The execution was described as "uneventful."[243]

91. HAROLD GILLETTE (a.k.a. Philip King). June 20, 1947. Fort Collins (Larimer County). W-W. Asphyxiation. Executed for the murder of Glen Cook, a ranch foreman; Gillette was standing outside when he shot Cook in the back while he was sitting in his living room. Gillette entered the house, tied Mrs. Cook to a bed, locked two children in a room, stole a small amount of property, and absconded in the victim's car. Gillette had worked as a ranch hand at the ranch and said that he killed Cook after the foreman learned that Gillette had been using an assumed name. At trial, Gillette pleaded guilty and was bitter that the jury still imposed a death sentence; later, he was angry that the governor did not

---

237. Martz v. People, 162 P.2d 408 (Colo. 1945).

238. *Martz May Be Given Stay of Execution*, DENVER POST, Nov. 23, 1945, at 1.

239. *Martz Loses His Appeal and Goes to Gas Death*, DENVER POST, Nov. 24, 1945, at 1.

240. Brown was described as having "mixed Negro and Indian blood." *Death Near for Slayer*, DENVER POST, May 22, 1947, at 32.

241. *Rejected Suitor's Gunshot Wound Fatal to Woman*, ROCKY MTN. NEWS, May 13, 1945, at 31; *Denver Woman Dies in Shooting Affray*, DENVER POST, May 13, 1945, at 3.

242. Brown v. People, 178 P.2d 948 (Colo. 1947).

243. Hugh Jennings, *Murderer Executed at Prison*, DENVER POST, May 24, 1947, at 16; *Denver Slayer of Woman Calmly Accepts Gas Death*, ROCKY MTN. NEWS, May 24, 1947, at 5.

commute it.[244] No appeal was taken. Gillette was thirty-one at the time of his death. He had served previous prison terms in five states.[245]

92. ROBERT S. ("BAT") BATTALINO. January 7, 1949. Golden (Jefferson County). W-W. Asphyxiation. A restaurant cook, Battalino was fired by the owner, Michael H. Randolph, who accused him of stealing money from the cash register. With another person who worked in the restaurant, Archie Miller, Battalino kidnapped Randolph at gunpoint, drove him to a rural area, and stole $450 from him. Battalino then shot Randolph in the forehead. The body was discovered several weeks later. Upon their arrests, both Miller and Battalino confessed. At trial, Battalino pleaded insanity, but this failed. His conviction was affirmed on appeal.[246] At the time of his execution, Battalino, thirty-nine, spat at a priest; told the warden, "I hate your guts"; and said he looked forward to joining his (Battalino's) friends in hell.[247] Miller was acquitted for his role in the crime.[248]

93. PAUL J. SCHNEIDER. December 16, 1949. W-W. Akron (Washington County). Asphyxiation. A triple murderer, Schneider was executed for the robbery-murder of gas station owner Frank J. Ford. Ford was abducted from his Denver gas station in September 1947, and his body was discovered one month later approximately one hundred miles northeast of the city. Death was caused by a concussion (a wound from a tire iron) and gunshot. One month after the murder, Schneider was apprehended in Kentucky when he tried to cash a check that was known to have been in Ford's possession. Schneider soon offered a complete confession—not only to Ford's murder but to two other robbery-murders of Michigan

---

244. *Condemned Slayer Visits with Mother*, DENVER POST, June 20, 1947, at 30.

245. *Ranch Hand Sought in Foreman's Death*, DENVER POST, Dec. 28, 1946, at 14; *FBI Joins Search for Man Wanted in Slaying*, ROCKY MTN. NEWS, Dec. 29, 1946, at 14; *Gillette Dies in Gas Chamber*, DENVER POST, June 21, 1947, at 16.

246. Battalino v. People, 199 P.2d 897 (Colo. 1948).

247. Bernard Beckwith, *"I'll Join My Friends In Hell": Battalino*, DENVER POST, Jan. 7, 1949, at 1. *See also Friendless Battalino Faces Gas*, DENVER POST, Jan. 7, 1949, at 36; *Battalino Surly on Eve of Execution; Warden Adds Deputy to Guard*, ROCKY MTN. NEWS, Jan. 7, 1949, at 10.

248. Pasquale Marranzino, *Battalino Dies Smiling*, ROCKY MTN. NEWS, Jan. 8, 1949, at 1.

gas stations committed after Ford was slain. This confession led authorities to Ford's body. At trial, Schneider pleaded not guilty by reason of insanity, but three physicians testified that he was sane. The Colorado Supreme Court affirmed the conviction,[249] and the US Supreme Court denied certiorari.[250] Among those who visited Schneider in his death row cell was the trial judge, who visited just three hours before the execution. Schneider was twenty-five at the time of his death. Approximately fifty people crowded outside the gas chamber to watch his final moments.[251]

94. JOHN J. BERGER, JR. October 26, 1951. Denver. W-W. Asphyxiation. Sentenced to death for murdering his wife, Pauline. For at least five years prior to the murder, Berger had beaten her, resulting in frequent arrests. He accused her of infidelity and a divorce was pending; he had an alcohol problem that caused him to be especially pugilistic. They had four children, the oldest of whom, Robert, was age seven at the time of the crime. Berger was convicted of arson in June 1947; while being transported to prison after that conviction, he said that upon his release, he planned to kill his wife. He was freed on January 26, 1948 (after a prison stay that included three months in a psychiatric ward).[252] He returned home and strangled her that night. He was thirty at the time of the crime. At trial, the chief prosecution witness was Robert,[253] who went on a vacation with the trial judge immediately after the trial.[254] The child's competency to testify was challenged on appeal. This challenge failed, although three justices dissented because they felt that the evidence of guilt, while strong, was circumstantial and not sufficient to sustain a death sentence.[255] Berger was executed after two psychiatrists

---

249. Schneider v. People, 199 P.2d 873 (Colo. 1948).

250. Schneider v. Colorado, 338 U.S. 862 (Colo. 1949).

251. Robert M. Cour, *Triple Killer Schneider Executed*, DENVER POST, Dec. 17, 1949, at 1; Sam Lusky, *Schneider Dies in Gas Chamber*, ROCKY MTN. NEWS, Dec. 17, 1949, at 1.

252. *Attorney Lost 3-Year Fight to Save Berger*, DENVER POST, Oct. 27, 1951, at 2.

253. *Berger Guilty in Wife's Murder*, DENVER POST, July 1, 1948, at 1.

254. *Berger Boy, Judge to Go on Vacation*, DENVER POST, July 1, 1948, at 19; *Bobby Berger Gets $20 To Spend "As You Like"*, DENVER POST, July 2, 1948, at 2.

255. Berger v. People, 224 P.2d 228 (Colo. 1950), *cert. denied*, Berger v. Colorado, 342 U.S. 837 (1951).

found him to be sane.[256] "I do not wish to have any part in the execution of an insane man," commented Gov. Daniel Thornton.[257]

95. BESALIREZ MARTINEZ. September 7, 1956. H-H. Eagle (Eagle County). Asphyxiation. Convicted of walking into a tavern and shooting its owner, Perfecto Cruz. Within a few hours, Martinez was arrested and had offered a full confession. Twenty-two months before the murder, Cruz had thrown Martinez out of the bar for causing a disturbance, and Martinez attacked Cruz with a knife (resulting in a six-month jail sentence for assault).[258] He was tried by an all-male jury and convicted; the conviction was affirmed on appeal.[259] After meeting with Martinez's wife and five of his eight children, Gov. Edwin C. Johnson denied clemency. Aged forty-four at the time of his death, Martinez, a miner, was the first to be executed in the newly built gas chamber.[260]

96. JOHN GILBERT GRAHAM. January 11, 1957. Denver. W-W. Asphyxiation. Convicted of killing his mother, Daisie E. King, by blowing up a United Airlines DC-6 airplane on which she was a passenger by packing twenty-five sticks of dynamite in her suitcase. Forty-three additional passengers and crewmembers were also killed. The bomb exploded eighteen minutes after the plane, en route to Portland, Oregon, departed from Denver's Stapleton Airport.[261] The plane departed fifteen minutes late. If it had left on time, the explosion would have occurred as the plane ascended over the Rocky Mountains, making the cause of the crash much more difficult to identify. Graham, age twenty-four at the time of his execution, had been employed primarily in construction work and

---

256. Fred Baker, *Berger Executed, Silent, Sullen to Last*, DENVER POST, Oct. 27, 1951, at 1; Fred Baker, *"I Am Signing Nothing"—Killer Defiant to End*, DENVER POST, Oct. 27, 1951, at 2.

257. Thor Severson, *Berger Sane; Dies Tonight*, DENVER POST, Oct. 26, 1951, at 1.

258. *Tavern Man Slain in Eagle Feud*, DENVER POST, Nov. 29, 1954, at 40.

259. Martinez v. People, 299 P.2d 510 (Colo. 1956).

260. Tom Gavin, *Martinez Dies in Gas Chamber*, ROCKY MTN. NEWS, Sept. 8, 1956, at 5; *These Are Events Leading to Execution of Martinez*, ROCKY MTN. NEWS, Sept. 8, 1956, at 27; *Father of Eight Executed in State Gas Chamber*, DENVER POST, Sept. 9. 1956, at 1; *Three on Death Row Ignored by Martinez*, DENVER POST, Sept. 9, 1956, at 3.

261. Al Nakkula, *44 Killed in Airliner Explosion*, ROCKY MTN. NEWS, Nov. 2, 1955, at 5; *44 Die in Plane Crash*, DENVER POST, Nov. 2, 1955, at 1.

truck driving, had completed one year of college, and had prior convictions for bootlegging, carrying a concealed weapon, and check forgery. Some alleged his motive was to receive $37,500 from a trip insurance policy purchased at the direction of his mother, but the bulk of the evidence pointed to a troubled relationship with his mother (who lived with Graham, his wife, and their two children).[262] Agents quickly determined that a bomb had brought down the plane, and two weeks after the crash, they interviewed Graham because of questions raised after they inspected the remnants of his mother's luggage. At that time he gave a full confession. Graham withdrew his insanity plea after six psychiatrists found him to be sane. After his conviction, Graham attempted to prevent his case from being appealed, but the Colorado Supreme Court nonetheless reviewed and affirmed it.[263] Before his death, Graham invited Zeke Scher, a *Denver Post* reporter who had covered his trial, to sit on his lap while the execution was taking place.[264] The invitation was declined. During the execution, Graham gasped, screamed, and strained at the straps, prompting the warden to comment that "this was not a normal procedure" but that it had happened before in other executions.[265]

97. LEROY ADOLPH LEICK. January 22, 1960. Denver. W-W. Asphyxiation. Convicted of beating and strangling his wife, Evelyn, to death. Evelyn's sister was also beaten, and initial reports of the crime also indicated that thugs attempting a robbery had also beaten Leick himself.[266] A day after the murder, however, a man came forward to say that two years earlier, Leick had tried to hire him to commit the murder. He had reported this to the police at the time, but no action was taken.[267] Two others said that

---

262. For a more thorough description of Graham's life history and mental status, *see* James A.V. Galvin & John M. MacDonald, *Psychiatric Study of a Mass Murderer*, AM. J. PSYCH. 115 (1959): 1057; JOHN M. MACDONALD, THE MURDERER AND HIS VICTIM 201–16 (1961); ALT & WELLS, MOUNTAIN MURDERS, 161–84.

263. Graham v. People, 302 P.2d 737 (Colo. 1956).

264. MACDONALD, THE MURDERER AND HIS VICTIM, 348.

265. Zeke Scher, *Graham Dies for Plane Bomb Murder*, DENVER POST, June 12, 1957, at 1.

266. *Denver Woman Kidnapped and Murdered!*, ROCKY MTN. NEWS, Dec. 2, 1953, at 1.

267. *Police Were Told of Plot; Mrs. Leick Wasn't; Why Not?*, ROCKY MTN. NEWS, Dec. 6, 1953, at 5.

Leick had (independently) approached them for the same mission.[268] Two days after the murder, both Leick and a man he hired to stage the robbery, Gene Dukes, confessed to the plot, stating that the motive was to win life insurance money.[269] At trial, Leick pleaded insanity. The Colorado Supreme Court reversed his first conviction,[270] but the conviction resulting from the second trial was affirmed.[271] Efforts to challenge his mental competency for execution also failed.[272] Shortly before the execution, Leick tried (unsuccessfully) to absolve Dukes (who had been sentenced to life imprisonment) from responsibility for the murder.[273] Leick, a thirty-six-year-old business executive for a Denver appliance firm, had a prior conviction for stealing an $800 diamond ring.[274] His execution ended six years of legal battles, almost all of which concerned his mental status.[275]

98. DAVID FRANCIS EARLY. August 11, 1961. Littleton (Arapahoe County). W-W. Asphyxiation. Convicted of the murder of Regina Knight and accused of (but not tried for) murdering her husband, Merrill, and the couple's fifteen-year-old daughter, Karen. The murders occurred four days after Early was released from a federal penitentiary (he had also served prison terms in New Mexico and Colorado).[276] According to one report, he had informed a psychologist at the penitentiary that he intended to commit a murder as soon as he could after his release.[277] He broke into the Knight home (Merrill was a prominent Denver attorney

268. *Was Slain Denver Woman Victim of Fiendish Plot?*, ROCKY MTN. NEWS, Dec. 3, 1953, at 1.

269. *Wife Killer Confesses!*, ROCKY MTN. NEWS, Dec. 4, 1953, at 1; *Gay Cafe Dinner Prelude to Death*, ROCKY MTN. NEWS, Dec. 5, 1953, at 1.

270. Leick v. People, 281 P.2d 806 (Colo. 195?).

271. Leick v. People, 322 P.2d 674 (Colo. 1958), *cert. denied*, 357 U.S. 922 (1958).

272. Leick v. People, 345 P.2d 1054 (Colo. 1959).

273. Al Nakkula, *Leick Absolves Dukes as Slay Accomplice*, ROCKY MTN. NEWS, Jan. 22, 1960, at 5.

274. Bill Brenneman, *Theft of $800 Diamond Ring Blots Leick's Record*, ROCKY MTN. NEWS, Dec. 3, 1953, at 5.

275. Zeke Scher, *Wife-Slayer Leick Dies Calmly in State Gas Chamber*, DENVER POST, Jan. 23, 1960, at 1; Al Nakkula, *Leick Is Executed!*, ROCKY MTN. NEWS, Jan 23, 1960, at 1.

276. *Self-Confessed Killer's Record Started at* 15, DENVER POST, Apr. 26, 1958, at 3.

277. MACDONALD, THE MURDERER AND HIS VICTIM, 249.

who had befriended him) and, finding no one at home, waited for the family to return. In the home he found a gun and a rifle. One by one over a six-hour period, as the family returned (including a son, who managed to escape and was not harmed), he bound them in different rooms in the house. He then shot them. He was quickly apprehended by neighbors and immediately confessed.[278] At trial, he pleaded not guilty by reason of insanity and supported this assertion with the testimony of two psychologists and four psychiatrists, who found him to be a paranoid schizophrenic. However, five psychiatrists testifying for the state found him to be sane. The jury rejected the insanity defense, and the conviction was affirmed on appeal.[279] As he entered the gas chamber, Early, thirty-two, apologized for his crimes.[280]

99. HAROLD DAVID WOOLEY. March 9, 1962. Golden (Jefferson County). W-W. Asphyxiation. Wooley, thirty-nine at the time of his death, was executed for the murder of a wealthy Denver "socialite," William Scott Wright. Mary Pearl Walker, Wooley's common law wife, was also convicted and sentenced to life imprisonment; she stood beside Wooley when he shot Wright and helped bury the body.[281] Wright was a friend of the duo and had invited the couple for a brief vacation in his mountain cabin. There, Wright was killed by a single bullet wound to his head as he slept. For three months thereafter, the couple cashed checks made out to Wooley and pretended that their friend had gone on vacation. On September 15, his body was discovered, and two days later both Wooley and Walker confessed that they had plotted the murder.[282] Wooley, who worked for his father in an upholstery shop, had no prior convictions. His insanity plea failed, and the conviction was affirmed on appeal.[283] Walker

---

278. *Ex-Convict Confesses Slaying Attorney, Wife and Daughter*, DENVER POST, Apr. 26, 1958, at 1.

279. Early v. People, 352 P.2d 112 (Colo. 1960), *cert. denied*, 364 U.S. 847 (1960).

280. William Hazlett, *Murderer of Three in Littleton Home Gassed to Death*, ROCKY MTN. NEWS, Aug. 12, 1961, at 5; Fred Baker, *David F. Early Executed in Gas Chamber*, DENVER POST, Aug. 12, 1961, at 24.

281. *Stood Beside Wooley at Killing, Helped Burial, Woman Admits*, DENVER POST, Sept. 18, 1959, at 3; *Mrs. Walker Faces Death Chair*, DENVER POST, Sept. 18, 1959, at 3.

282. *Ex-Con Confesses Killing Heir*, DENVER POST, Sept. 17, 1959, at 1; *$15,000 Cache "Missing" in Heir Slay Case*, DENVER POST, Sept. 18, 1959, at 1.

283. Wooley v. State, 367 P.2d 903 (Colo. 1962).

claimed shortly before the execution that she had fired the fatal shot, but the authorities did not find her statement to be credible. Shortly before the execution, Wooley was permitted to visit with Walker, and he gave her most of his possessions, including a parakeet that he had been allowed to keep.[284] Two months before his death, Wooley denied his previous confessions and pleaded that he was innocent, and he continued to maintain his innocence throughout the remainder of his life.[285]

100. WALTER J. HAMMIL (a.k.a. Hammill). May 25, 1962. Denver. W-W. Asphyxiation. Age thirty-one at the time of his death, the former circus animal trainer was convicted of strangling eleven-year-old Lester G. Brown, Jr., in a sex-related crime. Hammil was arrested the day after the crime and immediately confessed, explaining that he had invited the young boy to return to the circus one night, promising him a free ride on an elephant. Hammil choked him (to prevent him from alerting adults) when the boy refused his sexual advances. He was arrested the next day, confessed, led police to the body, and acknowledged that he would probably have to die for the crime.[286] He had a long record of prior convictions and delinquencies, dating back to when he was nine years old.[287] Physicians described Hammil as "mentally retarded" but legally sane.[288]

101. JOHN BIZUP, JR. August 14, 1964. Pueblo. W-W. Asphyxiation. Executed for the robbery-murder of a cabdriver, Roy Don Bussey.[289] Bizup, aged thirty, had been hitchhiking through Colorado at the time of the crime. He had been in reform schools and jails since age twelve.[290] Bizup

---

284. Dick Woodbury, *Wooley Executed in Prison*, DENVER POST, Mar. 10, 1962, at 1.

285. William Hazlett, *Wooley Is Executed at Cañon City Prison*, ROCKY MTN. NEWS, Mar. 10, 1962, at 1.

286. *Denver Boy, 11, Disappears; Police Quiz Circus Worker*, DENVER POST, Aug. 28, 1958, at 1; *Roustabout Admits Killing*, DENVER POST, Aug. 29, 1958, at 1; *Bereaved Parents Muted with Grief*, DENVER POST, Aug. 29, 1958, at 48; *"I'll Have to Die," Slayer Says*, DENVER POST, Aug. 30, 1958, at 1.

287. *Hammill* [*sic*] *Has Long Record*, DENVER POST, Aug. 30, 1958, at 3.

288. Hammil v. State, 361 P.2d 117 (Colo. 1961); Dick Woodbury, *Hammill* [*sic*] *Due to Die Tonight*, DENVER POST, May 25, 1962, at 2; Dick Woodbury, *Hammill* [*sic*] *Pays Full Penalty*, DENVER POST, May 26, 1962, at 2.

289. *Cab Man Killed by Bullet*, DENVER POST, Mar. 26, 1960, at 24.

290. *Killer Clings to Hope Until the Last*, DENVER POST, Aug. 15, 1964, at 3.

confessed to the murder and pleaded insanity; one psychiatrist supported that plea while three opposed it. The conviction was affirmed on appeal,[291] and his petition for a writ of habeas corpus was denied.[292] Shortly before his death, a psychiatrist concluded that Bizup was sane, and Gov. John Love refused to commute the sentence.[293] During the execution, cries of "killers" and "murderers" yelled by other prisoners and directed at the prison staff were heard in the death chamber.[294]

102. LUIS JOSÉ MONGE. June 2, 1967. Denver. H-H. Asphyxiation. Sentenced to death for the murder of his pregnant wife, Leonarda. Monge also killed three of the couple's ten children, Alan (age six), Vincent (age four), and Teresa (age eleven months). Monge was a native of Puerto Rico who grew up in New York. Immediately after the four murders, Monge called police and admitted his guilt. A salesman, Monge had no prior felony convictions, although in 1961 he abandoned his family for two months and served a short jail sentence in Louisiana for vagrancy.[295] The alleged motive for the murders was "to prevent exposure of sex crimes committed by defendant with his own children."[296] His wife was beaten to death with a steel bar as she slept, Teresa was stabbed, Vincent was choked, and Alan was bludgeoned with the steel bar.[297] After entering an insanity plea, Monge was evaluated and found to be sane. He then insisted on pleading guilty to first-degree murder. A jury that was

---

291. Bizup v. People, 371 P.2d 786 (Colo. 1962).

292. Bizup v. Tinsley, 393 P.2d 556 (Colo. 1964).

293. *Doomed Slayer Wills Eyes, But Clings to Clemency Hope*, DENVER POST, Aug. 13, 1964, at 2; *Killer's Fate Still Uncertain as End Looms*, DENVER POST, Aug. 14, 1964, at 5; *Rendall Ayers, Gov. Love Denies Clemency to Bizup*, DENVER POST, Aug. 14, 1964, at 3.

294. John Kokish, *Bizup Dies in Gas Chamber*, DENVER POST, Aug. 15, 1964, at 3; W. T. Little, *Bizup Executed for Pueblo Slaying*, ROCKY MTN. NEWS, Aug. 15, 1964, at 5. *See also Killer Clings to Hope*.

295. *Slayer's Disappearance Recalled; Described as Good Father*, DENVER POST, June 30, 1963, at 3.

296. Monge v. People, 406 P.2d 674, 676 (Colo. 1965). One of the children he sexually assaulted, Diann, later wrote a book about her experiences. Diann Kissell with Kathy Bird, A TURQUOISE LIFE (2014).

297. Bill Myers & Walt Lindenmann, *Father of Ten Kills His Wife, 3 of Children*, DENVER POST, June 29, 1963, at 1; Bill Myers & Walt Lindenmann, *Police Guard Slayer of Expectant Wife, Three Children*, DENVER POST, June 30, 1963, at 3.

convened for the penalty phase of the trial recommended death, and the conviction and sentence were affirmed on appeal. In January 1966, Governor Love suspended all executions in Colorado pending a referendum on capital punishment by voters. On November 8, 1966, the voters decided to retain the death penalty by a 3–1 margin. In March 1967, Monge attracted nationwide attention when he asked a Denver court to allow him to be hanged at high noon on the front steps of the Denver City and County Building. This request was denied.[298] The following month, Monge fired his attorneys and directed that no attempts should be made to save his life; nonetheless, his surviving children did appeal for clemency. Once more, Monge's mental status was evaluated, and he was found mentally competent for execution.[299] A week before his death, Monge shared a final meal with his surviving seven children.[300] On the eve of the execution, some seventy members of the Colorado Council to Abolish Capital Punishment gathered on the steps of the Capitol Building in Denver to protest the execution. Monge was forty-eight at the time of his death.[301] As he wished, after his death, one of his corneas was transplanted into a teenaged reformatory inmate.[302] He was the last person executed in the United States before all capital statutes, in effect, were voided by the US Supreme Court in 1972.[303]

103. GARY LEE DAVIS. Brighton. October 13, 1997. Convicted of the kidnap, rape, and murder of Virginia "Ginny" May in Byers, Colorado, a

---

298. R. Roger Harkins, *Some Thoughts on Watching a Man Suffocate*, BOULDER DAILY CAMERA, June 4, 1967, at 1.

299. Cary Stiff, *Killer Monge Slated to Die Friday, Wills Eyes to Boy*, DENVER POST, June 1, 1967, at 3; Martin Moran, *Monge Ruled Sane; Execution Slated Friday*, ROCKY MTN. NEWS, June 1, 1967, at 11.

300. Loy Holman, *Monge Visits with Son on Eve of His Execution*, ROCKY MTN. NEWS, June 2, 1967, at 5.

301. Loy Holman, *Monge Dies in Prison Gas Chamber*, ROCKY MTN. NEWS, June 3, 1967, at 5; Cary Stiff, *Monge Goes to His Death With Smile*, DENVER POST, June 3, 1967, at 24.

302. William Logan, *Monge Eye Transplant Is Called Success*, ROCKY MTN. NEWS, June 4, 1967, at 5.

303. Furman v. Georgia, 408 U.S. 238 (1972); Gary Gerhardt, *Last Man Executed also Wanted to Die*, ROCKY MTN. NEWS, Jan. 17, 1977, at 6. *See generally* STEPHEN H. GETTINGER, SENTENCED TO DIE: THE PEOPLE, THE CRIMES, AND THE CONTROVERSY 1–20 (1979).

small town in Adams County, fifty miles west of the county seat of Brighton (where the trial was held). May was abducted from her home in front of her two children. Her beaten nude body was found covered with brush in a ravine about eight miles from her home. Davis's (third) wife, Rebecca Fincham Davis, was sentenced to life imprisonment for her role in the crime.[304] In 1990 the Colorado Supreme Court upheld Davis's conviction.[305] In early 1997, Davis terminated his appeals, and Gov. Roy Romer denied his request for executive clemency.[306] By the time he was executed, he had spent eleven years on death row.

---

304. People v. Fincham, 799 P.2d 419 (Colo. App. 1990).

305. People v. Davis, 794 P.2d 159 (Colo. 1990); Davis v. People, 871 P.2d 769 (Colo. 1994).

306. Kit Miniclier, *Abducted Byers Woman Beaten before Dying*, DENVER POST, July 25, 1986, at B1; Steve Garnass, *Governor to Decide Davis' Fate; Death-Row Inmate to Quit Appeals Route*, DENVER POST, June 27, 1997, at B1; Kevin Simpson, *Davis Dies at 8:33 pm; Ginny May's Killer Fulfills Sentence after 11 Years*, DENVER POST, Oct. 14, 1997, at 1; Lisa Levitt Ryckman, *Davis Pays Final Price*, ROCKY MTN. NEWS, Oct. 14, 1997, at 1.

APPENDIX 2

People Sentenced to Death in Colorado, 1860–December 31, 2015, Not Executed and No Longer on Death Row (ordered by the year that the death sentence was imposed)[1]

1. WILLIAM F. HADLEY. Denver. 1860. Hadley was convicted of the murder of J. B. Card by a People's Court in Denver and was sentenced to be executed on June 25. "Unfortunately for the course of justice, he was able to escape the night before his scheduled execution by bribing a guard."[2] When last sighted, he was on his way "down the Platte," apparently headed for his home in Missouri.[3]

2. PAT FITZSIMMONS (a.k.a. Fitzgerald). Denver. 1866. Sentenced to death on April 28, 1866, for the murder of John Daly.[4]

---

1. These are examples only and it is not intended as a complete list. My intent is simply to list the names of people who I know were sentenced to death—not to give the complete story of how they were removed, only that they were not removed by execution.

2. Richard Burg, *Administration of Justice in the Denver People's Courts*, JOUR. OF THE WEST 7 (1968): 510–21, at 515.

3. *Wm. F. Hadley*, ROCKY MTN. NEWS, June 27, 1860, at 2; Francis S. Williams, *Trials and Judgments of the People's Courts*, COLORADO MAGAZINE 27 (1950): 287–302, at 297–98.

4. *Prisoners Sentenced*, ROCKY MTN. NEWS, Apr. 28, 1866, at 4.

DOI: 10.5876/9781607325123.c009

3. JAMES HILL. Arapahoe County. 1872. Sentenced to death on May 10, 1872. On appeal, the Colorado Supreme Court vacated the conviction and the sentence.[5]

4. BENJAMIN SMITH. Bent County (West Las Animas). 1876. Sentenced to death with James Miller, who was executed in 1877.[6] In January 1877, Gov. Frederick Pitkin commuted Smith's death sentence to life.[7]

5. MALACHI MONEYHAN (a.k.a. Minher, Monahan, Monyhan, Moynahan, or Moynehan).[8] Fremont County (Cañon City). 1876. Convicted of the murder of Patrick Fitzpatrick and sentenced to death.[9] He was originally scheduled to hang in January 1877 but won a reprieve because the original indictment first spelled the victim's name as "Fitz Patrick" (with a space and a capital *P*), but in two other places spelled it "Fitzpatrick."[10] The misspelling of the victim's name, not Malachi's, led the Colorado Supreme Court to vacate the conviction in August 1877.[11]

6. WALTER C. KNOWLES. Saguache County. 1881. Sentenced to death in the summer of 1881 for the murder of "Red" Lyons. Governor Frederick Pitkin commuted the death sentence to life on January 28, 1882.[12]

---

5. Hill v. People, Supreme Court of Colorado Territory, 1 Colo. 436 (February Term, 1872).
6. *See* appendix 1, case no. 11.
7. *Commuted: One of the Doomed Colored Soldiers Goes to Canyon for Life*, ROCKY MTN. NEWS, Jan. 16, 1877, at 4.
8. I have used the spelling "Moneyhan" because that is how his name is spelled in official prison records. He is buried under the name "Monyhan" in Greenwood Cemetery, Cañon City. The 1880 census spells his name "Moynhan." The Colorado Supreme Court spelled it "Moynahan." I am grateful to the Royal Gorge Regional Museum & History Center for their assistance in tracking down the details of this case.
9. *The Pistol: A Man Killed at Canon City*, COLO. WEEKLY CHIEFTAIN, Aug. 24, 1876, at 4; *Greenhorn Notes*, COLO. WEEKLY CHIEFTAIN, Nov. 30, 1876, at 4.
10. COLO. MOUNTAINEER, Jan. 3, 1877, at 2; CAÑON CITY TIMES, Jan. 4, 1877.
11. Moynahan v. The People, 3 Colo. 367 (1877), quoted at length in *Supreme Court Decisions*, DENVER DAILY TIMES, Aug. 24, 1877, at 2.
12. *No Rope Needed*, ROCKY MTN. NEWS, Jan. 29, 1882, at 4.

7. ALFERD PACKER. Hinsdale County (Lake City). 1883. Convicted of killing some traveling companions; the motive was food. After his original arrest, he escaped and was on the lam for nine years before being rearrested, convicted (April 13, 1883), and sentenced to death. The Colorado Supreme Court reversed the conviction and death sentence in 1885.[13]

8. EDWARD P. PETITE. Las Animas County. 1884. Convicted of killing a drinking companion, Charles Thorpe, in the small town of Starkville, near Trinidad. The murder occurred on January 26, 1884. On appeal in 1885, the death sentence was vacated by the Colorado Supreme Court.[14]

9. CHARLES CROSTHWAITE. Ouray County. 1888. "Chas. H. Crawthwaite [*sic*], who has been on trial in the District Court here for the past week, charged with the murder of Geo. W. Johnson on the night of September 17, during a quarrel over the ownership of a cabin near the city, was yesterday convicted . . . and the judge to-day sentenced Crosthwaite to be hanged January 25."[15] In March 1889, Gov. Job Cooper expressed doubts about Crosthwaite's sanity.[16] In early April, Cooper commuted the sentence to life imprisonment.[17]

10. JOHN B. KEARNEY. Pitkin County. 1888. Convicted in January 1888 and sentenced to be hanged for the murder of John J. Burt.[18] On appeal, the conviction was reversed.[19]

11. JAMES MEDLEY. Arapahoe County. 1889. Convicted of the murder (on May 13, 1889) of his wife and sentenced to death on November 29, 1889.

---

13. *See* discussion of Packer case in chapter 2, *infra*; Packer v. People, 8 P. 564 (Oct. 1885).

14. Petite v. People, 9 P. 622 (Dec. 1885).

15. *Death Sentence: Charles H. Crosthwaite at Ouray Sentenced to be Hanged*, ASPEN DAILY TIMES, Dec. 21, 1888, at 1.

16. WHITE PINE CONE (Gunnison County), Mar. 29, 1889, at 1.

17. WHITE PINE CONE, Apr. 5, 1889, at 1.

18. *Sentenced to Hang*, ASPEN DAILY TIMES, Jan. 26, 1888, at 3.

19. Kearney v. People, 17 P. 782 (Apr. 1888).

On March 3, 1890, the US Supreme Court vacated the conviction, as well as the conviction of James Savage.[20]

12. JAMES H. SAVAGE. Arapahoe County. 1889. Savage was charged with the June 25, 1889 murder of Emanuel Harbert, and on October 23 of that year, he was convicted and sentenced to death. On March 3, 1890, the US Supreme Court vacated the conviction and ordered Savage's immediate release.[21]

13. ROBERT HOLMES. Garfield County (Glenwood Springs). 1889. Holmes was sentenced to death in December 1889 for the murder of his brother, Henry.[22] The triggerman, William Chambers (the stepson of the victim) was sentenced to a prison term for his role in the murder. The murder was committed on June 17, 1889. On January 10, 1890, the Colorado Supreme Court granted a "supersedes" because of wrongful admission of testimony and refusal to admit certain evidence at the trial.[23] He was ultimately granted relief on grounds similar to those in the Medley (case no. 11, *infra*) and Savage cases (case no. 12, *infra*).[24] In November 1891, "Holmes . . . plead [*sic*] guilty to murder in the second degree, and was sentenced . . . to twelve years in the penitentiary."[25]

14. HENRY TYSON. Arapahoe County. 1889. Sentenced to death on July 26, 1889, for killing John King, who had eloped with Tyson's wife. The murder occurred on May 18, 1889. On appeal, the case was remanded

---

20. *See* case no. 12, *infra*; Medley, Petitioner, 134 U.S. 160 (1890) (hereinafter Medley); *Cannot be Hanged*, ROCKY MTN. NEWS. Mar. 4, 1890, at 1. In its day, the Medley case was important because of its stern denunciation of solitary confinement. The justices wrote, "It seems to us that the considerations which we have here suggested show that the solitary confinement to which the prisoner was subjected by the statute of Colorado of 1889, and by the judgment of the court in pursuance of that statute, was an additional punishment of the most important and painful character, and is, therefore, forbidden by this provision of the Constitution of the United States." Medley, at 171.

21. *See* case no. 11, *infra*; Savage, Petitioner, 134 U.S. 176 (1890); *Murderers Set Free*, ASPEN DAILY CHRON., July 3, 1890, at 1.

22. *Garfield's Necktie Party*, ASPEN DAILY CHRON., Dec. 21, 1889, at 1.

23. *Courts and Clients: The Supreme Court*, ROCKY MTN. NEWS, Jan. 11, 1890, at 2.

24. *The Holmes Case*, ASPEN WEEKLY TIMES, Mar. 8, 1890, at 1.

25. ADVOCATE (Glenwood Springs), Nov. 18, 1891, at 4.

because of errors in setting the range of dates for the execution.[26] From October 1889 through March 1895, he was judged to be insane, but on March 15, 1895, he was judged to be sane and the death sentence was restored. On further appeal, the conviction was affirmed.[27] Tyson was released from prison on August 31, 1895.[28]

15. MARK POWER (a.k.a. Powers). Montrose County. 1890. Convicted and sentenced to death on November 6, 1890, for the murder of Charles A. Baer, who was shot on July 2, 1890. Power was originally scheduled to be hanged in November 1890, but he won a stay from the Colorado Supreme Court.[29] On appeal, the conviction and sentence were affirmed.[30] On February 20, 1892, Gov. John Routt commuted the sentence to life imprisonment.[31]

16. WILLIAM T. ROBERTS. Arapahoe County. 1891. Convicted and sentenced to death on November 23, 1890, for the murder of Henry F. Kapella (a.k.a. Kapelli). In January 1890, Roberts's wife was granted a divorce on the grounds of desertion and non-support, but in August 1891, Roberts moved to have that decision set aside and instead to grant his counter motion for a divorce based on an adulterous affair that she had been having with Kapelli. The homicide was a consequence of the affair. On October 7, 1891, Roberts filed a motion for a new trial in trial court,[32] but on October 29, 1891, the motion was denied.[33] In an unpub-

---

26. In re Tyson, 22 P. 810 (1889).

27. In re Tyson, 39 P. 1093 (1895).

28. "Denver, Aug. 31—Henry Tyson, seven years ago, murdered John King in this city. He has spent three years in solitary confinement in Cañon City, has been sentenced to death three times, and was once within two days of execution. He was to-day declared free on a legal technicality, and walked out of prison." N.Y. TIMES, Sept. 1, 1895, at 5.

29. *The Supreme Court Interferes with the Power's* [*sic*] *Execution*, ROCKY MTN. NEWS, Nov. 23, 1890, at 4.

30. Power v. People, 28 P. 1121 (Feb. 1, 1892).

31. *Mark Powers to Remain in the Penitentiary for Life*, ROCKY MTN. NEWS, Feb. 21, 1892, at 7.

32. *Roberts' Motion for a New Trial*, ASPEN WEEKLY TIMES, Oct. 10, 1891, at 1.

33. *Will Roberts Hang?* ROCKY MTN. NEWS, Oct. 29, 1891, at 5; *Solitude Unpleasant*, ROCKY MTN. NEWS, Dec. 22, 1891, at 6.

lished opinion, Roberts won relief from the Colorado Supreme Court on December 22, 1892.[34]

17. LIBRADO MORA. Park County. 1891. On December 3, 1891, Mora was convicted of a double murder that occurred near Como on July 9, 1891. On appeal, the Colorado Supreme Court affirmed the decision.[35] On February 5, 1894, the sentence was commuted to life imprisonment.[36]

18. CHRISTIAN KUELBS. Arapahoe County. 1892. Convicted in 1892 of the murder of Young Murray and admitted to the prison on July 26, 1892.[37] Gov. John Routt commuted his death sentence on August 13, 1892.[38]

19. DR. THOMAS THATCHER GRAVES. Arapahoe County. 1892. A physician from Rhode Island (who had graduated first in his class at Harvard Medical School), Graves was convicted and sentenced to death for mailing a bottle of wine laced with arsenic to a friend, Mabel Barnaby, whose estate he managed and who was passing through Denver on her way to California. At the time, the trial was the longest murder trial in the history of the United States. The murder occurred on April 19, 1891. In January 1893, the Colorado Supreme Court reversed the conviction.[39] Graves took his own life before retrial.[40]

20–21. JUAN AMMON (a.k.a. Ammons) and PABLO LUCERO. Las Animas County. 1892. Ammon was convicted and sentenced to death on Octo-

---

34. *See Corrections Records*, COLORADO STATE ARCHIVES, accessed July 15, 2016, https://www.colorado.gov/pacific/archives/corrections-records (inmate number 2730).

35. Mora v. People, 35 P. 179 (1893).

36. FIFTH BIENNIAL REPORT OF THE STATE BOARD OF PARDONS, STATE OF COLORADO, 1901–1902, at 48–49; FAIRPLAY FLUME, Feb. 8, 1894, at 1.

37. BIENNIAL REPORT OF THE COMMISSIONERS OF THE COLORADO STATE PENITENTIARY FOR THE TWO-YEAR PERIOD ENDING NOVEMBER 30, 1900 (1901), at 113.

38. ASPEN DAILY LEADER, Aug. 13, 1892, at 8.

39. Graves v. People, 32 P. 63 (1893).

40. *Dr. Graves Death: End of the Barnaby Murder Defendant*, ROCKY MTN. NEWS, Sept. 4, 1893, at 1. The case was the subject of a book by the victim's great grandson. BARNABY CONRAD, A REVOLTING TRANSACTION (1983).

ber 3, 1892. On November 21, 1892, Gov. John Routt commuted the sentence.[41] As described by the State Board of Pardons,

> Juan Ammon was first tried for the murder of (Antonio) Riverra, convicted and sentenced to death, the principal witness against him being Pablo Lucero. His sentence was afterwards commuted to life imprisonment and, upon charges being filed against Lucero for the crime, Ammon was brought back from the penitentiary and testified against Lucero, with the result that Lucero was sentenced as above. Lucero claims that while he went with Ammon to Riverra's house, he left before Riverra was killed and had nothing to do with the murder.[42]

The State Board of Pardons denied Lucero's request for a full pardon on November 7, 1902.

22. WILLIAM NESBITT (a.k.a. Nesbit). Arapahoe County. 1893. Convicted July 8, 1893. Gov. Davis Waite commuted the sentence to life imprisonment through executive clemency on May 19, 1894.[43]

23. SANTIAGO TORRIS (a.k.a. "Indian Joe" or "Jose Torres"). Pueblo. 1893. Torris was sentenced to death on October 30, 1893, for the murder of a ranchman named Howard.[44] In March 1894, the Colorado Supreme Court affirmed the conviction on appeal.[45] In May 1894, Gov. Davis Waite commuted the sentence.[46]

24. LEVI STREETER (a.k.a. "Streetor"). Park County. 1894. On June 5, 1894, Streeter was convicted of killing Como marshal Adolph E. Cook and sentenced to hang. The murder occurred in April 1894.[47] The Colorado

---

41. *Sentence Commuted*, ASPEN DAILY LEADER, Nov. 22, 1892, at 1. "The sentence of Juan Ammon, convicted of the murder of Antonio Rivera [*sic*] at Trinidad and sentenced to be hanged, has been commuted [by Governor Routt] to life imprisonment." *To Life Imprisonment*, ASPEN DAILY CHRON., Nov. 22, 1892, at 1.

42. FIFTH BIENNIAL REPORT OF THE STATE BOARD OF PARDONS, 1902–1902, at 42.

43. *Id.* at 51; NEW CASTLE NEWS, May 19, 1894, at 1.

44. *Sentenced to Death*, ASPEN DAILY CHRON., Oct. 31, 1893, at 1.

45. Torris v. People, 36 P. 153 (Mar. 7, 1894).

46. BIENNIAL REPORT OF THE STATE BOARD OF PARDONS, at 51.

47. FAIRPLAY FLUME, Apr. 12, 1894, at 1, http://www.parkcoarchives.org/Streetor_Articles.pdf.

State Board of Pardons commuted the sentence to life on March 2, 1895. Streeter died in prison in 1896.[48]

25. A. W. VAN HOUTEN. El Paso County. 1895. On July 8, 1895, Van Houten was convicted and sentenced to death for the murder of Richard Newell. On February 25, 1896, acting governor David Coates commuted the death sentence.[49]

26. PABLO HATCH (a.k.a. Jimmie or James Hatch). Montezuma County. 1896. A Ute Indian, "Pablo the Ute" was convicted May 10, 1896, for killing Eweep, another Indian.[50] The murder occurred outside the limits of the reservation and thus it was tried in state court. On Oct. 27, 1896, Hatch died on death row in Cañon City from "consumption" (tuberculosis).[51]

27. WALTER DAVIS. El Paso County. 1896. Convicted December 15, 1896. The sentences for him and Allen Hense Downen[52] were commuted to life on April 19, 1897.[53]

28. ALLEN HENSE (OR HENCE) DOWNEN. Arapahoe County. 1896. Convicted and sentenced to death for killing Joel Ashworth on December 28, 1896. The sentences for him and Walter Davis were commuted to life on April 19, 1897.[54]

29–30. JOSE M. (J. M.) LUCERO and JUAN DURAN. Las Animas County. 1897. Both men were members of a gang who were involved with the murders of William Green and William Kelly, deputy sheriffs who were murdered in April 1896. Duran was convicted of killing the two sher-

---

48. VAN DUSEN, HISTORIC TALES, 120–24. Information about the case is also available thanks to work done by volunteers for the Park County Local History Archives. *See* FAIRPLAY FLUME, Apr. 12, 1894.

49. FIFTH ANNUAL REPORT OF THE STATE BOARD OF PARDONS, at 62–63; *Sentence Commuted*, TELLURIDE DAILY JOURNAL, Feb. 25, 1896, at 1.

50. *Pablo, The Ute*, ASPEN DAILY TIMES, May 27, 1896, at 2; Pablo v. The People, 46 P. 636 (Oct. 5, 1896).

51. *News Items*, COLO. MEDICAL JOUR. 2 (1896), at 362.

52. *See* case no. 28, *infra*.

53. *Around the State,* ASPEN DAILY TIMES, Apr. 23, 1897, at 2.

54. *Id.*

iffs and sentenced to death on September 22, 1897.[55] At the same time, Lucero was sentenced to death for killing another member of the gang, Miguel Reville.[56] Gov. Alva Adams commuted both sentences to life imprisonment on October 11, 1897.[57]

31. JOHN (JACK) COX. El Paso County. 1897. On April 11, 1897, Cox shot Robert (a.k.a. James or Bud) Daly after a fight over a pool game. The murder was committed on April 11, 1897, and Cox was sentenced to death in June. Gov. Alva Adams commuted the death sentence on July 9, 1897.[58]

32. LAWRENCE HEX. Pueblo. 1902. Hex was sentenced to death on January 2, 1902, for the murders of William White and Lizzie Alley. The State Board of Pardons commuted the death sentence on April 4, 1902.[59] On September 25, 1913, the prison sentence was commuted.[60]

33. HARVEY KING. El Paso County. 1903. "Colorado Springs, Colo., July 25. Judge Serds, of the District Court, on Thursday denied the motion for a new trial in the case of Harvey King, colored, convicted of the murder of his wife, and sentenced the prisoner to be hanged."[61] Despite the fact that King wanted to be hanged and refused to request a commutation, Gov. James Peabody commuted his death sentence to life imprisonment on November 7, 1903.[62] Before the commutation, King was scheduled

---

55. Four other defendants were also convicted of these murders and sentenced to prison terms: Rupeito Archuleta, Moses Frayter, Juan Pacheco, and Nestor Martinez. Martinez was pardoned in 1899; Archuleta and Pacheco died in prison in 1899 and 1901, respectively; and Frayter was paroled in 1913. Duran was paroled in 1911.

56. Reville was killed on April 17, 1896, three days before the deputies arrested him. *See* https://www.colorado.gov/pacific/csp/colorado-fallen-heroes-biographies (paragraphs on Deputies William Green and William Kelly, Las Animas County Sheriff's Office, murdered April 20, 1896).

57. *Murderers Not to Hang*, TRINIDAD DAILY ADVERTISER, Oct. 12, 1897, at 1.

58. *Sentence Commuted*, ASPEN DAILY TIMES, July 10, 1897, at 4.

59. FIFTH BIENNIAL REPORT OF THE STATE BOARD OF PARDONS, 1901–1902, at 34.

60. *Clemency for Murderers*, YAMPA LEADER, Sept. 25, 1913, at 2.

61. *Murderer Must Be Hanged*, WRAY RATTLER, July 31, 1903, at 7.

62. *Criminal Wants to Be Hanged but the Governor Intervenes*, CASTLE ROCK JOUR., Nov. 13, 1903, at 1.

to be the first inmate executed under the law that reinstituted capital punishment in 1901.

34. CHARLES PETERS. Denver. 1904. Sentenced to death for a 1903 murder with two codefendants, J. Newton Andrews and Fred Arnold, who were both hanged for the crime.[63] "Charles Peters escaped the noose when he became a raving maniac. He died, a madman, in the penitentiary."[64]

35. PATRICK BRENNAN. Lake County. 1905. On April 19, 1905, Brennan was convicted and sentenced to be hanged for killing his fiancé, Kate Looney. The murder occurred on Christmas Day 1904. In April 1906, the Colorado Supreme Court reversed the conviction.[65]

36. SANTIAGO TAFOYA (a.k.a. Juan Patoya). Las Animas County (Trinidad). 1907. Tafoya, "convicted of the murder of Pete Griego on March 1, 1907, and sentenced to be hanged this week, has had his sentence commuted to life imprisonment."[66]

37. ANDREW JOHNSON. Prowers County. 1907. "Lamar, Colo. To be hanged by the neck until dead is the fate of Andrew Johnson, convicted of the murder of Night Marshal J. H. Frisbie at Lamar."[67] On August 23, 1907, acting governor E. R. Harper commuted the sentence to life at the request of the widow of the victim.[68]

38. WILLIAM R. LONGINOTTI. Denver. 1908. Sentenced to death for the murder of Charles Reidel. On appeal, the Colorado Supreme Court reversed the conviction.[69] At retrial, he was convicted of second-degree murder.[70]

---

63. *See* appendix 1, case nos. 39 and 40.

64. *Lamar Bandits First Trio Put to Death for Same Crime*, DENVER POST, July 19, 1930, at 3.

65. Brennan v. People, 86 P. 79 (1906).

66. *Sentence Commuted*, ASPEN DEMO., July 3, 1907, at 1.

67. *Andrew Johnson Must Hang*, YAMPA LEADER, May 11, 1907, at 7.

68. *With Death Trap Set, Gov. Commutes Sentence*, DURANGO DEMO., Aug. 24, 1907, at 1.

69. Longinotti v. People, 102 P. 165 (1909).

70. *Longinotti Escapes the Death Penalty*, FORT COLLINS WEEKLY COUR., Aug. 4, 1909, at 6.

39. EDWARD HAGER. Pueblo. 1909. On May 1, 1909, Hager was sentenced to death for the murder of Elizabeth May Mae James, which occurred on October 26, 1908. The execution was scheduled to take place during the week of August 14, 1910. Hager had hoped to marry James, but after her former husband visited her, Hager shot James during a quarrel.[71]

40. FRED PIEL. Denver. 1910. Piel, a native of Russia who was unable to speak English, was sentenced to death for stabbing a friend to death at a gathering hosted by Piel's father-in-law. Piel was quite intoxicated at the time of the murder, which occurred during a quarrel at the party. On appeal, the Colorado Supreme Court vacated the conviction, finding, "No one can read the record before us without being impelled to the belief that the verdict is manifestly against the weight of the evidence."[72]

41. GEORGE KING. Elbert County. 1911. In July 1911, King and codefendant John Fields were convicted of the murder of Felix ("Pete") Jackson. Fields was sentenced to life and King was sentenced to death. King appealed, and the Colorado Supreme Court reversed the conviction because of faulty jury instructions.[73]

42. FRED WALKER. Pueblo. 1911. "Thomas Tynan, warden of the state penitentiary, today appealed to Governor [John] Shafroth to commute to life imprisonment the sentence of Fred Walker, a negro who is doomed to hang the week of October 12 . . . Walker is a negro who was convicted last winter of having killed another negro in Pueblo with a baseball bat."[74]

43. ROBERT HARRIS. Otero County. 1911. Harris was convicted of the murders of Jacob A. Kipper, the marshal of Rocky Ford, and his assistant,

---

71. *Hager, Convicted Murderer, Sentenced to Die in August*, PUEBLO CHIEFTAIN, May 2, 1909, at 7.

72. Piel v. People, 119 P. 687 (Sept. 1911).

73. King v. People, 129 P. 235 (Sept. 1912).

74. *Asks Commutation of Negro Slayer*, ASPEN DEMO.-TIMES, Sept. 21, 1912, at 1.

J. B. Craig, and sentenced to death.[75] In 1913, the Colorado Supreme Court reversed the convictions.[76]

44. LAURO GARCIA. Larimer County. 1912. "Lauro Garcia, the Mexican who several years ago was sentenced to death but later committed to life imprisonment for the murder of Policeman Brockman of Ft. Collins, has been declared insane."[77] Garcia was originally sentenced to death, but the Colorado Supreme Court vacated this conviction and sentence because his trial attorney did not have time to adequately prepare an insanity defense.[78] At retrial in 1916, he was sentenced to life. The murder occurred in 1912.[79]

45. HAROLD ("FRANK") HENWOOD. Denver. 1913. Henwood was prosecuted for the murder of two people in the bar of the Brown Palace Hotel in Denver on May 24, 1911. Henwood had been arguing with Sylvester Von Phul and shot him, but the indictment for this murder was dismissed in February 1913 under the speedy trial law. In the commotion he also shot and killed an innocent bystander, George E. Copeland. Henwood was originally convicted of second-degree murder and sentenced to life imprisonment for Copeland's murder, but this conviction was reversed because the jury was prohibited from considering a conviction for manslaughter.[80] At retrial in 1913, he was convicted of first-degree murder and sentenced to death.[81] This conviction and sentence were sustained on appeal.[82] On October 14, 1914, he was transferred from the county jail to Cañon City, where his execution was set for the week of October 25.[83] On October 16, Gov. Elias Ammons commuted the sen-

---

75. Charles Lee Bryson, *Trial of Aged Negro Follows Son's Conviction*, DENVER POST, Aug. 12, 1911, at 4.

76. Harris v. People, 135 P. 785 (Sept. 1913).

77. *Larimer County Prisoner Declared Insane*, FORT COLLINS COUR., Feb. 2, 1920, at 8.

78. Garcia v. People, 149 P. 614 (1915).

79. *First Degree Murder and a Life Term*, FORT COLLINS WEEKLY COUR., July 28, 1916, at 6.

80. Henwood v. The People, 129 P. 1010 (1913).

81. *Death Sentence for Harold F. Henwood*, ASPEN DEMO.-TIMES, July 26, 1913, at 1.

82. Henwood v. The People, 143 P. 373 (Sept. 1914).

83. *Henwood Goes to Death Cell*, ROCKY MTN. NEWS, Oct. 14, 1914, at 7.

tence to life. In 1922 Gov. Oliver Shoup granted clemency in the case and freed Henwood on the condition that he never return to Denver. In 1923 he was returned to prison for a parole violation, where he died in 1929.[84]

46. JOHN JONES. Moffat County. 1914. "John Jones, a negro charged with shooting and killing Bayle Herndon, wealthy stockman near Colorado-Wyoming line, Moffat county last fall, was found guilty of murder of the first degree at Craig and sentenced . . . to be hanged Friday, Nov. 13."[85] At retrial in 1916, Jones was again found guilty but sentenced to life imprisonment.[86]

47. WILLIAM L. RYAN. Larimer County. 1914. "Ft. Collins, Oct. 28. W. S. [*sic*] Ryan, who was recently convicted of murdering Attorney Newton Crosse on October 14, was today sentenced to be hung during the week of February 7."[87] The murder occurred August 1, 1914. On November 1, 1915, the Colorado Supreme Court vacated the conviction because of errors made by the trial judge in instructing the jury about the insanity defense.[88] The victim had previously represented both Ryan and his mother in various legal matters.

48. JAMES C. BULGER. Denver. 1914. Convicted of a murder that occurred on May 6, 1914, and on September 11 of that year he was sentenced to death. On appeal, his attorney argued that he was insane, but this appeal was denied.[89] In November 1916, Gov. George Carlson commuted the death sentence to life.[90]

---

84. Today's students of the death penalty are fortunate to have an outstanding book about the case. *See* DICK KRECK, MURDER AT THE BROWN PALACE (2003).

85. *Negro Who Killed Stockman to Hang*, BRANDON BELL, Aug. 21, 1914, at 2.

86. *Negro Found Guilty in His Second Trial*, STEAMBOAT PILOT (Steamboat Springs), Aug. 30, 1916, at 2.

87. *Ryan Sentenced to Be Hanged*, ASPEN DEMO.-TIMES, Oct. 28, 1914, at 5.

88. Ryan v. People, 153 P. 756 (Nov. 1, 1915) (lists victim as "Crose").

89. Bulger v. People, 156 P. 800 (Apr. 3, 1916).

90. *State Capitol News*, FAIRPLAY FLUME, Nov. 24, 1916, at 1.

49. NICK DAMAS (a.k.a. Damos). Huerfano County. 1915. Convicted and sentenced to death for the February 1915 murder of William Dick. On appeal in 1917, the Colorado Supreme Court reversed the conviction.[91]

50. CLYDE B. PEARSON. Larimer County. 1917. "A number of important decisions were handed down by the Supreme Court, including that of the People vs. Clyde B. Pearson, convicted and sentenced to hang by the District court of Larimer County (Colo.) for the murder of Sheriff Frank B. Roach of Laramie County, Wyoming."[92]

51. ELMER BEASLEY (a.k.a. Beazley). Pueblo. 1922. According to a newspaper report, Beasley was sentenced to death in late December 1922.[93] "Governor William E. Sweet today commuted the death sentence of Elmer Beazley [*sic*], aged 19 years, to life imprisonment. Beazley was sentenced to hang the last week in March for the killing of Oscar Kronke, a Pueblo filling station attendant, last September."[94]

52. JUAN SUTO. Walsenburg (Huerfano County). 1923. Sentenced to death for the murder of Michael Maroon. The murder occurred during a robbery of Maroon's clothing store on November 30, 1922.[95]

53. ARTHUR H. MITCHELL. Jefferson County (Golden). 1924. Sentenced to death for shooting Georgia Byrans and Andrew Sherie.[96] The conviction was affirmed on appeal.[97] In August 1925, Gov. Clarence Morley commuted the sentence to life because Mitchell had been erroneously prohibited from testifying at the original trial.[98]

---

91. Damas v. People, 163 P. 289 (Jan. 2, 1917).

92. *Pearson to Hang Next February*, RANGE LEDGER (Hugo), Nov. 10, 1917, at 1; Pearson v. People, 168 P. 655 (Nov. 5, 1917).

93. *Colorado News Notes*, AKRON WEEKLY PIONEER PRESS, Dec. 29, 1922, at 4.

94. *Death Sentence of Murderer is Commuted Today*, TELLURIDE DAILY JOUR., Mar. 6, 1923, at 1.

95. *Suto Not to Hang, Isn't a Sane Man*, FORT COLLINS COUR., Apr. 14, 1923, at 8.

96. *Arthur Mitchell, Slayer of Two, is Sentenced to Hang*, GOLDEN COLO. TRANSCRIPT, Jan. 31, 1924, at 1.

97. Mitchell v. People, 232 P. 685 (1924); *Mitchell is Taken to Pen; Still Hopes for Commutation*, GOLDEN COLO. TRANSCRIPT, Jan. 22, 1925, at 1.

98. *Governor Morley Saves Mitchell from Gallows*, ASPEN DAILY TIMES, Aug. 3, 1925, at 1.

54. ALEXANDER INGLES (a.k.a. Alex C. English). 1930. Denver. Convicted and sentenced to death for the murder of his wife's sister.[99] On appeal, the Colorado Supreme Court reversed the conviction.[100] At retrial, Ingles was again convicted and sentenced to death, but—again—the Colorado Supreme Court vacated the conviction.[101]

55–56. OSCAR CARLSON and WILLIAM PISKOTY. Denver. 1931. Both men were discovered burglarizing a garage and placed under arrest when Carlson shot and killed the police officer. Piskoty was granted a new trial and sentenced to life imprisonment. On October 3, 1932, Carlson was also granted a new trial.[102] As explained in the decision by the Colorado Supreme Court that vacated Carlson's conviction,

> Eight days after the crime and 13 days before trial, a new attorney with less than two years experience was appointed to represent defendant. Four days later, defendant pled guilty by reason of insanity and was committed for psychiatric examination for five days, during which time his counsel could not consult with him. The day after defendant's release, defense counsel moved for a continuance on the basis that out-of-state witnesses were required and that more than four days were needed to prepare for trial. The trial court denied the motion and convicted defendant.[103]

57–59. JOE SAIZ, ROY VIGIL, and CANDELARIO MONTOYA. Adams County. 1933. The three Mexican American teenagers were convicted of beating and burning the body of a seventy-four-year-old farmer named George Arnold in his Adams County home. The murder occurred on September 10, 1932. On appeal, the defendants alleged that their confessions were coerced, but the Colorado Supreme Court denied this appeal.[104]

---

99. *English Must Die for Killing Sister-in-Law*, DENVER POST, Nov. 2, 1930, at 1.
100. Ingles v. People, 6 P.2d 455 (Dec. 7, 1931).
101. Ingles v. People, 22 P.2d 1109 (Apr. 17, 1933).
102. Carlson, but not Piskoty, was on death row when James Foster was hanged in December 1931. *Greeley Torch Slayer Dies on Prison Gallows*, DENVER POST, Dec. 12, 1931, at 1.
103. Carlson v. People, 15 P.2d 625 (Oct. 3, 1932).
104. Saiz et al. v. People, 25 P.2d 1114 (Sept. 18, 1933).

60. WALTER RHINHOLD REPPIN. El Paso County. 1933. After pleading guilty, Reppin was sentenced to death for the murder of Vincent Regan. The crime occurred when Reppin was seventeen years old, but Colorado law allowed individuals to be eligible for the death penalty if they were aged eighteen or over at the time of sentencing. On appeal, the conviction was vacated because evidence of unrelated prior crimes by Reppin was introduced at trial.[105] At retrial, he was reconvicted, but the jury set the punishment at life imprisonment.[106]

61. LLOYD FRADY. Delta County. 1934. Codefendant of William Kelley, who was executed in June 1934.[107] On appeal, the judgment was affirmed.[108] Gov. Edwin Johnson commuted his death sentence in March 1935.[109]

62. CHARLES GRAHAM. Mesa County. 1934. Convicted of killing Vina Glasier; the date of the offense was January 14, 1934. In October of that year, the Colorado Supreme Court granted him a new trial because of the failure to properly consider the evidence of Graham's insanity.[110]

63. WILLIS WYNN. Pueblo County. 1937. Aged nineteen, Wynn was sentenced to death on February 21, 1937, for the murder of pawnbroker Isadore Schwartz during a robbery. The murder took place on November 15, 1936.[111] Wynn was unable to afford any appeals and his trial attorney stated that there were no errors and that Wynn had received a fair trial, so no appeal was taken. Gov. Teller Ammons commuted the sentence to life.[112] District Attorney Ralph Neary, who had prosecuted the case, denounced the commutation.[113]

---

105. Reppin v. People, 34 P.2d 71 (June 18, 1934).

106. *Life in Prison, Reppin Verdict*, ROCKY MTN. NEWS, Oct. 21, 1934, at 1.

107. *See* appendix 1, case no. 71.

108. Frady v. People, 40 P.2d 606 (1934).

109. *Under the Capitol Dome*, STEAMBOAT PILOT, Mar. 15, 1935, at 2.

110. Graham v. People, 38 P.2d 87 (Oct. 29, 1934).

111. *Jury at Pueblo Dooms Negro*, ROCKY MTN. NEWS, Feb. 22, 1937.

112. *Gov. Ammons is Still Undetermined What to Do with Schwartz' Slayer*, PUEBLO CHIEFTAIN, Sept. 9, 1937, at 12; *Fight to Save Wynn from Gas is Resumed*, PUEBLO CHIEFTAIN, Sept. 8, 1937, at 7; *Ammons Saves Life of Schwartz Slayer*, PUEBLO CHIEFTAIN, Sept. 10, 1937, at 1;

113. *Ammons "Weakling," Should Resign, Neary Declares in Sharply Worded Statement*, PUEBLO CHIEFTAIN, Sept. 10, 1937, at 1.

64. NORMAN WHARTON. El Paso County. 1938. Convicted of killing a detective, Arthur C. "Jack" Latting, of Colorado Springs during an attempt to rob a hotel room. The murder occurred on June 25, 1938. On appeal, the Colorado Supreme Court remanded the case back to trial court because one juror insisted that other jurors had coerced him into voting for death.[114] Because there were only eleven valid votes for death, the ruling also underscored the argument that the Colorado constitution prohibits the imposition of the death penalty with non-unanimous juries.

65. WILLIE DAVID MUNDY. Denver. 1938. On November 2, 1938, Mundy was convicted of murder and sentenced to death. In 1940 the conviction was reversed and the Colorado Supreme Court ordered a new trial because the jury was prohibited from considering a verdict of not guilty by reason of insanity.[115]

66. WILMER E. TOWNSEND. Boulder County. 1939. Convicted and sentenced to death for beating his wife to death. The murder occurred August 22–23, 1939. He was found guilty on November 17, 1939, and sentenced to death on November 27. On appeal, the conviction was reversed[116] and at retrial, Townsend was sentenced to life.[117]

67. GORDIE R. WRIGHT. Denver. 1944. Convicted and sentenced to death for killing his common law wife, Alberta, during a quarrel over romantic letters she had received from another man. The homicide occurred on November 8, 1943.[118] On appeal, the conviction was vacated because the judge's instructions about the possibility that the homicide may have resulted from self-defense may have been confusing to the jury.[119]

---

114. Wharton v. People, 90 P.2d 615 (May 8, 1939).

115. Mundy v. People, 100 P.2d 584 (Feb. 19, 1940).

116. Townsend v. People, 111 P.2d 236 (Feb. 24, 1941).

117. *Townsend, Not Satisfied with Escaping Gas Chamber, Wants Second Conviction Appealed*, BOULDER DAILY CAMERA, July 2, 1941, at 1; Carol Taylor, *Boulder's First Death Penalty Case was Reversed by the Colorado Supreme Court*, BOULDER DAILY CAMERA, Mar. 22, 2009, at 2D.

118. *Estranged Denver Wife Fatally Shot*, DENVER POST, Nov. 8, 1943, at 7.

119. Wright v. People, 171 P.2d 990 (Aug. 5, 1946). *See also* Lee Casey, *Gordie Wright—and the People*, ROCKY MTN. NEWS, June 2, 1947, at 13.

68. JUAN FREDERICO GALLEGOS. Denver. 1945. Gallegos, married with four children, was convicted and sentenced to death for the 1945 murder of Ida Baca, with whom he was having an affair. On appeal, Gallegos argued that prospective jurors who stood opposed to the death penalty were improperly excluded from the jury. This argument failed, however, and in 1947 the conviction and sentence were affirmed.[120]

69. OTONEIL MARTINEZ. Denver. 1949. Charged with killing Remiga Marie Ramirez and Bernie Trujillo in a Denver restaurant on March 22, 1949. Martinez had been dating Ramirez and became angry when Trujillo said unkind words about her mother. On August 27, 1951, the state Supreme Court affirmed the conviction.[121] On December 4, 1951, Gov. Daniel Thornton commuted the sentence to life: "Otoneil O'Neil is alive today because former Gov. Dan Thornton commuted the double slayer's sentence to life imprisonment in 1951."[122]

70. DOUGLAS PAUL BECKSTEAD. Adams County. 1954. On May 12, 1954, Beckstead killed an Illinois accountant near Stapleton Airport, and he was arrested in Nevada two days later with the victim's body in the trunk of his car. At trial, he was sentenced to death.[123] On appeal in 1956, the conviction and death sentence were vacated because the defendant had been denied the opportunity to substantiate his claim that he did not have malicious intent.[124]

71. FRANK (FRANCISCO) ARCHINA. Denver. 1955. On January 24, 1954, Archina killed his wife's parents and her brother and sister. He was sen-

---

120. Gallegos v. People, 179 P.272 (Mar. 24, 1947). "Gallegos, 48, convicted of the murder or Mrs. Ida Bacca, 40, in a Larimer street restaurant, Nov. 25, 1945, must die in the gas chamber." *Death Date Set for City Slayer*, DENVER POST, Mar. 24, 1947, at 20. It is unknown if the November 1945 date is the date of the murder or the date of the conviction, and no relevant articles could be found in the Denver newspapers around that date.

121. Martinez v. People, 235 P.2d 810 (1951).

122. Richard O'Reilly, *Sentences of 11 Murderers Commuted by Gov. Love*, ROCKY MTN. NEWS, Mar. 5, 1968, at 8.

123. *Becksted [sic] Sentenced to Death*, Denver Post, Dec. 11, 1954, at 1.

124. Beckstead v. People, 292 P.2d 189 (Colo. 1956).

tenced to death on April 24, 1955.[125] In 1957 the Colorado Supreme Court vacated the conviction and death sentence.[126]

72–73. ALBERT JOSEPH KOSTAL and ARTHUR JEROME WATSON. Jefferson County. 1958. After a joint trial, both men were sentenced to death. On initial review, the convictions were vacated, and both were remanded for a new trial.[127] At separate retrials, both men were reconvicted and given life sentences. These convictions were affirmed on appeal.[128]

74. LAVERN JACKIE JONES. Otero County (La Junta). 1959. Convicted of killing a man on February 10, 1959, during a robbery. On initial appeal, Jones won relief from the state Supreme Court.[129] However, once remanded to trial court, only the sentence was reconsidered, and Jones was resentenced to death. This caused the Colorado Supreme Court to again vacate the conviction and order a third trial.[130]

75. JAMES R. MARSHALL. Pueblo. 1959. On October 7, 1959, Marshall and a codefendant, David Penney, were convicted of murder.[131] Penney was sentenced to life and Marshall to death. The state Supreme Court stated, "The attorney general representing the People, with the candor required of him when the situation warrants, has admitted the conviction of Penney was erroneous and has admitted that at the conclusion of the evidence presented by the People, the court should have directed a verdict of not guilty in favor of Penney." On appeal, the Colorado Supreme Court ordered a new trial for Marshall before a new judge, because the trial judge had made up his mind before the trial that Marshall's insanity plea was unfounded.[132]

---

125. Al Nakkula, *Frank Archina Is Sane, Must Die, Jury Decides*, ROCKY MTN. NEWS, Apr. 24, 1955, at 5.

126. Archina v. People, 807 P.2d 1083 (Feb. 27, 1957).

127. Kostal et al. v. People, 357 P.2d 70 (Nov. 28, 1960).

128. Kostal v. People, 414 P.2d 123 (1966); Watson v. People, 394 P.2d 737 (1964).

129. Jones v. People, 360 P.2d 686 (1961).

130. Jones v. People, 393 P.2d 366 (1964).

131. William Hazlett, *Some of the Condemned Okay Death*, ROCKY MTN. NEWS, Dec. 21, 1960, at 94.

132. Penney and Marshall v. People, 360 P.2d 671 (Mar. 27, 1961).

76. SYLVESTER LEE GARRISON. Denver. 1960. In 1971, after eleven-and-a-half years on death row, Garrison's death sentence was vacated due to the improper exclusion of prospective jurors at his original trial because they had reservations about the death penalty.[133] In 1978 he was paroled.[134]

77. MICHAEL JOHN BELL. Denver. 1963. Sentenced to death for killing a Denver police officer. The conviction was affirmed on appeal.[135] On May 1, 1971, prison guards killed Bell and Ernest Alsip[136] during an escape attempt from their death row cells.[137]

78. JOE SEGURA. Pueblo. 1964. Sentenced to death for the murder of his seven-year-old son. On appeal, the conviction and sentence were affirmed in both state and federal court.[138] In 1971 his death sentence was vacated due to the improper exclusion of prospective jurors at his original trial because they had reservations about the death penalty.[139]

79. JOHN MAJOR YOUNG. El Paso County. 1966. Sentenced to death for the 1965 murder of a Colorado Springs gas station attendant. On appeal, the case was remanded back to trial court so the issue of sanity could be reconsidered.[140] He was removed from death row by the 1972 US Supreme Court case of *Furman v. Georgia*.[141]

80. ERNEST JOHN ALSIP. Denver. 1970. Jefferson County. Sentenced to death for killing a Denver woman in Jefferson County. On May 1, 1971,

---

133. Carol McMurrough, *Garrison Leaves Prison Death Row*, DENVER POST, June 30, 1971, at 21.

134. Bill McBean, *Slayer Cheated Death and Won*, DENVER POST, Apr. 26, 1978, at 3.

135. Bell v. People, 406 P.2d 681 (1965), Bell v. People, 431 P.2d 31 (1967).

136. *See* case no. 80, *infra*.

137. Alan Cunningham, *2 Inmates Die in Escape Try in View of Students*, ROCKY MTN. NEWS, May 2, 1971, at 5.

138. Segura v. Patterson, 402 F.2d 249 (1968).

139. Carol McMurrough, *Court Decisions Move 2 Men Off Death Row*, DENVER POST, June 29, 1971, at 3.

140. Young v. People, 488 P.2d 567 (1971).

141. Furman v. Georgia, 408 U.S. 238 (1972); Olsen, *2 in Colo. Death Row Spared.*

prison guards killed Alsip and John Bell[142] during an escape attempt from their death row cells.[143]

81. JAMES D. MANIER. Denver. 1970. Sentenced to death for the murder of his former wife.[144] He was removed from death row by the 1972 US Supreme Court case *Furman v. Georgia*.[145] Later, the Colorado Supreme Court affirmed the conviction.[146]

82–99. POST-*FURMAN* CASES (N = 18). Appendix 3 lists twenty-three men who have been sentenced to death in Colorado since 1972. Of the twenty-three, Nathan Dunlap,[147] Sir Mario Owens,[148] and Robert Ray[149] remained on death row as of December 31, 2015. Two others were executed—one in Texas[150] and one in Colorado.[151] Therefore, between 1972 and the end of 2015, there were eighteen defendants (all male) sentenced to death in Colorado who were not executed and who are no longer on death row.

142. *See* case no. 77, *infra.*
143. Cunningham, *2 Inmates Die in Escape Try.*
144. *Man Sentenced to Die in Colo. Gas Chamber*, DENVER POST, Dec. 3, 1970, at 3.
145. Furman v. Georgia, 408 U.S. 238 (1972); Olsen, *2 in Colo. Death Row Spared.*
146. People v. Manier, 518 P.2d 811 (1974).
147. *See* appendix 2, case no. 16.
148. *See* appendix 2, case no. 22.
149. *See* appendix 2, case no. 23.
150. *See* appendix 2, case no. 9.
151. *See* appendix 2, case no. 13 and appendix 1, case no. 103.

APPENDIX 3

Colorado Death Sentences: January 1, 1975–December 31, 2015 (N = 23) (ordered by date of offense)

1. DEAN LEWIS WILDERMUTH (a.k.a. Shane McKnight). January 18, 1975. Adams County (Brighton). W-W. Convicted in the stabbing death of Thelma C. Wrench in Northglenn, whom he had met a few days earlier in a local bar.[1] He was sentenced to death after the jury found that the murder was committed in "a heinous, cruel or depraved manner," an aggravating circumstance that made a death sentence mandatory.[2] In November 1975, prosecutors asked the trial court to vacate the death sentence because the trial judge had improperly denied requests by defense attorneys to question prospective jurors about their feelings regarding capital punishment.[3]

2. MICHAEL CORBETT. June 24, 1975. El Paso County (Colorado Springs). B-W. A former Fort Carson soldier, Corbett was sentenced to death for stabbing to death Winford Proffitt.[4] A codefendant, Freddie Glenn (see

1. *Woman Slain in Northglenn*, DENVER POST, Jan. 20, 1975, at 4.
2. Jim Kirksey, *Adams Slayer to Face Death; First Since '67*, DENVER POST, July 19, 1975, at 1.
3. Fred Brown, *Challenge to State Death Penalty Dropped*, DENVER POST, Nov. 25, 1976, at 19.
4. *Impassive Corbett Receives Death for Stabbing Proffitt*, COLO. SPRINGS GAZ. TELEGRAPH, Apr. 27, 1976, at 11; *Michae [sic] Corbett Is Sentenced to Die*, COLO. SPRINGS GAZ. TELEGRAPH, May 30, 1976, at 16G.

DOI: 10.5876/9781607325123.c010

case no. 3 below) was sentenced to life imprisonment for his role in the murder. Corbett also pled guilty and received life sentences for killing a cook, Daniel H. Van Lone, during a robbery at a restaurant, and for killing a friend, Winslow Douglas Watson.[5] The death sentence was vacated in 1978 when the Colorado Supreme Court found the state death penalty statute unconstitutional.[6]

3. FREDDIE GLENN. July 1, 1975. El Paso County (Colorado Springs). B-W. Sentenced to death for the murder of an eighteen-year-old waitress, Karen Grammer.[7] Grammer was kidnapped when she spotted Glenn (a Fort Carson soldier) and two accomplices preparing to rob a Red Lobster restaurant. She was taken to an apartment, where all three men raped her, and then to an alley, where Glenn slit her throat.[8] Prior to his conviction for the Grammer murder, Glenn was convicted of two other murders. He was sentenced to life imprisonment for the June 1975 murder of motel cook Daniel H. Van Lone during a robbery,[9] and in October 1975 (after a change of venue to Boulder), he pled guilty and was sentenced to life imprisonment for the murder of Winford Proffitt during a drug deal. The latter killing sent his codefendant, Michael Corbett (case no. 2 above), to death row.[10] Glenn's death sentence was vacated in 1978 when the state Supreme Court found the state death penalty statute unconstitutional.[11]

---

5. State v. Corbett, 713 P.2d 1337 (Colo. App. 1985); *Western Empire: Parole Board Denies Killer*, DENVER POST, Apr. 18, 1996, at B4. Freddie Glenn (q.v.) was sentenced to life for both the Proffitt and Van Lone murders.

6. People v. District Court, 586 P.2d 31 (Colo. 1978); Eric Lawlor, *Mom Expresses Fear for Life of Inmate*, ROCKY MTN. NEWS, Oct. 24, 1978, at 5.

7. *Glenn Is Found Guilty of Murder; Jury Deliberated 2½ Hours Tuesday*, COLO. SPRINGS GAZ. TELEGRAPH, Mar. 17, 1976, at 11; *Glenn Sentenced to Death*, COLO. SPRINGS GAZ. TELEGRAPH, Mar. 18, 1976, at 1; *Glenn Sentenced to Death for Killing of Young Girl*, COLO. SPRINGS GAZ. TELEGRAPH, May 8, 1976, at 1.

8. Jim Gibney, *Death Penalty in Springs Slaying*, DENVER POST, Mar. 18, 1976, at 27; *Glenn Sentenced to Death*.

9. *Carson Soldier is Convicted*, ROCKY MTN. NEWS, Feb. 15, 1976, at 46.

10. *Ex-Carson GI Gets Life in 3rd Murder Conviction*, DENVER POST, Oct. 15, 1976, at 17.

11. People v. District Court, 586 P.2d 31 (Colo. 1978); Lawlor, *Mom Expresses Fear*.

4. KENNETH H. BOTHAM, JR. August 23, 1975. Mesa County (Grand Junction). W-W. Sentenced to death for killing his wife, Patricia, in Grand Junction.[12] He was also convicted on three counts of second-degree murder for killing a neighbor and her two children.[13] The two women were suffocated and the children were shot. The bodies of all four were tied to scrap railroad iron and thrown into a river, where they were found one month later. The death sentence was vacated in 1978 when the state Supreme Court found the state death penalty statute unconstitutional.[14] Botham won a new trial in 1981 because "the failure of the trial judge to recuse himself, coupled with the failure to grant a change of venue, and erroneous and prejudicial evidentiary rulings, require[d] that a new trial be granted."[15] At retrial (after a change of venue to Golden), he was again convicted[16] and sentenced to life imprisonment (with a minimum of seventy years before parole eligibility).[17]

5. RONALD LEE FERRELL. February 17, 1976. Teller County (Cripple Creek). W-W. Convicted of killing Andrew J. Fullbright, a partner in various illegal drug transactions, because he had alerted another drug dealer that Ferrell and two companions planned to rob him.[18] The conviction was affirmed on appeal.[19] The death sentence was vacated in 1978 when the state Supreme Court found the state death penalty statute unconstitutional.[20]

---

12. Rich Mauer, *Botham Jurors Decide on Death*, DENVER POST, Dec. 15, 1976, at 1; Rich Mauer, *Botham Sentenced to Die; Appeal Likely*, DENVER POST, Jan. 26, 1977, at 3.

13. *Botham Convicted of Slayings*, ROCKY MTN. NEWS, Dec. 13, 1976, at 5.

14. People v. District Court, 586 P.2d 31 (Colo. 1978); Lawlor, *Mom Expresses Fear*.

15. People v. Botham, 629 P.2d 589, 603 (Colo. 1981).

16. Philip Reed, *Botham's Retrial in Killings Ends in Conviction*, ROCKY MTN. NEWS, Jan. 23, 1982, at 12.

17. Philip Reed, *Botham Gets 70 Years in Slayings*, ROCKY MTN. NEWS, Feb. 17, 1982, at 8.

18. Molly R. Parrish, *Ferrell Is Found Guilty of Murder*, COLO. SPRINGS GAZ. TELEGRAPH, Oct. 9, 1976, at 11; Molly R. Parrish, *Ferrell Is Given Death Sentence*, COLO. SPRINGS GAZ. TELEGRAPH, Oct. 10, 1976, at 4; *Murderer Will Die March 13–19*, COLO. SPRINGS GAZ. TELEGRAPH, Dec. 11, 1976, at 1.

19. People v. Ferrell, 200 Colo. 128; 613 P.2d 324 (Colo. 1980).

20. People v. District Court, 586 P.2d 31 (Colo. 1978); Lawlor, *Mom Expresses Fear*.

6. SCOTT ELLIOTT RAYMER. December 20, 1976. Jefferson County (Golden). W-B. Raymer (white) was convicted and sentenced to death for killing Doris Hargrove, an African American attendant at a Lakewood gas station who was shot during a robbery.[21] A second participant pled guilty to first-degree murder for his role in the killing and a third defendant pled guilty to manslaughter. Two weeks after being sentenced to death, Raymer pled guilty to felony murder and was sentenced to life imprisonment for killing a second gas station attendant (white) in Denver approximately twenty minutes after the first homicide.[22] The death sentence was vacated in 1978 when the state Supreme Court found the state death penalty statute unconstitutional.[23]

7. RICKY DILLON. August 14, 1977. El Paso County (Colorado Springs). B-W. Convicted and sentenced to death for bludgeoning to death Carl Taylor, who was killed as he slept in a moving van in the parking lot of a Colorado Springs apartment complex. The state contended that Dillon was among a group of soldiers from nearby Fort Carson who decided to burglarize the van.[24] No physical evidence linked Dillon to the murder; the only evidence against him came from self-confessed participants in the crime who implicated him. The death sentence was vacated in 1978 when the state Supreme Court found the state death penalty statute unconstitutional.[25] Dillon's initial appeal was denied.[26] However, in 1987 the Colorado Court of Appeals ordered a new trial because of ineffective assistance of counsel.[27]

8. EDGAR LEE DURRE (a.k.a. Duree). November 29, 1980. Weld County (Greeley). W-W. Convicted (with James Manners) of killing Gary L. Statler, the owner of a Denver antique shop and a member of the family that

---

21. Jerry V. Williams, *Raymer Given Death Penalty*, DENVER POST, June 29, 1977, at 21.

22. *Condemned Killer Gets Life Term*, ROCKY MTN. NEWS, July 8, 1977, at 29.

23. People v. District Court, 586 P.2d 31 (Colo. 1978); Lawlor, *Mom Expresses Fear.*

24. Joyce Trent, *Dillon Gets Death Penalty*, COLO. SPRINGS GAZ. TELEGRAPH, June 27, 1978, at 1; Joyce Trent, *Dillon's Execution Set During December*, COLO. SPRINGS GAZ. TELEGRAPH, Sept. 9, 1978, at 1.

25. People v. District Court, 586 P.2d 31 (Colo. 1978); Lawlor, *Mom Expresses Fear.*

26. People v. Dillon, 633 P.2d 504 (Colo. 1981).

27. People v. Dillon, 739 P.2d 919 (Colo. 1987).

owned the Statler Hotel chain (until the chain was sold to Hilton Hotels in 1954 for some $111 million).[28] The key witness at trial was Durre's son, Roger Baldwin, who testified that he had arranged a sexual encounter between Manners, Durre, and Statler at a Denver motel. However, it was a trap, and Statler was forced to write checks until his bank account was exhausted. He was later taken to a rural area in Weld County, where he was murdered. The jury first recommended a death sentence for Durre, but five jurors later wrote to the judge asking that Durre instead be sentenced to life imprisonment.[29] In 1984 the Colorado Supreme Court vacated the death sentence because the jury had not been told that a failure to agree unanimously on a death sentence meant that the defendant would be sentenced to life imprisonment.[30]

9. STEVEN PETER MORIN. November 6, 1981. Jefferson County (Golden). W-W. Convicted and sentenced to death for the kidnapping and murder of Sheila Ann Whalen, a Denver waitress who was found strangled to death in a motel room. Before his trial, he had already been given two death sentences for murders in Texas, and he was suspected of additional murders in several other states. At the trial in Golden, Morin refused to cooperate with his public defenders and offered no defense.[31]

---

28. Mark Byrnes, *The Rise and Fall of One of America's Most Innovative Hotel Chains*, CITYLAB, Feb. 15, 2013, accessed July 15, 2016, http://www.citylab.com/design/2013/02/hotel-chain-grew-americas-cities/4723/.

29. Frank Moya & Brad Martisius, *Trial in Greeley Will Be Test of Colorado Death Penalty*, DENVER POST, Aug. 19, 1981, at 2; Bill Myers, *Slayer Gets State's First Death Penalty*, DENVER POST, Oct. 1, 1981, at 1.

30. People v. Durre, 690 P.2d 165 (Colo. 1984); Howard Pankratz, *Death Sentence Overturned; Ruling May Limit Penalty's Use*, DENVER POST, May 22, 1984, at A1.

31. Pat McGraw, *Suspect Going to Trial Without Choice of Lawyer*, DENVER POST, July 10, 1984, at 4; Pat McGraw, *Unwanted, Morin Public Defenders on Job*, DENVER POST, July 11, 1984, at 4; Pat McGraw, *Trial of Morin, Charged With Motel Slaying, Expected to Begin*, DENVER POST, July 12, 1984, at 4; Pat McGraw, *Prosecution Outlines Case Against Morin*, DENVER POST, July 13, 1984, at 10C; Pat McGraw, *Jeffco Jury Convicts Morin in Kidnap, Murder of Woman*, DENVER POST, July 19, 1984, at C1; Pat McGraw, *Jurors Allowed to Consider Morin's Record*, DENVER POST, July 20, 1984, at 4; Pat McGraw, *Jury Recommends Gas-Chamber Death for Morin*, DENVER POST, July 24, 1984, at 4; Pat McGraw, *Morin Says He's a "Victim"; Faces 3rd Death Ruling*, DENVER POST, Aug. 13, 1984, at 4; Kit Miniclier, *Morin Sentenced to Death in Colorado's Gas Chamber*, DENVER POST, Aug. 14, 1984, at 7.

No appeal was taken. On March 13, 1985, seven months after receiving the Colorado death sentence, Morin was executed in Texas.[32]

10. JOHNNIE ARGUELLO. December 3, 1981. Weld County (Greeley). H-W. Sentenced to death for the murder of a Greeley gas station attendant, Rodney Russell (a student at the University of Northern Colorado), who was beaten to death with a hammer during a robbery.[33] In January 1983, the trial court denied his initial appeal.[34] The following week, Arguello committed suicide by hanging himself in his cell at Centennial Correctional Facility in Cañon City.[35]

11. RICHARD OWEN DRAKE. December 16, 1982. Mesa County (Grand Junction). H-W. Sentenced to death for masterminding the murder of his wife, who was stabbed to death by Drake's brother, James.[36] The alleged motive was to collect from her life insurance policy. James was subsequently convicted of being an accessory to murder and sentenced to eight years in prison.[37] In 1988 the state Supreme Court vacated the death sentence because of faulty jury instructions,[38] and Drake was resentenced to life imprisonment.

---

32. *Killer of Three Women Executed in Texas*, DENVER POST, Mar. 13, 1985, at 13.

33. Mike Peters, *Jury: Arguello Is Guilty*, GREELEY TRIB., July 22, 1982, at 1; Mike Peters, *Arguello to Die, Jury Determines in Russell Case*, GREELEY TRIB., July 23, 1982, at 1; Mike Peters, *Death Penalty Issued Arguello*, GREELEY TRIB., July 24, 1982, at 1. After the conviction and death sentence, the *Greeley Tribune* wrote a lengthy four-part series on the crime and trial. *See* Mike Peters, *What Price Life? Fourteen Dollars*, GREELEY TRIB., Aug. 1, 1982, at 1; Mike Peters, *Dec. 3, 1981, Was a Routine Day Until 9 p.m.*, GREELEY TRIB., Aug. 2, 1982, at 1; Mike Peters, *Diary of Russell Murder Probe*, GREELEY TRIB., Aug. 3, 1982, at 1; Mike Peters, *Confession, Innocent Plea Made Arguello Trial Unusual*, GREELEY TRIB., Aug. 4, 1982, at 1.

34. Mike Peters, *Arguello Appeal Denied*, GREELEY TRIB., Jan. 11, 1983, at 1.

35. Bob Diddlebock, *Convicted Slayer Is Found Hanged in Cell*, ROCKY MTN. NEWS, Jan. 17, 1983, at 9; Mike Peters, *Arguello Kills Self, Fulfills Warnings*, GREELEY TRIB., Jan. 17, 1983, at 1.

36. Karen Odom, *Two Brothers Possess Same Goal: Stay Alive*, DENVER POST, July 15, 1984, at 1E; *Jury Hands Spouse Death in Murder*, DENVER POST, Dec. 17, 1983, at D5; *Death Sentence Imposed*, DENVER POST, Jan. 17, 1984, at 8.

37. Karen Odom, *Brother Gets Prison for Providing Alibi*, DENVER POST, Dec. 1, 1984, at 8.

38. People v. Drake, 748 P.2d 1237 (Colo. 1988).

12. FRANK RODRIGUEZ. November 14, 1984. Denver. H-W. Sentenced to death for the murder of Lorraine Martelli, who was kidnapped, robbed, raped, and slowly stabbed to death. Frank's brother, Chris, was also convicted of first-degree murder for the crime.[39] On initial appeal, both the conviction and the death sentence were affirmed.[40] In 2002 Rodriguez died of complications from Hepatitis C while still on death row.[41]

13. GARY LEE DAVIS. July 21, 1986. Adams County (Brighton). W-W. *See* appendix 1, case no. 103.

14. JOHN O'NEILL. February 3, 1987. Jefferson County (Golden). W-H. Convicted of killing a friend and partner in a marijuana growing business, John Baca, because he believed that Baca was not sharing the proceeds. Baca's son pled guilty to being an accessory in the case.[42] In 1990 the state Supreme Court vacated the death sentence because of improper jury instructions.[43]

15. RONALD LEE WHITE. August, 1987. Pueblo. W-W. After guilty pleas, White was convicted on two counts of first-degree murder and given a sentence of life imprisonment. Shortly thereafter, he became a suspect in the murder of a former roommate, Paul Vosika. In 1991 he pled guilty to the Vosika murder and requested a death sentence, and this request was granted. On appeal, the conviction and death sentence were affirmed.[44] In May 1998, a district court judge set aside the death sentence after investigators discovered boxes of material in the possession of the sheriff that had not been turned over to the defense during the

---

39. Howard Pankratz, *Rodriguez Sentenced to Die*, DENVER POST, Dec. 18, 1986, at 1; Howard Pankratz, *Judge Orders Execution of Rodriguez*, DENVER POST, Jan. 29, 1987, at B1.

40. People v. Rodriguez, 794 P.2d 965 (Colo. 1990); People v. Rodriguez, 914 P.2d 230 (Colo. 1996).

41. Jenn Kostka, *Death-Row Inmate Dies of Illness; Murderer Had Nearly Exhausted Appeals*, DENVER POST, Mar. 10, 2002, at B1.

42. Thomas Graf, *Pot Dealer Found Guilty of Murder in Shooting Death of His Partner*, DENVER POST, Nov. 17, 1987, at 2B; George Lane, *O'Neill Ordered Executed for Killing "Best Friend"*, DENVER POST, Nov. 19, 1987, at 1C.

43. People v. O'Neill, 803 P.2d 164 (Colo. 1990).

44. People v. White, 870 P.2d 424 (Colo. 1994); Howard Pankratz, *State High Court Upholds Murderer's Death Sentence*, DENVER POST, Jan. 11, 1994, at B3.

trial.[45] After that new sentencing phase hearing in 2001 (before a judge only, not a jury), White was sentenced to life imprisonment.[46]

16. NATHAN DUNLAP. December 14, 1993. Arapahoe County (Aurora). B-W. Convicted of four counts of first-degree murder and sentenced to death for an after-hours killing spree in a Chuck E. Cheese restaurant in Aurora.[47] Dunlap, age nineteen, had been fired from his position as a cook in the restaurant; the murders were committed in revenge some five months later. The victims, all restaurant employees, included a fifty-year-old woman, Marge Kohlberg, and three teenagers, Sylvia Crowell, Ben Grant, and Colleen O'Connor. After a change of venue to Colorado Springs and a six-week trial, Dunlap was convicted. On March 7, 1996, the same trial jury recommended a death sentence.[48] He was formally sentenced to death on May 17, 1996.[49] On appeal, the conviction and sentence were affirmed.[50] As of October 2016, Dunlap remains on death row, but Gov. John Hickenlooper stayed his execution with a "temporary reprieve."

17. ROBERT ELIOT HARLAN. February 12, 1994. Adams County (Brighton). B-W. Convicted of the kidnap, rape, and murder of Rhonda Maloney. After Harlan forced Maloney's car off an interstate highway and sexually assaulted her, a motorist, Jaquie Creazzo, saw their car by the side of the road and stopped to offer assistance. Maloney jumped out of Harlan's car and into Creazzo's and explained to Creazzo that she had been kidnapped and raped. They then sped down the highway, with Harlan in pursuit and firing a gun at the two women. Creazzo's car exited the highway and flipped over on the front lawn of the Thornton Police

---

45. Tillie Fong, *Condemned Murderer to Receive New Hearing to Determine Penalty*, ROCKY MTN. NEWS, May 30, 1998, at 3.

46. Erin Emery, *Death Row Inmate Gets Reprieve—A Life Sentence*, DENVER POST, Aug. 23, 2001, at B2.

47. Ann Imse, *A Jury In the Dark?*, ROCKY MTN. NEWS, June 28, 2003, at 23A.

48. Ginny McKibben, *It's Death for Dunlap*, DENVER POST, Mar. 8, 1996, at 1.

49. Charlie Brennan, *Dunlap Erupts in Rage; Receives Death Sentence*, ROCKY MTN. NEWS, May 18, 1996, at 5; Ginny McKibben, *Condemned Killer Unleashes Rage in Court*, DENVER POST, May 18, 1996, at 1.

50. People v. Dunlap, 975 P.2d 723 (Colo. 1999); People v. Dunlap, 36 P.3d 778 (Colo. 2001).

Department; she had been shot in the spine, which resulted in lifelong paralysis. Harlan grabbed Maloney from the overturned car, drove away with her, and killed her shortly thereafter. This history is recounted in a decision by the Colorado Supreme Court that affirmed the convictions and death sentence.[51] On further appeal, the death sentence was vacated because the jury had consulted inappropriate materials (a Bible) during their deliberations.[52] Harlan was then resentenced to life imprisonment.[53]

18. GEORGE WILLIAM WOLDT. April 29, 1997. El Paso County (Colorado Springs). A-W. Convicted (with Lucas Salmon, who was sentenced to life imprisonment for his role in the crimes) and sentenced to death for the kidnapping, rape, and murder of a University of Colorado Colorado Springs student named Jacine Gielinski. The victim was kidnapped from a parking lot and taken to a nearby elementary school, where she was raped and stabbed.[54] In 2003, after the Supreme Court's decision in *Ring v. Arizona*,[55] the Colorado Supreme Court vacated Woldt's death sentence because it had been imposed by a three-judge panel and ordered that he be resentenced to life imprisonment without the possibility of parole.[56]

19. FRANCISCO MARTINEZ. May 31, 1997. Jefferson County (Golden). H-H. Convicted of first-degree murder for the kidnapping, rape, and murder of fourteen-year-old Brandaline "Brandy" Duvall.[57] Martinez was one of seven gang members involved in the crimes, although he was identified as the person who stabbed her to death. Before the penalty phase began, the Colorado Supreme Court rejected a challenge to the discovery requirements applicable in the penalty proceedings.[58] Martinez then became the first defendant to be sentenced to death in Colorado by a

---

51. People v. Harlan, 8 P.3d 448 (Colo. 2000).
52. People v. Harlan, 109 P.3d 616 (Colo. 2005).
53. Felix Doligosa, Jr., *Life Term for Harlan*, ROCKY MTN. NEWS, Dec. 20, 2005, at 29A.
54. Erin Emery, *Torture Murderer Gets Death Sentence: Judges Rule in Rape, Killing of Student*, DENVER POST, Sept. 7, 2000, at 1.
55. 536 U.S. 584 (2002).
56. Woldt v. People, 64 P.3d 256 (Colo. 2003).
57. Marilyn Robinson, *3 Held in Teen Girl's Slaying; Other Reputed Gangsters Sought*, DENVER POST, June 17, 1997, at B1.
58. People v. Martinez, 970 P.2d 469 (1998).

three-judge panel.[59] In 2003, after the Supreme Court's decision in *Ring v. Arizona*,[60] the state Supreme Court vacated Martinez's death sentence because it had been imposed by a three-judge panel and ordered that he be resentenced to life imprisonment without the possibility of parole.[61]

20. WILLIAM CODY NEAL. June 7, 1998. Jefferson County (Golden). W-W. Sentenced to death after pleading guilty to three counts of first-degree murder. The victims—Rebecca Holbertson, Angela Fite (Neal's girlfriend), and Candace Walters—were killed during a six-day spree, each with a wood-splitting maul. A fourth victim, who survived, was kidnapped, tied to a bed, raped, and forced to watch one of the murders.[62] Neal fired his public defender, acted as his own attorney at trial,[63] and was sentenced to death by a three-judge panel.[64] In 2001 chief deputy district attorney Mark Pautler was suspended from practicing law for three months and otherwise reprimanded by the Colorado Supreme Court for trying to get Neal to surrender by falsely telling him that he was a public defender.[65] In 2003 a district court vacated the death sentence and resentenced Neal to three consecutive terms of life imprisonment because the death sentence had been imposed by a three-judge panel,[66] in violation of *Ring v. Arizona*.[67]

21. EDWARD MONTOUR, JR. October 18, 2002. H-W. The offense occurred in Lincoln County, but there was a change of venue for the trial to Douglas County (Castle Rock), another county in Colorado's Eighteenth

---

59. Kieran Nicholson, *Judges Say Killer Must Die; Death Sentence a First by Panel*, DENVER POST, May 28, 1999, at 1.

60. 536 U.S. 584 (2002).

61. Woldt v. People, 64 P.3d 256 (Colo. 2003).

62. Kieran Nicholson, *Woman Tells of Murder Horror; Judges Weigh Penalty for Neal*, DENVER POST, Sept. 22, 1999, at B2.

63. Kieran Nicholson, *Neal Admits Killing 3 Women; Prosecutors to Seek Death Penalty*, DENVER POST, Feb. 26, 1999, at B1.

64. Kieran Nicholson, *Ax Killer Sentenced to Death*, DENVER POST, Sept. 30, 1999, at 1.

65. John Ingold, *Jeffco Deputy DA Censured; Pautler Not Sorry for Actions in Neal Case*, DENVER POST, Apr. 4, 2001, at B2; In the Matter of Mark C. Pautler, 47 P.3d 1175 (Colo. 2002).

66. *'99 Death Sentence Commuted for Neal*, DENVER POST, Dec. 14, 2003, at B2

67. 536 U.S. 584 (2002).

Judicial District. Montour was sentenced to life imprisonment without parole for the 1997 murder of his eleven-week-old daughter. He was serving that sentence at Limon Correctional Facility when he confessed to killing a prison guard, Eric Autobee. Autobee was the first correctional officer in Colorado killed by an inmate since 1929.[68] At trial, Montour represented himself, waived his right to a jury, and pled guilty before being sentenced to death by the trial judge. The murder occurred only seventeen days after a new death penalty law went into effect in the state, removing sentencing authority from a three-judge panel and putting it into the hands of jurors.[69] On April 23, 2007, the death sentence was vacated when the Colorado Supreme Court found that a guilty plea at trial did not mean that the defendant had also forfeited the right to a jury determination of sentence.[70] After six more years of litigation, on April 9, 2013, the trial court tossed out his guilty plea because of his history of mental illness and lack of adequate representation at the original trial.[71] Despite offers by Montour to plead guilty in exchange for a life sentence, prosecutors moved forward with a new trial and continued to pursue a death sentence. By early 2014, a total of 3,500 potential jurors were summoned for the retrial, but Bob Autobee, the victim's father, publicly appealed to them not to resentence Montour to death.[72] Questions were also raised about the validity of Montour's conviction for his daughter's death. Finally, the day after the retrial began, the district attorney abruptly decided to accept Montour's guilty plea because he believed that it was unlikely that the jury would return a death sentence. Montour was promptly sentenced to life imprisonment.[73]

---

68. Michael BeDan & Charley Able, *Limon Prison Kitchen Boss Slain*, ROCKY MTN. NEWS, Oct. 19, 2002, at 3.

69. Howard Pankratz, *Prison Slaying Brings Death Sentence: Convict Faces Execution for Murder of Worker*, DENVER POST, Feb. 28, 2003, at B1; Mike Patty, *Inmate Gets Death for Murder; Man was in Prison for Slaying Daughter Before Killing Officer*, ROCKY MTN. NEWS, Feb. 28, 2003, at 5A.

70. People v. Montour, 157 P.3d 489 (2007).

71. Karen Augé, *Prison-killing Case Goes Back to Court*, DENVER POST, Apr. 10, 2013, at 5A.

72. Jordan Steffen, *Victim's Dad to Protest Push for Death Penalty*, DENVER POST, Jan. 6, 2014, at 4A.

73. Jordan Steffen, *Emotional End: No Death Penalty*, DENVER POST, Mar. 7, 2014, at 4A; Jordan Steffen, *State Pays Millions before Abrupt End*, DENVER POST, Mar. 8, 2014, at 4A.

22–23. SIR MARIO OWENS AND ROBERT RAY. June 20, 2005. Arapahoe County (Centennial). Both Black. Convicted of killing Javad Marshall Fields (Black) and his fiancée, Vivian Wolfe (Asian). The alleged motive was the elimination of a witness. Fields planned to testify against Owens and Ray at Ray's trial for acessory to the murder of Gregory Vann (a crime for which he was later convicted, while Owens was convicted of first-degree murder in the case). Fields had graduated from Colorado State University just eleven days before his death, and Wolfe had graduated the previous semester. Owens and Ray were originally codefendants, but their trials were severed. Owens was sentenced to death on December 8, 2008, and on May 5, 2010, Ray followed him to death row. In 2010 Fields's mother, Rhonda, was elected to the Colorado House of Representatives, where she became an outspoken supporter of the death penalty.

INDEX

INDEX